THE CULTURE OF CHRISTINA ROSSETTI

Female Poetics and Victorian Contexts

Christina Rossetti, 1848. Oil portrait by Dante Gabriel Rossetti. (Private collection.)

THE CULTURE OF
CHRISTINA ROSSETTI

Female Poetics and Victorian Contexts

Edited by

Mary Arseneau, Antony H. Harrison,
and Lorraine Janzen Kooistra

Ohio University Press
ATHENS

Ohio University Press, Athens, Ohio 45701

Ohio University Press books are printed on acid-free paper ⊛™

05 04 03 02 01 00 99 5 4 3 2 1

Library of Congress Cataloging-in-Publication Data

The culture of Christina Rossetti : female poetics and victorian contexts / edited
  by Mary Arseneau, Antony H. Harrison, and Lorraine Janzen Kooistra.
     p.   cm.
   Includes bibliographical references and index.
   ISBN 0-8214-1243-4 (alk. paper)
     1. Rossetti, Christina Georgina, 1830-1894—Criticism and interpretation.
  2. Literature and society—England—History—19th century. 3. Women and
  literature—England—History—19th century. 4. Poetics. I. Arseneau, Mary.
  II. Harrison, Antony H. III. Kooistra, Lorraine Janzen, 1953-   .
  PR5238.C85   1999
  821'.8—dc21   98-49443
                                                              CIP

CONTENTS

   Christina Rossetti and the Significance of the Nonhuman
   KATHRYN BURLINSON

8 Astronomy of the Invisible   194
   Contexts for Christina Rossetti's Heavenly Parables
   LINDA E. MARSHALL

9 *Speaking Likenesses*   212
   Hearing the Lesson
   JULIA BRIGGS

                    III. FEMALE POETICS

10 Father's Place, Mother's Space   235
    Identity, Italy, and the Maternal in Christina Rossetti's Poetry
    ALISON CHAPMAN

11 Rossetti's Cold Women   260
    Irony and Liminal Fantasy in the Death Lyrics
    SUSAN CONLEY

12 Dying to Be a Poetess   285
    The Conundrum of Christina Rossetti
    MARGARET LINLEY

    Bibliography   315
    Editors and Contributors   335
    Index   338

ILLUSTRATIONS

ACKNOWLEDGMENTS

The editors would like to thank Dennis F. Evans for his editorial assistance in the early stages of this project; Jodi Sutherland for her help in producing a single document from the work of diverse hands; and Patricia Whiting for preparing the index. We are also grateful to Nipissing University and the University of Ottawa for the financial support which facilitated the preparation of the final manuscript and the publication of the volume. Sincere thanks to David Sanders, director of the Ohio University Press, for his generous support of this project and to Nancy Basmajian for her careful production work.

We would like to acknowledge those who have generously granted permission to reproduce material in this collection. A version of Margaret Reynolds's essay, "Speaking Unlikenesses: The Double Text in Christina Rossetti's 'After Death' and 'Remember,'" appeared in *Textual Practice* (January 1999). Linda E. Marshall's essay, "Astronomy of the Invisible: Contexts for Christina Rossetti's Heavenly Parables," is here reprinted, in slightly altered form, by kind permission of Triangle Journals Ltd., Wallingford, Oxfordshire, UK. The essay originally appeared in *Women's Writing: The Elizabethan to Victorian Period* 2, no. 2 (1995): 167–81. For permission to reproduce illustrations used in this book, the editors would like to thank the following individuals, institutions, and publishers: John Bolton; Nicholas G. Rossetti; Martin Ware; the British Library, London; the English Faculty Library, University of Oxford; the Fisher Library, University of Sydney, Australia; The Huntington Library, San Marino, California; The Osborne Collection of Early Children's Books, Toronto Public Library, Canada; David R. Godine, Publisher; The Medici Society Limited, London; *Playboy* magazine; and *Punch* magazine. Every effort has been made to ensure that all necessary permissions have been obtained.

ABBREVIATIONS

Armstrong   Armstrong, Isobel. *Victorian Poetry: Poetry, Poetics, and Politics* (London and New York: Routledge, 1993)

Bell   Bell, Mackenzie. *Christina Rossetti: A Biographical and Critical Study* (London: Hurst and Blackett; Boston: Roberts Brothers, 1898)

CP   *The Complete Poems of Christina Rossetti.* Variorum ed. Ed. R. W. Crump, 3 vols. (Baton Rouge and London: Louisiana State University Press, 1979-90). Unless otherwise noted, all citations of Rossetti's poetry are from this edition and will be noted parenthetically in the text.

FD   *The Face of the Deep: A Devotional Commentary on the Apocalypse* (London and Brighton: SPCK; New York: Young, 1892)

FL   *The Family Letters of Christina Georgina Rossetti.* 1908. Ed. William Michael Rossetti. (New York: Haskell, 1968)

Harrison, *CR*   Harrison, Antony H. *Christina Rossetti in Context* (Chapel Hill and London: University of North Carolina Press; Brighton: Harvester, 1988)

Kent   Kent, David A., ed. *The Achievement of Christina Rossetti* (Ithaca and London: Cornell University Press, 1987)

Leighton   Leighton, Angela. *Victorian Women Poets: Writing Against the Heart* (London and New York: Harvester; Charlottesville and London: University Press of Virginia, 1992)

LS   *Letter and Spirit: Notes on the Commandments* (London and Brighton: SPCK; New York: Young, 1883)

Marsh, *CR*   Marsh, Jan. *Christina Rossetti: A Literary Biography* (London: Jonathan Cape, 1994)

Maude   *Maude: Prose and Verse.* 1897. Ed. R. W. Crump (Hamden, Conn.: Archon Books, 1976)

Packer   Packer, Lona Mosk. *Christina Rossetti* (Berkeley and Los An-
                  geles: University of California Press, 1963)

PW   *The Poetical Works of Christina Georgina Rossetti.* Ed. with a
                  memoir and notes by William Michael Rossetti (London and
                  New York: Macmillan, 1904)

Rosenblum   Rosenblum, Dolores. *Christina Rossetti: The Poetry of Endurance*
                  (Carbondale: Southern Illinois University Press, 1986)

SF   *Seek and Find: A Double Series of Short Studies of the Benedicite*
                  (London and Brighton: SPCK; New York: Young, 1879)

TF   *Time Flies: A Reading Diary* (London and Brighton: SPCK,
                  1885; Boston: Roberts Brothers, 1886)

VP   *Victorian Poetry*

VN   *Victorian Newsletter*

VS   *Victorian Studies*

INTRODUCTION

MARY ARSENEAU

The essays in this collection offer a new appraisal of an unfamiliar Christina Rossetti, one more radical (even in her conservatism), more ironic, more critical of the literary traditions within which she positions herself, more diverse, and more engaged with political, economic, scientific, and social issues than once she was thought to be. This emergent Christina Rossetti has been "under construction" for almost two decades, her origins traceable to the crucial impetus of R. W. Crump's variorum edition of *The Complete Poems of Christina Rossetti* (1979-90) and the coincident rise of feminist criticism in the academy. In his review of Crump's edition, Jerome J. McGann helpfully suggested that Rossetti's poetry launches a full-scale critique of Victorian gender relations and amatory values,[1] thus inaugurating one of the most important streams of Rossetti scholarship in the 1980s. *The Culture of Christina Rossetti* extends critical understanding of Rossetti's female poetics, interrogates Victorian and current constructions of the woman poet, and re-evaluates Rossetti's relationship to female and male literary traditions. This collection also adds to the contextualization of Rossetti's art within Victorian culture by exploring for the first time her responses to contemporary issues in science, and by expanding knowledge of her engagement with ethics, economics, gender, politics, class structure, religion, and aesthetics.

The Culture of Christina Rossetti debunks the obsolete portrait of Rossetti as an unlearned and reclusive spinster, remote from current ideological debate,[2] writing sincere and spontaneous poetry that was perfect within a limited range but lacking in intellectual depth and substance.[3] Reconsideration of the characterization of Rossetti as unintellectual can begin by scrutinizing for bias two informing histories: the Victorian context in which Rossetti lived and the biographical record of her life. Lionel Stevenson, for example, sees in Rossetti the suppression of a "normally keen mind" and attributes that suppression to a number of forces, including Victorian gender roles, which prescribed that a young woman not be interested in "abstruse topics" or "entertain opinions of her own"; he also, however, remarks upon her lack of

both "curiosity" and "wide classical scholarship." Stevenson rightly, if conde-
scendingly, contextualizes Rossetti's (in his judgment) unexercised intellect
within the gender-, class-, and historically specific expectations of a "well-
brought-up young woman in the Victorian age," but he nevertheless cites
Elizabeth Barrett Browning's "wide classical scholarship" as evidence of
Rossetti's comparative deficiency, thus invoking the exception rather than the
rule.[4] Neither Christina Rossetti nor her sister, Maria, received a formal
education outside the home or instruction in the curriculum of classics,
maths, and sciences that remained a male preserve. As a family, the Rossettis
tended instead to pursue interests in the fine arts. Although brothers Dante
Gabriel and William Michael were exposed to a traditional program of study,
it was not in these disciplines that they would later make their marks. Dante
Gabriel, despite his six years of formal schooling at Mr. Paul's and then King's
College School, displayed no interest or competency in the classics, maths, or
sciences. "It may be feared that there was *no* solid reading—whether history,
biography, or anything else. . . . His intellectual life was nurtured upon fancy
and sympathy, not upon knowledge or information,"[5] states William Michael
(in a comment that betrays the strangely antiliterary prejudice that creative
works do not constitute "solid reading" and that they provide no "knowledge
or information"). In temperament, Christina seems much like Dante Gabriel,
who followed his own inclination in his explorations of art and literature.

Since the biographical record depends very heavily on William Michael's
memoirs, his reconstructions of his sister's life and career must be tested for
reliability. Although he shared a home with his sister for forty-six years,
William Michael's activities took him out of the house daily, beginning in
1836 when he went to day school and continuing after his employment in
the civil service in 1845. Perhaps he knew as few details of the female
Rossettis' daily routine as they knew of his office work. Certainly, in some of
his statements he underestimates his sister Christina; for instance, we must
weigh his report that "Of science and philosophy she knew nothing"[6] against
the clear evidence of her knowledge of both astronomy and biology, and also
against William Michael's own recollection that Plato held great appeal for
Christina—"she read his *Dialogues* over and over again, with ever renewed or
augmented zest."[7] Similarly, although William Michael asserts that Christina's faith was an unintellectual affair and states that she studied theology
"very little indeed" and did not read the Church Fathers,[8] a close reading of
her devotional prose suggests otherwise. Quite simply, here was an intellectual tradition in which William Michael had neither the interest nor the

expertise to judge his sister's knowledge. Finally, his and others' comments disparaging Christina's erudition demand closer scrutiny for gender-biased dismissals of self-education, for privileging of a classical curriculum provided exclusively to males, or for simple misinformation. Christina Rossetti came from a highly literate family, and while Mackenzie Bell notes that as a child she was "desultory in her habits of study," he also adds that "this disposition was compensated for by much wide general reading."[9] She had a high level of what we would today call "cultural literacy": she read in English, Italian, German, and French; knew Italian poets better than most scholars studying her poetry today; and read the important poets, novelists, and critics of her century including Coleridge, Shelley, Keats, Scott, Dickens, Carlyle, Ruskin, L.E.L. (Letitia Elizabeth Landon), Barrett Browning, Browning, Tennyson, and many more. Her letters also make clear that she was a tireless reader of periodicals, including the *Athenaeum, Macmillan's Magazine,* the *Saturday Review, Blackwood's,* and the *Edinburgh Review.* As an adult she approached Dante, Petrarch, Boccaccio, and Spenser as a scholar, spending innumerable afternoons at the British Museum.

Indeed, while there is no denying that Rossetti's primary legacy is poetic rather than scholarly, we should not overlook the latter. Rossetti published more than two thousand pages in a range of works whose focus was not primarily poetic or creative but rather biographical, critical, devotional, or exegetical, including numerous encyclopedia entries, two articles on Dante, and six volumes of devotional prose. The six devotional books demonstrate Rossetti's wide reading in and engagement with the traditions of biblical exegesis, hagiography, and the writings of the Church Fathers and of various divines. These meditative commentaries evince a sophistication and ambition in structure and scope that testify to the intelligence and care marshaled in their composition; furthermore, drawing as they do on a range of subjects including botany, geology, and astronomy, they belie the critical apprehension of Rossetti as narrow in learning. Her life and work provide evidence of a scholarly impulse that she was prevented from fully developing. Rossetti seriously considered undertaking literary biographies of Adelaide Proctor and Elizabeth Barrett Browning (in this instance she declined to proceed without Robert Browning's consent and cooperation), and she actually took a commission and began to research a life of Ann Radcliffe, until a lack of materials forced her to "reluctantly abandon the project."[10] Rossetti agreed to trace allusions to the Italian poets Dante, Petrarch, and Boccaccio for Dr. A. B. Grosart's scholarly edition of Spenser's *The Faerie Queene,* a project from which she withdrew due to ill health.[11] Although readers have valued these aspects of Rossetti's work less highly than her creative achievements, the scholarly and devotional writings attest to her varied interests and abilities and constitute a largely untapped resource for scholars.

Essays in this collection demonstrate how the recluse, saint, and renunciatory spinster of former studies was in fact an active participant in Victorian attempts to grapple with new developments in aesthetics, theology, science, economics, and politics. The contexts considered in the following essays are multiple, embracing both the production and reception of Rossetti's poems and ranging from an examination of contemporary discourses, such as the horticultural magazines that help locate Rossetti's "goblin fruit" technologically, economically, and historically, to a consideration of poems as products that reach the reader in a particular package, whether as illustrated texts or as part of an anthology of women poets. Richard Menke and Margaret Linley examine the commodification of poem and poetess that helps us understand poetic economies in the high Victorian period, while Lorraine Janzen Kooistra considers the commodification of *Goblin Market* in the Victorian and twentieth-century marketplace. Julia Briggs finds in *Speaking Likenesses* evidence of an almost Marxist class consciousness. Kathryn Burlinson and Linda E. Marshall consider Rossetti's work in relation to a cultural context largely unexplored by previous critics: Victorian science. Taken together, these essays revise our thinking about Rossetti's intellectual involvement with the materialist and scientific culture of her age.

Many essays also demonstrate how Rossetti's religion authorized and compelled her cultural critique. Rossetti rejected the values of her society; but the result of this abjuration is, paradoxically, not an escape from the world but an engagement of a most extreme kind. Such an approach runs counter to previous views: that since the life she ultimately valued was eternal and heaven her longed-for home, then quotidian realities must have left her unmoved; or, elsewhere, that since she maintained her faith in an age of increasing doubt, she stood somehow outside of history. As Edith Birkhead put it, "She was hardly touched by the many problems which agitated her age. Living at a time when the conflict between science and religion left Matthew Arnold watching the sea of faith ebb from him, hearing only its 'melancholy, long withdrawing roar,' she sang unclouded by the shadow of doubt."[12] The logic here premises that doubt was the only appropriate response to the challenges posed by scientific advances in Victorian England; Rossetti was not thrown into doubt, so therefore she must have simply ignored scientific discourse. The truth, however, is much more interesting, and essays in this collection show that Rossetti was responsive to the Victorian age's shifting world view. Rossetti's faith was integral to her evaluation of science, and instead of adopting a merely conservative stance of rejecting or ignoring new theories or discoveries, she thought and wrote about how new paradigms could be accommodated to her religion's eternal truths. Rossetti's religious values are likewise shown to inhere in her critique of class privilege and a commodity culture (Menke, Briggs, and Linley), in her reading of the amatory tradition in poetry (Mary Arseneau and Marjorie Stone), and in the formulations of love, desire, and death in her poetry (Alison Chapman and Susan Conley).

Margaret Reynolds and Conley reassess Rossetti's lyric voice and reveal the anger, resistance, and perversity lurking beneath the limpid surfaces of lyrics such as "After Death" and "Remember," effectively debunking the myths of artlessness and simplicity and re-envisioning these poems as formally intricate and radically ironic. Other essays in this collection attempt to situate Rossetti as a woman poet at a particular point in a literary tradition that includes precursors and contemporaries. Arseneau, Stone, Catherine Maxwell, Janzen Kooistra, Conley, and Linley all raise questions about the ways in which Rossetti emulates and critiques, is enabled or constrained by, that tradition. Conley and Linley examine how Rossetti's female poetics develops out of a woman writer's tradition that included Felicia Hemans, L.E.L., and Elizabeth Barrett Browning. While Conley and Linley interrogate from within the construction of the Victorian woman poet's tradition (an enterprise of considerable current interest), Stone and Maxwell, in contrast, suggest new gender-conscious models for positioning the female poet in a mainstream (that is, predominantly male) canon. These essays contribute to the ongoing retrieval of the tradition of the woman poet in the nineteenth century, highlight how Rossetti responds to both male and female traditions in revisionary ways, and engage in a crucial debate in Victorian poetics by examining the role of gender in negotiating Rossetti's position within canons continually under formation.

What does the future hold for Christina Rossetti studies? If this collection is any indication, then we will see more contextualizations of Rossetti's art within a variety of interrelated discourses, including those that address issues of gender, science, economics, politics, aesthetics, religion, or class structure. This is the "newly historicist, culturally materialist" trend that Herbert F. Tucker sees both across the discipline and particularly in the most recent major study of the poetry of Rossetti and her contemporaries, Isobel Armstrong's

Victorian Poetry: Poetry, Poetics, and Politics.[13] Retrieved from neglect by feminist critical attention, Rossetti's writing is now being scrutinized from an ever-expanding array of theoretical positions. Addressing issues of intertextuality (Arseneau, Stone, Maxwell), interdisciplinary positioning (Menke, Janzen Kooistra, Burlinson, Marshall), gender studies (Reynolds, Janzen Kooistra, Chapman, Conley, Linley), and Marxist analysis of class and consumption (Menke, Briggs, Linley), this collection indicates the multiple sites of future debate. Because scholarly attention to Christina Rossetti is belated, however, gaps still remain. McGann has noted that "not a single critic associated with the New Critical movement ever wrote anything about Rossetti," a neglect which he suggests results from the necessity of understanding the "social and historical particulars which feed and shape the distinctive features of her work."[14] Rossetti's technical proficiency, her mastery of form, the tensions, ambiguities, and local details of her poems yield much to good close reading, but Rossetti's unpopularity during the reign of New Criticism has left us even today with a dearth of formalist analysis of her poems. What would be valuable and timely would be close attention to text that takes into account McGann's "social and historical particulars," a critical mode Tucker calls "cultural neo-formalism," which he sees as the next wave of Victorian studies: "The theory of such a cultural neoformalism has yet to be written; we break ground for it, in the meantime, by writing the most locally alert and historically circumspect criticism we can."[15]

Rossetti's Anglo-Catholicism is perhaps both the most formative and the least understood influence on her poetry: scholars have yet to address fully the centrality of religious concepts, language, images, and affective modes in Rossetti's writing. Clearly, we need a more thorough knowledge of Rossetti's faith, and the later phases of her career and the devotional poetry and prose remain areas of neglect. Perhaps prejudiced by critical statements declaring that "at the age of twenty her style as a poet was completely formed" or that her "best poetry was written before she was twenty,"[16] scholarly attention has concentrated on a select few of the early narrative and lyrical poems, at the expense of a full examination of the range of Rossetti's work. The neglect of the later work and the unwillingness to see development in Rossetti's career are connected to a devaluing of the devotional writings. In contrast to the way critics have anatomized Milton's cosmology or Donne's religion, Rossettians often feel compelled merely to comment on the outdatedness of her faith or to lament the limitations it imposed on her life or art. More than ten years after G. B. Tennyson observed in his "Afterword" to *The Achievement of Chris-*

tina Rossetti (1987) that the "single most important lens through which to view Rossetti" is religion,[17] there is still a need to clarify and rehabilitate our view of the operations of religion in enabling, informing, and determining the shape and substance of Rossetti's art.

Much, however, has been achieved in the decades following William E. Fredeman's assessment of the narrowness of criticism on Christina Rossetti (1968).[18] Rossetti studies were given an "elixir of life" with the publication of Crump's edition; more recently, Jan Marsh's *Christina Rossetti: Poems and Prose* has made an ample selection of Rossetti's poetry and fiction affordably accessible for teaching. We have three full reprints of *Speaking Likenesses* (1992, 1994 and 1998), five new printings of *Maude* (1976, 1984, 1993, 1994, and 1998); a selected edition of Rossetti's fiction and nonfiction prose writings (1998); full-length critical studies by Dolores Rosenblum (1986), Antony H. Harrison (1988), Katherine J. Mayberry (1989), and Sharon Smulders (1996); a collection of fifteen essays in *The Achievement of Christina Rossetti* (1987); a centenary double issue of *Victorian Poetry* dedicated to Christina Rossetti (1994); two sustained comparative studies of Rossetti and Emily Dickinson (1987 and 1996); and four new biographies.[19] In the most recent and by far the most detailed and revisionary of these biographies, Jan Marsh thoroughly situates Rossetti's life and career within Victorian literary and social contexts. Christina Rossetti has also received serious treatment in the most recent comprehensive literary history of Victorian poetry, Armstrong's *Victorian Poetry* (1993), and unquestioned prominence in anthologies and studies of the Victorian woman poet including Angela Leighton's *Victorian Women Poets: Writing Against the Heart* (1992), Leighton and Margaret Reynolds's *Victorian Women Poets: An Anthology* (1995), Joseph Bristow's *Victorian Women Poets* (1995), Leighton's *Victorian Women Poets: A Critical Reader* (1996), and Armstrong and Bristow's *Nineteenth-Century Women Poets* (1996).[20] Antony H. Harrison's edition of Rossetti's collected letters, currently in progress (vols. 1–4, 1997–2000), will prove an essential research tool; almost two-thirds of these letters are previously unpublished.[21]

There is much scope yet for future work. Still lacking are scholarly and readily available editions of Rossetti's complete writings, including the prose works, many of which have been out of print for over a century. We need studies of Rossetti's textual revisions, analyses of her prosody, and an annotated edition of the poems that glosses Rossetti's literary allusions and her references to traditional iconography, floral emblems, the Book of Common Prayer, the Bible, and other sources.[22] Furthermore, even given the range of

Rossetti's writings addressed in this collection, some aspects of her work are unrepresented, namely, the poetry for children and the devotional poems, both of which, along with her fiction, merit further study. Such deficiencies, the legacy of an academy once too ready to allot Christina Rossetti the "lowest place" that she claimed for herself, are surely temporary; ahead lie opportunity, excitement, and discovery as scholarly interest and theoretical tools become equal to the complexity and variety of Rossetti's work.

NOTES

1. Jerome J. McGann, "Christina Rossetti's Poems: A New Edition and a Revaluation," *VS* 23 (1980): 237-54.

2. For instance, in *Women-Writers of the Nineteenth Century* (New York: Russell and Russell, 1923), Marjory A. Bald remarks: "The most essential fact of her nature was her singular independence of environment. It is hardly too much to say that the essentials of her art would not have been materially altered if she had lived in the England of either Elizabeth or Charles II." According to Bald, "Christina Rossetti was not a product of her age" and was not influenced by contemporary or past literary currents or by the Victorian era's "historical movements and great intellectual impulses" (pp. 239-40). Similarly, Edith Birkhead in *Christina Rossetti and Her Poetry* (London: Harrap, 1930) states, "A knowledge of the century in which Christina Rossetti lived is of slight assistance in the understanding of her poetry. She dwelt apart in a world of her own" (p. 18).

3. For a contemporary view of Christina Rossetti as a spontaneous poet exceptional in "artless art, if not in intellectual impulse," see Dante Gabriel Rossetti, qtd. in William Sharp, "Some Reminiscences of Christina Rossetti," *Atlantic Monthly* 75 (June 1895): 741. In the twentieth century, scholars have continued to draw a connection between lyrical purity and a lack of aesthetic and intellectual complexity. See Stuart Curran, "The Lyric Voice of Christina Rossetti," *VP* 9 (1971): 292, and Lionel Stevenson, *The Pre-Raphaelite Poets* (New York: Norton, 1972), p. 88. For an insightful discussion of these issues see Joseph Bristow's introduction to *Victorian Women Poets: Emily Brontë, Elizabeth Barrett Browning, Christina Rossetti,* ed. Joseph Bristow (London: Macmillan; New York: St. Martin's, 1995), pp. 1-31.

4. Lionel Stevenson, *The Pre-Raphaelite Poets,* p. 88.

5. William Michael Rossetti, "Memoir," in *Dante Gabriel Rossetti: His Family Letters,* ed. William Michael Rossetti (London: Ellis and Elvey, 1895), 1:83.

6. William Michael Rossetti, "Memoir," in *PW,* p. lxix.

7. William Michael Rossetti, "Memoir," in *PW,* p. lxx. It is difficult to determine what William Michael means by "philosophy" here. If he means philosophy in its primary sense, then the statement seems incompatible with Christina's enthusias-

tic reading of Plato, though perhaps this is explained by the fact that William Michael refers to Plato not as a philosopher but as "Among very great authors" (p. lxx). Possibly, by "philosophy" William Michael means "natural philosophy," with which, as chapters 7 and 8 in this collection show, Christina was more conversant than William Michael was aware.

8. William Michael Rossetti, "Memoir," in *PW,* pp. liv and lxix.

9. Bell, p. 15.

10. Marsh, *CR,* p. 496.

11. Marsh, *CR,* p. 457 and Bell, p. 37.

12. Edith Birkhead, p. 16.

13. Herbert F. Tucker, review of *Victorian Poetry: Poetry, Poetics, and Politics,* by Isobel Armstrong, *VP* 33 (1995): 175.

14. Jerome J. McGann, "The Religious Poetry of Christina Rossetti," *Critical Inquiry* 10 (1983): 128, 132.

15. Herbert F. Tucker, "Introduction," in *Critical Essays on Alfred Lord Tennyson,* ed. Herbert F. Tucker (New York: G. K. Hall, 1993), p. 8.

16. Edmund Gosse, *English Literature: An Illustrated Record,* vol. 4 (New York: Grosset and Dunlap, 1904), p. 350, and Stuart Curran, "The Lyric Voice of Christina Rossetti," p. 288.

17. G. B. Tennyson, "Afterword: Love God and Die—Christina Rossetti and the Future," in Kent, p. 351.

18. William E. Fredeman, "Christina Rossetti" in *The Victorian Poets: A Guide to Research,* ed. Frederic E. Faverty, 2d ed. (Cambridge: Harvard University Press, 1968), pp. 284-93.

19. *Speaking Likenesses* is reprinted in *Forbidden Journeys: Fairy Tales and Fantasies by Victorian Women,* ed. Nina Auerbach and U. C. Knoepflmacher (Chicago and London: University of Chicago Press, 1992); *Christina Rossetti: Poems and Prose,* ed. Jan Marsh (London: J. M. Dent, Everyman Library, 1994); and *Selected Prose of Christina Rossetti,* ed. David A. Kent and P. G. Stanwood (New York: St. Martin's, 1998). *Maude* has been reprinted in *Maude: Prose and Verse,* ed. and with an introduction by R. W. Crump (Hamden: Archon, 1976); *Christina Rossetti: Selected Poems,* ed. C. H. Sisson (Manchester: Carcanet Press, 1984); *Maude; On Sisterhoods; A Woman's Thoughts about Women,* ed. Elaine Showalter (New York: New York University Press, 1993); *Christina Rossetti: Poems and Prose;* and *Selected Prose of Christina Rossetti.* The publication of Sharon Smulders's *Christina Rossetti Revisited* (New York: Twayne, 1996), the second title on Rossetti in Twayne's English Authors Series, is further evidence of the current process of revaluation. The four recent biographies are Georgina Battiscombe, *Christina Rossetti: A Divided Life* (London: Constable, 1981), Kathleen Jones, *Learning Not to Be First: The Life of Christina Rossetti* (Moreton-in-Marsh: Windrush Press, 1991; New York: St. Martin's, 1992), Frances Thomas, *Christina Rossetti* (London: Virago, 1994), and Jan Marsh, *CR.* The comparative studies of

Rossetti and Dickinson are *The Language of Exclusion: The Poetry of Emily Dickinson and Christina Rossetti* (New York: Greenwood, 1987) by Sharon Leder with Andrea Abbott, and Claudia Ottlinger's *The Death-Motif in the Poetry of Emily Dickinson and Christina Rossetti* (Frankfurt: Peter Lang, 1996). The other critical works mentioned are found in the list of abbreviations for this collection.

20. *Victorian Women Poets: An Anthology,* ed. Angela Leighton and Margaret Reynolds (Oxford: Blackwell, 1995); *Victorian Women Poets: Emily Brontë, Elizabeth Barrett Browning, Christina Rossetti,* ed. Joseph Bristow; *Victorian Women Poets: A Critical Reader,* ed. Angela Leighton (Oxford: Blackwell, 1996); and *Nineteenth-Century Women Poets,* ed. Isobel Armstrong and Joseph Bristow with Cath Sharrock (Oxford: Oxford University Press, 1996).

21. *The Letters of Christina Rossetti: Volume 1, 1834-1873,* ed. Antony H. Harrison (Charlottesville and London: University Press of Virginia, 1997).

22. McGann called for such an edition in 1980 in "Christina Rossetti's Poems: A New Edition and a Revaluation," p. 240.

I: INTERTEXTS AND INFLUENCES

CHAPTER I

Speaking Unlikenesses

The Double Text in Christina Rossetti's "After Death" and "Remember"

MARGARET REYNOLDS

> Small though not positively short, she might easily be
> overlooked but would not easily be forgotten.
>
> —Christina Rossetti, *Maude: Prose and Verse* (1850)

> Indifferent to language, enigmatic and feminine, this space
> underlying the written is rhythmic, unfettered, irreducible to
> its intelligible verbal translation; it is musical, anterior to
> judgement, but restrained by a single guarantee: syntax.
>
> —Julia Kristeva, *Revolution in Poetic Language* (1974)

Once upon a time Christina Rossetti was simple. Her brother William Michael says that he "cannot remember ever seeing her in the act of composition." He admits that this is strange given that he and his younger sister were "almost constantly in the same house" from the date of her birth up to the year 1876, some forty-six years, woman and girl. Nevertheless, William Michael declares authoritatively that Rossetti's methods of composition were artless and unselfconscious:

Christina's habits of composing were eminently of the spontaneous kind.
I question her having ever once deliberated with herself whether or not
she would write something or other, and then, after thinking out a

subject, having proceeded to treat it in regular spells of work. Instead of this, something impelled her feelings, or "came into her head," and her hand obeyed the dictation. I suppose she scribbled lines off rapidly enough, and afterwards took whatever amount of pains she deemed requisite for keeping them in right form and expression.[1]

In spite of never having seen her at it, William Michael knows perfectly well how Christina writes and why. Or rather he knows perfectly well how girls write and why. They get taken over by something to do with feeling and then they take dictation. And they do it secretly. They live in the public eye, always accessible to family scrutiny, "almost constantly in the same house," and yet, like Jane Austen alerted by the creaking drawing-room door,[2] like Barrett Browning thrusting her manuscript scraps under the cushions,[3] like Christina's own Maude "slipping out of sight some scrawled paper,"[4] the practice of writing is hidden away, kept secret and separate from the performance of social engagement. That much of William Michael's observation is true and to be trusted. The part that is entirely unreliable is the fiction of spontaneity. To begin with it doesn't match with the determined control which made this hard-won space of privacy for writing. Then William Michael himself knows that it's not altogether true for even while saying that he never saw his sister at work he has to add a qualifier: "I cannot remember ever seeing her in the act of composition (I take no account here of the bouts-rimés sonnets of 1848)."[5] Obviously he did see her write those sonnets that were devised in public for immediate drawing-room consumption to entertain a family party at Brighton. In Christina's *Maude,* written two years later, her heroine also exerts herself "to amuse the party" but later, chastened, returns to writing alone in the privacy of her bedroom, and refuses to perform in public.[6] Rossetti herself knew what William Michael seems to have forgotten. She was not L.E.L., nor meant to be, and spontaneity and sprightly drawing-room entertainment, along with being impelled by "feelings" or whatever "came into her head" to be "scribbled" off, was the pride of the Improvisatrice as well as her doom.[7]

Just as the details of when, where, and how Rossetti wrote her poems were hidden from her brother, so *what* she wrote was equally obscured. Partly, Rossetti herself made it that way. At an early age Rossetti developed a scrupulous manner which meant, her brother teased, that "she would soon become so polite it would be impossible to live with her."[8] The hard-bound surface hides the vulnerable self. In a similar way Rossetti's own manuscript notebooks were elaborately tidy; William Michael refers to her "extremely neat but . . . rather timid and formal script"[9] and to her "usual excessive neatness of caligraphy [*sic*]."[10] Manners maketh the woman and by her hand you shall know her; for if Rossetti herself built up these defensive surfaces, her two brothers, and William Michael in particular in his later role of editor and literary executor, successfully obscured Rossetti further by creating a polished veneer that reflected back his own image of the woman poet. His 1904 edition of Rossetti is the main culprit here, carefully listing all extant portraits of the poetess, as if the likeness were the life, and neatly controlling the reader's interpretation of the poems by putting them all under individual headings described as "Some Leading Themes, or Key-Notes of Feeling, in the Poems of Christina Rossetti." These are: Personal Experiences and Emotions; Death; The Aspiration for Rest; Vanity of Vanity; Love of Animals; Winter; The Loveliness of the Rose.[11]

William Michael's list betrays his terms. His sister was a woman. Her poems must be feminine, so feminine he will make them: a particular nineteenth-century feminine that makes lyrical utterance into autobiography; death, especially her own death, into the ideal "most poetical topic" for a woman poet;[12] and all rounded off with devotional themes and subjects drawn from the nursery and the boudoir. The surface, the public image, once again intrudes and the real Rossetti is hidden from view. She is, like her own Maude, "easily overlooked."

This is a parable about what has also happened to her poetry. Scrupulously polite, excessively neat, redolently feminine, Rossetti's poetry is, nonetheless "not easily forgotten." In spite of having spent much of the twentieth century labeled as a "minor lyric voice,"[13] Rossetti has yet managed to hold on to her popular appeal. More than that, recently critics have begun to attribute Rossetti's unforgetableness to her "scandalous" tendencies, to her "capacity to unsettle," and to the "instability" of her texts.[14] Dualism, doubleness, repetition, alterity, have long been noted as prime influences and techniques in Rossetti's poetry, but, in fact, that double model is often the very essence of the disturbing quality which marks and which so richly empowers Rossetti's writing. Isobel Armstrong writes of the Victorian double poem, "The simpler the surface of the poem, the more likely it is that a second and more difficult poem will exist beneath it."[15] If the surface Rossetti is neat, polite and "simple," the hidden Rossetti underneath, the one William Michael never saw at work, is perverse, caustic, and complex.

Goblin Market, which so obviously is not the simple nursery tale it pretends to be, was the poem that first drew serious scholarly attention for its rich feast of repetitions, doublenesses, puns, and play with every form of orality going. Wearing its linguistic virtuosity on its dustjacket, the jouissance of *Goblin Market* has pleasured many textual analysts. In fact the rest of Rossetti's work, with its comprehensive Freudian panoply of dreams, puns, mirrors, dualities, and reiterations of desire and loss, lends itself to psychoanalytic analysis. And this is true of the most popular of anthology pieces, the most apparently transparent of Rossetti's lyrics, provided always that one remembers three things: first, that these are not in any way poems about Rossetti's own self or experience; they are imagined only and by no means the "love personals" she (rightly) feared they might be taken for. Second, that Rossetti knew what it was to work across and through oppositions; that "white" and "black" and "Heaven" and "Hell" both exclude and simultaneously imply one another. And third, that Rossetti's own literary ambition included an aim at "conciseness," which could often be so pared down that it ended up risking, even courting, "obscurity."[16]

The two sonnets "After Death" and "Remember" were both composed in 1849, "After Death" on April 28 and "Remember" on July 25. Both were written out by Rossetti in the same manuscript notebook, now in the Bodleian, and the two poems appeared consecutively, "Remember" first, in the 1862 edition of *Goblin Market and Other Poems*. Both poems are very well known, much reprinted and, especially in the case of "Remember," much loved. And yet, while they often receive honorable mentions in Rossetti criticism, very little sustained attention has been given to them.[17]

After Death

The curtains were half drawn, the floor was swept
    And strewn with rushes, rosemary and may
    Lay thick upon the bed on which I lay,
Where thro' the lattice ivy-shadows crept.
He leaned above me, thinking that I slept
    And could not hear him; but I heard him say:
    "Poor child, poor child:" and as he turned away
Came a deep silence, and I knew he wept.
He did not touch the shroud, or raise the fold
    That hid my face, or take my hand in his,
      Or ruffle the smooth pillows for my head:
      He did not love me living; but once dead
    He pitied me; and very sweet it is
To know he still is warm tho' I am cold. (*CP*, 1:37–38)

In the editions of Rossetti's poetry published in her lifetime (1862, 1865, and the American edition of 1875) both "After Death" and "Remember" were subtitled "Sonnet," drawing attention to the tight literary formula they use. Each has a clear-cut octet followed by a sestet, and although each employs a strict rhyme scheme, they still manage to sound intimate and colloquial. In the case of "After Death" the two parts of the rhyme scheme are each palindromic (ABBAABBA and CDEEDC); "Remember" uses the palindrome for the octet while the sestet is slightly irregular (ABBAABBA and CDDEECE). That the surface of each poem is so restrained in form, in syntax, in grammatical exactitude, in precision of vocabulary, sets the reader up for the more wayward texts underneath. "A Sonnet is a coin: its face reveals / The soul, its converse, to what Power 'tis due," wrote Dante Gabriel in the introductory poem to his sonnet sequence, *The House of Life*.[18]

"After Death" already suggests its two-sidedness in its title. There was a life, now there is death (and continuing life), and the one state will be measured against the other. Whether or not this is a "real" death is open to question. Generally, and because Rossetti so insistently returns to a landscape beyond the grave where a speaking self still feels and knows and haunts the living, it is taken that Rossetti's speaker here is dead and laid out prior to burial. In fact, linguistically speaking, all the phrases the poem uses, "dead," "slept," "shroud," "cold," could be used, as they conventionally are, as synonyms, euphemisms, or exaggerations for some other state dramatically declared to be a death in life. The example that particularly comes to mind, suggestively in this case, is the way that Barrett Browning uses exactly these terms and phrases to describe the abjection and self-loathing of the raped and abused Marian in her *Aurora Leigh* (1856/1857). Using a vocabulary common in Victorian sexual morality, Marian repeatedly describes her rape as a change which is "death" or "murder" and says that she cannot now return to life and respectable marriage because she cannot "get up from my grave, / And wear my chin-cloth for a wedding-veil."[19]

The shifting context of Rossetti's poem is suggested by the physical scene-setting in the first four lines. The curtains are "half drawn"; the floor is "strewn," that is, partly covered, with rushes; "rosemary and may" lie on the bed, and presumably, on her, the poet-speaker. Everything is half covered, both revealed and concealed, not light, nor dark, but both at once. And this is confirmed in the fourth line where "thro' the lattice ivy-shadows crept." The lattice, as Catherine Maxwell rightly says, along with the rushes and the detail of the flowers on the bed, situates the poem within a mock medieval tradition of the enclosed lady, the "high-born maiden" invoked by Tennyson in "The Lady of Shalott" and by Browning in "Porphyria's Lover."[20] But in its simplest descriptive image it also points to the black and white crisscross, that is double and contradictory, the half-seen, half-hidden that is the literary essence of the poem. And, "thro' the lattice ivy-shadows crept."

This line is, literally, creepy. While the half-seen, half-hidden is economically set up in the first lines, there is also a clear sense of barriers crossed, divisions broken down, laws of place transgressed. The outside world has come into the inside, death has invaded life (or vice versa), and the seen/not-seen of the "lattice" is no protection. "Ivy-shadows" creep (crept/creep/crypt) from the outside to the inside . . . and on the inside . . . what happens? "He leaned above me, thinking that I slept / And could not hear him." Close juxtaposition of words and phrases in Rossetti is never accidental. The shadows creep through, and "He," now introduced into the poem's consciousness for the first time, "he" leans above "me" in a privacy where he (wrongly) believes himself unobserved and where, consequently, he believes it unnecessary to constrain or curb himself. We don't know who this "he" is, but there is a hint. In this secret space, unobserved, "he" says, "Poor child, poor child." Now doubleness and reciprocity, meaning one term by saying another, are trademarks in Rossetti poems. Maxwell begins to grasp this by pointing out that the trick is to turn this, apparently conventional, term around. If he calls her "child," then what does she call him? The answer is "Father." Maxwell (correctly) positions the poem in the Confessional mode, deduces (correctly) that this must be a privileged male given that he is permitted a private interview with a woman alone in her bedroom, puzzles (incorrectly) over who such a man can be "with no familial or projected familial ties"—and comes up with the ingenious suggestion that this "he" is a priest.[21]

It's easier than that, of course, and worse than that. The absent term here, the one that cannot be spoken out, but only gestured at, is the name of Father. And why is the word unsaid? Because the act of naming would name more than the father, for it would label the argument of the poem too; fix its "meaning" too overtly. In Lacan's terms the "nom-du-père" represents the Law of the Father which marks out the border between Culture and "nature abandoned to the law of copulation."[22] Those borders, those barriers, are all broken down in this poem and the key term that fixes the transgression, that names the crime, is left out. In the silences of the poem, through the opposition of one term (child) which obliquely spells another term (father), the semiotic signals its coded message from within the body of the text, while the law of the symbolic remains written on its skin. That the meaning conveyed by Kristeva's semiotic is associated with the child's pre-Oedipal stage contact with the mother's body is significant here. The speaker in this poem may indeed be a "child" ("poor child, poor child") and the poem may speak exactly at the moment of transition on to the Oedipal phase. The rhetoric in "After Death" is "artless," childlike, uncomplicated, apparently naive, and from within that "innocence" a message spells itself out. The poem refuses to name the father, and in that absence, that silence, a new knowingness marks the entry into the symbolic. Maud Ellmann says that "For Lacan . . . incest is bad grammar."[23] The taboo against it is "identical with an order in language."[24] Rossetti's poem, so grammatically precise, so coolly ordered, leaves out the naming to keep her grammar and syntax intact.

But everything else is breached. The sestet of the poem, where one would expect to find some change in theme, argument, or mood, hots up the sense of anxiety and threat of transgression. "He did not touch the shroud, or raise the fold / That hid my face, or take my hand in his, / Or ruffle the smooth pillows for my head." It begins with a negative, "He did not." But language works in linear progression and functions, as explained by de Saussure and endorsed by Lacan, only on differences, for there are no positive terms. So we can only go about the process of imagining the negative here by first conceiving the action to be negated. We are invited to imagine him doing exactly all these things; touching the shroud, raising the fold to expose her face, taking her hand. If he does not actually carry out these actions—and we are told so only once, so that we are inclined to forget the negative as the list goes on—he still could do them, might do them, might long to do them. "He did not ruffle" the pillows so that they are no longer "smooth" but some implied "different" term. Rough? Roughed up? Both are suggested by the assonance in spite of the apparent transparency of "ruffle." Like Emily Dickinson's poem "He fumbles at your soul" Rossetti's sonnet places us in a readerly discomfort. We know "He did not" do these things on this occasion. But has he done them before? By prioritizing the negative the poem invites us to imagine some surprise in the speaker's voice, some assumption that the familiar pattern will be, could well be repeated yet again.

The obscure sense of invasion that governs the opening section of the poem is made very strong here. A should-be-externalized object intrudes threateningly into a discrete space. In this particular context first the room is invaded, and then the garments, wrapping up, closing off, protecting, identifying ("the fold that hid my face") the very body of the speaker, are all twitched aside by linguistic sleight of hand. In Rossetti's language "differences" are all, and the pull between the said and the not-said is always making spaces filled with meaning. Or a space where meaning can be thrown out.

Kristeva's account of the processes of abjection includes a story about "The Improper/Unclean":

> Loathing an item of food, a piece of filth, waste or drug. The spasms and vomiting that protect me. The repugnance, the retching that thrusts me to the side and turns me away from defilement, sewage, muck. . . . But since the food is not an "order" for "me," who am only in their (mother and father) desire, I expel myself, I spit myself out, I abject myself within the same motion through which "I" claim to establish myself. That detail, perhaps an insignificant one, but one that they ferret out, empha- size, evaluate, that trifle turns me inside out, guts sprawling; it is thus that they see that "I" am in the process of becoming an other at the expense of my own death. During that course in which "I" become, I give birth to myself amid the violence of sobs, of vomit.[25]

Kristeva's language sounds extravagant beside Rossetti's reflecting surfaces, but it tells a truth about what is being thrown out, abjected in Rossetti's poetry.

In "After Death" (and in "Remember") Rossetti's speaker spits out, vomits up, the "unclean" that weighs into her silences. What she has to say is unpalatable. She spews out a truth (which may or may not be a personal truth) about dominance, about power and sex relations, and that truth is nauseating. Like the bulimic who exercises control over her body (and her self-image) by puking up all that she deems unnecessary, redundant, ugly, Rossetti's verse throws up the weighty burden of her message. And, like the bulimic, she does it in secret, for that story is not on the public surface. The body evacuates; the social self closes over. The semiotic splurges; the symbolic tightens.

And yet even in this "involuntary" spasm there may be a positive process of self-creation. For in the process of throwing up this waste, the speaker/ poet/Rossetti, otherwise hidden from view, does become "I," gives birth to an assertive self at the cost of her own death. The death part is often portrayed literally; that is partly why Rossetti employs so many living-beyond-death speakers. But the speaking-out self also gets born here, though the reader has to pay close attention to hear "the violence of sobs, of vomit."

In the last three lines of "After Death" Rossetti's "I" becomes an "other" separating herself from the father who "names" her ("Poor child, poor child") but whom she dare not name. We are told that "He did not love me living." How anyone who reads nineteenth-century literature, with its many ironic female corpses, can take this at face value baffles me. He did not love me. Maybe true, but doubtless he used me, controlled me, perhaps he even hated me. And once "dead"—as opposed to alive, vital, demanding, assertive, self-directed—then certainly he may "pity" me. Just as Porphyria's lover pitied her, as Lancelot pitied the Lady of Shalott, as the Duke pitied his Last Duchess, as Dickens pitied Little Nell, as Hardy pitied Tess.

So he pities me . . . "and" . . . Rossetti's speaker here uses "and," notice. Not "but" or "yet" or "still." Her conjunctions, like everything else, are telling. "And" means that the sentiment which follows, her sentiment, her feeling, expressed for the very first time in the poem, has some direct connection to what went before—that is, his "not loving" her, but now weeping and "pity-ing" her. She feels this not in spite of what he feels, has felt, about her, but because of it. And what she feels is pleasure . . . cruel, "cold," dispassionate pleasure. A pleasure that is "sweet" with all the erotic and physically realized sensuality (of food and of sex) that the word can bear.

In her reading of "After Death" Maxwell is troubled by the "perversity" of "sweet" here, and rightly so. She points out that its freakish insistent power is connected to the fact that the words "warm" and "cold" in the last lines, descriptions of each of the poem's protagonists' respective positions—he is now "warm" and she is "cold"—might function as synonyms for "emotionally susceptible" and "emotionally detached."[26] This is the right track, but there is more, much more, here. As Isobel Armstrong has shown, "warm" and "warmth" in Rossetti's vocabulary very often carry connotations of an intense erotic.[27] In "After Death" he—the man who invades, breaks laws, enters in—"still is warm." If anything, he is even hotter than before, the restraint of "He did not" pushing at the boundary of suggestion hinting that now, more than ever now, in a moment of intense but rigidly policed desire, would he like to do the things he once did. But now she, the speaker, is "dead" and another taboo, perhaps stronger and yet more deliciously tantalizing than the one she fails to name, denies and bars. And the effects of his thwarted taunted desire are "sweet" for the speaker. Now, at last, she is "cold"—calculating, detached, in charge, indifferent, cruel—a dominatrix whose power of denial (so long denied to her) is indeed "sweet."

"Perverse" the poem is, not least because the "père-version" it uncovers, and deconstructs, is written over with a new text that asserts "I." But only if the reader sees. Or rather, only if the reader hears. For Rossetti's readers have to listen to her talking poem and to analyze the hidden traumas described. In the meantime they return as compulsive repetitions. Listen to what she says in "Remember."

> Remember me when I am gone away,
>   Gone far away into the silent land;
>   When you can no more hold me by the hand,
> Nor I half turn to go yet turning stay.
> Remember me when no more day by day
>   You tell me of our future that you planned:
>   Only remember me; you understand
> It will be late to counsel then or pray.
> Yet if you should forget me for a while
>   And afterwards remember, do not grieve:
>   For if the darkness and corruption leave
> A vestige of the thoughts that once I had,
> Better by far you should forget and smile
>   Than that you should remember and be sad. (*CP,* 1:37)

The first question to ask is then: remember . . . what? Of course, the answer looks like "me." "Remember me" is repeated three times in the first eight lines and the title of the sonnet is often mistakenly given as "Remember me." But it's a Rossetti trick. As the poem moves on to the sestet the instruction to "remember" appears twice, but in neither case is it made clear exactly what may, or may not, be remembered there. Everyone knows, or feels as if they know, this poem. It's in all the anthologies, it's on all the poetry request programs. It's popular because it's short, neat, and has no difficult words in it (with the possible exception of "vestige"), and perhaps above all, because it seems to embody the romantic ideal of self-sacrificing womanhood that is to be demanded of a poem where the signature at the bottom relentlessly over-determines interpretation. Rossetti scholars fall into the trap. W. David Shaw says that in this lyric of "barely repressed pain"

> Rossetti discovers that the most exquisite and refined torture is, not to be forgotten by her beloved, but to inflict suffering on *him.* Tactful concern for the lover now displaces any self-centered desire to live on in his memory. . . . "Harsh towards herself, towards others full of ruth." That line (5) from "A Portrait" seems to me the best single comment on

the courtesy and ease with which the sonnet "Remember" absorbs the
pain of death, turning self-regard into an exquisitely refined contest in
gentility and tact.[28]

Exquisite, refined, genteel, selfless, tactful; William Michael would have
recognized this Christina.

"Remember" looks like a love poem. But then that might mean that we
have already made assumptions about who is speaking to whom that go
beyond what is actually in the text. Apart from knowing a woman to be the
author, why do we take it that this is a woman speaking? Because, in de
Beauvoir's terms, "He is the Subject, he is the Absolute—she is the Other."[29]
The (supposed) listener/man in this poem is obviously someone out there in
the world doing things, he is "one"; she, the speaker/woman, is clearly
"Other"—she doesn't have an independent existence beyond this relationship.
She is anxious that he should remember her (and she goes on about it so much
that the implication is that he won't), so that she will exist.

The active/passive opposition set out in this poem further implies a feminine
signature. Cixous's "Sorties" diagram lines up activity, along with sun, culture,
day, father, head, logos, with the masculine principle while the feminine
principle lines up with passivity, moon, nature, night, mother, heart, pathos.[30]
The ultimate passivity for women, enacted so often in Rossetti's poems, explicit
in "After Death" and hinted at in "Remember," is death. Not that there's any
reason here to explain why this speaker is about to die. The referent is absent,
but presumed, because the condition of (assumed) femininity includes the
condition of passivity and death. "The silent land" is pretty vague, and "the
darkness and corruption" not much better, but nonetheless the idea that this
speaker is about to die is quite acceptable in our cultural positioning; women
die, men mourn, it's a classic literary trope and one that Rossetti exploits to
the full. Interestingly it's quite hard to turn it the other way around, because
then what would a he-speaker be dying of? going to war? There are few
possibilities. Men have to die for a reason; women just do.

So. The nice version of this poem goes: "Please remember me when I'm
dead, but on the other hand, if it's going to make you unhappy to remember
me, then I love you so much ('For if the darkness and corruption leave / A
vestige of the thoughts that once I had') that I'd rather that you did forget
about me so that you can be happy."

It is true that this reading is in the poem. But it's not the only one. As
Angela Leighton has observed, "Behind Rossetti's 'Aesthetic of Renunciation'

it is possible to discern an alternative aesthetics of secrecy, self-containment, and caprice."[31] And the clue to the capricious reading lies in the verbs. The first verb to appear is the odd construction applied to the speaker, "when I am gone away." That the verb here is "to be" used in the present tense to convey a future idea, and without any active verb-construction—like "When I have gone away"—applied to the speaker, makes the sentence feel oddly passive. By contrast in the opening octet the listener is given active verbs lining him (it/they/she) up with the masculine principle and making the *listener* the dominant party. "When you can no more hold me by the hand" . . . so he does the holding; "I half turn to go yet turning stay" . . . so she makes a move away, but doesn't quite manage that bid for independence; "when no more day by day / You tell me of our future that you planned" . . . *our* future? that *you* planned? . . . so she didn't have a say in it; "It will be late to counsel then or pray." . . . O.K., is that what he does all the time? goes on at her, giving advice and asking her to do things?

The way these verbs work means that this speaker manages, almost secretly, subtextually, to reveal that the he-listener is the chief actor in their relationship. In life she, the speaker, is "use-value."[32] He uses her for whatever agenda it is that he has in mind, personal or social, and she has no say in anything. (Except, of course, through the medium of the poem.) He acts and she is acted upon.

Just as he acts and she is acted upon in "After Death." Interestingly, in both poems the same image, the same idea of action, appears. In "Remember" the speaker looks toward the day "When you can no more hold me by the hand." In "After Death" the he-presence in the poem does not "take my hand in his." It's a resonant absence—or presence. The father takes the child by the hand; the lover takes the beloved by the hand; patriarchy takes a hand and she is taken, wherever this père-verted discourse is organized.

What about the pretty end then?—"if the darkness and corruption leave / A vestige of the thoughts that once I had." What thoughts are these? Thus far, they all seem to be cross, fed-up thoughts about how he is bullying her and lecturing her. Maybe then *these* are the thoughts that will get left behind, the traces, like fossils left on the face of the earth. And maybe the "darkness and corruption" here is not death (as in the nice version), but the darkness and corruption of her anger, her distress, at his conventional use of her. No wonder then that he should "forget and smile" because, maybe, just maybe, what is going on here is not that she wants him to forget so that he can be happy because she loves him so much, but that if he remembers, and remembers the truth, then he will be sad. And the implication is that so he should be, because he's going to realize what a shit he's been all along. "Better by far" does not sound much like a generous valedictory wish any more; it sounds like a curse, a threat, a bitter promise that is perverse and "sweet" and cruel in the mouth of the vengeful speaker.

Once upon a time Christina Rossetti was simple.

But Christina loved games, puns, parodies, and secrets, and while William Michael and so many later readers have mooned over the "broken-hearted"-ness of her poetry, Rossetti has played a joke.[33] Self-effacing, hidden, secret, behind, underneath, are words that are often associated with Rossetti, yet what goes on in that underneath, still needs excavation. The curiously throw-away reference to an evolutionary context that appears in "Remember" may provide a model. "Darkness and corruption" may, after all, be the troubled present, the nineteenth century itself, the period of Rossetti's own lived life, fraught with personal and social prohibitions that make indirect speaking necessary. But still in that place a trace may be left of the individual life, a vestige of (self) creation.[34] Others coming after, remembering Rossetti, will be able to read the trace of the hidden life beneath the cover story. Not that the one excludes the other. "After Death" and "Remember" both have (at least) two readings. In each case a subversive text is inscribed within a complaisant poem, but they are simultaneously compatible.

In 1856 Christina Rossetti wrote a story about a picture called "The Lost Titian." It was published in *The Crayon* in New York and was later included in Rossetti's *Commonplace and Other Short Stories* (1870). Dante Gabriel called this collection "the most everyday affair possible" but he misses the point. Compiling the commonplace book, a scrapbook or family album containing favorite quotations, recipes, autographs, and illustrations, provided a famil-iar domestic occupation for Victorian women; and scrapbooks, with all their implications for doubleness, text and revised text, fragments reworked, were a preoccupation with his sister. There is also a curious echo here in the title, which Christina said she just couldn't manage to improve. Years since, when Dante Gabriel had shown John Ruskin Christina's *Goblin Market,* Ruskin had declared

> no publisher—I am deeply grieved to know this—would take them, so full are they of quaintness and other offences. Irregular measure . . . is the calamity of modern poetry. . . . Your sister should exercise herself in the severest commonplace of metre until she can write as the public like.[35]

Doubtless Dante Gabriel showed the letter to Christina; doubtless she remembered it; doubtless she replied with her title. Another Christina pun,
another joke, another hidden text.

"The Lost Titian" tells the story of Gianni, a colleague and rival of Titian's
in Renaissance Venice. Gianni is a successful and popular painter, but his life
and his methods are suspect, and his position is threatened by Titian's preeminence, soon to be confirmed by the unveiling of his latest masterpiece.
One night, in an apparently friendly game of dice, Titian, drunk with wine
and success, stakes his newly created work—and Gianni wins. Jealous of the
Master's fame, Gianni daubs over the picture with coarse pigments, and then,
on the blank surface, he paints "a dragon flaming, clawed, preposterous."
Falling from favor and into debt, Gianni is beset by his creditors, who are
unaware of the presence of Titian's masterpiece, while Titian himself does not
recognize his own painting. To Gianni's horror, the dragon is nonetheless
claimed by another creditor who takes a fancy to its gaudy show and sets it
up as an inn sign. Gianni spends the rest of his life trying to paint a new
dragon that will be accepted in satisfactory exchange, but to no avail. So when
Gianni dies, still silent, Titian's masterpiece remains hidden, lost forever. Or
"perhaps not quite lost": "Reader, should you chance to discern over wayside
inn or metropolitan hotel a dragon pendent, or should you find such an effigy
amid the lumber of a broker's shop, whether it be red, green or piebald,
demand it importunately, pay for it liberally, and in the privacy of home scrub
it. It *may* be that from behind the dragon will emerge a fair one, fairer than
Andromeda, and that to you will appertain the honor of yet further exalting
Titian's greatness in the eyes of a world."[36]

The double texts of Rossetti's poems are the other way round, of course.
Underneath the "fair one" with her smooth surface is a "preposterous" dragon
who nonetheless is an Andromeda waiting to be unchained. And when that
cruel-perverse-Rossetti-dragon is revealed, it will contribute to Rossetti's
greatness: "Reader . . . in the privacy of home scrub it." In the privacy of
"home" the "unheimlich" will be uncovered.[37] "Uncanny" is a word often
associated with Rossetti's poetry and it's a right word. As a good Victorian
daughter and sister Rossetti is always at home—"almost constantly in the
same house." And yet her poetry is "unheimlich" because it speaks, and it
says more than it means. Rossetti wrote in secret and she wrote secrets. Not
necessarily her own, but everybody's secrets. Her poetry is our talking-cure.
Her protagonists speak, confess, tell.[38] In their nightmares and their dreams
they compulsively repeat the traumas of desire and loss. Her dead women are

the corpses who have fallen (cadaver/cadere) and lost themselves in decay, but they paradoxically project (abject/throw out/throw up) a hidden self, a vital self, in the process.[39] Squeezed in between, or out between, the spaces in the text is the secret message, written "in white ink" that seeps and oozes through the page.[40] In Kristeva's terms, the semiotic speaks through, or beyond, or out of, the symbolic. The symbolic in Rossetti is always that "excessively neat" surface held together by the decorum of the "single guarantee: syntax." But "underlying the written," and quite as meaningful, even more powerful, is the silent speaking space, "enigmatic and feminine . . . rhythmic, unfettered, irreducible to its intelligible verbal translation . . . musical, anterior to judgement."[41] But you have to listen hard. At the center of both "After Death" and "Remember" there is a silence. In "After Death" there "Came a deep silence" just before the speaker lets out the second bitter text. In "Remember" the speaker projects herself into a time when she will be gone away "into the silent land" and her second bitter text might be remembered. But it has, mostly, been forgotten, or rather, not heard. In the double texts of Rossetti's poems her "two lips" may speak together but they may also mumble into silence.[42]

Yet I suspect Rossetti herself knew this well enough. Her "conciseness" could lead to "obscurity," and that condition of obscurity, of being hidden from view, of being overlooked, probably appeared to her an inevitable condition of her status as a Victorian woman who was also a poet. In her prose story *Speaking Likenesses* (1874) Rossetti tells a tale about feminine acquiescence and propriety. Flora dreams about a tea-party where a game called "Self-Help" is invented to be played by a group of grotesque children: "The boys were players, and the girls were played (if I may be allowed such a phrase)." The bodies of the boys here are spiky—"One boy bristled with prickly quills like a porcupine"—or they are sharply angled, or covered in fishhooks. The girls, on the other hand, are gelatinous, oozing, slidey, fluid, and liable to be rubbed away: "One girl exuded a sticky liquid and came off on the fingers; another, rather smaller, was slimy and slipped through the hands."[43] Rossetti's girls, slimy and liable to slide away, prefigure Irigaray's account of the "mucosity" and flow in a "feminine syntax."[44] They also anticipate Kristeva's account of the irony in the critic's slippery task of fixing meaning. "It is," she writes of Freud's economy of laughter in *Jokes and their Relation to the Unconscious,* "a discharge with two meanings between sense and nonsense."[45]

Rossetti's work, then, may be distinctively feminine after all. Like the girls in her story, her poetry slips through the fingers. And this is Rossetti's joke:

that she will always slip away, dissolve, evaporate, disappear, and the poor critic will be left juggling the remnants of surface and subtext, attempting to "coagulate an island of meaning upon a sea of negativity."[46] If the semiotic is "the nonsense woven indistinguishably into sense,"[47] then Rossetti's nonsense story makes sense and the surface-sense of her best-loved poems may be nonsense. For they secrete a secret that "might easily be overlooked" but will "not easily be forgotten."

NOTES

1. William Michael Rossetti, ed., Introduction, *New Poems of Christina Rossetti Hitherto Unpublished or Uncollected* (London: Macmillan, 1900), pp. xii-xiii.

2. J. E. Austen-Leigh, "A Memoir of Jane Austen," in *Persuasion,* ed. D. W. Harding (Harmondsworth: Penguin, 1965), pp. 339-40.

3. Alexandra Sutherland Orr, *Life and Letters of Robert Browning* (London: Macmillan, 1908), p. 202.

4. Christina Rossetti, *Maude,* p. 29.

5. W. M. Rossetti, Introduction in *New Poems,* p. xiii.

6. Christina Rossetti, *Maude,* pp. 35, 37, 48-49, 50.

7. For an account of Letitia Elizabeth Landon and the cult of the Improvisatrice, see Leighton, pp. 58-64 and Angela Leighton and Margaret Reynolds, eds., *Victorian Women Poets: An Anthology* (Oxford: Blackwell, 1995), pp. 39-42.

8. *PW,* p. lx.

9. W. M. Rossetti, Introduction in *New Poems,* p. ix.

10. Christina Rossetti, *Maude,* p. 79.

11. *PW,* pp. xliii-xliv. The most amusing example of William Michael's willful rehabilitation here is his listing of *Goblin Market* under the heading "Love of Animals."

12. "[T]he death of a beautiful woman is, unquestionably, the most poetical topic in the world" (Edgar Allan Poe, "The Philosophy of Composition," in *Essays and Reviews* [New York: Literary Classics of the United States, 1984], p. 19). For a comprehensive study of this theme in the nineteenth century, see Elisabeth Bronfen, *Over Her Dead Body: Death, Femininity, and the Aesthetic* (Manchester: Manchester University Press, 1992), including a chapter on Dante Gabriel Rossetti and his reification of the dead Lizzie Siddal.

13. Stuart Curran, "The Lyric Voice of Christina Rossetti," *VP* 9 (1971): 287-99.

14. See, for example, Armstrong; Leighton; Isobel Armstrong, "Christina Rossetti: Diary of a Feminist Reading," in *Women Reading Women's Writing,* ed. Sue Roe (Brighton: Harvester, 1987); and Steven Connor, "'Speaking Likenesses': Language and Repetition in Christina Rossetti's *Goblin Market,*" *VP* 22 (1984): 439-48.

15. Armstrong, p. 324. Armstrong's analysis of the "deeply sceptical" form of the

Victorian double poem is important to my readings here. I also acknowledge McGann's useful essay on the techniques of Rossetti's poetry that "test and trouble the reader by manipulating sets of ambiguous symbols and linguistic structures" (Jerome J. McGann, "Christina Rossetti's Poems: A New Edition and a Revaluation," *VS* 23 [1980]: 243) and Leighton's chapter on Rossetti in *Victorian Women Poets: Writing Against the Heart* (pp. 118-63). Other works that deal with the idea of doubleness in Rossetti's work include Winston Weathers, "Christina Rossetti: The Sisterhood of Self," *VP* 3 (1965): 81-89; Theo Dombrowski, "Dualism in the Poetry of Christina Rossetti," *VP* 14 (1976): 70-76; Helena Michie, "'There is No Friend Like a Sister': Sisterhood as Sexual Difference," *English Literary History* 52 (1989): 401-21; and Mary Arseneau, "Incarnation and Interpretation: Christina Rossetti, the Oxford Movement, and *Goblin Market*," *VP* 31 (1993): 79-93.

16. "Only I must beg you will not fix upon any [poems to show Thomas Woolner] which the most imaginative person could construe into love personals. . . . [T]hat something like this has been the case I have too good reason to know" (qtd. in Antony H. Harrison, "Eighteen Early Letters by Christina Rossetti," in Kent, p. 199). Note that this letter was written on the same day as the sonnet "After Death." "And whilst it may truly be urged that unless white could be black and Heaven Hell my experience (thank God) precludes me from hers [that of the 'fallen woman'], yet I don't see why 'the Poet mind' should be less able to construct her from its own inner consciousness than a hundred other unknown quantities" (qtd. in Janet Camp Troxell, ed., *Three Rossettis: Unpublished Letters to and from Dante Gabriel, Christina, William* [Cambridge: Harvard University Press, 1937], p. 143).

17. The two poems are treated briefly in Rosenblum (pp. 129 and 209-10). More recently Catherine Maxwell has dealt with one, in "The Poetic Context of Christina Rossetti's 'After Death,'" *English Studies* 76 (1995): 148-55. While I would agree with and extend some of her propositions, especially in relation to the placing of the poem within the context of works by Tennyson and Browning, her reading comes only tentatively at the dark, willful perversity that is at the center of the poem and that, in my opinion, explains its peculiar power to attract, and more insidiously, to repel.

18. Dante Gabriel Rossetti, *The House of Life,* in *The Collected Works of Dante Gabriel Rossetti,* ed. W. M. Rossetti (London: Ellis and Elvey, 1888), p. 176.

19. Elizabeth Barrett Browning, *Aurora Leigh,* ed. Margaret Reynolds (Athens, Ohio: Ohio University Press, 1992; New York: Norton, 1996), 6:812-13 and 9:392-93.

20. Maxwell, pp. 145-50.

21. Maxwell, pp. 145-46.

22. Jacques Lacan, *Ecrits: A Selection,* trans. Alan Sheridan (London: Tavistock, 1977), p. 67.

23. Maud Ellmann, *Psychoanalytic Literary Criticism* (London: Longman, 1994), p. 7.

24. Lacan, p. 66. I suppose I must (resignedly) make it clear here that just as

Lacan's "nom-du-père" or the symbolic father is clearly differentiated from any idea of the real father, so the "father" that I find in this poem is related only to the symbolic function and, perhaps tangentially, to Victorian patriarchy, but is not necessarily related to any real father including Christina's own.

25. Julia Kristeva, *Powers of Horror: An Essay on Abjection,* trans. Leon S. Roudiez (New York: Columbia University Press, 1982), pp. 2–3.

26. Maxwell, p. 154.

27. Armstrong, p. 359.

28. W. David Shaw, "Poet of Mystery: The Art of Christina Rossetti," in Kent, pp. 34–35.

29. Simone de Beauvoir, introduction to *The Second Sex,* trans. H. M. Parshley, in *New French Feminisms,* ed. Elaine Marks and Isabelle de Courtivron (Brighton: Harvester, 1981), p. 44.

30. Hélène Cixous, "Sorties," in *The Newly Born Woman,* trans. Ann Liddle, in Marks and de Courtivron, *New French Feminisms,* p. 90.

31. Sandra M. Gilbert and Susan Gubar, *The Madwoman in the Attic: The Woman Writer and the Nineteenth-Century Literary Imagination* (New Haven and London: Yale University Press, 1979), pp. 549–54, qtd. by Angela Leighton, "'When I Am Dead, My Dearest': The Secret of Christina Rossetti," *Modern Philology* 87 (1990): 376.

32. Luce Irigaray, *This Sex Which Is Not One,* trans. Claudia Reeder, in Marks and de Courtivron, *New French Feminisms,* p. 105.

33. "Touching these same verses, it was the amazement of every one what could make her poetry so broken-hearted as was mostly the case" (*Maude,* p. 31). Leighton makes the point that Rossetti's secret was that there was no secret, and that "At the heart of this unremittingly lovelorn poetry, there is a freakish freedom of purpose and meaning. Over and over again, Rossetti makes a joke of the predictably tragic monotony of love" ("When I Am Dead," p. 379).

34. I suspect that Rossetti's use of "vestige" in "Remember" owes something to the title of Robert Chambers's *Vestiges of the Natural History of Creation* (London, 1844). *Vestiges* included an interesting passage about the loss of the individual life (as opposed to the race), which may be recalled by Rossetti's close juxtaposition of and punning on the word "once": "if the darkness and corruption leave / A vestige of the thoughts that once I had." (Like Tennyson, Rossetti made contemporary evolutionary theory into a subject of poetry.) "It is clear, moreover, from the whole scope of the natural laws, that the individual, as far as the present sphere of being is concerned, is to the Author of Nature a consideration of inferior moment. Everywhere we see the arrangements for the species perfect; the individual is left as it were, to take his chance amidst the mêlée of the various laws affecting him" (Chambers, p. 377).

35. William Michael Rossetti, ed., *Ruskin: Rossetti: Preraphaelitism: Papers 1854–1862* (London: George Allen, 1899), pp. 258–59.

36. Christina Rossetti, *Commonplace and Other Short Stories* (London: F. S. Ellis,

1870), p. 161. Leighton makes a similar point: "this image of the double painting, the secret masterpiece below and the vivid decoy above, also expresses something of Rossetti's own art; its moral nonsense, whether goblins, crocodiles or dragons, its obliqueness and disguises and, above all, its secret meanings which have been forever concealed, forever lost" (p. 158).

37. Freud's explanation of how the word "unheimlich," or uncanny, derives from the word "heimlich," homely or familiar, is in his 1919 essay on Hoffman's "The Sandman." See *The Complete Psychological Works of Sigmund Frued,* trans. James Strachey (London: Hogarth, 1953-74), 17:217-56.

38. From *Studies in Hysteria* (1893-95) on, Freud construes the process of psychoanalysis as one that begins with a therapeutic confession—hence Anna O.'s designation of his "talking cure." That the analysand has to talk, to shape stories about the self, to confess, makes psychoanalytic literary criticism a peculiarly appropriate tool for reading Rossetti's intimate and telling poems. That readers are so willing to act as analyst is partly connected to what Foucault describes as a "metamorphosis in literature," which takes place in the nineteenth century and where literary texts are no longer seen as fictions, but as a "confession" extracted "from the very depths of oneself, in between the words" (Michel Foucault, *The History of Sexuality, Volume One: An Introduction* [Harmondsworth: Penguin, 1984], p. 59).

39. Hélène Cixous, "The Laugh of the Medusa," trans. Keith Cohen and Paula Cohen, in Marks and de Courtivron, *New French Feminisms,* p. 251.

40. Irigaray, *This Sex,* p. 134.

41. Julia Kristeva, "Revolution in Poetic Language," trans. Margaret Waller, in *The Kristeva Reader,* ed. Toril Moi (Oxford: Basil Blackwell, 1986), p. 97.

42. Luce Irigaray, "Sexual Difference," in *The Irigaray Reader,* ed. Margaret Whitford (Oxford: Basil Blackwell, 1991), p. 175.

43. Christina Rossetti, *Speaking Likenesses* (London: Macmillan, 1874), pp. 36 and 28. The sexualized character of the boys' and girls' physical characteristics has been noticed by Roderick McGillis: "these two games . . . reveal a deep fear of sexual violence and a disturbing disrespect for humanity" ("Simple Surfaces: Christina Rossetti's Work for Children," in Kent, p. 227), and by Julia Briggs: "the symbolism of the boys with their projecting quills or hooks and the sticky, slippery women is disturbingly sexual" ("Women Writers and Writing for Children: From Sarah Fielding to E. Nesbit," in *Children and Their Books,* ed. Gillian Avery and Julia Briggs [Oxford: Clarendon, 1989], p. 17).

44. Irigaray, *This Sex,* p. 134.

45. Julia Kristeva, "How Does One Speak to Literature?" in *Desire in Language: A Semiotic Approach to Literature and Art,* ed. Leon S. Roudiez, trans. Thomas Gora, Alice Jardine, and Leon S. Roudiez (Oxford: Basil Blackwell, 1981), p. 109.

46. Kristeva, "How Does One Speak," p. 109.

47. Ellmann, p. 25.

CHAPTER 2

"May My Great Love Avail Me"

Christina Rossetti and Dante

MARY ARSENEAU

I n her article "Dante, an English Classic" Christina Rossetti remarks that anyone lucky enough to have been born Italian has the privilege of securing "the Divina Commedia as his birthright."[1] As Londoners of Italian lineage and as the children of Gabriele Rossetti, the Rossetti siblings were doubly entitled to this heritage. But while Maria, Dante Gabriel, William Michael, and Christina all published either translations of or commentary on Dante, the Dante each of them embraced resembled only in varying degrees the political, sectarian figure who was the subject of their father's lifelong study. Christina Rossetti's own published contribution to this field includes two articles: "Dante, an English Classic," a commendatory article written in support of Charles Bagot Cayley's *terza rima* translation of the *Divine Comedy* and published in *The Churchman's Shilling Magazine* in 1867, and the more ambitious "Dante. The Poet Illustrated out of the Poem" which appeared in *The Century* in 1884.[2] Of at least equal interest, moreover, are the views expressed in a less public forum, the unpublished annotations that Christina elaborated in the margins of two copies of her sister Maria's study, *A Shadow of Dante* (1871).[3] Christina Rossetti's commentary on Dante is inextricable from what amounts to a Rossetti family obsession and cannot be fully understood apart from the dialogue among five Rossettis' interpretations of Dante's work.[4] When seen in this context, it becomes clear that gender, religion, and poetics are all decisive factors in Christina Rossetti's response to Dante, informed as it is by her various roles as a daughter and sister of Dante scholars, as a Christian, as a poet, and as a specifically female poet. Christina considers herself the last and the least of the Rossettis to say her "little say" on Dante,[5] but underneath the characteristically self-effacing rhetoric unfolds a consistently literal and Christian reading of the *Commedia,* one pursued with confidence and authority.

Common as it is for scholars to note the significance of Dante in the Rossetti household, there has been no consensus on the extent or importance of Christina Rossetti's interest in this enormously influential poet, nor any close study of her published and unpublished commentary on Dante. Humphry House notes that Christina, like all the Rossetti children, knew Dante better than she knew any English poet,[6] and William Michael Rossetti records that "The one poet whom she really gloried in was Dante,"[7] but it is difficult to ascertain when this intense interest began. Presumably, William Michael's statement regarding Dante Gabriel's early attitude to Dante pertains to Christina as well: "Dante Alighieri was a sort of banshee in the Charlotte Street house; his shriek audible even to familiarity, but the message of it not scrutinized."[8] Mackenzie Bell dates Christina's study of Dante as beginning in 1848 (she would have been seventeen years old), but this seems not to be an interest at the same high level as that manifested in the allusions and quotations in the later poetry such as *"Monna Innominata,"* as well as the illustrations, annotations, and articles of her maturity; and Bell elsewhere states that "She was as deeply influenced by Dante as was any other member of the Rossetti family, but this was not until a subsequent period."[9] R. D. Waller, meanwhile, underestimates Christina's early attention to Dante when he says that she showed "no sign of interest in problems of interpretation until almost at the end of her life,"[10] for the publication of "Dante, an English Classic" in 1867 and the annotations that attest to Christina's contributions to Maria's *A Shadow of Dante* both demonstrate the close attention Christina paid to Dante's work through her thirties. Dantesque studies may have held little interest to the Rossettis as children, but at least by 1860, according to Caroline Gemmer's reminiscences, Dante was a topic of intense interest.[11]

Although none of the grown children would share his views on the hidden meaning of the *Commedia,* the family's interest in Dante clearly originated with Gabriele Rossetti,[12] whose writings on Dante include his commentary *La Divina Commedia di Dante Alighieri con Comento Analitico* appearing in 1825 and 1827;[13] *Lo Spirito Antipapale che produsse la Riforma* in 1832;[14] the five-volume *Il Mistero dell' Amor Platonico del Medio Evo derivato dai Misteri Antichi,* printed but not circulated in 1840; and *La Beatrice di Dante* in 1842. According to Gabriele Rossetti, the *Commedia* is a political allegory written in a secret code understandable to, among others, an underground society of fellow Ghibellines.[15] After expounding Dante's antipapist leanings in the *Comento,* Gabriele Rossetti became convinced that Dante was not only antipapal but also anti-Christian. As his theories and field of study broadened, Rossetti became persuaded that the mystical symbolism and cryptic language that he believed Dante used to communicate with other sectarians was only one example of a coded language, or *gergo,* and he set out to prove that this code disguises the real meaning of a whole array of medieval literature concerned with sectarian aims of establishing a world Emperor.[16] His theory expanded as he traced a secret tradition, associated with Freemasonry, and evident in various ages from the classical to Gabriele Rossetti's own day; and the *gergo* was seen as the key to works of literature by writers as diverse as Plato, Chaucer, Dante, Bunyan, and Milton (Waller, p. 90). In *La Beatrice di Dante,* Rossetti returned to his original focus on Dante, restated his long-held opinion that Beatrice had "no objective existence at all" (Waller, p. 92), and attempted to demonstrate that Beatrice is the emblem of, among other things, the secret brotherhood he described (Waller, p. 93). Central to all these works is Rossetti's rejection of the literal level of interpretation; as he reiterates so often, "we must not forget that, in this language, words are used in a sense quite at variance with their literal acceptance." The surface meaning was no more than a ruse, one of many means "devised to delude the general reader, and enlighten the sectarian."[17]

The extravagances of Gabriele Rossetti's theory are undeniable, and as a result it is tempting to be dismissive of all of his writings. Assessments of his work mention his "unscholarly self-confidence," "his often ridiculous verbosity and longwindedness" (Waller, p. 93), and "numerous inaccuracies of deduction, mis-statements of historical fact, and self-contradictions."[18] Such judgments, while true, do not tell the whole story, for some aspects of his work (especially his political reading of the *Divine Comedy* in the *Comento*) are convincing; indeed, he commanded a breadth of knowledge in Dantean studies that would be hard to duplicate. In some ways this makes the works more problematic, for one never knows when to trust his comprehensive knowledge of Dante and related scholarship and when to dismiss his interpretations as the progeny of his *ideé fixe.*

Flawed as it is, Gabriele Rossetti's work has not been relegated to obscurity.

Oscar Kuhns cites his influence as important in the nineteenth-century revival of Dante studies in England; Robert Hollander lists Gabriele Rossetti among the dozen "major names" in nineteenth-century Dante criticism in Italian. Even today, his theories retain a certain profile or notoriety, the *Humanities Citation Index* showing frequent current references to his work, and a hefty extract from *Disquisitions on the Antipapal Spirit which Produced the Reformation* appearing in *Dante: The Critical Heritage* (1989). According to Leon Surette in *The Birth of Modernism,* Gabriele Rossetti's theories have had "extraordinary staying power" and despite the limited circulation of his writings (only the *Comento* and the *Disquisitions* being readily available) they have had their influence in the twentieth century through, for example, Jessie Weston and Ezra Pound.[19] Certainly, serious criticisms arise in modern assessments: in *Interpretation and Overinterpretation,* Umberto Eco presents a careful critique of the fallacies of Gabriele Rossetti's "suspicious interpretation" of Dante's texts. Eco cites Rossetti's theories and proofs as an example of what he terms "Hermetic semiosis," a method of interpreting whose "criterion of similarity displayed an over-indulgent generality and flexibility." Rossetti's commentaries, argues Eco, are "a blatant case of overinterpretation," the primary flaw of such interpretation being "an excess of wonder" that "leads to overestimating the importance of coincidences which are explainable in other ways."[20]

In his own day, Gabriele Rossetti's work earned him both discipleship and ridicule,[21] but an even-handed critique—the only one that Rossetti speaks of with respect, though at a much later date (Waller, p. 97)—came from the pen of Tennyson's friend, Arthur Henry Hallam. According to Hallam, "There are two fatal errors in the Professor's mode of reasoning. He sees his theory in everything; and he will see no more in anything." Hallam acknowledges the grain of truth at the heart of Rossetti's *Spirito Antipapale* and finds persuasive the exposition of political allegory in the *Divine Comedy;* what Hallam criticizes is Rossetti's complete rejection of the literal meaning in any of the works he discusses. Hallam cites his denial of the existence of a living Beatrice, his rejection of any meaning in the *Commedia* that is moral or religious rather than political, and his assertion that medieval love poems are not at all about love but rather all about politics. Hallam sees the smaller truths that Rossetti has buried under his monolithic theory and admits that there are political allegories "scattered through the poem, as the *'Polysensum'* seems to intimate, and as Signor Rossetti's book has, we confess, made more probable to us than before." But unlike Rossetti, Hallam refuses to renounce the literal level of meaning and continues to "adhere to the plain words of Dante."[22]

The mixed reviews that Gabriele Rossetti's work has historically received were paralleled in the reaction of the Rossetti siblings, who from childhood were "alternately overawed and amused by their father's absorption in his theme" (Waller, p. 120). As adults, they viewed their father's scholarship with skepticism, and though apparently reluctant to denounce his views in so many words, each attempted to provide a corrective to his speculations. The points of divergence in the Rossetti family members' interpretations of Dante follow a discernible pattern operating on generational, gendered, and religious lines of division. Each of the four siblings in turn expresses an unwillingness to discard the literal sense of Dante's poem, but they are divided regarding the primary significance of the text: the agnostic brothers see the poem in amatory terms, while the Anglo-Catholic sisters read it for its spiritual meaning.

William Michael Rossetti's dedication to his book *Dante and His Convito* — "Inscribed to the memory of my father Gabriele Rossetti, bold and often helpful as a Commentator on Dante" — with its mingling of filial respect, faint praise, and suggested criticism, typifies the ambivalent tone of the Rossetti siblings' references to their father's work.[23] In his translation of the *Inferno* William Michael dismisses his father's ideas, if not in theory at least in practice, for he declines to "express adherence to or dissent from any of the various theories and interpretations" of Dante's work, advocating instead a concentration on the literal sense which his father dismisses: "To take him literally is enough, and more than enough, for most men."[24] This adherence to the literal level of Dante's writings is central to the second generation's views on Dante and forms an insurmountable division between their readings of the poet and their father's.

Perhaps none was more openly dismissive of the father's theories than Dante Gabriel. Theodore Watts-Dunton writes that "Gabriel could speak of his father's symbolizing (as in 'La Beatrice di Dante') as being absolutely and hopelessly eccentric and worthless."[25] In writing, Dante Gabriel was inclined to be less contemptuous and more nostalgic: "The first associations I have are connected with my father's devoted studies which, from his own point of view, have done so much towards the general investigation of Dante's writings."[26] Thus muting his disapproval, the son at least intimates that his father's "devoted studies" were less useful than he thought them to be and that the senior Rossetti had deluded himself. Elsewhere, Dante Gabriel articulates a faithfulness to the literal meaning of Dante's writing that places him decisively at odds with his father's reading: he affirms that which lies at "the heart of all true Dantesque commentary; that is, the existence of the actual events even where the allegorical superstructure has been raised by Dante himself."[27]

This contested status of the literal meaning, which I suggest is at the root of the fundamentally different approaches of the father and his children, has a focal point in the diverse readings of Beatrice. Gabriele Rossetti regarded her as an allegorical figure; for Dante Gabriel, Beatrice was a living, breathing woman. The elder son's fascination with the Beatrice theme is obvious in his work, in his translation of the *Vita Nuova,* in his drawings and paintings on Dantesque subjects, in poems such as "The Blessed Damozel," and even in his attempt to shape his love for Elizabeth Siddal within this frame of reference. For Dante Gabriel the figure of Beatrice is the inspiration for an exploration of the transcendent possibilities of erotic love. The love that Dante the pilgrim bore for Beatrice is likewise central to Christina's under-standing of the *Divine Comedy,* and she focuses on it in "Dante, an English Classic" as she summarizes the poem: "the lost love of earth is found again as one higher, lovelier, and better loved in paradise" (p. 201). But for Christina the poem means more than this, and in this conviction she departs decisively and critically from Dante Gabriel's emphasis and from the Pre-Raphaelite focus on the amatory theme. Christina highlights the recovery of the lost love "as one higher, lovelier, and better loved in paradise," but she goes on to say that "even this sainted and exalting passion pales at last, and is, as it were, no more accounted of before the supreme revelation of the love of God."[28] In reading the poem as transcending amatory concerns in the final revelation of the Godhead, Christina sees the import of the *Divine Comedy* as fundamentally theological.

Dante Gabriel's and Christina's depictions of ideal, inspirational women are deeply informed by their divergent readings of Beatrice, Dante Gabriel's recurring theme of the aspiration for the idealized and eternal union of the human lovers contrasting markedly with Christina's focus on the union of both lover and beloved with God. Dante Gabriel's focus on the *Vita Nuova* and Dante's love for Beatrice has its rebuttal in Christina's emphasis on the *Divine Comedy* and its redirection of the pilgrim Dante's love from Beatrice to God. In this theocentric reading of Dante's writings, Christina transcends the Pre-Raphaelite amatory preoccupations and conceives of a far different state of heavenly blessedness than the one achieved by Dante Gabriel's lonely "Blessed Damozel." It is thus Christina, and not Dante Gabriel, who is most aligned with Dantean values, for her poetry attempts to achieve that focus on God that Dante's persona, emulating Beatrice, finally attains in the *Paradiso:*

"I prayed thus; and she, so far off as she seemed, smiled and looked at me, then turned again to the eternal fount."[29]

As the rejection of the literal separates Gabriele Rossetti's interpretation from each of his children's, so too the Christian perspective divides Christina's and Maria's readings from those of the men in the family. Gabriele's belief that Dante was anti-Christian was unacceptable to the deeply religious Rossetti women. Indeed, upon his death, his wife, Frances, destroyed all extant copies of his *Il Mistero dell' Amor Platonico*. Maria Rossetti's *A Shadow of Dante* and Christina's responses to it exemplify the daughters' divergence from the views held by their father. Although Maria Rossetti dedicates her book "to the beloved memory of my father" and acknowledges her obligations to her "late dear Father," her interpretation of the *Divine Comedy* is diametrically opposed to his: she reads the poem as Christian and takes an almost prayerful attitude toward it, emphasizing that as much as the mind profits from a study of the *Commedia*, "greater, far greater, is the profit accruing to the soul."[30] Without naming her father or drawing undue attention to her defection, Maria rejects his theory of a nonhistorical, solely allegorical Beatrice and matter-of-factly places herself in the opposing camp: "The Beatrice of Dante remains to this day the perplexity of scholars and of commentators, some regarding her as a personage from first to last purely allegorical. I adopt the view of Boccaccio and the majority."[31]

Christina is not inclined to criticize her father and brothers openly; therefore, her commentary on Dante must be read very carefully for its subtext of opposition. She begins her critical discussion in "Dante. The Poet Illustrated out of the Poem" by humbly admitting her trepidation; for her it is "a grave if not formidable undertaking to treat of that soldier, statesman, philosopher, above all poet." She continues:

> If formidable for others, it is not least formidable for one of my name, for *me*, to enter the Dantesque field and say my little say on the Man and on the Poem; for others of my name have been before me in the same field, and have wrought permanent and worthy work in attestation of their diligence. (p. 566)

In Christina's case, the sense of belatedness and the anxiety of influence stem not only from the greatness of the poet she contemplates but perhaps more oppressively from the immediate "family romance." In fact, Christina spends the entire second paragraph of her article citing the contributions that members of her family have made to Dante studies. In what is perhaps a misprision of

her father's career, she names only his earliest and in many ways least controversial commentary, the *Comento Analitico sull'Inferno di Dante,* which has "left
to tyros a clew and to fellow-experts a theory" (p. 566). This faint praise is
counterpointed by her expressed admiration for Maria's *A Shadow of Dante,*
which, Christina says, "eloquently expounded the Divina Commedia as a discourse of most elevated Christian faith and morals" (p. 566); thus, Christina
implicitly distances herself from her father's views. Although this is the only
time she mentions her father overtly in "Dante. The Poet Illustrated," the essay
quite methodically subverts the cornerstones of her father's theory as it pertained
to an interpretation of the *Divine Comedy:* his suggestion that the poem contains,
above all else, a political meaning; his denial of the historical existence of
Beatrice; and his rejection of the religious meaning in the poem.

Of course, such a critique of Gabriele Rossetti's theories presupposes some
familiarity on Christina's part with her father's work. Waller questions this,
arguing that "it may be doubted whether she had ever read any of her father's
work on the subject," his primary evidence of her ignorance being a 19 July
1892 letter in which Christina asks William Michael "Does anyone dispute the
existence of Beatrice Bardi, nata Portinari?" (Waller, p. 119). But the full text of
the letter does not evince the kind of naivety that Waller's excerpt betrays, for
Christina elaborates, "I should fancy the point of any such controversy might
be limited to the question of her identity or otherwise with the surnameless
Beatrice of Dante's immortalization."[32] Christina is making a more subtle point
here than Waller gives her credit for. She is not asking whether anyone questions
that the figure of Beatrice in Dante's writings should be read as a flesh-and-blood
woman, which she of course knows is indeed open to dispute. She asks instead
whether the existence of the historical personage Beatrice Portinari is universally
acknowledged (independent of any issues related to interpretations of Dante's
works), and then remarks that still controversial, even with evidence of Beatrice
Portinari's existence, would be the *identification* of that real woman with the
Beatrice of "Dante's immortalization." First, she is seeing through the biographical or genetic fallacy that would leap from the proof of the historical fact of
Beatrice Portinari's existence to the conclusion that this Beatrice and Dante's
creation are one and the same. Dante might well have known a Beatrice
Portinari, Christina implies, and yet the Beatrice of the *Vita Nuova* and *Divine
Comedy* might nevertheless be an imaginative construct unrelated to that historical woman. Secondly, Rossetti is aware of the inevitable gap between the
poet's "immortalization" and the individual who might inspire such an ideal-
ization, a difference she explored in *"Monna Innominata."*

That Christina was familiar with the broad outlines of her father's theory is supported by the content of her article "Dante. The Poet Illustrated out of the Poem" as well as by her allusion in the prose preface to *"Monna Innominata"* to what William Whitla calls "that complex of events and ideas which constituted the subject of her father's lifework."[33] What she knew of her father's more controversial later books, however, probably came second-hand: it is hard to believe that Christina would pore through five volumes of *Amor Platonico,* a book so heretical that her revered mother saw fit to burn all unreleased copies.[34]

"Dante. The Poet Illustrated out of the Poem" has three main sections following the introductory remarks relating to the Rossetti family: the first section deals with the public, political Dante; the second takes up his private life and his love for Beatrice; and the third offers a plot summary of the *Divine Comedy.* The discussion of the public Dante offers a fairly complete biographical sketch of the poet as "a portion of the history of his age and nation" (p. 571), including numerous details pertaining to the political controversies of his day. But details of political intrigue here remain first and foremost biographical facts and do not become the handmaids (as they do in her father's work) of a political reading of the poem.[35] Christina sees the writings of Dante in exile as motivated not by a covert political agenda but by a new wisdom; Dante has been "taught by bitter experience in what scales to weigh this world and the things of this world" (p. 570), the same vanity-of-vanities lesson that is central to so many of Christina's own poems.

Just as she tacitly rejects her father's political reading of the *Commedia,* Christina also implicitly counters his reading of Beatrice as a purely allegorical figure and his dismissal of the spiritual pilgrimage the poet's persona undertakes in his poem. Although Christina leaves open the possibility of an allegorical reading of Beatrice, she is willing to regard Beatrice as symbolic only to the extent that she stands for a shaping influence in Dante's life, and she rejects any reading that dismisses the professed meaning of the narrative—Dante's progress toward spiritual enlightenment.[36]

As Rossetti moves into the final section of her essay and the summary of the *Commedia* that it contains, she underlines her fidelity to the "obvious signification" (p. 572) of the narrative in what appears an explicit criticism of her father's theories. She writes that "Some students speak of hidden lore underlying the letter of our poet's writings: in Beatrice they think to discern an impersonation rather than a woman, in the Divine Comedy a meaning political rather than dogmatic." These interpretations she rejects: "So obscure a field of investigation is not for me or for my readers; at least, not for them through any help of mine." This last phrase is intriguing. One could read in it the modesty regarding Dante scholarship Rossetti had expressed earlier in her article when she compared herself to her father and siblings: "I, who cannot lay claim to their learning, must approach my subject under cover of *'Mi valga . . . il grande amore'* ('May my great love avail me'), leaving to them the more confident plea, *'Mi valga il lungo studio'* ('May my long study avail me')" (p. 567). But Rossetti's phrasing, "not for them through any help of mine," also suggests a digging in of her heels and a refusal to play any part in the kind of heretical studies her father pursued. She continues in her rejection of her father's "obscure . . . field of investigation" with the statement "to me it is and it must remain dim and unexplored" (p. 572), a resistance that could express not only insufficient knowledge, ability, and motivation, but also a resolute determination not to explore a theory that ran counter to her religious principles.

While Christina takes a public stand in her two articles on Dante, her annotations to Maria Rossetti's 1871 edition of *A Shadow of Dante* reveal preoccupations perhaps even closer to her heart. An interest in close textual readings and a Christian and biblical emphasis are keynotes in these annotations, along with a bent toward subtle reasoning, risk-taking originality, and forceful argument—the self-effacing public persona evident in "Dante. The Poet Illustrated out of the Poem" is remarkably absent here. Scholars have often emphasized Christina Rossetti's submission to both male and religious authority, whether familial, clerical, or biblical, but have tended to overlook the ways in which her Christianity empowered her critical and creative voice and provided her with an authoritative position from which she could both engage a strong poet like Dante Alighieri and evaluate the male Rossettis' critical and creative responses to his work.

There are two extant copies of *A Shadow of Dante* with annotations by Christina, both privately held.[37] One copy, presented by the author "To my dear Sister / Christina G. Rossetti / with much love. / 13th October 1871" contains Christina's pencil illustrations, added at the beginning of each chapter, as well as some brief annotations. The second copy, inscribed by Maria "To my dearest Mother / with my chief earthly love / 13th October 1871," became part of Christina's library and contains several lengthy annotations by Christina.[38] The illustrations and annotations in Christina's own presentation copy attest to her emphasis on the literal in her reading of Dante: her sketches of Dante, Virgil, Beatrice, and the multifoliate rose among other figures highlight the obvious meaning of the passage depicted rather than any obscure symbolic meaning (see figs. 2.1 and 2.2). Christina's annotations in her mother's copy continue in this vein of literal reading.

Christina clearly read carefully her copy of *A Shadow of Dante* shortly after its presentation to her and probably was reading with an editorial eye charged with making corrections for subsequent editions. Many annotations show a concern with precision and fine matters of diction; for example, Christina underlined and criticized the phrase "convex edge" on the grounds that "*Edge* could I think only apply to a *section* of a sphere" (p. 12). She suggests "Would not *convexity* be more accurate?" (p. 12), and, indeed, the 1872 and later editions show the offensive "convex edge" replaced with the more accurate "convex summit." Similarly, Christina found the word "mid-circumference" (p. 205) exceptionable, and later editions show a change in wording to "two opposite points of the circumference." These editorial comments almost certainly date to the period between the first and second editions in 1871–72; moreover, the conversational tone of the notes suggests that these comments were addressed directly and helpfully to Maria. While the annotations to Christina's presentation copy offer textual evidence that allows for fairly precise dating, there is little in the annotations in the second copy that indicates the period of their composition. It is notable, however, that in place of the editorial advice and direct address to Maria in the 1871–72 annotations, the comments in Frances's presentation copy refer to Maria in the third person.[39] These notes probably postdate Maria's death in 1876. It also seems plausible to date them after Frances's death in 1886, for it was presumably at this time that her copy was passed on to Christina. During the intervening years Christina had engaged in more formal study of Dante's work, attending lectures on the *Inferno, Purgatorio,* and *Paradiso* at University College 1878–80;[40] her additional study provides some explanation for the greater sophistication and complexity of the later comments.

There are some passages, however, that attract similar comment in each set of annotations. For example, Christina indicates in both copies of *A Shadow of Dante* that she is the source of the "curious theory" Maria recounts in a footnote:

> The following curious theory has been conversationally suggested. The Pit of Hell being vast enough to harbour so large a number out of all generations of mankind, the Western Mountain, consisting of the earth thrown up from that pit, is necessarily of the same proportions,

CHAPTER III.

DANTE'S LIFE-EXPERIENCE.

Nel mezzo del cammin di nostra vita.
In midway of the journey of our life.

Inf. I. I.

L ET us now inquire what he was, who, born, as he believed, into an universe in the main so constructed
and so governed, lived in it fifty-six years, and departed not
till he had tracked a path to aid future generations safely
to work their way from its lowest to its highest sphere :—
what she was, at whose prompting he began, by whose
guidance he completed the pilgrimage wherein he gained
his own experience of that path. Not that this latter inquiry
can be answered as confidently as the former. The
Beatrice of Dante remains to this day the perplexity of
scholars and of commentators, some regarding her as a
personage from first to last purely allegorical. I adopt the
view of Boccaccio and the majority.

Dante Allighieri was born at Florence in May 1265, of
a noble family adhering to the Guelph party. When nearly
nine years old he was taken by his father to a festival held
at the house of Folco Portinari. He there beheld his host's
daughter ; and this first great event of his conscious life,
colouring all its after course, he himself thus narrates :

‘ Nine times already since my birth had the Heaven of

18

Fig. 2.1. Christina Rossetti's pencil drawing for chapter 3 in Maria Rossetti, *A Shadow of Dante* (London: Rivingtons, 1871), p. 18. Reproduced with the kind permission of Mr. Nicholas G. Rossetti.

CHAPTER IV.

THE WOOD, AND THE APPARITION OF VIRGIL.

Questa selva selvaggia ed aspra e forte.
What this wood was, savage, and rough, and strong.
Inf. I. 5.

I N A.D. 1300, the year of the Jubilee ; at dawn on the
25th of March, the Feast of the Annunciation, then
reckoned as New Year's Day, and happening that year to
be also Maundy Thursday ; Dante, then nearly thirty-five,
and approaching the time of his election to the Priorato,
perceived himself to have wandered while half asleep from
the right path, and to be actually entangled in the mazes of
a dark wood. Before him rose a hill whose sides were
clothed with sunshine ; but no man walked thereon. Dante
took courage to begin the ascent, and had made some little
progress in climbing, the lower foot being ever the firmer,
when he found himself successively withstood and repelled
by three wild beasts, a swift Leopard, a raging Lion, and a
craving greedy Wolf. These, but chiefly the last, were
gradually and irresistibly forcing him back upon the sun-
less plain, when suddenly he became aware that he was no
longer alone.

> While I was crushing down to the low place,
> To me was offered one before mine eyes
> Who seemed by reason of long silence hoarse.

Fig. 2.2. Christina Rossetti's pencil drawing for chapter 4 in Maria Rossetti, *A Shadow of Dante* (London: Rivingtons, 1871), p. 32. Reproduced with the kind permission of Mr. Nicholas G. Rossetti.

and may have sufficed for the dwelling of the entire race until the Deluge, after which event the Ark was providentially guided to deposit its freight on Mount Ararat in the Eastern hemisphere. (p. 15)

The concerns here are not as outlandish as they might first appear, for the *Divine Comedy* is encyclopedic: Dante hopes to take into account science, history, theology, philosophy, and astronomy, among other disciplines, and Christina's attempt at explaining an apparent conundrum of geography and biblical history would not be inappropriate in the context of the commentary tradition. Nevertheless, it reveals a fascinating concern with practicalities such as the size of the Pit of Hell and the Western Mountain, the amount of space necessary to accommodate the generations before the flood, and modes of transportation. It also suggests the concrete, physical aspect that Dante's cosmology presented to Christina and indicates that she drew no divisions among Dante's masterpiece, the Bible, and human history.

In both sets of annotations Christina also attempts to explicate the suitability of punishments for which Dante does not explain their ironic appropriateness.[41] Again, the focus is on the concrete detail, and the annotations are concerned with demonstrating that when read most attentively the literal level does not fade to insignificance but rather opens itself to layers of other meanings as well. For example, three separate annotations pertain to Canto 23 of the *Inferno,* in which Dante describes how Caiaphas, Annas, and the rest of the Council that condemned Christ are impaled naked in the form of a cross, trampled continuously by the heavily laden hypocrites of Pit 6 in the eighth circle of hell.[42] Christina's presentation copy indicates that her imagination was engaged in the graphic details of the punishment of Caiaphas and the others—she drew a cruciform figure in the margins of Maria's description of the Arch-hypocrites "impaled naked in the form of a cross" (p. 57). Meanwhile, the annotations in Frances's copy reveal that Christina attempted a close reading of the passage, trying to explain the appropriateness of this punishment. She wrote, "It struck me (CGR) but the idea did not seem to commend itself to dear MFR that he who had sacrificed all to save 'place & nation' is here punished by having so literally no place allowed him on the face of the earth (i.e. hell) as to be made part & parcel of that ground whereon others tread" (p. 57). Christina's note indicates that she offered some of her own interpretations to Maria while she was writing *A Shadow of Dante,* this suggestion being one that Christina thought demonstrated Dante's fine sense of poetic justice, though Maria apparently was not convinced.[43]

Christina refers, very characteristically, to the Bible in explicating this passage. Like Maria and most other commentators, Christina recognizes as Caiaphas he whom Dante describes as having "counselled the Pharisees that it was expedient to make one man suffer for the people" (*Inferno* 23.116-17) and picks up on the reference to John 11:50. Christina turns to the implied biblical context to demonstrate how the punishment is particularly fitting. In John 11:48, some who had witnessed Jesus' raising of Lazarus go to the Pharisees, describe how Jesus is performing miracles, and express their fear that "If we let him thus alone, all men will believe on him: and the Romans shall come and take away both our place and nation." It is altogether typical to find Rossetti here comparing earthly concerns of "place and nation" with the ultimate rewards and punishments such concerns will bring. Having "sacrificed all to save 'place & nation,'" Caiaphas had misplaced priorities and now finds himself without that transitory "place & nation" which, as the verses from John's Gospel show, Caiaphas valued more highly than he valued Christ.

This biblical emphasis is consistent throughout Christina's lengthy comments in Frances's presentation copy. In her note on evil counselors, who are doomed to being enclosed in tongues of flame (*Inferno,* canto 26), Christina writes:

> May we not connect with this?—Moses was divinely appointed to be *as God* to Aaron: thus an *evil* counsellor might find his appropriate punishment in being made as it were "a consuming fire"—plus for endless *self*-destruction[.] consider also the text "His Name shall be called Counsellor"—, also our Lord's Name of "the Word—". Of Akitophel we read that men sought to him as to the Oracle of God. So that an evil counsellor is in a degree a counterfeiter of the Divine Person. (p. 58)

She does not remark upon an obvious biblical parallel—this punishment as a parody of the tongues of flame and gift of tongues of the New Testament. Instead, Rossetti engages in some intricate word play.[44] First she alludes to Exodus 4:16, where Moses, after complaining to the Lord that he is not eloquent, is told that Aaron will be his "spokesman unto the people: and he shall be, even he shall be to thee instead of a mouth, and thou shalt be to him instead of God." Christina's point seems to be that whereas Moses, divinely appointed to convey God's intentions to Aaron, had beheld the burning bush that was not consumed (Exod. 3:2), conversely, the false coun-

selor, who is not God's appointed conduit, becomes "'a consuming fire.'" Then
Rossetti highlights the difference between an evil counselor and Christ, citing
Isaiah 9:6, "and his name shall be called Wonderful, Counsellor," implicitly
comparing the true "Counsellor" to the evil counselors in the *Inferno,* and
recalling that Christ is called "the Word," while the damned evil counselors
speak only false words. Finally she turns to the biblical figure of Akitophel
whose counsel was sought "as if a man had enquired at the oracle of God" (2
Sam. 16:23). Akitophel, who counselled Absalom in his rebellion against his
father, David, is an evil counselor who does not in fact appear among the
sinners in this pit of hell though his name is raised as a comparison to Bertran
de Born in Canto 28. But the description that Rossetti's note offers of
Akitophel as the sham "Oracle of God" is a biblical, and not a Dantean,
reference. Not only is the reference scriptural, the point of the reference and
the reading of the passage is intensely Christian. In most commentaries the
evil counselors are condemned for having used their "high mental gifts for
guile"[45] and for "cunningly" having hidden their thought within "flaming
speech."[46] But Rossetti turns to the Bible and to the figure of Akitophel for
her condemnation: her false counselors mislead not through a "misuse of
superior mental power,"[47] but by posing as the one "Counsellor," the true
"Word," that is, by counterfeiting Christ.

Similar aggressively Christian readings of Dante are found elsewhere in
this later set of annotations. At one point in *A Shadow of Dante* Maria suggests
that Pontius Pilate is not in hell because his role in Christ's crucifixion is
countenanced by Dante. Referring to Dante's political treatise *De Monarchiâ,*
Maria (though she herself finds this line of reasoning and its conclusion
"inadmissable") argues that Dante believed Christ sanctioned the temporal
jurisdiction of the Roman Empire; therefore, in acting as its judge, Pilate was
not sinning when his office involved sitting in judgment over Christ (*Shadow,*
pp. 222-23). This, suggests Maria, is "the key to a perplexing problem — why
Pontius Pilate is nowhere met with in Hell" (*Shadow,* p. 223). This hypothesis
occasions yet another marginal note by Christina in which she suggests that
it is Pilate who appears, unnamed, among the Neutrals in Canto 3 as "him
who from cowardice made the great refusal."[48] Christina knew that virtually
all commentators understood this to refer, not to Pilate, but to Pope Celestine
V[49] (who resigned the papal office, thus allowing Dante's enemy Boniface VIII
to become Pope), but she nevertheless argues for her reading with some
perseverance. Her lengthy annotation reads:

Is it certain that he is not "Colui che per viltà fei il gran rifiuto"?[50]
Such a definition would closely correspond with his perverted response
to his wife's "Have thou nothing to do with—." Thus he washed his
hands in repudiation, & formally disconnected himself from the Blessed
Blood. "See you to it."

WMR aptly suggests thus D. could not know "Esaw" by sight: but
a careful reading of the passage in question suggests a possible distinction between "riconobbi" & "guardai e vidi."[51] Nor does it follow that
Virgil was unacquainted with the person of Pontius Pilate, for V. gives
a list of the translated out of Limbo which includes individuals perhaps
as likely to have been hidden from him:[52] & what V knew he often
communicated to D. tho' here the *name* admitted not of *record*.

I think "Poscia ch'io V'ebbi alcun riconsciuto Guardai, e vidi—"[53]
may even be intended to suggest the distinction between what D. recognized and what by some different channel ascertained." (p. 223)

This line of argument reveals Christina's interest in close textual reading and
in fine distinctions in expression. She refers to William Michael's note regarding the suggestion by some commentators that Esau is the one who made the
"great refusal"; William Michael points out a logistical problem "but how
could Dante know him by sight?"[54] Christina contests William Michael's
objection on the grounds that Virgil elsewhere in the *Comedy* lists individuals
he could not have known in his lifetime. But the point of her refutation is
not to defend the Esau reading that William had dismissed, but rather to
dismiss an argument that might be held against her own suggestion that the
great refuser is Pilate. Her subtle reasoning, her familiarity with traditional
interpretations of this passage, and her confidence in explicating Dante in
Christian rather than political terms are all evident here.

Taken as a whole, Christina Rossetti's published and unpublished comments on Dante both demonstrate her desire to forge her own critical
position in a field haunted by family members and highlight the divergences
in the Rossettis' ideological and aesthetic positions. In her Dante commentary Rossetti resists the antiliteralness as well as the interpretive excesses, or
"overinterpretation," of her father's theories and instead espouses an aesthetic
based on compatible and mutually reinforcing levels of meaning not unlike
Dante's own *"polysensum."* This interpretive practice has clear parallels with
Christina Rossetti's own poetic in which the literal or physical signification
points beyond itself to the moral and spiritual interpretations evolved from

it. If for Gabriele Rossetti in poetry things are not what they seem, for Christina they are what they seem, but at the same time so much more. The result is that in a poem such as "An Apple-Gathering" (*CP,* 1:43–44) the literal and natural details are as true as the sexual, moral, or religious readings interpretable in those details. Rossetti's reading of Dantesque poetics sheds light on her own understanding of the relationship of literal, symbolic, and allegorical meanings; and thus, the implications of her reading of Dante redound beyond the conspicuous intertextuality of *"Monna Innominata,"* the acknowledged allusions in *Later Life* and "An Old-World Thicket," the *Inferno*-indebted fate of the Ghost and Bride in "The Hour and the Ghost" who will, like Paolo and Francesca, "In the outcast weather / Toss and howl and spin," or the adaptation of the Dantesque materials such as the dream-vision in "The Dead City," the beatific vision in "From House to Home," or the purgatorial ascents of "The Convent Threshold" and "Faint, Yet Pursuing."

In *A Shadow of Dante* Maria Rossetti evokes Dante's preeminence, saying that he "rises before us and above us like the Pyramids" (p. 3), a description that Christina found so suggestive that she chose the image for one of her illustrations. Strikingly, Rossetti was not overwhelmed by this daunting presence, but instead engaged the Dantesque poetic and commentary traditions, using her gender and her religion as entry points. It is from a Christian position that Christina questioned the authority of the Rossetti men and offered a reading of Dante that ran counter to theirs. In addition, Christina defined herself against her poet-brother Dante Gabriel in ways that have implications for our understanding of the amatory ideals in the poetry of both siblings. For instance, while the suitability of Dantesque materials to a male poet's purposes is fairly obvious, the adaptability of a genre such as the medieval dream vision or of a figure such as the inspirational woman to the woman poet's needs is more problematic. Christina's solution is to let "such a lady [speak] for herself" (*CP,* 2:86) in *"Monna Innominata,"* and the result, as Marjorie Stone demonstrates, contests both the gender dynamic of Dante and the secularized values of her brother.[55] While her brother Gabriel Charles Dante re-christened himself Dante Gabriel and thus signaled his adoption of the poet's mantle, Christina assumed the even more daunting task of adapting to her poet's voice the subject position of Beatrice, and there is evidence that it is in this persona that succeeding male and female poets such as Gerard Manley Hopkins and Michael Field (Katherine Bradley and Edith Cooper) confronted Christina Rossetti.[56] Christina Rossetti's poetic strategies for coping with Dante's literary legacy extend well beyond her explicit confrontation with it in *"Monna Innominata"* and promise to provide a crucial insight into the gender dynamics of her poetry.

NOTES

1. Christina Rossetti, "Dante, an English Classic," *The Churchman's Shilling Magazine and Family Treasury* 2 (1867), p. 200. Subsequent references to this work will be cited parenthetically in the text by page number.

2. Christina Rossetti, "Dante. The Poet Illustrated out of the Poem," *The Century* 27 (1884): 566-73, n.s. vol. 5. Subsequent references to this work will be cited parenthetically in the text by page number.

3. Maria Francesca Rossetti, *A Shadow of Dante: Being an Essay towards Studying Himself, His World, and His Pilgrimage* (Boston: Roberts Brothers, 1872).

4. See *Christina Rossetti in Context* where Antony H. Harrison contextualizes Christina Rossetti's interest within various circles and traditions including the nineteenth-century literary debt to Dante, mainstream Victorian readings of Dante, the Pre-Raphaelite adaptation of the Dantean materials, and the Dantean obsessions of the Rossetti family.

5. "Dante. The Poet Illustrated out of the Poem," p. 566.

6. Humphry House, "Pre-Raphaelite Poetry," in *Pre-Raphaelitism: A Collection of Critical Essays,* ed. James Sambrook (Chicago and London: University of Chicago Press, 1974), p. 130.

7. William Michael Rossetti, "Memoir," in *PW,* p. lxix.

8. William Michael Rossetti, "Memoir," in *Dante Gabriel Rossetti: His Family Letters,* with a Memoir by William Michael Rossetti, ed. William Michael Rossetti (London: Ellis and Elvey, 1895), 1:64.

9. Bell, p. 355.

10. R. D. Waller, *The Rossetti Family, 1824-1854* (Manchester: Manchester University Press, 1932), p. 119. Subsequent references to Waller's work will be noted parenthetically in the text.

11. Caroline Gemmer tells of "a small party," to which she was invited by Christina, at which Gemmer was "introduced to [Christina's] mother brothers and elder sister." Other guests included Charles Bagot Cayley who "had just brought out his book on Dante." Gemmer relates that "Maria Francisca, [*sic*] explained to us that evening with word and pencil '*Dante's* World,' as she called it." Gemmer's reminiscences, as transcribed by Mackenzie Bell, are held in the Troxell Collection, Princeton University Library.

12. Christina acknowledges the primacy of her father's influence but also cites

her maternal grandfather Gaetano Polidori's appreciation for Dante's poetry. In a letter of 20 March 1892 to Lucy Rossetti, Christina comments, "Perhaps it is enough to be half an Italian, but certainly it is enough to be a Rossetti, to render Dante a fascinating centre of thought; moreover, I am not sure that my dear old Grandfather did not outrun my Father in admiration for the poet *as* a poet" (*FL,* p. 184).

13. The two volumes deal only with the *Inferno,* though commentary on the *Purgatorio* and part of the *Paradiso* was written.

14. This was published in an English translation as *Disquisitions on the Antipapal Spirit which Produced the Reformation: Its Secret Influence on the Literature of Europe in General, and of Italy in Particular,* trans. Caroline Ward, 2 vols. (London, 1834).

15. The Ghibellines, politically opposed to the Guelphs, were members of the aristocratic party that supported the claims of the German emperors against the papacy.

16. See Waller, p. 88 and E. R. Vincent, *Gabriele Rossetti in England* (Oxford: Clarendon, 1937), p. 73.

17. Gabriele Rossetti, *Disquisitions on the Antipapal Spirit which Produced the Reformation,* 1:133 and 1:142.

18. Vincent, p. 72.

19. Oscar Kuhns, *Dante and the English Poets from Chaucer to Tennyson* (New York: Holt, 1904), pp. 120-21; Robert Hollander, "Dante and His Commentators," in *The Cambridge Companion to Dante,* ed. Rachel Jacoff (Cambridge: Cambridge University Press, 1993), p. 232; *Dante, The Critical Heritage 1314(?)-1870,* ed. Michael Caesar (London: Routledge, 1989); and Leon Surette, *The Birth of Modernism: Ezra Pound, T. S. Eliot, W. B. Yeats, and the Occult* (Montreal and Kingston: McGill-Queen's University Press, 1993), p. 120.

20. Umberto Eco with Richard Rorty, Jonathan Culler, Christine Brooke-Rose, *Interpretation and Overinterpretation,* ed. Stefan Collini (Cambridge: Cambridge University Press, 1992), pp. 45, 50, 52.

21. Two of Gabriele Rossetti's main benefactors were the enthusiastic Charles Lyell, father of the famous geologist, and the more cautious but usually encouraging John Hookham Frere. Both encouraged Rossetti in taking his theories to implausible lengths and actually supplied some of the more improbable ideas that made their way into his work (Waller, p. 99). E. R. Vincent writes that Lyell was "grossly ignorant" on the subject of Dante (pp. 100-101); Lyell's suggestions to Rossetti were profuse, questionable, and often accepted.

22. Arthur Henry Hallam (T.H.E.A.), *Remarks on Professor Rossetti's* Disquisizioni sullo Spirito Antipapale (London, Edward Moxon: 1832), pp. 48, 41, 22-23, 49, 41.

23. William Michael Rossetti, *Dante and His Convito: A Study with Translations* (London: Elkin Mathews, 1910).

24. William Michael Rossetti, *The Comedy of Dante Allighieri: Part I—The Hell* (London: Macmillan, 1865), p. iv.

25. Theodore Watts-Dunton, *Old Familiar Faces* (Freeport, N.Y.: Books for Libraries Press, 1970), p. 186.

26. Dante Gabriel Rossetti, Preface to the First Edition (1861), *Dante and His Circle* in *The Works of Dante Gabriel Rossetti,* ed. William Michael Rossetti, rev. and enl. ed. (London: Ellis and Elvey, 1911), p. 283.

27. Dante Gabriel Rossetti, *Dante and His Circle* in *The Works of Dante Gabriel Rossetti,* p. 343.

28. "Dante, an English Classic," p. 201. Harrison sets Christina's reading of Dante in the context of "the Pre-Raphaelites' obsessive concern with the great Italian poet's transposition of erotic passion to a spiritual object and condition," citing as evidence the first passage I quote from "Dante, an English Classic" (Harrison, *CR,* p. 146). Harrison does not quote the second part of the passage and thus emphasizes Christina's affinities with the Pre-Raphaelite treatment; meanwhile, I am concerned with the ways in which her Christian emphasis diverges from Dante Gabriel Rossetti's fascination with the Beatrice theme as an expression of the transcendent possibilities of erotic love.

29. Dante Alighieri, *The Divine Comedy of Dante Alighieri,* trans. John D. Sinclair, 3 vols. (New York: Oxford University Press, 1939), *Par.* 31.91-93. Subsequent references to this work will be noted parenthetically in the text by book, canto, and page numbers.

30. Maria Francesca Rossetti, *A Shadow of Dante,* pp. 5, 7. Maria cites her father's *Comento* at various points in her discussion of "Dante's Pilgrimage through Hell" (pp. 50, 52, 57, 61, 87), but does not invoke his political reading.

31. *A Shadow of Dante,* p. 18. Michael Caesar remarks that fourteenth-century commentators generally took for granted that Beatrice represented Theology (or Holy Scripture), and that "it is Boccaccio in his *Trattatello* who complicates the issue by introducing various details concerning Dante's actual relationship with the historical Bice Portinari" (*Dante, The Critical Heritage 1314{?}-1870,* p. 180).

32. *FL,* p. 188.

33. William Whitla, "Questioning the Convention: Christina Rossetti's Sonnet Sequence '*Monna Innominata,*'" in Kent, p. 88.

34. Jan Marsh likewise surmises that Christina did not "read deeply in [Gabriele Rossetti's] prose works in adulthood, not least because of the implications of heresy." Marsh does not focus on the aesthetic issues in debate; rather she comments on the considerable impact of the father's theories on the emotional and psychological development of the children, claiming that "indeed none of the Rossetti family can be understood without reference to this arcane paternal activity" (Marsh, *CR,* p. 37).

35. Christina's own political views, particularly her dislike of imperial power, are apparent in her somewhat half-hearted defense of Dante's transformation from a Guelph into a Ghibelline, when "from having been champion of an Italian Italy, free and sole mother and mistress of her own free children, he became, whether from

personal disgust or sheer despair or from whatever other motive, as ardent a champion of that Imperial power which aspired to rule over her." She even acknowledges that "we may feel disposed to wonder at the transformation, perhaps to condemn the citizen." In defending him against potentially rash judgment on the part of her audience, Rossetti urges readers to study in his writings "his own lofty view and exposition of a world-wide political theory" ("Dante. The Poet Illustrated out of the Poem," p. 570), a statement indicating some familiarity on her part with the views on a temporal monarchy as expressed in the *Convito, De Monarchiâ,* and the *Divine Comedy.*

36. Elsewhere, Christina makes a parallel rejection of her father's allegorical reading of Petrarch's Laura, whose actual existence he denied in reading Laura as a symbol for a masonic lodge (Waller, p. 91). Christina engages in an oblique manner this whole subject of the symbol's connection to the concrete in her entry on Petrarch in John Francis Waller's *Imperial Dictionary of Universal Biography* (London: William MacKenzie, 1863), where she returns the focus to the physicality of "flesh and blood" in her claim that Laura is her "own ancestress, as family documents prove" (3:544).

37. I would like to express my gratitude to Mrs. Cicely Rossetti and Mr. Nicholas Rossetti for their kindness and generosity in allowing me to study the contents of their private libraries. Citations will distinguish between the two copies of *A Shadow of Dante* by indicating the original owner (Frances *Shadow* and Christina *Shadow*), and will be noted parenthetically in the text.

38. The volume is inscribed by William Michael, "from Christina's books / 1894."

39. For example, "It struck me (CGR) but the idea did not seem to commend itself to dear MFR . . ." (Frances *Shadow,* p. 57).

40. Marsh, *CR,* pp. 457, 471.

41. The question of the aptness of the punishment Dante describes is important in the *Inferno.* For example, in Canto 28, Mahomet explains that sowers of scandal and schism are cloven in hell. Rossetti chooses to address passages where the appropriateness of the punishment to the crime is not explained or is not obvious.

42. In addition to the two annotations I discuss, Rossetti also questions Maria's verdict that "truth is spoken" by the hypocrites in this pit. Christina underlines three times the words "truth is" and places an "X" in the margin beside the underlined phrase (Christina *Shadow,* p. 85).

43. This rejected suggestion to Maria regarding Caiaphas's punishment (in addition to Christina's "curious theory," which Maria did include in a footnote) confirms Jan Marsh's surmise that Dante was being "discussed over tea and supper" (Marsh, *CR,* p. 392), and demonstrates how closely involved Christina was in Maria's study of Dante.

44. The wordplay that is central to this discussion on the consuming flame is likewise evident in a discussion with William Michael dated 20 March 1892:

Don't you think something (additional to your exposition) might be made of Mastro Adamo's dropsy? His crime was to debase coin; his punishment to have his blood debased; that by alloy, this by water. And, if (as I think I saw somewhere) the circulation of the blood was not unsurmised as long ago as would be required, would or would not a play upon words suggest itself between the circulating vital fluid and the circulating medium? (*FL*, p. 184)

45. John D. Sinclair, *The Divine Comedy of Dante Alighieri with Translation and Comment*, 3 vols. (New York: Oxford University Press, 1939), 1:329.

46. C. H. Grandgent, *Companion to the Divine Comedy, as edited by Charles S. Singleton* (Cambridge: Harvard University Press, 1975), p. 89.

47. Grandgent, p. 89.

48. *Inferno* 3.59-60. Charles S. Singleton indicates that some modern commentators have also identified this figure as Pilate (*The Divine Comedy, Translated with a Commentary. Inferno: Commentary*, Vol. 1.2, Bollingen Series 80 [Princeton: Princeton University Press, 1970], p. 59). For a discussion of this passage see Giorgio Padoan, "*Colui Che Fece Per Viltà Il Gran Rifiuto*," *Studi Danteschi* 38 (1961): 75-128.

49. She was certainly aware of this because she cites William Michael's note on Esaw, which also mentions the generally received reading of the figure as a reference to Celestine (William Michael Rossetti, *The Comedy of Dante Allighieri: Part I—The Hell*, p. 18).

50. The passage in question is translated by Sinclair as "him who from cowardice made the great refusal." Christina is working from memory; the line is actually "*colui / che fece per viltà il gran rifiuto*" (*Inferno* 3.59-60). I am grateful to my colleague Dominic Manganiello for his assistance with Rossetti's Italian annotations and for numerous informative conversations on Dante.

51. Again Rossetti's memory is faulty: "*riconobbi*" is actually "*Conobbi*" (*Inferno* 3.59) in the text; "*guardai e vidi*" is "*riguardai, vidi*" (*Inferno* 3.52).

52. Those freed from Limbo by Christ include Adam, Abel, Noah, Moses, Abraham, David, Jacob and his twelve sons, and Rachel (*Inferno* 4.51-63).

53. Translated by Sinclair as "After I had recognized some of them I saw and knew." The actual line is "*Poscia ch'io v'ebbi alcun riconosciuto, vidi e conobbi*" (*Inferno* 3.58-59).

54. William Michael Rossetti, *The Comedy of Dante Allighieri: Part I—The Hell*, p. 18.

55. See "'*Monna Innominata*' and *Sonnets from the Portuguese*: Sonnet Traditions and Spiritual Trajectories," chapter 3 in this collection.

56. Jerome Bump suggests that for Hopkins Christina Rossetti was "like Beatrice in Dante's poetry, . . . the lady who is spiritually more advanced, clearly superior in holiness" ("Hopkins, Christina Rossetti, and Pre-Raphaelitism," *VN* 57 [1980]: 4).

Meanwhile, in Michael Field's elegy "To Christina Rossetti" (*Victorian Women Poets: An Anthology,* ed. Angela Leighton and Margaret Reynolds [Oxford and Cambridge, Mass.: Blackwell, 1995], p. 506), the elegist suggests that the subject fails to live up to this identification with Beatrice:

> Lady, we would behold thee moving bright
> As Beatrice or Matilda 'mid the trees,
> Alas! thy moan was as a moan for ease
> And passage through cool shadows to the night:
> Fleeing from love, hadst thou not poet's right
> To slip into the universe? . . .

See Susan Conley's "'Poet's Right': Christina Rossetti as Anti-Muse and the Legacy of the 'Poetess,'" *VP* 32 (1994): 365-86, for a discussion of this elegy and the tradition of women poets.

CHAPTER 3

"*Monna Innominata*" and *Sonnets from the Portuguese*

Sonnet Traditions and Spiritual Trajectories

MARJORIE STONE

In a quietly audacious bid for fame, Christina Rossetti invites comparison in the preface to *"Monna Innominata": A Sonnet of Sonnets* with Dante, Petrarch, and Elizabeth Barrett Browning, the "Great Poetess" of her "own day" (*CP,* 1:86). Yet, despite her explicit mention of the author of the "'Portuguese Sonnets,'" the literary connections between Barrett Browning's famous sequence and Rossetti's have remained largely unexplored. In the two most illuminating studies of *"Monna Innominata"* to date, William Whitla and Antony H. Harrison approach the sequence in the context of the Dantean and Petrarchan tradition, but give relatively little attention to the context created by the *Sonnets from the Portuguese.*[1] As Rossetti's preface implies, however, her engagement with Dante and Petrarch is inseparable from her engagement with Barrett Browning. Moreover, her response to all three poetical precursors seems to have been shaped by her ambivalent reaction to Dante Gabriel Rossetti's *The House of Life,* which appeared, in a revised and expanded form, the same year as *"Monna Innominata."*[2] This essay explores some of the echoes, parallels, and counterplots linking *"Monna Innominata"* to Dante's *Divine Comedy,* to Dante Gabriel Rossetti's *The House of Life,* and above all, to the *Sonnets from the Portuguese.*[3] Among these, the artistic connections to the "Portuguese Sonnets" would seem to be the most obvious, given Rossetti's prefatory remarks. But they remained practically uninvestigated for almost a century because of prevailing approaches to women writers. Just as Barrett Browning's sequence was traditionally read as a transparently autobiographical text hiding behind the "mask" of its title, *"Monna Innominata"* was assumed to be a "personal utterance" concealed by the "blind" of its preface.[4] More recent criticism has rightly challenged such readings, in Barrett Browning's case as in Rossetti's, yet critics of the two poets seem not to have been in dialogue with one another.[5] Or like Harrison, Rossetti critics have been so concerned to establish her superior artistry and innovation that they emphasize the ways in which she departed from Barrett Browning's example, to the exclusion of the ways in which she followed it.

As I hope to show, the close connection between *"Monna Innominata"* and the *Sonnets from the Portuguese* simultaneously manifests itself in their points of greatest divergence and convergence: in the diametrically opposed spiritual trajectories these two sequences trace, as well as in their parallel subversions of a masculine sonnet tradition. The opposing spiritual trajectories of the two sequences are brought into view by Rossetti's "'They Desire a Better Country'" (*CP*, 1:195-96), a three-sonnet sequence written in 1867 or 1868 that anticipates *"Monna Innominata"* in both form and subject matter.[6] Passed over in most studies of Rossetti, "'They Desire a Better Country'" is particularly significant for my argument here because it opens with a pointed critique of the movement from divine to human love embodied in the *Sonnets from the Portuguese*. In *"Monna Innominata"* this critique expands into a subtler and more multi-faceted engagement with the idolization of earthly love Rossetti discerned in the plot and imagery of the *Sonnets from the Portuguese*. "I yield the grave for thy sake, and exchange / My near sweet view of Heaven, for earth with thee!" Barrett Browning's speaker exclaims in Sonnet 23 of her sequence. This was not an "exchange" Rossetti was likely to accept. Heaven is seldom "near" in her more soberly realistic vision of spiritual struggle; in fact, in Sonnet 11 of *"Monna Innominata,"* "heaven is out of view." But even "out of view," it is not something to be "exchanged" for love on earth. In *"Monna Innominata"* Rossetti presents a directly opposing trajectory to Barrett Browning's in moving from *eros* to *agape,* from earthly love to the spiritual love associated with the "better country" of heaven.

Rossetti represented this spiritual ascent with all the more quiet urgency because she confronted an intensified version of Barrett Browning's absorption in earthly love in her brother Dante Gabriel Rossetti's *The House of Life.* Dorothy Mermin notes that *The House of Life* is reminiscent of the *Sonnets from the Portuguese* in its "marmoreal cadences, personifications, archaisms, and heated slow simplicities."[7] The personification of Love as a palpably physical presence — as an earthly angel — is one of the more striking parallels between Dante Gabriel Rossetti's sequence and Barrett Browning's. The sensuous personifications and the narrative trajectories of both sequences, together with the spiritual values they reflect, are countered in Rossetti's *"Monna Innominata."* Mary Arseneau has shown how Rossetti's *The Prince's Progress* registers her resistance to the transformations in her brother's spiritual beliefs and "his gradual unhinging of his symbolic method from any stable system of signification."[8] The critique of Barrett Browning in both "'They Desire a Better Country'" and *"Monna Innominata"* suggests that Rossetti objected to an analogous, though less dramatic, transformation in Barrett Browning's vision and symbolic practice.

Nevertheless, despite the opposing spiritual trajectories of their sonnet sequences, Rossetti was by no means completely hostile to Barrett Browning's achievement in the sonnet form. As I have argued elsewhere, Rossetti markedly differed from Barrett Browning in her spiritual vision and aesthetic principles, but at the same time, learned much from her precursor's revisionary gynocentric perspectives and textual practices.[9] A similarly complex though opposite pattern characterizes her textual engagement with Dante and Petrarch, a circumstance that helps to explain why her textual engagement with these masculine precursors in *"Monna Innominata"* is inseparable from her engagement with the "Great Poetess" of her own day. On the one hand she turned to the ascent to heavenly love represented in Dante's *Divine Comedy* as a corrective for the emphasis on human love in the *Sonnets from the Portuguese* and her brother's *House of Life.* But on the other hand, she turned to Barrett Browning's example in refashioning courtly love conventions to accord with a female center of consciousness. An appreciation of the doubleness of Rossetti's response to Dante and Petrarch, as well as to Barrett Browning, helps to reconcile the divergent though equally persuasive arguments of Harrison and Whitla concerning Rossetti's relation to the sonnet tradition. Thus, Whitla rightly emphasizes Rossetti's "questioning" of Dantean and Petrarchan sonnet conventions (though without addressing the precedent set by Barrett Browning) in observing that *"Monna Innominata"* decenters "the sonnet tradition from the poet or the poem to the muse," and also radically revises "Dante's own estimate of the muse's qualities."[10] Harrison argues to the contrary that Rossetti "accepts and imitates Dantean tradition rather than attempting to supersede or transform it as her brother does" in order to distance her "poetry from its immediate historical contexts" and present "a forceful ideological critique of those contexts."[11] Such apparently contradictory arguments are alike well grounded because Rossetti's critique cuts both ways. She turned to the revisionary strategies of the "Great Poetess" of her "own day" to underline the limitations of the masculine sonneteers of the past; but she simultaneously turned to the past, and in particular to Dante, to reveal the inadequacies of spiritual vision in the increasingly secular world that surrounded her.

The first section of this essay analyzes the paradoxes of Rossetti's enigmatic preface, giving particular attention to her subtly gynocentric *métissage* of allusions to Dante's *Divine Comedy,* her identification of Petrarch as an "inferior bard," and her equivocal tribute to Barrett Browning. The second section considers the ways "'They Desire a Better Country'" functions as a critique of the spiritual trajectory manifested in *Sonnets from the Portuguese.* Section three explores the counterplot to this trajectory that Rossetti creates in *"Monna Innominata,"* and the striking differences between her representation of human and divine love and both Barrett Browning's in the Portuguese *Sonnets* and Dante Gabriel Rossetti's in *The House of Life.* The final section analyzes some of the equally striking parallels in Rossetti's and Barrett Browning's revision of the love sonnet tradition. Through their similar use of the metaphor of translation, their subversions of female silence and the male gaze, and their creation of a new discourse of reciprocal love, Rossetti and Barrett Browning modify sonnet conventions to express a newly articulate female subjectivity.

Unpacking the Preface: The Velvet Gauntlet

That *"Monna Innominata"* constitutes a bid for poetic fame is announced immediately in the preface not only by the choice of Dantean quotations but also by the way in which Rossetti uses them to challenge her poetical precursors. Whitla, who has identified all of the Dantean and Petrarchan quotations in the sequence, points out that the Dantean epigraphs extend the intertextuality of Rossetti's work by invoking numerous poets aside from Dante and Petrarch, including Virgil, Sordello, Casella, Guinizelli, Statius, Matilda, Saint Bernard, and Piccarda, Dante's sister-in-law: "[t]he epigraphs' oblique references either involve a direct address by one of Dante's fellow poets or are spoken in the presence of those poets by Dante . . . or allude to the invocation of the god of poetry."[12] The first quotation from Dante in the preface is also true to this pattern, suggesting how much Rossetti saw Dante as a "poets' poet," and how much she was seeking to establish herself as a similar kind of writer.

In its focus on the great poets of the past, and Dante above all, *"Monna Innominata"* is like "A Vision of Poets" (1844), the work in which Barrett Browning most clearly attempts to walk in Dante's footsteps. This allegorical dream vision, much praised by Victorian reviewers, portrays an anonymous pilgrim-poet who aspires to join the immortal company of "king poets," each of whom is invoked and summed up in turn with an unusual concision stimulated by Barrett Browning's use of a simplified version of Dante's *terza rima*. And her catalogue of king-poets of course includes both Dante and Petrarch, writers whom Barrett Browning greatly admired, even to the point of translating portions of their works.[13] Much as Barrett Browning indirectly signals her aspiration to join the company of immortal poets in "A Vision of Poets" by saluting and memorializing each dead great poet in turn, Rossetti signals her aspiration in *"Monna Innominata"* by saluting Dante with the tribute ("altissimo poeta") accorded to Virgil in Dante's hearing. Moreover, the salutation she chooses appears in *Inferno* 4.80, just before Virgil introduces Dante to Homer "who all poets hath surpassed" (88), followed by Horace, Ovid, and Lucan—in other words, by others among the "king poets," to use Barrett Browning's terms. Significantly, however, Rossetti's choice of tribute implicitly singles out the Christian Dante, not the pagan Virgil or Homer, as the greatest of her precursors. By contrast, despite her use of a Dantean poetic form, Barrett Browning pays tribute to both pagan and Christian poets in "A Vision of Poets," beginning with Homer.

Rossetti's self-reliant critical judgment is further revealed as she proceeds to place Petrarch firmly in Dante's shadow as the lesser poet, and simultaneously, to criticize both for their representation of their muses:

> Beatrice, immortalized by "altissimo poeta . . . cotanto amante"; Laura, celebrated by a great tho' an inferior bard,—have alike paid the exceptional penalty of exceptional honour, and have come down to us resplendent with charms, but (at least, to my apprehension) scant of attractiveness.

The compressed resonance of this opening is matched only by the boldness of its critique. The steady poise of the parallel syntactic structures—"the exceptional penalty of exceptional honour," "resplendent with charms" but "scant of attractiveness"—speaks with a quiet but undeniable authority. In the midst of such stylistic precision, the parenthetical disclaimer reads less like a modesty trope than an assertion of faith in the writer's own "apprehension." Initiating a pattern that recurs throughout the preface and the sequence of sonnets, Rossetti sets up a parallelism and/or a rhetorical doubling that immediately folds into a paradox. In this instance the rhetorical doublings crystallize, in a few apt words, the "paradox of the pedestal" that underlies Rossetti's incisive critique of Dante, Petrarch, and, by implication, all of their masculine imitators.

The subtle play of Rossetti's paradoxes is particularly apparent in her identification of Dante not simply as "altissimo poeta," but as the greatest poet with such a lover ("cotanto amante"). This pair of allusions united by an ellipsis braids together passages that in fact appear in different cantos of *The Divine Comedy*.[14] While the tribute to Virgil by Dante comes from *Inferno* canto 4, the phrase "cotanto amante" comes from *Inferno* 5.134, where the doomed Francesca describes how Guinevere's smile, "so thirsted for," was "kissed by such a lover" as Lancelot. This is also the critical point when the burning passion of Francesca and Paolo is ignited by the act of reading about Guinevere and Lancelot, and, in Francesca's words, her own lover "[A]ll trembling kissed my mouth" (5.136). Rossetti's *métissage* of allusions seems to have multiple functions. Most obviously, it epitomizes the struggle between sensuous and spiritual love that her sequence explores, and implies, through its connection of Dante with Lancelot (and Paolo and Francesca), that the author of *The Divine Comedy* experienced the same struggle. At the same time, however, her intertwined allusions also mark her distance from her masculine precursors, whose representation of women she finds so "scant of attractiveness." Enacting an intriguing gender reversal, Rossetti's syntax displaces the passionate Lancelot with a (passionate) Beatrice, while also making Dante's greatness conditional upon the fact that he has "such a lover" as she. Moreover, the phrase she chooses to cite comes from a passage in which intense passion—the burning first kiss—is described from a doubled female perspective (Francesca's and Guinevere's), creating a woman-centered and surprisingly erotic subtext for her apparently chaste sequence. The shrewdness of Rossetti's strategy is apparent in the way she decenters the work of her most daunting male precursor by using his own words: the words he portrays Francesca as speaking in what is arguably the most hauntingly romantic passage of the *Inferno*, as the responses of Keats and Dante Gabriel Rossetti alike suggest.[15] By taking the words from Dante's mouth, so to speak, Rossetti implies that he had the power—if only he had had the eyes to see her—to portray a woman who was not only as "resplendent" and pure as Beatrice, but also as passionate and as articulate in conveying her passion as Francesca. In short, he had the power to portray a muse who was also a woman possessing her own intense center of consciousness.

Rossetti prompts the reader to reflect upon her interwoven Dantean allusions by opening her preface with a much more conspicuous revisionary swerve. Unexpectedly, she begins by naming Beatrice and defining (but not directly naming) Dante relative to her, and then repeats the same pattern with the introduction of "Laura, celebrated by a great tho' inferior bard." In a work in which the title throws the attention on an unnamed though particular lady from the very start, this is surely a deliberate strategy.[16] Through her substitution of Beatrice's name for Dante's, and Laura's for Petrarch's, Rossetti prepares the way for her suggestion that "many a lady" among the Troubadours may have "shared her lover's poetic aptitude." Marsh points out that Rossetti may have been led to imagine an unnamed lady writing a sonnet sequence herself in part because Francis Hueffer's *The Troubadours* identified "some fourteen gifted women" among the ranks of four hundred or so twelfth-century troubadours—a suggestively apt number, Marsh adds, given the total of fourteen poems in Rossetti's "sonnet of sonnets."[17] Or it may be, as Whitla suggests,[18] that Rossetti took her idea from Dante Gabriel Rossetti's mention in *The Early Italian Poets* of a lady named Nina, the love of Dante da Maiano, "herself it is said a poetess." In either case, Rossetti believed that her idea of imagining an unnamed female troubadour was a new one. "I rather wonder," she wrote to Gabriel, "that no one (so far as I know) ever hit on my semi-historical argument before for such treatment,—it seems to me so full of poetic suggestiveness."[19]

What Rossetti does not do, either in this private letter or in the preface to *"Monna Innominata,"* is present herself as the first woman poet in her own age to write a sonnet sequence from the female perspective. On the contrary, she acknowledges the precedent set by the *Sonnets from the Portuguese*—though not without indirectly advancing her own claim to innovation. Thus she observes that, if a poetically gifted female troubadour had "spoken for herself" in a situation where "mutual love" was not "incompatible with mutual honour,"

> the portrait left us might have appeared more tender, if less dignified, than any drawn even by a devoted friend. Or had the Great Poetess of our own day and nation only been unhappy instead of happy, her cir-

cumstances would have invited her to bequeath to us, in lieu of the "Portuguese Sonnets," an inimitable "donna innominata" drawn not from fancy but from feeling, and worthy to occupy a niche beside Beatrice and Laura.

Harrison describes this passage as a "curious invocation" of Barrett Browning, while Joan Rees terms it an "equivocal tribute,"[20] terms more than justified by the circumlocutions of Rossetti's conditional phrasing.

It is an "equivocal tribute," I believe, because, like the invocation to Dante and Petrarch, it simultaneously acknowledges the legacy Barrett Browning has "bequeathed" and expresses Rossetti's bid to surpass the "Great Poetess" of her own age. The first reading, interpreting the passage as tribute, is reinforced by the probable echo of the opening lines of *Aurora Leigh* in the first sentence. Just as Rossetti indicates that a lady's own portrait of her thoughts and feelings is preferable to a portrait drawn "even by a devoted friend," so Aurora begins her book ("I write") by emphatically indicating her preference for her own self-portrait over a portrait by a masculine "friend": a friend who, in Aurora's ironic words, "keeps [his portrait of you] in a drawer and looks at it / Long after he has ceased to love you, just / To hold together what he was and is."[21] The second reading, interpreting the "tribute" as a tactfully indirect challenge, emerges from Rossetti's suggestion that, if the "Great Poetess of our own day" had "only been unhappy instead of happy," she might have written an "inimitable 'donna innominata' drawn not from fancy but from feeling and worthy to occupy a niche beside Beatrice and Laura." Since Barrett Browning was happy, however, she clearly did not create an "inimitable" peer of Beatrice and Laura, and the field is open to Rossetti to do so. In other words, one might say, taking a cue from Rossetti's opening reference to a ranked male pair of poets, and from her use of the modifier "great" for both Petrarch and Barrett Browning, the field is open to Rossetti to become the Dante to Barrett Browning's Petrarch.

Indeed, Rossetti's reference to the author of the "'Portuguese Sonnets'" has been interpreted in an even more negative light than this. Hall Caine in the nineteenth century and Lona Mosk Packer in the twentieth found in this passage the implication that the *Sonnets from the Portuguese* were written not from feeling, but from fancy.[22] Dolores Rosenblum more obliquely suggests that Rossetti's opposition between fancy and feeling is "peculiarly ambiguous."[23] I would agree with Whitla that the interpretations of Caine and Packer involve a misreading, given that Rossetti herself was "sorry" that Caine seemed "to have misapprehended [her] reference to the Portuguese Sonnets." As Rossetti explains, "Surely not only what I meant to say but what I do say is, not that the Lady of those sonnets is surpassable, but that a 'Donna innominata' by the same hand might well have been unsurpassable. The Lady in question, as she stands, I was not regarding as an 'innominata' at all,—because the latter type, according to the traditional figures I had in mind, is surrounded by unlike circumstances."[24] Nevertheless, one cannot help but note the ambiguities of even this gloss on the convoluted prefatorial reference to Barrett Browning, though in the case of the letter the ambiguities are created not by conditional phrasing but by negative constructions. Once again, what Rossetti seems to say is that "the Lady" of the *Sonnets from the Portuguese* is not "unsurpassable"—ironically, the preface suggests, because she was happy and not unhappy in love.

Spiritual Trajectories: "They Desire a Better Country"

The reasons Rossetti considered the *Sonnets from the Portuguese* "surpassable" have everything to do with her spiritual convictions, as her earlier, more direct critique of Barrett Browning in "'They Desire a Better Country'" indicates. First published in 1869 in *Macmillan's Magazine*, "'They Desire a Better Country'" seems to be closely related to "By Way of Remembrance," dated 1870 in manuscript (*CP*, 3:485). Both are three-sonnet sequences proleptic of the more extended *"Monna Innominata."* Indeed, as Linda Schofield has pointed out, Rossetti "cannibalized" portions of "By Way of Remembrance" in writing *"Monna Innominata."*[25] All three sequences articulate a love unfulfilled on earth yet hopeful of fulfillment in heaven, although the degree of hope differs for each sequence and only in the third does it become clear that the speaker is a woman. The earliest of the three, "'They Desire a Better Country,'" seems to reflect Rossetti meditating on the pattern she had chosen for her life in the years immediately following her rejection of Charles Bagot Cayley's marriage proposal "some time in August of 1866."[26] She chose to take stock of her life, notably, by echoing and responding to a pivotal sonnet in Barrett Browning's canon.

Opening with the emphatic lines, "I would not if I could undo my past / Tho' for its sake my future is a blank," the first sonnet in "'They Desire a Better Country'" almost certainly invokes a sonnet by Barrett Browning entitled "Future and Past" (3:247). "Future and Past" was first published as a separate poem in Barrett Browning's 1850 *Poems,* but subsequently incorporated as Sonnet 42 in the revised version of *Sonnets from the Portuguese* included in her 1856 *Poems.*[27] The intertextual dialogue Rossetti activates by invoking "Future and Past" is further complicated by the fact that this sonnet itself echoes and plays against a still earlier sonnet entitled "Past and Future" (2:228), published by Barrett Browning in her 1844 *Poems.* "Past and Future" embodies a spiritual trajectory focused on Christ and heaven, in keeping with the prevailing religious impulses that David G. Riede has identified in Elizabeth Barrett's works up to 1844.[28] The later sonnet, "Future and Past," epitomizes the very different spiritual trajectory focused on earth that emerges in the *Sonnets from the Portuguese.* Since neither sonnet is among Barrett Browning's best known, I include both here, followed by the opening sonnet of Rossetti's "'They Desire a Better Country,'" which recalls the vision and the images of "Past and Future" in order to contest the reversal that occurs in "Future and Past."

Past and Future

My future will not copy fair my past
On any leaf but Heaven's. Be fully done,
Supernal Will! I would not fain be one
Who, satisfying thirst and breaking fast,
Upon the fullness of the heart at last
Says no grace after meat. My wine has run
Indeed out of my cup, and there is none
To gather up the bread of my repast
Scattered and trampled; yet I find some good
In earth's green herbs, and streams that bubble up
Clear from the darkling ground,—content until
I sit with angels before better food:
Dear Christ! when Thy new vintage fills my cup,
This hand shall shake no more, nor that wine spill.

Future and Past

[subsequently Sonnet 42 of the *Sonnets from the Portuguese*]
"My future will not copy fair my past" —
I wrote that once; and thinking at my side
My ministering life-angel justified
The word by his appealing look upcast
To the white throne of God, I turned at last,

And there, instead, saw thee, not unallied
To angels in thy soul! Then I, long tried
By natural ills, received the comfort fast,
While budding, at thy sight, my pilgrim's staff
Gave out green leaves with morning dews impearled.
I seek no copy now of life's first half:
Leave here the pages with long musings curled,
And write me new my future's epigraph,
New angel mine, unhoped for in the world!

"They Desire a Better Country"

I would not if I could undo my past,
   Tho' for its sake my future is a blank;
   My past for which I have myself to thank,
For all its faults and follies first and last.
I would not cast anew the lot once cast,
   Or launch a second ship for one that sank,
   Or drug with sweets the bitterness I drank,
Or break by feasting my perpetual fast.
I would not if I could: for much more dear
   Is one remembrance than a hundred joys,
      More than a thousand hopes in jubilee;
   Dearer the music of one tearful voice
   That unforgotten calls and calls to me,
"Follow me here, rise up, and follow here."

(*CP*, 1:195-96)

Although there is no overt sign that Rossetti is responding to Barrett Browning's "Past and Future" and "Future and Past" in this reflection on her own past and future, the terms in her opening lines seem too close to her precursor's opening terms—in not one but two sonnets—to be coincidental. Equally important, she appears to be echoing two sonnets that, taken together, made the autobiographical nature of the *Sonnets from the Portuguese* unequivocal, as Robert Browning's comments in 1864 indicate.[29] Nor should we forget that such details were more likely to appear significant in Rossetti's lifetime than they do today, because of the initial uncertainty expressed in the reviews of Barrett Browning's 1850 *Poems* concerning the subject matter of the sequence. The probability that Rossetti's echoes are intentional is further suggested by the overtly signaled critique in the sequence "Three

Nuns" of the focus on earthly love in Barrett Browning's "Catarina to Camoens," a poem closely linked to the *Sonnets from the Portuguese,* given the title of the latter.[30] Nor is it difficult to see why Rossetti may have seen the sentiments expressed by Barrett Browning in "Future and Past," which in effect reverse those expressed in the earlier "Past and Future," as requiring a strong and direct response. In her eyes, these sentiments may well have been tantamount to blasphemy or, at the very least, backsliding.

Like several of Barrett Browning's other accomplished sonnets of 1844 on religious subjects, "Past and Future" expresses a vision very close to Rossetti's own, using some of the same biblical images (of fasting and feasting, of Christ's cup of wine, of Christ as bridegroom, of an imperfect earth redeemed by the "new vintage" of heaven) that recur in her work. In "Future and Past," however, Christ and the angels of "Past and Future" are replaced by a man "not unallied / To angels" in his soul. Furthermore, in turning away from the past ("I seek no copy now of life's first half"), Barrett Browning turns away as well from the heaven in which she had once hoped to find a "fair copy" of her youthful happiness on earth. At the same time, in asking Robert Browning to "write me new my future's epigraph," she places her reliance on another human being in a manner that Rossetti may well have found very troubling. In other words, Barrett Browning places the pen in her lover's, not God's, hand—though we should remember that, paradoxically, this statement takes the form of a command and that it appears in a sequence where the pen is clearly in her hand from start to finish.

In stark contrast to Barrett Browning, Rossetti repudiates such a turning away from "remembrance" and such a reliance on other mortals. "I would not if I could undo my past," she asserts, emphasizing her responsibility for determining the pattern of her own life: "My past for which I have myself to thank." She holds to the fasting metaphor used by Barrett Browning herself in the earlier "Past and Future," refusing to "drug with sweets the bitterness" she drank, or "break by feasting" her "perpetual fast." She holds to the faith that is called for throughout Hebrews 11, the source of her title. Hebrews 11 begins, "Now faith is the substance of things hoped for, the evidence of things not seen," and goes on to describe how the faithful "desire a better country, that is, an heavenly [country]" (Heb. 11:16).[31] Most of all, Rossetti holds fast to "the music of one tearful voice," the voice not of a lover who can raise her up, but of a suffering Christ who calls on her to rise and "follow here": calling not once, but many times as in the Gospels, and thus again in the final line of the sequence, "Follow me hither, follow, rise, and come."

REVISING BARRETT BROWNING'S REVISION OF THE SONNET TRADITION: ECHOES AND REVERSIONS

Rossetti's critique in "'They Desire a Better Country'" of "Future and Past," Sonnet 42 of the *Sonnets from the Portuguese,* expands in *"Monna Innominata"* to a revision of the entire love sonnet tradition and simultaneously, as Harrison suggests, registers her resistance to the secularism of her age. In the process, she engages in a more multifaceted critique of the spiritual trajectory embodied in Barrett Browning's sequence, a trajectory which her brother followed out to its disillusioned end, in the context of unhappy rather than happy love, in his own ironically titled sequence, *The House of Life.*[32] As Shaakeh Agajanian and Glennis Stephenson have shown, in contrast to the love Dante portrays in his *Vita Nuova,* the love Barrett Browning represents becomes "progressively physical"—appropriately enough, one might argue, in a sequence that often echoes Spenser's *Amoretti* and ends, as it does, with a celebration of wedded love.[33] By contrast, Rossetti's *"Monna Innominata"* begins, as Harrison observes, with a "wish for a physical meeting with the beloved" and progresses to "a desire for perfection of the beloved" and a "transcendent union of the lovers with God" that occurs "beyond phenomenal reality."[34] The speaker of the Portuguese *Sonnets* celebrates a heavenly bliss on earth so intense the angels might aspire to enter its "deep, dear silence" (Sonnet 22); the lady of *"Monna Innominata"* awaits an eternity in which "life reborn annuls / Loss and decay and death, and all is love" (Sonnet 10). Barrett Browning's speaker, looking "only for God," finds instead a human lover who becomes indistinguishable from the personified figure of "Love" who saves her from "Death" in Sonnets 1 and 27. Rossetti's lady similarly declares that "love is strong as death" (Sonnet 7), but the love she alludes to is God's love, the love she directs her beloved to embrace in Sonnet 13: "And therefore I commend you back to Him / Whose love your love's capacity can fill." In fact, throughout *"Monna Innominata,"* as in "An Echo from Willowwood," Rossetti eschews the personifications of Love that feature so prominently in *Sonnets from the Portuguese* as well as in her brother's *House of Life.*

The contrast between Rossetti's and Barrett Browning's approach to human and divine love is especially apparent in the ways in which their speakers "think" of the beloved. For example, in Sonnet 29, written at a point when Barrett Browning's speaker is feeling joyously assured of her lover's regard, she writes "I think of thee!" and proceeds to describe the exuberance of her loving thoughts in images of budding, fertile vitality: "my thoughts do twine and bud / About thee, as wild vines about a tree." Yet "o my palm-tree," she playfully exclaims, "be it understood / I will not have my thoughts instead of thee / Who art dearer, better!" The imagery, as Agajanian suggests, is wittily metaphysical, involving an allusion to "the ivy plant that twined around the stark mast of the Greek pirate ship harboring Dionysus," signaling the presence of a god, and the ivy that concealed Prospero's "princely trunk."[35] Once again, then, we see the equation of the lover with a divine being (and a pagan one in this instance) that runs through the *Sonnets from the Portuguese*, as in Sonnet 20 where the speaker compares her inability to foresee her meeting with her lover to atheists who "cannot guess God's presence out of sight." No such equation of human and divine is ever contemplated in *"Monna Innominata."* Nor are pagan and Christian allusions freely mingled. Sonnet 9 of Rossetti's sequence begins much like Sonnet 29 in Barrett Browning's, with the words "Thinking of thee." But it presents very different thoughts as Rossetti's speaker places her love in the context of "all that was, and all / That might have been and now can never be," before going on to indicate her commitment to the "happier call" of a spiritual love that entails continual struggle—wrestling like Jacob with the angel "till the break / Of day." Sonnet 9 is pivotal in that it constitutes the *volta* of Rossetti's "sonnet of sonnets." In this instance the "turn" clearly marks a spiritual transition, emphasized by the biblical allusions Rossetti makes at this point. Helen H. Wenger notes at least five in the space of ten lines.[36]

A related contrast between the vision of these two poets is apparent in the very different images of love folding its wings like a dove or the Holy Spirit in the two sequences. Barrett Browning explicitly uses this image at least twice in *Sonnets from the Portuguese*: in Sonnet 31, where the speaker calls on her lover to dispel her fears that love cannot last—"Ah, keep near and close / Thou dovelike help! . . . Brood down with thy divine sufficiencies"; and in Sonnet 35, where a compressed allusion to the dove associated with Noah's ark permits a veiled reference to the deep grief she experienced after her brother Edward's death by drowning. Thus she asks her lover to "Open thine heart wide, / And fold within the wet wings of thy dove." Two features are especially notable in these uses of the dove image. First, even though Barrett Browning is clearly activating biblical associations in both cases, the reference of the dove shifts, much as the reference of religious signifiers does in Dante Gabriel Rossetti's poetry.[37] Secondly, the allusion in Sonnet 31 again implies the equation of her human lover with God, in this case in the form of the Holy Spirit.

Noting the ways in which the human lover of the Portuguese *Sonnets* takes on the role of the Holy Ghost in the dramatic Annunciation scene of Sonnet 1, and the revivifying role of Christ in Sonnet 23, Agajanian points out that Barrett Browning clearly departs from the Italian sonnet tradition in attributing divine powers to her beloved: "for while Beatrice . . . and Laura partook of some divinity, they were never raised above the rank of angels or compared to the Virgin or Venus, let alone the Holy Ghost, God, Christ or Zeus."[38] This is a revision of the tradition Rossetti set about revising again in her turn by reverting to Dante's and Petrarch's more orthodox religious views. At no point does she suggest that the beloved has divine powers. Thus, her use of the dove image in Sonnet 10 of *"Monna Innominata"* invokes a more traditional image of divine love that does not transgress orthodox Christian beliefs, as the lady alludes to the time when "[l]ife wanes" and "love folds his wings above / Tired hope," bringing sleep and peace.

The contrasting visions of love expressed by Barrett Browning and Rossetti are further apparent in their use of a common metaphor of mutability in the love sonnet tradition: the waxing and waning moon. In Sonnet 1 of *"Monna Innominata,"* the lady writes, "My hope hangs waning, waxing, like a moon / Between the heavenly days on which we meet," in describing the "pang of parting" from her beloved. A similar antithesis of sun and moon appears in Sonnet 32 of the Portuguese *Sonnets*, which opens with the lines: "The first time that the sun rose on thine oath / To love me, I looked forward to the moon / To slacken all those bonds." In other respects, however, this parallel points to the strong contrast between the spiritual visions embodied in the two sequences. As Agajanian points out, the recurring doubt provoked by the lover's absence in the Portuguese *Sonnets* reflects an important departure from the tradition:

> While the fears and sorrows of the traditional lover, occasioned by the absence of the beloved, were of psychological and metaphysical origin (as expressed in Petrarch's Sonnets CXC and CCXVI . . .), the doubt expressed by the Victorian poet is ontological and epistemological. In this new concept where love is not an external metaphysical entity but the constituent element of the lover's being, when the lover is absent the emotion is absent as well. Near or far, reciprocated or not, the Tuscan, Petrarchan, and Elizabethan lover never doubted the ontological reality of love.[39]

The "ontological" doubt that troubles the speaker in the *Sonnets from the Portuguese* becomes an even more pronounced element in Dante Gabriel

Rossetti's *The House of Life*. But such doubt does not figure in *"Monna In-nominata,"* with its reversion to a Dantean vision, even though Rossetti does engage in a sophisticated exploration of the epistemological uncertainties that perplex human lovers. Significantly, Rossetti chooses to use the image of the waxing and waning moon at the beginning of her sequence, where the lady is still most tied to earthly "pleasures" and to "one man" who is "my world of all the men / This wide world holds." In the Portuguese *Sonnets*, however, where we do not see the same progression from earthly to heavenly love, this image occurs in the final third of the sequence, when both lovers are well advanced in their relationship. The emphasis on mutability at this late point reflects the degree to which Barrett Browning's speaker depends upon one man's love. And what if, being human, he should prove to be less than an angel after all? Although such anxieties seem finally to be dismissed in Sonnet 32 because the lady sees them as a "wrong" to her lover, her very insistence on casting him as an angel suggests how much nevertheless she remains subject to ontological doubt.[40]

Revising the Masculine Tradition: Sisterly Affinities

Thus far, I have focused on Rossetti's resistance in *"Monna Innominata"* to the secular values reflected in the *Sonnets from the Portuguese.* But such resistance and the revisionary impulse it generated constitute only half of the story of Rossetti's textual engagement with the "Great Poetess" of her age in *"Monna Innominata."* Although she was sharply critical of Barrett Browning's turn away from the "better country" of heaven, Rossetti was also much indebted to her precursor's rewriting of the masculine paradigms that shaped the sonnet sequences of the Italian and English Renaissance.[41] And once again, her response to Barrett Browning seems to have been connected to her response to her brother, who replicated many of these masculine assumptions in a sequence that obsessively focused on ladies never given the chance to speak. In Sonnet 10 of *The House of Life*, for instance, entitled "The Portrait," Dante Gabriel Rossetti assumes his ability to present the beauty of his unnamed lady's "inner self"; and since "Her face is made her shrine" by his art, he concludes, "They that would look on her must come to me." Little wonder that his sister preferred not to "come" to him or to sonneteers like him, but instead chose to follow the example set by the Portuguese *Sonnets* and *Aurora Leigh* in creating a "portrait" of a lady speaking (or rather writing) "for herself."

To date, critics have not engaged in comparative analyses of the ways in which Barrett Browning and Rossetti rewrite sonnet conventions to accord with a female subject. While a full treatment of this subject is beyond the scope of this essay, a brief indication of certain parallel strategies in *"Monna Innominata"* and the *Sonnets from the Portuguese* may suggest how similar the two poets' revisionary impulses are. First and most obviously, we may note the ways in which both poets use the translation tropes reflected in the title of each sequence. Given that Barrett Browning deliberately positioned her Portuguese *Sonnets* immediately after "Catarina to Camoens" in her 1850 *Poems* (her instructions to the printer in the manuscript at Wellesley College Library clearly state, *"Go on to the Sonnets from the Portuguese.* MS"),[42] mid-Victorian readers were encouraged to speculate that the sonnets may have been written by a Portuguese lady older and happier in love than the unfortunate Catarina. Similarly, Rossetti's title, together with her preface, encourages readers to speculate that her sequence may have been written by an Italian female troubadour.

Critics have assumed that the title of the *Sonnets from the Portuguese* was merely a "blind" tacked on at the last minute to disguise their personal nature, and it is true that Barrett Browning herself referred to publishing them in 1850 "under some sort of veil."[43] But if the title was a "veil," it was a carefully chosen one, related both to the scenes and images of the sequence itself (palaces, minstrels, lutes, and mandolins), and to Robert Browning's association of his love for Elizabeth Barrett with her "Catarina." I stress this point because in reading the *Sonnets from the Portuguese* as a personal outpouring of love, critics have implicitly assumed that its scenes take place in English and mid-Victorian domestic settings. Consequently, they have objected to the references to palaces, lutes, mandolins, and minstrels as Petrarchan trappings; Mermin also criticizes the erotic images of "grapes, androgynous angels, palm trees, dolphins, and the like" as being out of keeping with "the domestic realities of Victorian life."[44] But many of these details are in keeping with the Portuguese setting of "Catarina to Camoens," while no details in the sequence itself explicitly suggest the Victorian domestic settings critics bring to the poem based on popularized images of "The Barretts of Wimpole Street."

Nevertheless, if Barrett Browning's title with its suggestions of translation from the Portuguese was a carefully chosen veil,[45] it was also an imperfect one, particularly once the addition of "Future and Past" in 1856 made the autobiographical narrative of the sequence clear. One suspects that Rossetti may have recognized as much, and that the recognition led her to fashion a more artful veil for her own sequence. She does this by using the trope of translation more pervasively: employing the Italian language for her title, expanding on the idea of an Italian source or prototype (she is cleverly ambiguous as to which) in her preface, and incorporating epigraphs in the original Italian of Dante and Petrarch throughout the sequence itself. With her usual enigmatic reserve, she did not at any point include or add a sonnet that revealed the sequence's clear connection to events in her own life.

Despite these differences, however, the translation trope is a revisionary strategy serving similar ends in both the *Sonnets from the Portuguese* and *"Monna Innominata."* First, in providing a "veil," it permits both poets to articulate female desire without sacrificing the appearance of modesty necessary to preserve their artistic reputations. As well, the translation motif reflects the limitations in communication between lovers that both poets recognized as inevitable. Yopie Prins has noted that "ancient Greek" became a "special language of desire" for the Brownings in their love letters, providing "the potential for mediating between two selves" while also implying that each self was ultimately "untranslatable to the other."[46] One might say that, for Rossetti, Italian similarly functioned as the language of desire, a language she used in writing love lyrics to Cayley.[47] And like the Brownings, Rossetti clearly recognized the essentially untranslatable aspects of even the most intimate love, as the lady's comments on hermeneutical indeterminacies in Sonnet 4 of *"Monna Innominata"* make clear: "I love and guessed at you, you construed me / And loved me for what might or might not be." Finally and most importantly, the translation trope employed by Barrett Browning and Rossetti implies that for a woman to write about love in the context of an overwhelmingly masculine amatory discourse entails a continuous process of translation. In "Roundtable on Translation," Jacques Derrida writes that any marriage contract involves a double act of translation: "a promise, a marriage, a sacred alliance—can only take place, I would say, in translation, that is, only if it is simultaneously uttered both in my tongue and the other's."[48] But such a "double act of translation" is likely to be experienced most acutely by those who have traditionally been assigned, not the role of the (masculine) speaking subject, which Derrida assumes here, but the role of the "other" whose "tongue" Derrida does not even explicitly mention. In the context of countless sonnet sequences in which the lady remains the silent "other," a woman poet writing of love is particularly apt to feel that she is speaking in a foreign tongue—that in effect her text requires continuous translation.

Another notable parallel between the *Sonnets from the Portuguese* and *"Monna*

Innominata" springs from the breaking of this centuries-old convention of the sonnet lady's silence. Both sequences not only transform the silent muse into a speaking subject; they also play upon the paradoxes her conventional silence inevitably entails. "And wilt thou have me fashion into speech / The love I bear thee. . . ?" Barrett Browning asks in Sonnet 13, only to answer, "Nay, let the silence of my womanhood / Commend my woman-love to thy belief." Yet all the while she is not only speaking, as Leighton observes, but also indicating reasons for her silence "that reveal not the impotence, but the very force of her words."[49] With similar, though more strategically placed paradox, Rossetti closes her eloquent articulation of "woman-love" with the question, "Youth gone and beauty gone, what doth remain?" and answers, "A silent heart whose silence loves and longs; / The silence of a heart which sang its songs . . . / Silence of love that cannot sing again." But, of course, the "songs" of the sequence she has written do remain even as she bids farewell in this palinode to the earthly love that first inspired them, a paradox powerfully conveyed by her allusion to Dante's sister-in-law Piccarda who "literally vanishes into song" in the *Paradiso*.[50] Such paradoxes need to be kept in mind in assessing the apparent conventionality with which the speakers in both the *Sonnets from the Portuguese* and *"Monna Innominata"* accept the role of "help-meet" to their male counterparts.[51]

In the realm of the visual as opposed to the auditory, both women poets also use similar strategies to subvert the dynamics of the dominant male gaze. For instance, both sequences represent the thoughts and feelings of an aging female speaker in place of a man's thoughts and feelings about an idealized and objectified woman. Rossetti's final sonnet, speaking of beauty "gone if ever there / Dwelt beauty in so poor a face as this," is the first and only reference to the speaker's appearance in the entire sequence, and para-doxically it speaks of it only when it is absent. Both poets likewise avoid an inventory of the beloved's appearance—thereby wisely negotiating what Leighton describes as "the politics of subject and object" in love poetry written from a woman's perspective.[52] More intriguingly, both choose not to include the conventional sonnet describing the first meeting (even though this must have been an intensely dramatic moment in Barrett Browning's case)—perhaps because typically such a sonnet focuses on the impact of the woman's beauty on the poet. Similarly, both poets emphasize that they did not foresee the coming of love, Rossetti in Sonnet 2 and Barrett Browning in Sonnet 20.

Rossetti's Sonnet 2 merits special attention because it ironically deconstructs the conventional representation of the first meeting so artfully in describing a "day of days" as "traceless as a thaw of bygone snow." As the unexpected use of the verb "thaw" as a substantive suggests, this day fades before it is recognized as an entity, preparing for the sonnet's concluding focus on the final anonymity of an impersonally phrased exclamation—"Did one but know!"—which underlines the instabilities of memory and perception the sequence explores. Granted, the lady tells her lover that she *wishes* she could remember the "first moment of your meeting me." But her very terms of speech further emphasize the epistemological and linguistic difficulties she is grappling with, given that the reversal of subject and object (not my meeting you, but "your meeting me") implies a conventional order in which the dramatic moment of meeting is represented from a male perspective that is unavailable to her.

Here and in Sonnet 4, where the lady speaks of her lover's love waxing more strong "one moment," Rossetti may possibly have had her inconstant brother's sonnet sequence in mind. The prefatory poem of *The House of Life* defines the sonnet as "a moment's monument,— / Memorial from the Soul's eternity / To one dead deathless hour." In *"Monna Innominata"* Rossetti subtly critiques such an obsession with earthly moments, focusing instead on the lady's and her lover's difficult progress towards God's eternity.

"Monna Innominata" most strikingly differs from *The House of Life* and resembles the *Sonnets from the Portuguese,* however, in rejecting the traditional inequality between the Petrarchan lover and a lady who is simultaneously worshipped and silenced—an inequality reinscribed in her brother's sequence. In the place of this inequality, Christina Rossetti and Barrett Browning develop a discourse of reciprocal love, using a range of strategies too complex to be addressed in detail here. These include the representation of debate or exchange with the beloved, often involving a very precise use of logic; striking gender reversals in imagery; rhetorical doublings linking speaker and beloved (especially pronounced in Rossetti's sequence, as in the opening of Sonnet 5—"My heart's heart, and you who are to me / More than myself myself"); and an emphasis on their shared identity as poets, as in Sonnet 19 of Barrett Browning's sequence and Sonnet 4 of Rossetti's.[53] What Agajanian observes of the *Sonnets from the Portuguese*—"the English notion of reciprocal love intimated by Sidney . . . becomes an actuality in this sequence"[54]—is equally true of *"Monna Innominata,"* despite Rossetti's more consistent adherence to the Italian tradition. Likewise, Betty S. Flowers's comment concerning *"Monna Innominata"* applies equally well to the *Sonnets from the Portuguese*: "although

the sonnets are love sonnets, the persuasion is not directed toward seduction but towards understanding. In effect, the Lady says not, 'Look at me and love me,' but 'Listen to me and agree with me.'"[55]

The force and resonance of the lady's words in each sequence are intensified by the way in which both poets engage from the start with the European literary tradition. Rossetti, as we have seen, uses her preface to initiate her engagement with Dante, Petrarch, a "school of less conspicuous poets" in the early Italian Renaissance, and Elizabeth Barrett Browning; while Barrett Browning uses the range of allusions in her opening two sonnets to develop a similar intertextual resonance. "Greek pastoral, the rebirth of Adonis, Achilles' injured love and pride, Satan's banishment from heaven, Shakespeare's celebration of human love—these are the contexts in which *Sonnets from the Portuguese* first establishes itself," Mermin observes; while Agajanian notes, along with the allusions to Theocritus's *Idylls*, Homer's *Iliad*, Milton's *Paradise Lost*, and Shakespeare's sonnets, an echo of Spenser's *Amoretti* in the second sonnet as well.[56]

The invocations of heroic feminine figures of the classical and Biblical past reflect one especially notable feature of the allusions in both sequences, in part because they also point to a key difference between the two poets I have already mentioned. Whereas Barrett Browning draws freely and eclectically on the classical tradition, mixing references to Theocritus, Homer, and Sophocles with echoes of the Bible, and especially the sensuous Song of Solomon, Rossetti scrupulously restricts her principal allusions to the Christian tradition. Their uses of Electra and Esther respectively can serve to illustrate both their parallel gynocentric revisionism and their differing aesthetic and moral creeds. In the justly praised fifth sonnet of her sequence, Barrett Browning adds to the epic and tragic dimensions of her speaker by comparing the magnitude of her grief to Electra's: "I lift my heavy heart up solemnly / As once Electra her sepulchral urn." Similarly, in the climactic Sonnet 8 of "*Monna Innominata*," Rossetti turns to a heroic woman from the past to reveal the magnitude of her lady's love. But she chooses not a classical tragic heroine like Electra, but the Christian figure of Esther, who used her beauty to save her people: "'I, if I perish, perish'—Esther spake: / And bride of death or life she made her fair."

The point of this astonishing description of an Esther who is "[h]armless as doves and subtle as a snake" in the wiles of her beauty becomes apparent only in the sonnet's concluding lines, where the lady expresses her desire to be as heroic and successful in her life and love as Esther:

> If I might take my life so in my hand,
> And for my love to Love put up my prayer,
> And for love's sake by Love be granted it!

But, of course, the lady cannot be so successful as Esther. In the following sonnet, marking the *volta* of her sequence, Rossetti turns away from such visible heroic action to a focus on inward spiritual sacrifice. Yet the sonnet on Esther remains the most vivid in the series, a testimony to a Christian woman's epic stature. Significantly too, the representation of Esther poses a striking contrast to Dante Gabriel Rossetti's representation of Lady Lilith in *The House of Life*, a woman who is demonic rather than heroic in the use of her beauty. Both poets emphasize the beautiful hair of the women they describe and the "snare" created by their beauty. But Dante Gabriel's concluding image of a hapless youth trapped by "one strangling golden hair" of Lilith the self-involved "witch" is very different from his sister's description of the selfless Esther trapping the powerful King Ahasuerus with "one mesh of silken hair."[57]

The richness of the biblical, classical, and literary allusions in *"Monna Innominata"* and the *Sonnets from the Portuguese* makes it all the more surprising that they were approached so uniformly as merely personal utterances, hidden behind the "blinds" of their titles and, in Rossetti's case, of her preface. The predominance of such approaches manifests the inveterate nature of the gendered paradigms that both poets sought to deconstruct. Hall Caine said of the *Sonnets from the Portuguese* in 1882, a year after *"Monna Innominata"* appeared, that it is "essentially woman's love poetry" in its "absolute saturation by the one idea which bears out Byron's familiar dictum that 'Love is in man's whole life a thing apart, / 'Tis woman's whole existence.'"[58] In our time, many might see Caine, and not the female writers he describes, as the one who is absolutely saturated "by one idea" about women's nature and existence. Such a ruling assumption imposes a homogenizing sameness on women's love poetry, obscuring the ideological and aesthetic differences between works like the *Sonnets from the Portuguese* and *"Monna Innominata."* As these two sequences indicate, the ideological contexts and the aesthetic traditions shaping women's writing are as complex and diverse as they are in the case of male writers like Barrett Browning's husband or Rossetti's poet-brother, Dante Gabriel. Moreover, in many instances, intertextual influences cross gender lines, as the similarities between the *Sonnets from the Portuguese* and *The House of Life* reveal.

The spiritual trajectory in *Sonnets from the Portuguese,* tracing Barrett

Browning's turn away from the religious and otherworldly vision of her earlier works to an engagement with the earth and its realities, stands as a striking embodiment of the increasingly secular vision of the mid-Victorian age—the vision that Rossetti encountered, in a later phase of development, in her own brother Gabriel. The opposing trajectory of *"Monna Innominata"* provides one of the strongest contemporary critiques of this increasing secularism. But at many points the two sequences meet in their shared use of images, in their shared discourse of mutual love, and, paradoxically, in the roots of their opposing visions of human and divine love. "Belovèd, thou has brought me many flowers," Barrett Browning concludes, writing an envoy in which she offers in return only the "bitter weeds," the "eglantine" and "ivy" of the thoughts that have unfolded in her love sonnets. "[T]ake them, as I used to do / Thy flowers," she tells her lover: "Instruct thine eyes to keep their colours true, / And tell thy soul their roots are left in mine." Rossetti, for her part, forcibly repudiates such flowers in her concluding sonnet: "I will not seek for blossoms anywhere." Writing a palinode in the tradition of the Renaissance sonneteers like Sir Philip Sidney ("Leave me, O Love! which reachest but to dust"), she prepares for the completion of her "Sonnet of Sonnets" by her "Double Sonnet of Sonnets," *Later Life*—a text that remains unjustly neglected, as Linda E. Marshall points out.[59] Yet despite their dramatically different conclusions, and despite the dramatically different lives of their authors, one might say that the "roots" of *"Monna Innominata"* and of the *Sonnets from the Portuguese* are often intertwined.

NOTES

1. Harrison, *CR* and William Whitla, "Questioning the Convention: Christina Rossetti's Sonnet Sequence *"Monna Innominata"* (in Kent, pp. 82-131). Joan Rees provides an extended comparison of *"Monna Innominata"* and *Sonnets from the Portuguese* in *The Poetry of Dante Gabriel Rossetti: Modes of Self-Expression* (Cambridge: Cambridge University Press, 1981), pp. 146-54. But her study predates recent rereadings of *Sonnets from the Portuguese* and takes a very different view of the connections between Christina Rossetti's sequence and Barrett Browning's than this essay does.

2. Betty S. Flowers notes this chronological conjunction in "'Had Such a Lady Spoken for Herself': Christina Rossetti's *'Monna Innominata,'*" in *Rossetti to Sexton: Six Women Poets at Texas,* ed. Dave Oliphant (Austin: Harry Ransom Humanities Research Center, University of Texas at Austin, 1992), p. 17.

3. Dante Alighieri, *The Divine Comedy*, ed. Paolo Milano, trans. Laurence Binyon, *The Portable Dante* (New York: Viking, 1975); Dante Gabriel Rossetti, *The House of Life*, in *The Pre-Raphaelites and Their Circle*, ed. Cecil B. Lang, 2d ed. (Chicago

and London: University of Chicago Press, 1975), pp. 79-129; and Elizabeth Barrett Browning, *Sonnets from the Portuguese* in *The Complete Works of Elizabeth Barrett Browning*, ed. Charlotte Porter and Helen A. Clarke, 6 vols. (1900; rpt. New York: AMS, 1973). Subsequent references to these works will be noted parenthetically in the text.

4. For summaries and critiques of biographical readings of the *Sonnets from the Portuguese*, see Angela Leighton, *Elizabeth Barrett Browning* (Brighton: Harvester, 1986), pp. 97-98; and Glennis Stephenson, *Elizabeth Barrett Browning and the Poetry of Love* (Ann Arbor: UMI Press, 1989), pp. 69-72. Robert Browning referred to the "mask" disguising the personal nature of the *Sonnets from the Portuguese* (see note 29, below); while William Michael Rossetti similarly identified the preface to "*Monna Innominata*" as a "blind" for an "intensely personal" utterance, "interposed to draw off attention from the writer in her proper person" (*PW*, p. 462). Harrison and Whitla both condemn what Harrison calls the "usual mistake" of reading Rossetti's sequence "biographically" (*CR*, p. 174). As Whitla observes, William Rossetti's identification of the preface as a "blind" transforms it into a "pretext" rather than a "pre-text," creating a "'blind' alley" that shuts down "the free play" Rossetti's intertextuality invites (in Kent, p. 92). Despite much over-determined sleuthing by critics and biographers, readers can still do little more than speculate about the "personal" story that lies behind "*Monna Innominata*." Was it Rossetti's relationship with the shy scholar Charles Bagot Cayley who proposed to her in 1866, only to be rejected? Was it her earlier uncertain courtship with James Collinson, the religiously vacillating and shy member of the Pre-Raphaelite Brotherhood (Marsh, *CR*, p. 93)? Or was it a more illicit and passionate desire of the sort that Lona Mosk Packer pieced together in her discredited hypothesis that Rossetti was in love with the married painter William Bell Scott (Whitla, in Kent, p. 84)? Jan Marsh, who has explored the "enigmatic" nature of Rossetti's emotional life most sensitively and fully, concludes that, while "*Monna Innominata*" "seems to accord" with Rossetti's relationship with Cayley, "the sonnets are infinitely more than that. They are the culmination of a literary tradition tied not to affection for a particular man, but articulating love in all its aspects—romantic, wistful, steadfast, self-denying, painful, heroic, serene—as it was alive in her heart and imagination" (Marsh, *CR*, pp. 474-75).

5. Rees criticizes biographical interpretations of "*Monna Innominata*," yet sees the *Sonnets from the Portuguese* as a text in which its author too naively takes to heart Sir Philip Sidney's injunction, "look in thy heart and write" (p. 146). Harrison argues that, "[u]nlike Rossetti's sequence, Browning's surrenders entirely to tradition," content with "the baggage of conventional Petrarchan desires, expectations, and fulfillment" (*CR*, pp. 156-57). Yet several critics writing on Barrett Browning have demonstrated how she altered or subverted the tradition. See, in particular, Shaakeh Agajanian, "*Sonnets from the Portuguese*" *and the Love Sonnet Tradition* (New York: Philosophical Library, 1985); Leighton's groundbreaking rereading in *Elizabeth Barrett Browning*, pp. 91-113; Helen Cooper, *Elizabeth Barrett Browning: Woman and Artist*

(Chapel Hill: University of North Carolina Press, 1988), pp. 99-110; Dorothy Mermin's *Elizabeth Barrett Browning: The Origins of a New Poetry* (Chicago and London: University of Chicago Press, 1989), pp. 128-46; and Glennis Stephenson, *Elizabeth Barrett Browning and the Poetry of Love*, pp. 69-89. Agajanian offers the most detailed reading of the ways in which Barrett Browning modifies or subverts sonnet conventions, while Harrison and Whitla provide the fullest treatment of Rossetti's revisions of the tradition.

6. Jan Marsh discusses the circumstances surrounding the genesis of "They Desire a Better Country" in *CR*, p. 373.

7. Mermin, *Elizabeth Barrett Browning*, p. 140. Rees also notes some of the connections between the *Sonnets from the Portuguese* and *The House of Life* in *The Poetry of Dante Gabriel Rossetti*.

8. Mary Arseneau, "Pilgrimage and Postponement: Christina Rossetti's *The Prince's Progress*," *VP* 32 (1994): 279-98.

9. Marjorie Stone, "Sisters in Art: Christina Rossetti and Elizabeth Barrett Browning," *VP* 32 (1994): 339-64. Rossetti had a high regard for Barrett Browning despite her religious and artistic differences with her; see "Sisters in Art," p. 344.

10. Whitla, in Kent, p. 88.

11. Harrison, *CR*, pp. 167, 159.

12. Whitla, in Kent, p. 103.

13. Barrett Browning's translations of Petrarch's *Rimes* and the opening section of *The Divine Comedy* are listed in *The Browning Collections: A Reconstruction with Other Memorabilia,* compiled by Philip Kelley and Betty A. Coley (Winfield, Kansas: Armstrong Browning Library of Baylor University, The Browning Institute, 1984); see entries 1245 to 1255, and entries D1210 to D1213. On the Dantean elements in "A Vision of Poets" and the Victorian reception of this poem—including Robert Browning's description of its catalogue of "king-poets" as "perfect, absolutely perfect . . . a line, a few words and the man there,—one twang of the bow and the arrowhead in white"—see Marjorie Stone, *Elizabeth Barrett Browning* (London: Macmillan, 1995), pp. 85-93.

14. I am indebted to Whitla's identification of these two passages (in Kent, p. 87), although he does not comment on the fact that they appear in different cantos.

15. "The fifth canto of Dante pleases me more and more," Keats wrote to George and Georgiana Keats in April of 1819; "it is that one in which he meets with Paulo and Francesca—I had passed many days in rather a low state of mind, and in the midst of them I dreamt of being in that region of Hell. The dream was one of the most delightful enjoyments I ever had in my life—I floated about the whirling atmosphere as it is described with a beautiful figure to whose lips mine were joined at *for as* it seem'd for an age. . . ." This dream led to Keats' sonnet, "On a Dream," with the closing lines, "Pale were the sweet lips I saw / Pale were the lips I kiss'd and fair the form / I floated with about that melancholy storm—" (*The Poetical Works and Other*

Writings of John Keats, ed. H. Buxton Forman, 8 vols. [1939; rpt. New York: Phaeton Press, 1970], 7:271-72). Dante Gabriel Rossetti began a design of Paolo and Francesca in 1849, and in 1854-56 "produced a triptych" showing "the lovers' kiss, and their souls in Hell, and in the centre Dante or some other figure"; he returned to the subject in the 1862-68 period, according to William, and produced an "exceptionally successful" watercolour" (*Dante Gabriel Rossetti: His Family Letters*, ed. William Michael Rossetti, 2 vols. [London: Ellis and Elvey, 1895], 1:187-88; 239-40).

16. Whitla notes that the title comes from "one of the names for 'Lady' (when used with a proper name) in the *Vita Nuova* (in Kent, pp. 101-2). The passage he cites, referring to Monna Vanna, is apt to have been particularly significant to Rossetti given her brother Gabriel's painting of that figure. Another of Dante Gabriel Rossetti's paintings was entitled "Monna Pomona" (*Dante Gabriel Rossetti: His Family Letters*, 2:239, 242). Betty S. Flowers identifies *monna* as a "shortened form of '*madonna*'" and suggests that it indicates Rossetti's reference to the "archetypal Lady who leads, through love, to Heaven"(p. 16).

17. Marsh, *CR*, p. 472.

18. In Kent, p. 102.

19. *FL*, p. 98.

20. Harrison, *CR*, p. 156, and Rees, p. 154.

21. Elizabeth Barrett Browning, *Aurora Leigh*, ed. Margaret Reynolds (Athens, Ohio: Ohio University Press, 1992; New York: Norton, 1996), bk. 1, lines 6-8.

22. Qtd. by Whitla (in Kent, pp. 90-91).

23. Rosenblum, p. 204.

24. *FL*, p. 98. William Rossetti further confuses the interpretation of this passage because he mistakenly reads "[t]he Lady in question" in the last sentence as a reference to the speaker in *"Monna Innominata,"* and not, as the context makes clear, to the speaker in the *Sonnets from the Portuguese*, "the Lady of those sonnets." Thus he observes in his headnote, "What she says in her letter—that the speaker in her sonnets was not intended for an 'innominata at all'—is curious, and shows that her mind was conversant with very nice shades of distinction." He then goes on to insist that the speaker in *"Monna Innominata"* is "Christina herself, giving expression to her love for Charles Cayley" (*FL*, p. 97).

25. Linda Schofield, "Displaced and Absent Texts as Contexts for Christina Rossetti's 'Monna Innominata,'" *The Journal of Pre-Raphaelite Studies*, n.s., 6 (spring 1997): 39. Schofield provides an insightful analysis of the changes Rossetti made in the portions of "By Way of Remembrance" that she wove into *"Monna Innominata."*

26. Marsh, *CR*, p. 359.

27. Warner Barnes, *A Bibliography of Elizabeth Barrett Browning* (Austin: University of Texas Press, Armstrong Browning Library of Baylor University, 1967), pp. 37, 50.

28. David G. Riede, "Elizabeth Barrett: The Poet as Angel," *VP* 32 (1994): 121-39.

29. As Browning explained to Julia Wedgewood in 1864, the personal nature of the Portuguese *Sonnets* was initially disguised "by leaving out one sonnet which had plainly a connexion with the former works: but it was put in afterwards when people chose to pull down the mask" (qtd. in Mermin, p. 142). The importance of "Future and Past" as a pivotal sonnet was emphasized by Barrett Browning even when it was published separately, however, since in her 1850 *Poems* she positioned it, like a figure of Janus, at the close of Volume I, at the end of her series of sonnets—looking forward to Volume II, which concluded with the *Sonnets from the Portuguese*.

30. See my analysis of this critique in "Sisters in Art," pp. 345-49. "Catarina to Camoens" contains a similar play on the trope of past and future, in Catarina's lament to her absent lover, "You may cast away, Belovèd, / In your future all my past," as she imagines him attracted to some "fairer bosom-queen." The conclusion of "Catarina to Camoens," in which the dying heroine blesses her lover's future romantic relationships, seems to be echoed in Sonnet 12 of *Monna Innominata*," where the speaker insists that she will not "grudge" being displaced by another woman.

31. This was clearly a biblical text important to Rossetti's personal creed; see also the brief lyric, "'Now They Desire a Better Country,'" first published in 1885 (*CP*, 2:313-14).

32. "Despite its title, death is among the most common words to be found in *The House of Life*," Paul Jarvie and Robert Rosenberg point out in "'Willowwood,' Unity and *The House of Life*," *The Pre-Raphaelite Review* 1 (1977-78): 115. They reject William E. Fredeman's view that the sequence moves through disillusionment to a higher faith, seeing it instead as mapping a "general downward pattern of despair and helplessness," marked by solipsistic withdrawal and detailing "separation, not communion" (pp. 113, 116-17).

33. Agajanian, p. 76; Stephenson, pp. 73-89. Stephenson perceptively analyzes Barrett Browning's celebration of a sensuous love and her substitution of tactual images for the tropes of distance between lovers characteristic of many Renaissance sonnet sequences.

34. Harrison, *CR*, pp. 178-79.

35. Agajanian, p. 98.

36. Helen H. Wenger, "The Influence of the Bible in Christina Rossetti's '*Monna Innominata*'," *Christian Scholar's Review* 3 (1973): 21-22.

37. This characteristic is particularly pronounced in D. G. Rossetti's later poetry, where he shifts from "Allegory to Indeterminacy" (to use D. M. R. Bentley's words) or "Erases the Art-Catholic" (to use David G. Riede's words), or sterilizes "completely the religious potency" of his images, as Jerome J. McGann points out. See D. M. R. Bentley, "From Allegory to Indeterminacy: Dante Gabriel Rossetti's Positive Agnosticism," *Dalhousie Review* 70 (1990): 70-106; 146-48; David G. Riede, "Erasing the Art-Catholic: Rossetti's *Poems, 1870*," *Journal of Pre-Raphaelite Studies* 1 (1980-81): 50-70; and Jerome J. McGann, "Rossetti's Significant Details," *VP* 7 (1969): 233.

In "Pilgrimage and Postponement," Arseneau summarizes these interpretations and comes to a similar conclusion that "by the middle and later phases of his career, Dante Gabriel had ceased to locate his symbols within a Christian tradition in which each object could claim an authorized and preordained meaning" (pp. 293–94).

38. Agajanian, pp. 112, 101–2.

39. Agajanian, p. 99.

40. In Sonnet 32, the lover is represented in terms reminiscent of the Dantean "chief angel" who plays on the instrument of mortal poets' hearts in "A Vision of Poets" (*The Complete Poems of Elizabeth Barrett Browning*, 2:320). Like this angel, he has "master-hands" that obtain "perfect strains" from "instruments defaced."

41. How much Rossetti and Barrett Browning may have been indebted to earlier revisions of masculine sonnet conventions by Romantic women poets such as Mary Robinson (in her sequence, *Sappho and Phaon*) remains to be investigated. On Romantic women poets' innovative use of sonnet conventions, see Daniel Robinson's "Reviving the Sonnet: Women Romantic Poets and the Sonnet Claim," *European Romantic Review* 6 (1995): 98–127.

42. I am grateful to the English Poetry Collection of Wellesley College Library for permission to examine and cite the printer's copy for Barrett Browning's 1850 *Poems*.

43. Qtd. in Mermin, pp. 264–65.

44. Mermin, p. 141.

45. Agajanian (p. 17) speculates that the title was borrowed from John Adamson's 1810 translation of Camoens' love sonnets, entitled *Sonnets from the Portuguese*.

46. Yopie Prins, "Elizabeth Barrett, Robert Browning and the *Différance* of Translation," *VP* 29 (1991), p. 437.

47. Marsh, *CR*, p. 291.

48. Qtd. in Prins, p. 436.

49. Leighton, *Elizabeth Barrett Browning*, p. 111. Leighton offers a particularly perceptive reading of the paradoxes that inform Barrett Browning's representations of womanly silence in the *Sonnets from the Portuguese*.

50. Whitla in Kent, p. 108.

51. "God's will devotes" her lover's art to serve His ends, and "mine to wait on thine," Barrett Browning's speaker observes in Sonnet 17. Rossetti's speaker in Sonnet 5 describes "woman" as the "helpmeet made for man." I am indebted to Diane D'Amico's work-in-progress on "The Helpmeet" for revealing the subtleties of Rossetti's views concerning woman as "helpmeet."

52. Leighton, *Elizabeth Barrett Browning*, p. 104.

53. Harrison notes a similar parallel to the last of these in commenting on the "dialogue" between Sonnet 1 of *"Monna Innominata"* ("Ah me, but where are now the songs I sang / When life was sweet because you called them sweet?") and Sonnet 7 of the Portuguese *Sonnets*: ". . . this lute and song . . . loved yesterday, . . . are only

dear / Because thy name moves right in what they say" (*CR*, p. 175). But he does not find a discourse of reciprocal and equal love in Barrett Browning's sequence, noting that the "speaker repeatedly embraces her subordinate role" (*CR*, p. 156). While it is true that such gestures of subordination appear in the *Sonnets from the Portuguese*, Leighton, Agajanian, Cooper, and Stephenson have argued that, paradoxically, these gestures frequently permit the speaker to assert her identity as a woman and poet. Indeed, in "Strategic Self-Centering and the Female Narrator: Elizabeth Barrett Browning's *Sonnets from the Portuguese*," *Browning Institute Studies* 17 (1989): 75–91, Sarah Paul has argued that, "[f]ar from being a self-abnegating figure, the speaker of the [Portuguese] *Sonnets* is a profoundly self-centered one whose elaborate (false) modesty serves a number of strategic functions" (p. 77). Paul also demonstrates the speaker's "propensity for giving orders" (p. 86), a feature Harrison notes in *"Monna Innominata"* in observing that Rossetti's poet-lover "speaks characteristically in imperatives" (*CR*, p. 157).

54. Agajanian, p. 77.

55. Flowers, p. 18.

56. Mermin, p. 138; Agajanian, p. 72.

57. Harrison argues that Rossetti portrays Esther with a Keatsian sensuality, transforming her from "a prototype of Christ" into a "morally equivocal" "Lamia figure" (*CR*, p. 180). Although Rossetti's speaker ultimately rejects Esther as a model for her own inward struggle, I find the representation of Esther less equivocal than Harrison suggests. As Rosenblum notes, Rossetti emphasizes Esther's wisdom and altruism (Rosenblum, p. 208). The graphic sensuousness of the portrayal may be attributable in part to Rossetti's critique of her brother's portrait of "Lady Lilith," rather than to her desire to make Esther "equivocal." In short, Christina Rossetti's Esther may be less a "Lamia figure" than a heroic female counterpoint to the Lamia figures that pervade her brother's poetry. D. G. Rossetti portrays demonic female figures like Lady Lilith and Sister Helen, while Christina Rossetti, as *Goblin Market* suggests, portrays demonic male figures.

58. Qtd. in Agajanian, p. 9.

59. In "'Abstruse the Problems!': Unity and Division in Christina Rossetti's *Later Life: A Double Sonnet of Sonnets*, *VP* 32, nos. 3–4 (1994): 299–314, Linda E. Marshall observes that *Later Life* is a text "pointedly inviting comparison" with the single macrosonnet *"Monna Innominata"* and similarly experimenting with Petrarchan structures of octave and sestet. In this later sequence, Rossetti more fully develops "an explicitly devotional art" which speaks to "the mysteries of Love's rule" (pp. 299–300).

CHAPTER 4

Tasting the "Fruit Forbidden"

Gender, Intertextuality, and Christina Rossetti's Goblin Market

CATHERINE MAXWELL

> The golden apple, the golden apple, the hallowed fruit,
> Guard it well, guard it warily,
> Singing airily,
> Standing about the charmèd root.
>
> —Tennyson, "The Hesperides" (14-18)

I s there a separate tradition of women's poetic writing in the nineteenth century? If such a tradition exists, what is its relation, if any, to the male poetic tradition? Modern feminist criticism has responded in different ways and has devoted more attention to the first than to the second of these questions. Elaine Showalter and Ellen Moers were among the earliest critics to raise the possibility of a separate women's literary tradition, and subsequent critics such as Sandra M. Gilbert and Susan Gubar, Adrienne Rich, Margaret Homans, Angela Leighton, and Isobel Armstrong have given accounts or descriptions of how such a tradition might be constituted.[1] While these descriptions differ, all seem to endorse the idea of a female tradition as enabling: women writers derive a sense of their legitimacy as writers from their female precursors and inherit models that they can adopt or transform.

On the other hand the male tradition is implicitly or explicitly seen as disabling for women writers, the basic premise being that "although masculine language and poetic traditions are pervasive, . . . it is difficult for women poets either to insert themselves into this tradition, or to appropriate its material for their own use, since these prove extremely opaque to the light of female, let alone feminist definition."[2]

The propounding of male and female traditions has led to some interesting tensions. Gilbert and Gubar's idea of a women's tradition is reactive or, as Jan Montefiore points out, "oppositional, not independent."[3] In their account, women writers struggle with the repressive misogynist myths and images of "patriarchal poetry" in order to refigure positive positions for themselves. This struggle is not, however, straightforward in that its staging is interior, revealing the woman writer's divided consciousness: the good patriarchal daughter must be quelled by her rebellious alter ego—"the madwoman in the attic." Gilbert and Gubar pay lip service to the idea of an enabling female tradition. In contrast to Harold Bloom, who envisages an essentially male tradition emerging from a series of aggressive Oedipal encounters between poetic fathers and sons,[4] they suggest that the woman writer's relation to her literary foremothers is benign, even if her struggle with her poetic fathers is not. She "can begin such a struggle only by actively seeking a *female* precursor who, far from representing a threatening force to be denied or killed, proves by example that a revolt against patriarchal literary authority is possible."[5] They also note with approval how Moers and Showalter demonstrate that "by the nineteenth century there was a rich and clearly defined female literary subculture, a community in which women consciously read and related to each other's works."[6] However, in practice they seem comparatively uninterested in the process by which one woman might inherit her female precursors' figures of rebellion and they detail very few direct relationships of influence between women. For example, Sandra Gilbert's reading of Christina Rossetti's poetry precedes her discussion of Elizabeth Barrett Browning. The casual chronological inversion signals to the reader that the issue of Barrett Browning as precursor will not be part of this discussion.

The female tradition that Gilbert and Gubar see emerging in the eighteenth and consolidating in the nineteenth century is founded in its reaction to a male tradition. For all its negations and deprecations, the male tradition as described by them seems more productive of nineteenth-century women's writing than do the writings of earlier women. Yet this dependence is occluded because the woman writer is pictured as battling against her patriarchal self rather than the male writers themselves—a depiction that has the effect of erasing women's relationships with particular male writers. While men's texts are alluded to continually, they are rarely instanced as playing a major constructive role. The stress on female internal conflict predominates, often with the effect of emphasizing negative, sometimes masochistic tendencies in women's writing. Moreover, writing that lacks or moderates some overt figuration of female rage and rebellion is seen as conformist or repressive. Gilbert brings to her reading of Rossetti's *Goblin Market* critical and historical assumptions about the poet's religious beliefs and gender ideology that lead her to understand the poem as displaying the "aesthetics of renunciation."

A less ambiguous and more celebratory treatment of a women's tradition of poetic writing has emerged more recently in the work of Angela Leighton and Isobel Armstrong. Leighton's elegant and informative *Victorian Women Poets: Writing Against the Heart* (1992) was the first concerted attempt to assert "that women's poetry of the nineteenth century, much more than the novel, was written and read as part of a self-consciously female tradition."[7] Leighton explores significant and productive relationships between nineteenth-century women poets such as the one between Rossetti and Barrett Browning ignored by Gilbert. But her study, perhaps in its effort to be corrective, overplays the idea of a separate women's tradition without ever really explaining its relation to a male tradition. Both Felicia Hemans and Letitia Landon are important to Barrett Browning, but arguably Shelley, Tennyson, and Robert Browning (to name but a few male influences) are equally if not more so. Nonetheless, feminist criticism subsequent to Leighton's has tended to concentrate on an independent female poetic tradition. This is exemplified, as Herbert F. Tucker points out, by Isobel Armstrong's wide-ranging survey *Victorian Poetry: Poetry, Poetics, and Politics* (1993). In an otherwise generally approving review, he complains that "the separatist decision to give women a chapter to themselves purchases local coherence at the cost of dealing women out of the larger reckoning that the book as a whole conducts. . . . The extent to which men's and women's poetry constituted disparate traditions has been if anything overemphasized already."[8] Tucker comments that by denying "reference to masculine poetic tradition, neither Armstrong nor anybody else can get far with *Sonnets from the Portuguese* or *Aurora Leigh*." This is supported by Marjorie Stone in *Elizabeth Barrett Browning* (1995): "since Barrett Browning was not an underground writer in her age or a writer always marginalized by her own gender, it is also important to conceptualize her achievement in the context of a poetic tradition conventionally defined in terms of predominantly male writers."[9] Tucker's sense of "the reciprocal influence of male and female poets"[10] is corroborated by recent work on nineteenth-century male poets' adoptions of "feminized" or "androgynous" styles, plots, and personae. The terrain of "the feminine" proves not to be an exclusively female preserve, but an area shared and sometimes contested by men and women writers.[11]

Of course, more traditional or nonspecifically feminist criticism has no particular theoretical brief against charting the influence of men's texts on women (or vice versa), but in practice the persistent undervaluation of women's texts, which endured until quite recently, has meant that their writings have rarely attracted either serious scholarly source study or theoretical speculations about relations with precursors or followers. Consequently examination of women's texts in relation to the male tradition has been sporadic rather than sustained. Where examinations have taken place, they often fail to address the issue of gender directly. Yet might there not often be particular gendered implications for one poet's borrowings from a writer of the opposite sex? The reclamation of Rossetti's work by feminist scholars such as Rebecca Crump prepared the ground for Antony H. Harrison's scholarly monograph *Christina Rossetti in Context* (1988), which situates the poet in relation to many of her male precursors. Yet although this thoughtful and useful study explores Rossetti's often revisionary engagement with the ideological values of those poets, it does not specifically reflect upon the part played by gender in shaping those revisions. Harrison's later article, "Christina Rossetti and the Romantics: Influence and Ideology," underlines the intensity of Rossetti's engagement — "her poetry most often stands as a powerful corrective to what she saw as the misguided amatory, spiritual and political values — the secular ideologies of those Romantics most important to her"[12] — again without speculating on whether she might "correct" specifically masculine values. Whereas feminist critics insist (perhaps overmuch) on the "difficulty" of women using the male tradition, critics working without a feminist framework or an analysis of gender may make the relationships between male and female writers too straightforward.

In the rest of this essay I propose to reconsider the issue of the woman writer's relation to the male tradition through a new reading of *Goblin Market*. This reading sees the poem as an allegory of the woman writer's negotiations with her male precursors' texts, but it also charts how individual male-authored writings are absorbed into the body of the poem. While it shows that Rossetti was aware of the difficulties a women might experience in relation to the work of poetic "fathers" and "brothers," it also demonstrates that she sees women's contact with men's writing as a potential source of strength that can be appropriated and adapted to female use.

At this point it seems pertinent to recall Jan Montefiore's reminder that "however necessary it may be to think in terms of 'the woman poet' or 'the woman writer,' she is entirely mythical; she doesn't exist in real life, any more than 'the archetypal male poet' does. What does exist is an immense variety of women poets, often divided by major differences of class, race and circumstances." She adds that "the necessary task for feminists is not creating a 'woman's tradition,' but asking in *which* tradition, feminine and otherwise, do particular writers belong?"[13] My ensuing reading is necessarily premised on the assumption that Rossetti is an educated middle-class mid-Victorian woman writer responding predominantly to British middle-class male precursors, most of whom are also writing in the nineteenth century. And yet I would also want to affirm Angela Leighton's proposition that Barrett Browning's *Aurora Leigh,* with its images of male currency, female fallenness, and sisterly redemption, is also an important influence on *Goblin Market.* Indeed *Goblin Market* is a crucial text for establishing the woman poet's sense of a female tradition—a sense which I think only truly comes into being in the middle of the nineteenth century. It comes into being because Rossetti experiences and acclaims Barrett Browning as a strong woman precursor. Barrett Browning, who while she acknowledged earlier female writers bemoaned her own lack of "grandmothers,"[14] is for Rossetti the first emulatable poet of persuasive female strength.[15] *Goblin Market* simultaneously recognizes "sisterly influence" in its figuration of an emergent women's tradition (Laura saved by Lizzie, Laura's story as told to her daughters) and demonstrates how this tradition is born out of its contact with the male tradition. Barrett Browning, whom we can read as "Lizzie" to Rossetti's "Laura," is an effective female precursor because, as a woman writer deeply influenced by male predecessors, she has herself learned to deal productively with the male tradition. Her own treatment of the problems of equal exchange between men and women in the mid-Victorian period recognizes the need for female autonomy, but also suggests that women need to explore and transform their relationships with men. Both Barrett Browning and Rossetti after her stress the necessity of women's learning to negotiate. However, while Barrett Browning ends *Aurora Leigh* by replacing relationships between women with a revisionary and reconciliatory heterosexual union, Rossetti proves more radical than her precursor, establishing a new female genealogy that nonetheless has its roots in male as well as female sources.

Sandra M. Gilbert's reading of *Goblin Market* offers a useful parallel to my proposed reading because it also sees the poem as allegory, though in this case it is an allegory of limitation. For Gilbert, the poem pictures the woman writer who wishes to experience the full fruits of her imagination, but Rossetti, too much bound by conventions, is unable to let herself or her female characters have this freedom. Rebellious Laura must suffer for her impetuosity when she gives in to her desire to eat the goblin fruit. However, prudent Lizzie intervenes to save her sister and restore her to the safe but conservative sphere of home. The focus in this reading is as much on the initially conflicting desires of the sisters as on the encounters with the goblin men. Nonetheless the reading as a whole is supported by a wealth of allusions to men's texts and patriarchal traditions. The biblical story of the Fall in Genesis, Milton's retelling of this story in *Paradise Lost,* the New Testament narrative of Christ's temptation, and the Eucharistic liturgy are identified as underlining the poem's moral message about temptation and redemption, its "bitter repressive wisdom." Gilbert also cites Keats's poem "La Belle Dame Sans Merci" as an analogy to (rather than an influence on) *Goblin Market,* but while she sees Keats's poem as daring advocacy—"Art . . . is ultimately worth any risk"— she roundly condemns Rossetti's poem for playing safe.

While Gilbert's allegory does not specify direct male sources for the poem, it does identify the goblins with male precursors:

> the goblin men . . . are of course integrally associated with masculinity's prerogatives of self-assertion, so that what Lizzie is telling Laura (and what Rossetti is telling herself) is that the risks and gratifications of art are not "good for maidens," a moral Laura must literally assimilate. . . . Young ladies like Laura . . . and Christina Rossetti should not loiter in the glen of imagination, which is the haunt of goblin men like Keats and Tennyson—or like Dante Gabriel Rossetti and his compatriots of the Pre-Raphaelite Brotherhood.[16]

Furthermore the allegory associates the goblin fruits with the literary imagination: "works of art—the fruits of the mind." Laura is seen as "metaphorically eating *words.*"[17] Gilbert never quite declares that these artful verbal fruits are poems. I would propose that not only are they poems but that they are men's poems. The fruit is directly identified as goblin produce ("goblin fruits").[18] Its flesh and juice, described as "Goblin pulp and goblin dew" (470), suggest that it partakes of the same bodily nature as the goblin men, that it is a synecdoche for the goblins' own fleshly, masculine, and potent juices. However, Rossetti evokes multiple echoes that connect the fruits not only with masculinity but with male-owned or male-identified texts.

The most fundamental references are biblical. The scriptures not only belong to a venerable patriarchal tradition, they are also regarded by Protestants as the Word of God, authored by his Holy Spirit. The forbidden fruit consumed by Eve in Genesis is the exclusive property of the paternal Creator God. This fruit, which confers knowledge of good and evil, has the capacity to make the partaker intellectually powerful like God who, recognizing the threat of usurpation, ejects the disobedient human couple from Eden before they gain immortality by eating from the Tree of Life (Gen. 4:22). Human beings are punished for eating God's fruit, but in the New Testament they are actively encouraged to redeem themselves and have "eternal life" by ingesting the Word of God as embodied in Christ. Christ's redeeming blood, symbolized by wine, revives Old Testament fruit imagery, as does his claim to be "the true vine" (John 15:1). Fruit and the male body are also connected in the Old Testament Song of Solomon. Most modern readers would read the Song simply as an erotic poem but, in the interpretation traditionally approved by ecclesiastic authority, the Song is a spiritual allegory of Christ's relationship to his Bride, the Church, conveyed through a series of sensual love lyrics.[19] At the beginning of the Song, the female speaker identifies her lover with apple trees and their fruit—fruit that will satiate her longing for him. "As the apple tree among the trees of the wood, so is my beloved among the sons. I sat down under his shadow with great delight, and his fruit was sweet to my taste. He brought me to the banqueting house, and his banner over me was love. Stay me with flagons, comfort me with apples: for I am sick of love" (Song 2:3-5). These biblical texts form a web of associations which connect fruit with male authority and knowledge as well as with the male body and its potency.

But Rossetti is also trading on the associations formed by the male poetic tradition. Milton, often seen as the father of modern poetry, launches the figure of potent fruitfulness into English verse when he retells the story of the Fall in *Paradise Lost*. Milton's serpent enlarges on the Biblical serpent's tempting promise "ye shall be as gods" (Gen. 3:5) in a flood of eloquence, declaring that the tree's fruit has not harmed but rather empowered him. Impressed by the evidence that the fruit "Gave elocution to the mute," Eve succumbs to temptation and eats the "intellectual food."[20] Milton's emphasis on the superior powers of articulation bestowed by the fruit, powers exercised by Eve immediately after eating, strengthen the links between fruit and verbal artistry. Like Eve who returns home to try out her persuasive speech on Adam, fallen Laura returns to Lizzie, meeting her sister's reproachful warnings with a paean in praise of the banquet she has just consumed. Her language, notably more elaborate than anything previously voiced by the maidens, now directly imitates the goblin men's persuasive cries, but it is also infiltrated by Romantic poeticisms such as "pellucid," "odorous," "mead," and "velvet."[21] She continues her oral gratification by filling her mouth with verbal evocations of the pleasure-giving fruit that has stimulated both her physical appetite and her love of language.

Milton describes the Tree of Knowledge as infused with "sciential sap, derived / From nectar, drink of gods."[22] This inspiring, honey-sweet juice, the sap of Edenic forbidden fruit, seeps into the writings of his male followers, where it is imbibed by Rossetti. In Keats's "La Belle Dame Sans Merci," the faery's seduction of the knight-at-arms involves a bewitching song and enchanted foods—"roots of relish sweet, / And honey-wild, and manna dew."[23] Rossetti revises Keats's "faery's song" into the goblins' "iterated jingle / Of sugar-baited words" (233–34) and "tones as smooth as honey" (108), and glamorizes Keats's sweetmeats into an altogether more exotic collection of fruits, which seduces the reader as much as it does Laura. However, the glamour she imparts to them is partly derived from other Keatsian texts such as "The Eve of St. Agnes" (30.265–70) where luscious fruits are an aid to seduction.[24] Keats's more earthy "roots" (and thus some of the roots of Rossetti's poem) are preserved in Laura's ingenuous question about sources— "Who knows upon what soil they fed / Their hungry thirsty roots?" (44–45)—and Keats's knight, stricken as he is, nonetheless offers us and Rossetti an example of the powers of the creative imagination under enchantment.

Coleridge's visionary youth in "Kubla Khan" is also drunk with his inheritance from Milton: "For he on honey-dew hath fed, / And drunk the milk of Paradise,"[25] and Tennyson, too, experiences the enticement of the sap "liquid gold, honeysweet" which fills the closely guarded apples of "The Hesperides" ("The luscious fruitage clustereth mellowly, / Goldenkernelled, goldencored / Sunset ripened") and the sedative enchanted fruits of "The Lotos-Eaters."[26] Both these Tennyson poems are about the allure of poetic imagination. The first and earlier poem defends the place of the imagination, founded on its likeness to Milton's Eden, against all who try to rob it of its fruitfulness.[27] The second poem reminds us of "The Palace of Art" with its admonitions about the poet isolating himself from the "real" world, but the

actual recreation of Lotos-land is dreamily evocative enough for us to understand it as a temptation.

Rossetti, allured by the visions of her male predecessors, is an intruder in
the Hesperean garden of English poetry. Her goblin men and goblin fruits
are her way of indicating a tradition of male-authored poems that use fruit,
fruit-juice, and honey-dew as motifs for imaginative inspiration and poetic
influence, and her poem shows how women poets can claim their place in this
tradition by appropriating this "sciential sap" for themselves through theft.
In this, *Goblin Market* resembles the strategies of female authorship discussed
by Patricia Yaeger in her book *Honey-Mad Women,* which employs the image
of honey stealing and drinking to illustrate the woman writer's relationship
to the male tradition.

Yaeger cites passages from a poem by the American poet Mary Oliver in
which a "she-bear," who stands in for the female writer, steals honey to
illustrate "the seriously playful, emancipatory strategies that women writers
have invented to challenge the tradition." She comments: "In Oliver's 'Happiness' we meditate upon the female poet's good appetite; her possession of
language is equated with the possession of a delicious excess of meaning that
is forbidden, but therefore twice delicious. Once found it lightens the
speaker's clamorous burden of feeling." While Rossetti's forbidden fruits with
their "delicious excess" of sexual, economic, religious, and intertextual meanings offer an excellent analogy to Yaeger's allegory, Yaeger's treatment of
appropriation is much more idealized than Rossetti's:

> The scenes that Mary Oliver depicts in her poem are such scenes of theft:
> we may recall Derrida's insistence that the *"letter,* inscribed or pro-
> pounded speech, is always stolen. . . . It never belongs to its author or
> to its addressee." Oliver reproduces the female writer's pleasure in dis-
> covering this ownerlessness, in lightening the fictions that weigh her
> down, in stealing and incorporating the languages that, until she claimed
> them, did not belong to her.[28]

Although the letter may always be stolen, this does not mean that the female
writer sees it as "ownerless." Part of her difficulty in negotiating with a male
literary tradition is that poetic language, even though it may always be
without an ultimate author or owner, *seems* very much a male property,
although this can also increase her pleasure in stealing. Yaeger tends to
simplify the difficulties of theft, but she does usefully note that "male

language" can also be represented by women as a poison, as dangerous. She cites Monique Wittig's *Les Guérillères,*[29] but we might also think of those fruits "like honey to the throat / But poison in the blood" (554–55). Yaeger picks up this last reference in her own treatment of *Goblin Market,* but her discussion of the poem is surprisingly brief and marred by the fact that she confuses Lizzie with Laura. She uses the poem as a personal allegory of the dangers and pleasures experienced by the woman critic drawing upon male theory: "I would like to argue, as Laura implicitly does, that this gathering of male texts can also represent a feminist harvest."[30] While this is true, Yaeger misses the opportunity of seeing the whole poem as a commentary on women's dangerous yet necessary relation to the male literary tradition.

Rossetti's poem reveals that women cannot enter this tradition on the same footing as men, any more than they can compete with men on equal terms in the mid-Victorian marketplace. Yet it also suggests that female interaction with the male tradition, however complicated and risky, is inevitable. Although the goblins are presented as dangerous creatures to be outwitted and escaped, they also give this poem its motivating energy. In other words, the goblins and the need to conquer them are necessary, as the poem charts a typical path from innocence to experience. The goblin fruits are also the fruits of experience, but Rossetti shows women learning to control that experience in order to maintain their own fruitfulness. (One thinks of another of her poems, "An Apple Gathering," which warns against the risk of picking flowers too early and thus losing the chance of fruit.) Women poets need to develop different strategies to avoid being overpowered by male influence to the extent that they can no longer write poems of their own. Trying to buy the goblins' fruit, Laura compromises herself by giving away part of her female identity—her golden curl. When she subsequently dines on the goblins' fruit, she loses all taste for her home-produced food, and from this we might infer that an exclusive diet of male texts seems to starve the female literary imagination. But Lizzie, like a woman poet who realizes she cannot simply buy into the male tradition, is resistant to the blandishments of the goblins, refusing to swallow their sales pitch. Rossetti's depiction of goblin aggression writes in what is missing from Gilbert and Gubar's account, as the woman struggles with or resists her male precursors. Resistance means that Lizzie obtains the fruit-juice surreptitiously without paying for it; she steals rather than buys. Following her own intuition she knows that if she takes away the juice *on* rather than *in* her body, she can transform it into something of her own—"my juices" (468). Like many readers, the Victorian poet Alice Meynell was puzzled by the different effects of the fruit juice, writing that "we miss any perceptible reason why the goblin fruits should be deadly at one time and restorative at another."[31] But in a poem that is all about sources, context becomes all important. Given by the goblin men, the fruit juice is like a poison, but mediated by a loving sister, sucked from a woman's body, it becomes a restorative antidote.

When Laura tastes this female-mediated potion, the description of her reaction uses the language of poetic inspiration: "Writhing as one possessed she leaped and sung" (496). The antidote releases a flood of energy which makes her into a poet:

> Her locks streamed like the torch
> Borne by a racer at full speed,
> Or like the mane of horses in their flight,
> Or like an eagle when she stems the light
> Straight toward the sun
> Or like a caged thing freed,
> Or like a flying flag when armies run. (500–506)

Once Laura has returned to health, the poem concludes with a picture of the maidens grown to full womanhood. Although we are told that they are wives, no husbands or men are visible, and the children, who appear to be girls, seem like clones of their mothers. The poem ends with a celebration of female community and a new female tradition as it seems that an inspiring story of women's strength will be passed from mother to daughter down the generations.

The final lines of the poem apparently support the modern ideal of a separate female tradition, but the ambiguity about absent fathers is telling. Dorothy Mermin makes the interesting suggestion that it is through their contact with the goblins that the women become fertile, and readers curious about the children's paternity might well wonder if the restorative fruit-juice is more than antidote. Mermin implies that she sees the sisters' separate encounters with the goblins as symbolic impregnations,[32] but this doesn't seem quite accurate as Laura declines as a result of her initial transaction. I see both women becoming fruitful solely as a result of Lizzie's daring theft and transformation of the juice. Lizzie effectively steals the goblins' potency— "Goblin pulp and goblin dew" (470)—which, smeared on her body, becomes hers. When she lovingly administers it to her sister, the fantasy logic and the metaphorical logic of the poem prescribe a symbolic act of insemination. Once they have been in contact with the juice, both maidens will eventually become "wives," mature women capable of motherhood. They have transformed male potency and male poetry into something that will help them generate creations of their own. Male writers have often used the language of insemination, pregnancy, and childbirth to describe their acts of literary production. (The male poet describes himself as either giving birth to his own creations or begetting children on his muse. It seems that Rossetti may be playfully revising these figures in order to show how the sisters become authors in their own right.) Her specific reclamation (or "stealing back") of the figure of maternity means that Laura's and Lizzie's children symbolically represent their mothers' poems as well as the younger female poets who will be generated by a women's tradition. However, we cannot forget that these new poets and poems are also the children of male precursors, hostile goblin "brothers" who are unwittingly made into fathers.

The poem advocates stealing and appropriation as a positive strategy for the woman poet, and the image of daring or dangerous theft may itself be stolen from the male Romantics' Prometheanism and revised for feminine purposes.[33] (While the male tradition is dangerous in that it can overwhelm an inexperienced woman writer and cut her off from her own creativity, it can provide resources and a valuable energy for the woman writer who is more secure; in other words, a woman writer who understands her own position and differences in relation to the male tradition, who knows that she can calculate what she can take from it at the same time as she takes her distance. This writer is able to assess what can be taken and transformed to suit women's needs, turning her appropriations into new expressive forms for women.)

One pertinent question might be whether this process of revision, like that envisaged by Harold Bloom and Gilbert and Gubar, is necessarily aggressive. Bloom sees belated and precursor poets locked in male struggle, while Gilbert and Gubar see the divided woman poet struggling with herself rather than with male precursors. Certainly nineteenth-century women's poems do contain significant motifs of aggression in that they are alert to men's abuse of women through sexual coercion, violence, or exploitation, and some of these representations of abuse may also do duty for the female poet's perception of herself as vulnerable in the male literary marketplace. The retaliatory violence of women poets may be more covert—the "castrational" blinding of Romney in *Aurora Leigh* or Rossetti's mocking diminishment of her precursors as grotesque goblin men. However, the overt strategies of "strong" women's poems show women not so much fighting men as resisting them or transforming losses into gains. Lizzie outfaces the goblins and steals their potency while Marian in *Aurora Leigh* claims the baby engendered by her rape as compensation for herself. Augusta Webster's Castaway bravely plunges into a stringent analysis of self and society, while Amy Levy's dying Magdalen concludes her monologue with a declaration of emotional emancipation.[34] Angela Leighton has written of the Victorian woman poet's identification of herself with the "fallen" woman,[35] and it may be that where the fallen woman or the poet as narrator offers a reassessment or redemption of female fallenness, we are likely to be reading the poet's sense of her own engagement with a male tradition. Male Tradition

Finally we also have to ask whether women poets show aggression or resistance to female forbears and contemporaries. Both *Aurora Leigh* and *Goblin Market* are important texts in that they show a midcentury consciousness of the emergence of the strong woman poet and endorse the idea of sisterhood, of women enabling other women. However, as Marjorie Stone demonstrates, both Barrett Browning and Rossetti were also aware of strife and rivalry between sisters, and Rossetti's treatment of the less positive aspects of the sororal bond in poems like "Sister Maude," "Noble Sisters," and "The Lowest Room" can also be read as commentary on the more troubling aspects of her relation to her "older sister in art."[36] Even in *Goblin Market* Rossetti's representation of precursor and belated poet as sisters rather than mother and daughter may be an attempt "to close the gap" between poets, to make the earlier poet nearer and thus less anxiety-provoking. The seeming interchangeability of Laura and Lizzie, their much-stressed likeness, also effectively cancels the distance between them. Laura (Christina), even though she is represented as "weaker," still resembles Lizzie (Elizabeth), and can become essentially like her.[37]

In her poem "Wine of Cyprus," Barrett Browning remembers herself thirstily drinking in the male classical tradition which she images as "œnomel," a mixture of wine and honey, used as a beverage by the ancient Greeks.[38] Citing "Wine of Cyprus" as example, the *OED* explains that œnomel is also figuratively "applied to language or thought in which strength and sweetness are combined." We have already seen that the English poetic tradition uses the image of honeysweetness to figure poetic strength and influence but, as Barrett Browning undoubtedly knew, the image of honey or sweetness as influence derives from the classical tradition. In a letter discussing imitation, Petrarch (of whom, Jan Marsh asserts, Rossetti "had an intimate knowledge")[39] writes: "This is the substance of Seneca's counsel, and Horace's before him, that we should write as the bees make sweetness, not storing up the flowers but turning them into honey, thus making one thing of many various ones, but different and better."[40] And in a letter to Boccaccio he writes: "I quote the authors with credit, or I transform them honorably, as bees imitate by making a single honey from many various nectars."[41] When Laura/Rossetti sucks the antidote from Lizzie's body, she is taking strength from a female precursor who had had the rare advantage of a masculine classical education and therefore was not overawed by it, but the image may also carry the sense of ingesting or consuming the precursor, absorbing her into the body of one's own text where she is no longer a threat.

The term "consumption" has been widely used by critics in association with Rossetti's poem. Laura's bingeing and fasting resemble what we might now call an eating disorder and various feminist critics have written eloquently about the significance of eating disorders to the poem and the part that such disorders can play in the construction of young women's female identity.[42] On a different tack other critics, notably Elizabeth Helsinger, have explored "consumption" as a metaphor for transactions concerning exchange and purchase in the economic marketplace—a marketplace dominated by the entrepreneurial middle-class male. Helsinger has shown how the Victorian woman, when she leaves her domestic sphere and strives to be a consumer in an arena where she lacks bargaining power, always risks being consumed. Her anomalous position aligns or even conflates her with that other problematic female agent in the marketplace—the prostitute or "fallen woman"—whose sole economic power consists in selling her body, in making herself into an object of consumption.[43] But another way that "consumption" operates in the poem draws on both these metaphors and extends them. Implicit in my argument so far is the idea that the marketplace is not merely the economic sphere closed to most Victorian women but also the place where literary texts are circulated for consumption. Consumption here represents not just reading, but a process of intertextual purchase, investment, and employment. The potential writer as consumer buys up what attracts him, claiming the ownership and use of language, figures, and meaning. But the literary marketplace, like the economic marketplace, is one in which Victorian women are at a disadvantage, especially with regard to poetry, in that they appear to lack the credentials, the means and authority, for easy purchase. *Goblin Market* therefore illustrates the complex tactical process by which women might enter a male-dominated literary arena and negotiate with male texts in order to secure materials with which to enlarge their own sphere.

The poem, however, simultaneously insists on the physicality of consumption. Where imaginative influence is represented as "sciential sap," writers do not just buy up or into literary texts; they also consume or ingest them as the means of nourishing their own writing. Consumption can also be a way of subduing the precursor by devouring his or her poems, incorporating or internalizing them into the body of one's own text. This feeding on one's precursor, eating his or her words, also trades on the destructive connotations of the word "consumption," its allied meanings of "wasting," "doing away with," and "causing to vanish." Rossetti's "consumption" of Barrett Browning may be a way of neutralizing a threat from her major female precursor, but Barrett Browning, the woman who has consumed her poetic fathers without misadventure, is also the figure who enables Rossetti to ingest her male precursors productively.

So which male texts does Rossetti consume in *Goblin Market*? Although her appetite is mainly stimulated by nineteenth-century male writers, an important early source is Shakespeare and his fairy play *A Midsummer Night's Dream*. Various commentators have pointed to Rossetti's use of contemporary fairy material such as that found in *Traditions, Legends, Superstitions, and Sketches of Devonshire on the Borders of the Tamar and Tavy* (1838) and *A Peep at the Pixies* (1854) by her own cousin Anna Eliza Bray, and in the anthology *The Fairy Mythology* (1828, revised ed. 1850) by Thomas Keightley, a friend of the Rossetti family.[44] Keightley's book was much enjoyed by the Rossetti children, while Christina's original title for *Goblin Market*—"A Peep at the Goblins"—shows her familiarity with her cousin's collection of tales. However, it also needs to be acknowledged that a major source for much nineteenth-century fairy writing is Shakespeare's play, and B. Ifor Evans's early article on the sources of *Goblin Market* notes the importance of *A Midsummer Night's Dream* to Keightley, who excerpted the following lines spoken by Titania to her Elves: "Feed him with apricocks, and dewberries, / With purple grapes, green figs, and mulberries."[45]

Evans points out the likeness of these lines to those describing fruit in *Goblin Market*, explaining how they are reinforced by an illustration "of the 'little men' who are bearing the tempting fruit to Bottom"[46] However, if on the hint of this evident echo, we further examine the relation between poem and play, we cannot fail to notice the way in which Rossetti revises and improves on Shakespeare's portrayal of female friendship. His Helena and Hermia (another pairing of alliterative names) are initially bonded by a powerful symmetry. When Helena accuses Hermia of disloyalty to their friendship with its "sister-vows," she reminds her of their shared past:

> We, Hermia, like two artificial gods,
> Have with our needs created both one flower,
> Both on one sampler, sitting on one cushion,
> Both warbling of one song, both in one key,
> As if our hands, our sides, voices, and minds
> Had been incorporate. So we grew together,
> Like to a double cherry, seeming parted,
> But yet an union in partition,
> Two lovely berries moulded on one stem;
> So with two seeming bodies, but one heart. (3.2.203-12)

Shakespeare's language of sisterly symmetry can be reheard in *Goblin Market*'s vision of female unity:

> Golden head by golden head,
> Like two pigeons in one nest
> Folded in each other's wings,
> They lay down in their curtained bed:
> Like two blossoms on one stem,
> Like two flakes of new-fall'n snow,
> Like two wands of ivory
> Tipped with gold for awful kings. (184-91)

In Shakespeare's play the bond between women is emotional. Helena and Hermia are physically differentiated: the first is tall and fair, the second small and dark. Rossetti strengthens the idea of likeness and sisterhood by accentuating physical resemblance. Moreover, she replaces Shakespeare's image of the double cherry on one stem with her own image of "two blossoms on one stem" (188), because in her poem fruit imagery is connected with masculinity and potency.[47] Throughout *Goblin Market,* the maidens are predominantly described by means of floral imagery, an imagery which hints that they need protection against male threats such as deflowerment. It is only at the end of the poem, when Lizzie is braving the goblins' assault, that the fruit and flower imagery comes together and she is "Like a fruit-crowned orange-tree / White with blossoms honey-sweet" (415-16). The important juxtaposition of male- and female-identified imagery suggests that at this critical point in the poem, Lizzie has proved herself equal to resist the goblins without losing her female integrity.

In *A Midsummer Night's Dream,* Helena makes it clear that she thinks sisterhood has been betrayed because of male influence. She accuses Hermia of being corrupted by Demetrius and Lysander:

> And will you rent our ancient love asunder,
> To join with men in scorning your poor friend?
> It is not friendly, 'tis not maidenly:
> Our sex, as well as I, may chide you for it,
> Though I alone do feel the injury. (3.2.215-19)

We, the audience, know that the disruption is really due to the magic of Puck, also called "Hobgoblin," who has caused mayhem by mistakenly sprinkling an enchanting "love-juice" on the eyes of the wrong lovers. As his master Oberon tells him, in doing this, he has damaged "some true-love's sight" (2.1.40 and 3.2.89). In *Goblin Market,* male influence and goblins' influence combine to disrupt the harmony of this female household. As Laura begins to suffer the ill-effects of the fruit-juice, Rossetti turns again to Shakespeare's description of female unity with its images of women sewing and singing together to indicate change. While both maidens still sew together, only Lizzie warbles for "bright day's delight" (213), for Laura is now alienated from her home and sister.

Rossetti turns Puck's floral "love-juice" into an enchanting fruit-juice, but both these juices have a powerful effect on the senses. Both poem and play also include the notion of a restorative "antidote" which undoes the negative effects of the juice; however, Rossetti's narrative applies itself vigorously to the preservation of the women's relationship. Although in Shakespeare's play harmony is restored, men and marriage will still diminish the women's friendship. Rossetti, on the other hand, seems determined to keep the bond intact and primary: "For there is no friend like a sister" (562). There is no possibility that this ancient love will be rent asunder. Male influence, at first a threat to the women's unity, is artfully cannibalized into something that can only strengthen their productive relationship.

Male poets' treatment of sisterhood and the ways one woman might help another continued to attract Rossetti's revisionary gaze. Another important source for *Goblin Market* occurs in a poem of Robert Browning's, "The Flight of the Duchess," about a woman's rescue by another woman.[48] While Rossetti's major enthusiasm was for Barrett Browning's poetry, we know that

she admired Robert Browning's work, in later life citing "Cleon" and "Karsh-
ish" as among those poems she liked best.[49] Dante Gabriel, a passionate reader
of Browning from as early as 1847, was noted for his evangelistic recitations
of the poetry and had even met and communicated with the poet himself; it
seems more than likely that Rossetti would also have been familiar with some
of Browning's early work.[50]

The theme of "the lady imperilled by a dastardly male"[51] is recurrent in
Browning's work, often generating a corresponding theme of rescue. Browning's
own "rescue" of Elizabeth Barrett from her father's house gave an added personal
meaning to this theme that cannot have been lost on Victorian readers, Rossetti
among them, who were familiar with the story of the poets' romance. Usually
in Browning's poetry the woman's rescue is undertaken by a man, but "The
Flight of the Duchess" shows rescue by female agency. This poem, always
popular with readers of Browning, benefited from the revisionary comments of
Elizabeth Barrett. It was also one of her favorites—she refers to it more than
any other poem in the love letters, and it may have been used by Browning as
a courtship poem in persuading her to flee her father.[52]

Rossetti's own involvement as a lay-sister in a community dedicated to the
redemption of "fallen women" meant that she was already committed to one
particular kind of rescue of women by women. Browning's poem with its
central motif of one woman aiding another to escape male cruelty would have
reinforced her own sense of the need to demonstrate sisterhood to more
vulnerable women, but the apparent personal subtext of the poem, the fact
that the poem at one level can be read as figuring the projected rescue and
"redemptive healing" of the woman poet Barrett Browning, must also have
made an impression.[53] Rossetti's rewriting of this story with Lizzie (Elizabeth)
as the strong woman poet who then rescues her sister Laura shows her
adaptation of Browning's fable for her own purposes, as the rescued woman
poet becomes a rescuer in her own right.

In Browning's poem, the newly married Duchess is at first lively and
energetic, "active, stirring all fire," but her husband's contemptuous treatment of her ensures that she "grew silent and thin, / Paling and ever paling, /
As is the way with a hid chagrin" (174, 208-10). The Duke is annoyed by
his wife's ill-health, which he reads as a personal affront. He meets a grotesque old Gypsy woman while he is out hunting and sends her off to see
the Duchess in the hope that she will give her a salutary fright. The huntsman who narrates the story is commissioned to take the Gypsy to his
mistress and, curious about the interview between them, watches through

the lattice. Instead of witnessing the punitive shock prescribed by the Duke, he beholds the women bonded in mystic sympathy. Gazing up into the Gypsy's mesmerizing eyes and absorbed by her song, the Duchess is revitalized by her contact with the other woman, a contact which is imaged as a restorative draught or elixir:

> For it was life her eyes were drinking
> From the crone's wide pair above unwinking,
> —Life's pure fire received without shrinking,
> Into the heart and breast whose heaving
> Told you no single drop they were leaving,
> —Life, that filling her, past redundant
>   Into her very hair, back swerving
> Over each shoulder, loose and abundant,
>   As her head thrown back showed the white throat curving;
> And the very tresses shared in the pleasure
> Moving to the mystic measure,
> Bounding as the bosom bounded.
> I stopped short, more and more confounded,
> As her cheeks burned and eyes glistened,
> As she listened and she listened. (540-44)

The Duchess drinks in the other woman's gaze like an antidote. The huntsman gleans from the Gypsy's song that she had immediately recognized the Duchess as her own Gypsy kin. She vows to return her to her lost tribe who will support her as a member of their community. The Gypsy's promise of loyal kinship sets the pattern for Rossetti's later declaration that "there is no friend like a sister":

> Lo, hast thou kept thy path or swerved,
> We are beside thee in all thy ways,
> With our blame, with our praise,
> Our shame to feel, our pride to show,
> Glad, angry—but indifferent, no! (655-59)

The Duchess, restored to glowing health and accompanied by the Gypsy, escapes with the help of the male narrator and is never seen by her husband again. As Mrs. Sutherland Orr, an early commentator on Browning, pointed out, "the poetic truth of the Duchess's romance is incompatible with rational explanation, and independent of it."[54] Rossetti is also working to a fabular logic in which one woman can be magically restored and strengthened by contact with another. Echoes of the earlier text in *Goblin Market* seem persuasive. Laura finds the female-mediated "fiery antidote" (559) "wormwood to her tongue" (494), but it nonetheless "possesse[s]" her (496), manifesting its liberating energy in her writhing body and streaming locks, just as "Life's pure fire" fills the Duchess. After her recovery, Laura exhibits the abundant vitality of the Duchess's glistening eyes and luxuriant tresses:

> Her gleaming locks showed not one thread of grey,
> Her breath was sweet as May
> And light danced in her eyes. (540-42)

Browning provides Rossetti with a story that includes male abuse of a woman, her consequent suffering, and her recovery by the "consumption" of a female-mediated antidote. It also contains important motifs of female kinship, solidarity, and rescue, and finally the creation of a loving and redemptive community.

But while Browning's narrator is sympathetic, there is inevitably something voyeuristic about his gaze, especially as we realize his attraction to the Duchess. He also plays his own small part in aiding the rescue. Rossetti's revisions cut him out, focusing the reader's attention directly on the women, their relation and actions, and not on male surveillance, desire, or intervention. *Goblin Market,* originally titled "A Peep at the Goblins," privileges the female rather than the male gaze as the maidens learn about looking, its rewards and dangers. Rossetti's erasure of Browning's narrator has the symbolic effect of excising Browning himself, allowing her to recreate the story not as an oblique courtship poem addressed by a male to a female poet, but as an allegorical tale by a woman poet about an enabling poetic sister.[55] Rossetti also reserves grotesquerie for the goblins, preferring to stress not merely the sisters' likeness but also their fair purity of demeanor. That this purity can be completely restored even after Laura's fall reinforces Rossetti's belief in the power of sisterly relations and her positive faith in a "better" nature, which inheres even when a woman has gone "astray."

A final source text for *Goblin Market,* Dante Gabriel Rossetti's poem "Jenny," raises the issue of sisterhood appraised by Christina.[56] Dante Gabriel worked on several versions of "Jenny," and although the poem was not published until 1870, when it appeared in his collected *Poems,* it seems likely that Christina was responding to a version he completed toward the end of

1858.[57] Rossetti's poem resembles her brother's in several details, and one specific cryptic echo suggests her indebtedness. As Jan Marsh points out, "Jeanie" as remembered by Lizzie in *Goblin Market* may be pronounced "Jenny" to rhyme with "many" in line 149, evoking the fallen women in Dante Gabriel's poetic monologue.[58] Moreover, both poets figure pure and sullied female chastity by means of floral imagery and identify men's sexual exploitation of women with "beastliness"—Christina's depiction of the animalistic goblins corresponding to Dante Gabriel's image of predatory male sexuality: the "flagrant man-swine whets his tusk" (349). Both poets see how women are bought and consumed as sexual objects in the marketplace ("when Saturday night is market-night / Everywhere" [140-41], as Dante Gabriel puts it) and both show men identifying women's golden hair with money, making the female body into a form of currency. Laura pays the goblins with her golden curl, while the speaker of "Jenny" pays the sleeping prostitute by dropping his gold into her golden hair (340-42).

The poems, however, diverge fundamentally in their different attitudes toward the essential kinship or sisterhood of women. The speaker in "Jenny" (who of course does not necessarily represent Dante Gabriel's own views) is concerned by the sleeping prostitute's fate, but states the conservative wisdom that pure women risk contamination if they help sexual sinners. He sees the desirability of women's rescue by other women, but believes that the conventions of the day prevent pure women from even contemplating their fallen sisters' plight:

> If but a woman's heart might see
> Such erring heart unerringly
> For once! But that can never be. (250-52)

These lines are themselves a disguised echo of Byron's lines in *The Giaour* about women for whom "every woe a tear can claim / Except an erring sister's shame."[59] In reply to Byron and the speaker of "Jenny," Rossetti asserts the sacrificial imperatives of sisterhood. "Tender" Lizzie, able to view her sister's heart unerringly, fulfills the wistful desire of her brother's speaker.

This speaker is nonetheless disturbed when he compares the impure Jenny with his pure cousin Nell. For all their differences of caste, the sleeping Jenny recalls the innocence of Nell, and on closer examination it seems Nell shares Jenny's fondness for clothes and amusement. Graveled by the puzzle of this sisterhood, and trying to distinguish Jenny as other, the speaker declares:

Two sister vessels. Here is one.

It makes a goblin of the sun.

So pure,—so fall'n! How dare one think
Of the first common kindred link? (205–8)

If the "It" in "It makes a goblin of the sun" refers to Jenny, the speaker
suggests that the fallen woman disfigures or makes mock of the inherent grace
of her womanhood, and more generally perverts the relations between beauty
and truth.[60] In contrast, Christina Rossetti's poem movingly redeems the
fallen woman by insisting that it is men, not women, who are the goblins.
For her the fallen woman is "goblin-ridden" (484), the victim of goblin men.
Her response exposes the speaker of "Jenny"; for, in his thoughts as well as
in his actions as client, he goblinizes or makes a goblin of Jenny. *Goblin
Market,* on the other hand, insists unabashedly on the "common kindred link"
or likeness of women and their mutual responsibilities. Rossetti's insistence
on symmetry, on the maidens' essential likeness, not only reinforces the fact
that even fallen women are redeemable, but also reminds pure women that
they too are frail, and might in other circumstances have suffered the same
fate. Sisters share both a fallible human nature and a nature redeemed by
grace. Recognizing their own fallibility and the contingencies that can make
another fall, saints are the best sisters to sinners.

While interpretation of Rossetti's revisionary response to "Jenny" emphasizes the contemporary sociological message in *Goblin Market,* this reading
need not be, even in its own terms, exclusive. If depictions of female fallenness
encode the woman poet's sense of her relation to the male tradition, we can
read fallen Laura's rescue by Lizzie as a fable of poetic enablement, resistance,
and appropriation, which is partly engendered by Rossetti's own poetic resistance to "Jenny." When, early in *Goblin Market,* Lizzie admonishes Laura to
"remember Jeanie" (147), she reminds her sister of the woman who has fallen
due to male influence. But she also makes us recall "Jenny," the image of the
unredeemable fallen woman as constructed by a brother poet. Jeanie/Jenny at
first figures as a fatal precursor, setting up a pattern that Laura will be forced
to repeat, but Lizzie's brave intervention breaks the chain. "Mindful of Jeanie"
(364), she obtains what she wants from the goblins without succumbing to
their powers. It is Lizzie, not Jeanie, who becomes Laura's precursor, and
"remembering Jeanie" becomes a way of reminding oneself about the necessary dangers of negotiating with men's texts and men's images of women.
This kind of remembering leads to revision. Correcting the conservative views

of her brother's speaker, Rossetti appropriates and revises his language and imagery for her own devices.

Men's texts about sisterhood provide Rossetti with a sure point of entry into the male literary market. Her confident beliefs about the mediating work of supportive sisters mean that she can use these texts in a revised and "strengthened" form to mediate her own relationship with the male tradition. Barrett Browning, an enabling sister, is also her mediatrix who shows how it is possible to experience the fruits of a male poetic tradition without losing a sense of one's female difference. The exemplary strength of the poetic sister provides an antidote so that men's texts can be consumed without the fear that they may eat up one's own imaginative energies.

Goblin Market suggests that underlying and informing the language of Oedipal or sexual rivalry that we have used to describe relations of influence is a more primitive and instinctual vocabulary of feeding and forbidden fruit. While the poem itself literally and figuratively demonstrates how each new text consumes other texts, is ceaselessly chewing over and redistributing the language of other texts, it also intimates that male-authored writings require extra-careful digestion by a woman poet's intertext. The female poet's management of consumption suggests a scrupulous evaluation of what will best nourish her and how it can be made to satisfy her needs. That she can be nourished and satisfied, however, is clear, and while *Goblin Market* manifests the poet's feigned innocence about sources—as in the allusion to the "unknown orchard" (135)—it is possible to see Rossetti as banqueting, not on bitterness as Gilbert suggests,[61] but on the purloined spoils of her travels "in the realms of gold."

NOTES

1. Elaine Showalter, *A Literature of Their Own: British Women Novelists from Brontë to Lessing* (London: Virago, 1978); Ellen Moers, *Literary Women* (London: The Women's Press, 1978); Sandra M. Gilbert and Susan Gubar, *The Madwoman in the Attic: The Woman Writer and the Nineteenth-Century Literary Imagination* (New Haven and London: Yale University Press, 1979); Adrienne Rich, *On Lies, Secrets, and Silence* (London: Virago, 1980); Margaret Homans, *Women Writers and Poetic Identity* (Princeton, N.J.: Princeton University Press, 1980); Leighton, *Victorian Women Poets;* and Armstrong, *Victorian Poetry.*

2. Jan Montefiore, *Feminism and Poetry: Language, Experience, Identity in Women's Writing,* 2d ed. (London: Pandora, 1994), p. 57.

3. Montefiore, p. 58.

4. Harold Bloom, *The Anxiety of Influence: A Theory of Poetry* (London, Oxford, and New York: Oxford University Press, 1973).

5. Gilbert and Gubar, p. 49.

6. Gilbert and Gubar, p. xii.

7. Leighton, p. 1.

8. Herbert F. Tucker, review of *Victorian Poetry: Poetry, Poetics, and Politics,* by Isobel Armstrong, *VP* 33 (1995): 182.

9. Marjorie Stone, *Elizabeth Barrett Browning* (London: Macmillan, 1995), p. 48.

10. Tucker, p. 183.

11. See, for example, Dorothy Mermin's article, "'The Fruitful Feud of Hers and His': Sameness, Difference, and Gender in Victorian Poetry," *VP* 33 (1995): 149-68.

12. Antony H. Harrison, "Christina Rossetti and the Romantics: Influence and Ideology," in *Influence and Resistance in Nineteenth-Century English Poetry,* ed. G. Kim Blank and Margot K. Louis (London: Macmillan, 1993), p. 131.

13. Montefiore, p. 59.

14. Elizabeth Barrett Browning, *Letters of Elizabeth Barrett Browning,* ed. Frederic G. Kenyon, 2 vols. (London: Macmillan, 1898), 1:232.

15. This is a point also made by Marjorie Stone in her excellent article "Sisters in Art: Christina Rossetti and Elizabeth Barrett Browning," *VP* 32 (1994): 357.

16. Gilbert and Gubar, pp. 573, 574, 573.

17. Gilbert and Gubar, p. 569.

18. *CP,* 1:23, line 469. Subsequent citations of *Goblin Market* by line number will refer to this edition, pp. 11-26.

19. Mary Arseneau demonstrates Rossetti's familiarity with the Song of Solomon, its traditional interpretation, and the poet's use of it in her poetry, in "Pilgrimage and Postponement: Christina Rossetti's *The Prince's Progress,*" *VP* 32 (1994):. 280. *Goblin Market,* like the traditional reading of the Song, brings together spirituality and eroticism but in a more integral fashion, although again modern readers tend to see the poem's religious images as subordinate to its sexual connotation.

20. John Milton, *Paradise Lost,* ed. Alastair Fowler (London: Longman, 1971), 9.758 and 9.768.

21. *CP,* 180, 178, 179. "Odorous," "mead," and "velvet" as adjectives describing organic texture are all to be found in Keats's poem *Endymion,* in *The Poems of John Keats,* ed. Miriam Allott (Harlow and New York: Longman, 1970), 2.424, 514; 4.362; 1.484; 2.951; 1.874, 2.414. "Pellucid" is Shelleyan and Rossetti may have taken it from Shelley's fairy poem "Queen Mab"; *Shelley: Poetical Works,* ed. Thomas Hutchinson, rev. G. M. Matthews (Oxford and New York: Oxford University Press, 1970), 1:82.

22. *Paradise Lost* 9.835-37.

23. Keats, 25-26.

24. Keats, 30.265-70.

25. Samuel Taylor Coleridge, *Poems,* ed. John Beer (London and Melbourne: J. M. Dent, 1974), lines 53–54.

26. Alfred Tennyson, *The Poems of Tennyson,* ed. Christopher Ricks, 3 vols. (Harlow: Longman, 1989), 1:461–67, lines 37, 101–3; and 1:467–77. I cannot be sure that Rossetti knew "The Hesperides," which Tennyson did not reprint after its initial publication in 1832, but the poem's lyrical irregular metrics and the themes of forbidden fruit and potential theft provide tantalizing points of comparison with *Goblin Market.* For Rossetti's own poem "The Lotus-Eaters: Ulysses to Penelope," composed October 1847, see *CP,* 3:144–45.

27. In his prefatory note to the poem (*Poems* 1:461), Christopher Ricks writes: "The apples would be associated with Eden (Hesperean fruit is mentioned in *Paradise Lost*)."

28. Patricia Yaeger, *Honey-Mad Women: Emancipatory Strategies in Women's Writing* (New York: Columbia University Press, 1988), pp. 20, 21, 22.

29. Yaeger, p. 22.

30. Yaeger, p. 247.

31. Alice Meynell, *Prose and Poetry* (London: Jonathan Cape, 1947), p. 147.

32. Dorothy Mermin, "Heroic Sisterhood in *Goblin Market,*" *VP* 21 (1983): 113–14.

33. See Marjorie Stone, *Elizabeth Barrett Browning,* pp. 76–77.

34. Elizabeth Barrett Browning, *Aurora Leigh,* ed. Margaret Reynolds (Athens, Ohio: Ohio University Press, 1992; New York: Norton, 1996); Augusta Webster, "A Castaway," and Amy Levy, "Magdalen," in Angela Leighton and Margaret Reynolds, eds., *Victorian Women Poets: An Anthology* (Oxford: Blackwell, 1995), pp. 433–48 and 602–4.

35. Angela Leighton, "'Because Men Made the Laws': The Fallen Woman and the Woman Poet," in *New Feminist Discourses: Critical Essays on Theories and Texts,* ed. Isobel Armstrong (London and New York: Routledge, 1992), pp. 343–60.

36. Marjorie Stone, "Sisters in Art," p. 358.

37. Jan Marsh points out that Rossetti "wrote an extended entry on Petrarch for the *Universal Dictionary of Biography,* in which she referred to family documents showing herself to be descended from Laura" (*Christina Rossetti: Poems and Prose,* [London: J. M. Dent, 1994], p. xxiii). Marsh, *CR,* pp. 211–12, appears to date the composition of this entry to 1857. D. M. R. Bentley, in his essay "The Meretricious and the Meritorious in *Goblin Market*" (in Kent, p. 72, n. 34), sees Laura and Lizzie's names as gesturing towards secular and religious love as respectively embodied by Petrarch's Laura and St. Elizabeth of Hungary.

38. Elizabeth Barrett Browning, *The Poetical Works of Elizabeth Barrett Browning* (London: Smith, Elder, 1897), p. 280.

39. Marsh, *Christina Rossetti: Poems and Prose,* p. xxiii.

40. Francesco Petrarch, *Letters from Petrarch,* trans. Morris Bishop (Bloomington: Indiana University Press, 1966), p. 199.

41. Petrarch, p. 183.

42. See Paula Marantz Cohen, "Christina Rossetti's 'Goblin Market': A Paradigm for Nineteenth-Century Anorexia Nervosa," *University of Hartford Studies in Literature* 17, no. 1 (1985): 1–18; and Deborah Ann Thompson, "Anorexia as a Lived Trope: Christina Rossetti's 'Goblin Market,'" *Mosaic* 24, nos. 3–4 (1991): 89–106.

43. Elizabeth Helsinger, "Consumer Power and the Utopia of Desire: Christina Rossetti's 'Goblin Market,'" *English Literary History* 58 (1991): 903–33.

44. William Shakespeare, *A Midsummer Night's Dream,* in *The Riverside Shakespeare,* ed. G. Blakemore Evans et al. (Boston: Houghton Mifflin, 1974); Anna Eliza Bray, *Traditions, Legends, Superstitions, and Sketches of Devonshire on the Borders of Tamar and the Tavy* (London: John Murray, 1838), and *A Peep at the Pixies, or, Legends of the West,* with Illustrations by H. K. Browne (London, 1854); Thomas Keightley, *The Fairy Mythology,* 2 vols. (London, 1828) and *The Fairy Mythology, Illustrative of the Romance and Superstition of Various Countries,* enl. and rev. ed. (London, 1850). See also Marsh, *CR,* pp. 230–31 and her article "Christina Rossetti's Vocation: The Importance of Goblin Market," *VP* 32 (1994): 235–36. All subsequent references to *A Midsummer Night's Dream* will be noted parenthetically in the text.

45. B. Ifor Evans, "The Sources of Christina Rossetti's 'Goblin Market,'" *Modern Language Review* 28 (1993): 156–65; Keightley, 2:131; *Midsummer Night's Dream,* 3.1.166–67.

46. Evans, p. 157.

47. In her essay "Verses with a Good Deal about Sucking: Percy Bysshe Shelley and Christina Rossetti," in *Influence and Resistance in Nineteenth-Century English Poetry,* ed. G. Kim Blank and Margot K. Louis (London and Basingstoke: Macmillan, 1993), Barbara Charlesworth Gelpi has attributed Rossetti's "Like two blossoms on one stem" to a line in Shelley's "Fiordispina"—"like two flowers / Upon one stem" (lines 15–16), but admits (p. 164) that both passages have links with *A Midsummer Night's Dream.* Her essay is suggestive, but in view of the many links between Rossetti's poem and the play, I am inclined to think Rossetti was directly indebted to Shakespeare.

48. Robert Browning, "The Flight of the Duchess," in *Robert Browning: The Poems,* ed. John Pettigrew and Thomas J. Collins, 2 vols. (New Haven: Yale University Press; Harmondsworth: Penguin, 1981), 1:424–47. Subsequent references to this poem will be cited parenthetically in the text by line number.

49. Marsh, *CR,* p. 175. *Childe Roland,* Browning's anti-quest poem, was also to make a significant impact on Rossetti's own poetic depiction of a failed quest, *The Prince's Progress* (published 1866), which draws on the earlier poem's description of a barren landscape.

50. For D. G. Rossetti's early reading of Browning, see Oswald Doughty, *A Victorian Romantic: Dante Gabriel Rossetti* (London: Frederick Muller, 1949), p. 55, and also the introduction to *The Works of Dante Gabriel Rossetti* (London: Ellis, 1911), p. xv, where W. M. Rossetti mentions his brother's recitations.

51. R. Browning, 1:1097.

52. William Clyde DeVane attests the poem's popularity in his *A Browning Handbook,* 2d ed. (New York: Appleton-Century-Crofts, 1955), p. 176. On the different versions of the poem, see the editorial comments in *Robert Browning: The Poems* 1:1096-97. Browning published the first nine sections of the poem in *Hood's Magazine* III, April 1845, 313-18, and the longer revised version in *Dramatic Romances and Lyrics,* 6 November 1845 (*Bells and Pomegranates* no. VII). W. M. Rossetti (see above) mentions his brother reciting from *Bells and Pomegranates,* and in a letter to William of 18 September 1849 D. G. Rossetti mentions his acquisition of "the original editions of the lyrical numbers of *Bells and Pomegranates,* which you remember contain variations" (*Letters of Dante Gabriel Rossetti,* ed. Oswald Doughty and John Robert Wahl, 4 vols. [Oxford: Clarendon, 1965-67], 1:56).

53. DeVane, drawing on the work of earlier scholars, sees sections 10-16 of the poem as "written with Miss Barrett very much in mind" (p. 175). The editorial comment in the Penguin edition accepts the possibility that the poem played a part in the Brownings' courtship: "The argument . . . is not seriously affected by doubts about dates of writing—that Browning may have used the poem as suggested does not necessarily imply that he wrote it for that purpose" (*Poems* 1:1097).

54. Mrs. Sutherland Orr, *A Handbook to the Works of Robert Browning* (London: G. Bell and Sons, 1927), p. 276.

55. While Daniel Karlin, in *The Courtship of Robert Browning and Elizabeth Barrett* (Oxford: Clarendon, 1985), refuses to see the poem as an allegory of Elizabeth Barrett's domestic situation, he does identify the huntsman with Browning: "Browning may have seen in the huntsman's relation to the Duchess a model of his desired relation to Elizabeth Barrett" (p. 91).

56. D. G. Rossetti, "Jenny," in *Works,* pp. 36-43. Subsequent references to this work will be cited parenthetically by line number in the text.

57. Dante Gabriel Rossetti wrote the first version of "Jenny" in 1847-48. It is reprinted by Paull F. Baum in his article "The Bancroft Manuscripts of Dante Gabriel Rossetti," *Modern Philology* 39 (1941): 48-52. According to William Michael Rossetti's note on "Jenny" in his edition of his brother's works (p. 649), Dante Gabriel "finished" the poem toward the end of 1858 when it seems to have first assumed the monologue form. That this later version bears a strong likeness to the one published in the collected *Poems* of 1870 is apparent from Ruskin's brief description of the poem in a letter of 1859 in *Ruskin: Rossetti: Preraphaelitism: Papers 1862 to 1870,* ed. W. M. Rossetti (London: George Allen, 1899), pp. 233-35. Christina Rossetti's manuscript of *Goblin Market* is dated 27 April 1859.

58. Marsh, *Christina Rossetti: Poems and Prose,* p. 443.

59. George Gordon, Lord Byron, *The Works of Lord Byron* (Ware: Wordsworth Editions, 1994), p. 249. These lines are quoted by Emma Shepherd in an article in *The Magdalen's Friend* 1 (1860): 13-14, a journal for those involved in the rescue of fallen women. A substantial excerpt which includes this quotation is reproduced in

Marsh, *CR,* p. 586. Shepherd does not attribute the Byronic quotation but implies it is well known, as it obviously was to Dante Gabriel. Like his sister he shows an awareness of the contemporary prejudice against pure women coming into contact with impure women. While Shepherd writes against this moral separatism, the sermons by Bishop Wilberforce and Canon Burrows mentioned in Mary Wilson Carpenter's article, "'Eat me, drink me, love me': The Consumable Female Body in Christina Rossetti's *Goblin Market,*" *VP* 29 (1991): 415–34, display an anxiety that the pure can be corrupted by the impure.

60. Daniel Harris, in "D. G. Rossetti's 'Jenny': Sex, Money, and the Interior Monologue," *VP* 22, no. 2 (1984): 210, takes the "It" as referring not to the just-mentioned "vessel" (Jenny), but to the resemblance between Jenny and Nell, a resemblance which confuses moral certainties.

61. Gilbert and Gubar, p. 575.

II. CONTEXTS AND CRITIQUE

GOBBLING MARKET

"Leering at each other,
  Brother with queer brother;
Signalling each other
  Brother with sly brother . . .

'Come buy, come buy' . . .
  In tones as smooth as honey,
The cat-faced purr'd,
  The rat-paced spoke a word . . ."

Fig. 5.1. E. H. Shepard, "Gobbling Market." From *Punch or The London Charivari* (March 11, 1942), p. 189. Reproduced with the kind permission of *Punch* magazine.

CHAPTER 5

The Political Economy of Fruit

Goblin Market

RICHARD MENKE

I f more than a century of critical response is any guide, Christina
Rossetti's *Goblin Market* would seem to remain as delicious and mystifying as the goblin fruit it describes. In response to the speculations it
provoked, Rossetti herself claimed that the poem was only a fairy story,
utterly without "any profound or ulterior meaning,"[1] but notwithstanding
her pronouncement, *Goblin Market* has remained the subject of innumerable
interpretations, especially religious, psychological, and biographical ones.
Artless children's story or sophisticated allegory, unconscious fantasy or carefully crafted fable, *Goblin Market* does in fact possess the texture of a fairy
tale, with its singsong repetitions, its mingling of the mundane with the
outré, its curious mixture of otherworldliness and acute materiality. Indeed,
this materiality is one of its most memorable and attractive, even seductive,
qualities. I wish to consider the materiality of the poem, especially as it
centers around representations of fruit as physical object and commodity, and
to offer a reading of the poem that brings Rossetti's so-called "aesthetics of
renunciation"[2] into line with what I consider her sharp but subtle economic
critique—that is, to read Rossetti's renunciatory poetics alongside Victorian
political economy, the "science of *wealth*" that is "simultaneously the science
. . . of want, of *thrift,* of *saving,*" of *"asceticism"* and "[s]elf-denial": the science
of renunciation.[3]

Terrence Holt has complained that most contemporary readings of *Goblin*

Market emphasize "the goblins, and the issues of sexuality and gender they seem to represent," at the expense of "the market," but recently several accounts of the poem have attempted to redress the situation.[4] Holt himself discusses *Goblin Market* in terms of the various patterns of exchange—linguistic, psychological, economic, and sexual—that structure it. Elizabeth Campbell draws upon the work of Julia Kristeva to examine the interaction of gender and market relations in the poem's contrast between male linearity and female cyclicality. Working from Nancy Armstrong's claim that "the 1860s represent a new moment in the history of desire in which consumer culture changed the nature of middle-class femininity," Mary Wilson Carpenter considers the double way in which the poem treats women's bodies as "consumable," that is, both as able to be consumed and destroyed by men, and as sustaining and life-generating. By focusing on the shadow figure of the prostitute, Elizabeth K. Helsinger explores *Goblin Market*'s treatment of the relationship between women and the marketplace, and incisively questions the poem's ultimate utopian solution to the problems this relationship presents.[5] But if *Goblin Market* is indeed a poem about consumers and markets, what might goblin fruit—its central representation of the consumable and marketable—mean?

The *OED* traces the movement of the word *fruit* through its centuries of use in English: from its core meaning of physical botanical product, to its biblically inflected extension into metaphor ("the fruit of the righteous is a tree of life," "the fruit of the womb"), and finally to a point where the metaphorical again becomes material (fruit as the result of labor, fruit as financial profit). In a curious way, the motion of *Goblin Market* itself parallels and reiterates the movement of *fruit,* its drift from the physical to the metaphorical and back to the physical, and does so, I argue, largely through the lavishly described yet always mysterious "goblin fruit" itself. Inspired first of all by the long list that foregrounds the goblin fruit, and even the words used to represent the fruit, as sensuous and firmly particular, the first sections of this essay consider the fruit of the goblin market as fruit in the mid-Victorian market. My emphasis then shifts to the metaphorical or metonymic meanings of the goblin fruit, especially in terms of dominant Victorian political economy and John Ruskin's attempts to rewrite economics along aesthetic and ethical lines. Finally, the essay attempts to re-materialize the fruit in order to interrogate its imaginary status as the realization of that abstract concept, a "commodity," and by doing so, to recapture the poem's critical power—and to recognize its crucial equivocations.

Unseasonable Frosts

Such a reading of *Goblin Market* must begin by defining the site of the poem's production, locating it not merely discursively but also spatially and temporally, finding its starting point before tracing its trajectory. Indeed, this site seems intriguingly antithetical to the imaginary setting of the poem. In place of a picture-book countryside we have London (in which Christina Rossetti spent most of her life, and about which she wrote few of her poems);[6] in place of fairy-tale timelessness, a particular year and even a specific day: April 27, 1859, the date written on the manuscript.[7]

It was an unusual spring in England, to say the least, and one that had followed an unusual winter. An 1859 article in *Turner and Spencer's Florist, Fruitist and Garden Miscellany* compares the mild English winter just past to one in "the south of Italy." In the wake of such a warm season, Christina Rossetti might well have anticipated that the coming spring would be a green and pleasant one. If she did, she must have been terribly disappointed, for after this uncommonly gentle winter, the "extraordinary vicissitudes" of English weather soon proved disastrous to the trees and flowers she loved and wrote about. In fact, these vicissitudes seem exceptionally likely to have decisively affected the composition, possibly even the original conception, of *Goblin Market*. The *Florist*'s writer continues:

> Very early in February a number of shrubs were fast breaking into leaf, and Apricots opening their blooms; during March all went on unchecked, so much so, that . . . the woodlands and pasture grounds presented all the appearances usually shown by the first week in May, and every description of garden produce partook also of the general earliness of the season.[8]

But these early blossoms and fruit, like Jeanie's "gay prime" in *Goblin Market*—and almost like Laura's "early prime"—come to an end when a frost brings premature destruction (316, 549):

> On the 31st of March we had 10° of frost, which, following after a snow the previous evening, did a vast amount of mischief to such fruit trees in bloom, besides destroying in several places the crops of Apricots, which were then of considerable size. Peaches had partly set, and suffered more or less throughout the country; and early Pears and Plums also.

Even at this point, one gardener notes the many plants lost and the "fruit trees shorn of promising crops."[9] But the unusual conditions continue:

> The weather became warmer, and the 4th, 5th, 6th, and 7th of April were remarkable for their great heat, the day temperature having been 82° in this neighborhood on the 7th, and between 70° and 80° the greater part of the former three days, an extraordinary temperature for the first week of April. . . . The weather next became sensibly colder, and on the 14th and following days indications of winter made their appearance, followed by snow storms, cold north-west winds, and frosty nights. On the morning of the 20th we had 8° of frost, accompanied by an easterly wind; this frost has almost completed the ruin of our crops of Pears, Plums, and Cherries, excepting perhaps those in some favored locality, or which had ample protection, things almost impossible to effect within the means of an ordinary garden expenditure, to say nothing of orchards and open garden fruits.[10]

Another writer notes the results of this "most disastrous" frost in more detail:

> Apricots were a most abundant crop on the walls, and as large as Damsons. On trees unprotected, or protected only with nets, every fruit is destroyed; on trees protected with tiffany, even double, some few are left, perhaps one in 1000, but these, although green and apparently sound, have their kernels brown and dead. Peaches and Nectarines under the same circumstances seem all destroyed; they had set an immense crop. I never remember them blooming more kindly or setting their fruit better, owing to their shoots being so well ripened by the warmth of the summer and autumn last year. Some few kinds of Plum were in full bloom . . . the germs of all the expanded blossoms are destroyed. . . . Pear trees here had not unfolded their blossoms, but they seem to have suffered much.[11]

After the abundant harvests and well-supplied fruit market of the preceding seasons,[12] in the spring of 1859 Britain seemed likely to grow precious little fruit in the coming season. One gardener in Lincolnshire reports the loss of all his peaches, and many of his gooseberries, currants, pears, and both early and late apples.[13] A Yorkshire correspondent to the *Gardeners' Chronicle and Agricultural Gazette* notes the widespread lamentation over the recent weather's effect on the British fruit crop: "Expectations of abundant crops are blighted, and now the cry is that the severe frosts of the last two days of March and the greater part of April have all but destroyed our fruit."[14] No doubt nearly everyone in England in the spring of 1859 would have been painfully conscious of the extremely intemperate weather between the end of March and late April,[15] but further awareness of the resulting state of British fruit was hardly restricted to a handful of disappointed fruiterers writing in horticultural magazines. The *Economist*'s weekly account of foreign goods on the British market outlines the increasing scarcity of lemons and oranges, some of the most popular varieties of fruit for importation, from the end of March to the end of April. On April 23 it reports a "[m]arket bare of oranges," a week later one emptied not only of oranges but now also of lemons. By May 7, the "backward season for fruit of home growth" seemed "likely to clear the market of foreign produce" as well, as Britons substituted imported for homegrown fruit.[16] Anyone in England who sought a sweet orange to eat or wanted a lemon for punch would very likely have had to do without. Given the destruction of the new fruit crop and the subsequent scarcity of imported fruit, England in late April 1859 must have been a particularly fruit-less place.

According to the manuscript of *Goblin Market,* Christina Rossetti completed the poem or at least wrote out this most important draft on April 27, 1859. Even if the unhappy situation of British horticulture and the fruit trade did not positively determine the representation of the conspicuously plentiful and luscious fruit in *Goblin Market,* it cannot help but have informed it. In place of a "renunciatory aesthetics" that simply and unquestioningly spurns present pleasures, here perhaps is a poetics that takes genuine enjoyment in displacing absence, or at least one acutely sensitive to the dynamic relationships between desire and constraint, pleasure and imagination. The fulfillment of such desires, the realization of such pleasures, may depend on the consumption of goods, but poetic imagination may provide a substitute—or may make the ache of desire more acute. If the inventory of fruit in *Goblin Market* seems dreamlike in its intense physicality, the reasons for this paradox may in fact be legitimately historical: at the time the poem was written, fresh fruit would indeed have been largely the stuff of fantasy. In the context of a real market barren of lemons or oranges, of orchards with apricots, pears, peaches, and cherries dead on the boughs, how great must have been the sheer extravagance, and perhaps the level of denial, involved in producing such a fantastic catalogue. Or how great must have been the power of such a call as the goblin men incessantly make to their prospective customers. "Morning and evening / Maids heard the goblins cry," begins *Goblin Market* (1–2). The poem then proceeds to mimic its goblins by articulating their cry, a marvelously encyclopedic and paratactic call that includes twenty-nine kinds of fruit in twenty-nine lines:

> "Come buy our orchard fruits,
> Come buy, come buy:
> Apples and quinces,
> Lemons and oranges,
> Plump unpecked cherries,
> Melons and raspberries,
> Bloom-down-cheeked peaches,
> Swart-headed mulberries,
> Wild free-born cranberries,
> Crab-apples, dewberries,
> Pine-apples, blackberries,
> Apricots, strawberries;—
> All ripe together
> In summer weather,—
> Morns that pass by,
> Fair eves that fly;
> Come buy, come buy:
> Our grapes fresh from the vine,
> Pomegranates full and fine,
> Dates and sharp bullaces,
> Rare pears and greengages,
> Damsons and bilberries,
> Taste them and try:
> Currants and gooseberries,
> Bright-fire-like barberries,
> Figs to fill your mouth,
> Citrons from the South,
> Sweet to tongue and sound to eye;
> Come buy, come buy." (3–31)

"Bloom-down-cheeked peaches," "Figs to fill your mouth"—it certainly seems a list to fill one's mouth, exquisitely "sweet to tongue and sound to eye"; simply to read the list aloud is almost to "taste them and try." In another poet, in another poem, the effect of the cry's penultimate line might be to give a whiff of synaesthesia, mere sensory shift. But here, language and food, sight and taste, the visual and the auditory and the physical ("sound to eye") all begin to merge. The combination will soon prove dangerous to Laura, for whom "a peep at goblin men" seems almost automatically to entail trafficking with them and consuming their fruit (49). The power of the fruit and the power of the merchants' language overlap in this visionary introductory catalogue. And in its sheer profusion, the list works at least temporarily to keep things in the realm of the material, to "overload the senses and . . . impair the observer's ability to see beyond the physical."[17]

PROTECTING, FORCING, TRADING

This account helps locate some the materiality of the poem in the (over-) insistent physicality of the missing but fantasized fruit of the spring of '59; the remaining task is to locate the fruit, economically, technologically, and even politically—to explore the nature of goblin fruit in relation to other kinds of fruit and other discourses. John Stuart Mill's figurative use of plants at a memorable point in *On Liberty,* published in 1859, seems curiously relevant to *Goblin Market:*

> If it were only that people have diversities of taste, that is reason enough
> for not attempting to shape them all after one model. But different
> persons also require different conditions for their spiritual development;
> and can no more exist healthily in the same moral, than all the variety
> of plants can in the same physical, atmosphere and climate.[18]

Mill's words contrast sharply with the goblins' description of their fruit as "All ripe together / In summer weather." He uses the commonsense observation that all plants cannot thrive in the same physical setting to validate his claim that all people cannot flourish in the same "moral" setting; his assumption that human nature reiterates a stable and consistent vegetable nature informs the connection between the tenor and vehicle of his metaphor. Yet even as Mill, a devoted amateur botanist himself,[19] was making this botanical comparison, British scientists and horticulturists were attempting as never before to cultivate an enormous variety of foreign plants, many of them highly exotic, in the gardens and greenhouses of Britain. In the process, they were creating a reality much more reminiscent of the goblins' world than of the one casually invoked by Mill.

Although the insight that artificially manipulating the environment of plants could improve their growth was hardly new, in the nineteenth century not only was this knowledge rapidly improved, circulated, and systematized, but it was extended into new techniques for cultivating many plants, including tropical ones, that could not have grown in Britain at all without elaborate human intervention. Such intervention included two basic techniques: protecting and forcing. Protecting, that is, applying a "material . . . to prevent the parts developed from being injured by sudden atmospheric changes," as the cheaper and easier technique, was also the more widespread.[20] The simplest type of protection consisted merely of planting a bush or tree against a wall, typically a south-facing one, in order to maximize warmth and sunlight and to minimize wind and frost. Such measures were especially recommended for "peaches, nectarines, and apricots, . . . the more delicate pears, and the earliest cherries . . . likewise . . . any particular tree that it is desired should bring its fruit early towards maturity."[21] In fact, the amateur gardener Laura employs this technique after she has tasted the goblin fruit but finds she cannot buy more:

> One day remembering her kernel-stone
> She set it by a wall that faced the south;
> Dewed it with tears, hoped for a root,
> Watched for a waxing shoot,
> But there came none;
> It never saw the sun,
> It never felt the trickling moisture run. . . . (281–87)

Perhaps Laura should have tried some of the more elaborate new protective procedures available to the gardener manqué in the pages of popular books and journals, schemes involving not only garden walls but also various configurations of nets, ties, trellises, and wooden or iron supports. Soon after the terrible spring of 1859, and with reference to the havoc it had wrought, one writer reiterates the necessity of just such complex measures.[22]

Yet it is hard to imagine that any amount of protection would have allowed Laura's kernel-stone to grow; maybe the situation called instead for forcing, that is, "heat applied artificially to obtain natural results." Forcing causes an "acceleration of vegetable growth" and "induces earlier development"; in many cases, especially when undertaken in a greenhouse, it could compel plants to bear fruit that otherwise never would have developed in England.[23] Forcing in Victorian Britain depended not simply upon raw physical heat, often supplied—as in any other mill—by coal, "hard coke, such as is used in the locomotive," but on detailed knowledge of plants and increasingly sophisticated machinery.[24] As advertisements and articles in horticultural journals show, forcing was rapidly becoming more and more intricate, audacious, and technologically advanced—and becoming big business. One expert predicts that, thanks to the development of better greenhouses (of which the Crystal Palace of the Great Exhibition of 1851 was the most famous example), the "cultivation of exotic fruits" will soon be "carried much farther than it ever yet has been . . . adding to the dessert a variety of handsome and delicious fruits, which are now only known by reputation, or procured with difficulty from foreign countries."[25]

Were the types of fruit in the goblin catalogue real fruit grown in England, almost a third of them—citrons, dates, figs, lemons, melons, oranges, pineapples, pomegranates, and grapes if they are to grow "so luscious" (61)—would almost certainly have been forced. Indeed, the forcing of pineapples in particular had become a popular competitive pursuit, with special prizes awarded for superior specimens.[26] But Victorian horticulture recommended forcing not only for exotic varieties of fruit but also for much more common types, some of them native to England or grown there for centuries: cherries, raspberries, plums (i.e., the damsons, greengages, and bullaces of *Goblin Market*), peaches, apricots, strawberries. The reason for this painstaking treatment is not merely to preserve them from the vagaries of the weather, a task that "protecting" might have performed with less trouble, but to provide "a valuable addition to the dessert in spring," that is, to accommodate the vagaries of the market.[27]

Growing fruit out of season would help satisfy unseasonable appetites. Although Mill uses the example of plants to argue that society should not attempt to mold people "all after one model," in fact both plants and people were being shaped by and for the exigencies of market society. With the intrusion of the market and its rhythms into such natural cycles, it is not surprising that after her indulgence in goblin fruit Laura knows "not was it night or day"; the very first thing we learn about the goblins is that they cry their fruit "[m]orning and evening," as if the market never closed (139, 1). She might also be forgiven if she forgot the season, surrounded as she is by twenty-nine kinds of goblin fruit

"All ripe together
In summer weather,—
Morns that pass by,
Fair eves that fly . . ." (15–18)

Obviously, then, the popularity of forcing and hot-houses represents not only one of the fruits of imperialism, the desire to cultivate the exotic at home and to reproduce the Empire in the greenhouse, but also the growing ascendance of the market as an organizing social institution. This growth, the growth of consumer capitalism, predicates itself on such tasks as the reorganization of biological cycles into market ones through technology and scientific knowledge; the process amounts precisely to a version of Weberian rationalization realized on the shoots and fruits of plants and assumes a parallel transformation of their consumers' palates.[28] The complementary development of the fruit trade and consumer tastes might be taken by a Victorian political economist as a demonstration of Jean-Baptiste Say's "law" that, in the long run, markets always clear, "that every commodity put on the market creates its own demand, and that every demand exerted in the market creates its own supply," a dictum that plays an important part in the work of nineteenth-century economists such as David Ricardo.[29]

In contrast, the economics of *Goblin Market* confirms one half of Say's equation but cannily distrusts the other. Fruit may provoke hunger as supply provokes demand, but, as poor Laura discovers, mere hunger calls forth no fruit—an observation characteristic of Rossetti's poetry. In *Goblin Market,* economic supply initially presents itself as a physical reality, but consumer demand is desire (typically "baulked desire," in the poem's skeptical view), metaphysical and subjunctive (267). In fact, the poem's second half confirms what its initial, incantatory, overinsistent catalogue has strongly hinted, that supply too may be contingent and insubstantial, like goblin fruit that can ripen out of season or disappear from the market altogether; in the short run, markets may "clear" in a sense very different from Say's complacent pronouncement of eternal equilibrium and leave desirous consumers like Laura to starve.

Were the goblin fruits real, the growing popularity of hot-houses and the obvious unnaturalness of so many types of fruit "all ripe together" at the same time would amount to a virtual guarantee that many of them had been forced, a guarantee only strengthened by the grievous state of unforced English fruit in late April 1859. Furthermore, the preternaturally fresh and untouched state of "grapes fresh from the vine" and especially "plump unpecked cherries" strongly hints at an origin in the greenhouse. The goblins, however, make explicitly contradictory claims. "Come buy our orchard fruits," they start their sales pitch: *orchard* fruits, not hot-house flowers. Accordingly, their merchandise list includes "Wild free-born cranberries" and "Pears red with basking / Out in the sun" (11, 358-59); their words carefully deny any possibility that the fruit is not "free-born" and unconstrained but a product of technological intervention.

In spite of the bold assertions made in testimonials to the power of forcing, not all goblin fruit could have been forced reliably or effectively in England. Dates were only rarely grown there, for example. The pomegranate occasionally ripened fruit in England, but "under no circumstances [was] it likely to repay the labour bestowed on it."[30] Fortunate it may have been for seekers of such goblin fruit, then, that throughout the nineteenth century, Great Britain also imported a large and growing quantity of fruit, despite the "difficulty" alleged by promoters of forcing. Some of the most popular at midcentury were citrus fruits, imported individually wrapped in paper or leaves: oranges from Iberia and Italy; lemons from these countries and from France; and citrons, candied and preserved, from the Madeira archipelago. Grapes arrived from Portugal, and pomegranates reached England from southern Europe and the West Indies.[31] In addition to the fresh fruit there, merchants stocked Covent Garden Market with great quantities of dried fruit from the Levant: figs, dates, and currants.[32]

Clearly, the list of goblin fruit includes "not just common, home-grown apples and cherries, but also a rich variety of gourmet fruits imported from foreign climes," that is, "luxury fruits that appeal to 'sundry refined tastes' such as have been cultivated by Britain's colonial Empire";[33] a yen for exotic fruit seems a classic imperial taste. But England also imported more familiar varieties of fruit, to help satisfy an immense and growing domestic demand for "valuable addition[s] to the dessert": apples, plums, cranberries.[34] Like so many goods in the nineteenth and twentieth centuries, fruit was an item that, once considered a luxury, was gradually becoming a staple for middle-class consumers.[35] In *London Labour and the London Poor* (1851-61), Henry Mayhew observes that the poor purchase only a "small quantity" of costermongers' fruit; the buyers of this "luxury . . . consist mostly of clerks, shopmen, small tradesmen, and the children of mechanics or the lower grade of middle class people."[36] Far from Mayhew's London, the genteel but none too wealthy Misses Jenkyns of Elizabeth Gaskell's *Cranford* (1851-53) habitually eat oranges for dessert (which they consume in private, in order to avoid any embarrassment from the noises of sucking them). Other goods such as sugar and tea (another key commodity in *Cranford*) experienced a similar shift, a type of economic and cultural change both strongly determined by and strongly determining the course of nineteenth-century imperialism.[37]

In *Goblin Market,* the goblin men are also emphatically *"merchant* men," hawking their wares on a mobile market for which the appearance of unfettered free trade only masks the fact that they set the terms of exchange (474; emphasis added). Moreover, the poetically archaic term calls to mind another, far more current meaning for "merchant man" in the nineteenth century: a "vessel employed in conveying freight or passengers, as distinguished from a national vessel, and from vessels in the revenue service, coast survey, *etc.*";[38] a private, commercial ship involved in the movement of people or goods; that is, a trading ship. If the "quaint fruit-merchant men" (553) are also in some measure merchantmen bearing quaint fruit, they are ships whose previous ports of call are apparently unknowable. This situation seems rather appropriate for such traders, since as Adam Smith reminds us, a "merchant . . . is not necessarily the citizen of any particular country."[39] The origins of the goblins remain hidden, and such secrecy extends to their stock. It is precisely this mystery that occasions Laura's initial warning about goblin fruit:

> "We must not look at goblin men,
> We must not buy their fruits:
> Who knows upon what soil they fed
> Their hungry thirsty roots?" (42–45)

Even Laura's words of caution portend danger; the rhetorical question "Who knows upon what soil they fed / Their hungry thirsty roots?" slides into the real and apparently unanswerable question of where they are from and how they were produced. Her temptation begins in earnest when Laura starts, almost unconsciously, to speculate about such origins:

> "How fair the vine must grow
> Whose grapes are so luscious;
> How warm the wind must blow
> Thro' those fruit bushes." (60–63)

After she eats the fruit, her imagination becomes far more vivid:

> "Odorous indeed must be the mead
> Whereon they grow, and pure the wave they drink
> With lilies at the brink,
> And sugar-sweet their sap." (180–83)

Finally, the "waves" she has envisioned enter her dreams and make her "baulked desire" for goblin fruit even more unbearable (288-92, 267). Laura plants her kernel-stone and "hope[s] for a root," but she should know by now that goblin fruit never offers roots (283). For Laura, desire first enters through the epistemological aporia between the product and the knowledge of its production, the gap between perceiving the fruits and imagining their roots. In fact, one function of the goblins' catalogue itself is to reinforce this mystery by piling fruit upon fruit, exotics upon domestics, "wild free-born" berries upon the likely products of forcing, so that it hopelessly confuses descriptions and mystifies origins. The goblins' merchandise embodies a certain unknowability; they offer fruits with no apparent roots. In terms of the poem's imagery, they enforce the same state on Laura; as she pines for more goblin fruit, "[h]er tree of life droop[s] from the root," and as she drinks the "fiery antidote" from Lizzie's face and neck, she falls "[l]ike a wind-uprooted tree" before she is restored (260, 559, 517). In their encounter with Lizzie, the goblins try to pull "her hair out by the roots" (404), as if their goal were to deracinate even hair, which they have previously accepted from Laura in exchange for fruit.

Beyond Laura's fantasies, seldom does the poem offer even a vague sense of where the goblins' offerings may actually have originated, just where or what "that unknown orchard" might be (135). Lizzie recalls that, before dwindling away and dying, abandoned by the goblins, poor Jeanie "Ate their fruits and wore their flowers / Plucked from bowers / Where summer ripens at all hours" (150-52); this description of perpetual warmth could refer equally well to a forcing-house or to the eternally sunny lands of imperial fantasy. Somewhat more helpfully, there are the "citrons from the South," the final item in the goblins' original list. Tantalizingly, at least one mid-Victorian "authority" considered the forbidden fruit of the Bible to have been "a variety of Citron."[40] But regardless of whether "the fruit forbidden" (439) corresponds to the biblical forbidden fruit, the citron passage offers one of the only hints about where the goblin fruit may come from: "the South."

Whether or not the fruits themselves come from the South, their sellers may. The goblin men, far from being simply goblins or men, look and act like various animals. Like some of the fruits they sell, some of the animals the goblin merchants resemble are common, completely ordinary ones in England: cats, rats, snails, birds, magpies, pigeons, and fish (71-74, 114, 345-47). Others are much more unusual: wombats, ratels, and parrots (75-76, 112). In part, the references simply echo Rossetti's long-standing interest in small, exotic animals; even before she moved to Albany Street in 1854, she often visited the Zoological Gardens at nearby Regent's Park. Rossetti regularly mentioned creatures such as tortoises, alligators, armadillos, and wombats in letters to her family and enjoyed sketching them; in the early 1860s, Dante Rossetti assembled a collection of small creatures outside his house in London, a menagerie to which Christina was a frequent visitor.[41] Yet it seems more than coincidental that the homelands of the exotic animals associated with the goblin men describe the Southern hemisphere in general and Britain's colonies there in particular: parrots from the tropical Americas (British Guyana), ratels from South Africa (Cape Colony), and wombats from Australia (New South Wales). At the very least, these ambiguously colonial hybrids hint at the dangers of intimacy and confusion between home and abroad.[42]

Insofar as the goblin men and their goods are identifiable with the foreign, they clearly threaten Lizzie and Laura, whose daily work of milking cows, cleaning house, and preparing food confirms their strong affiliation with the domestic, in at least one sense. John Ruskin, among others, emphasizes in his economic writing that the source of *economics* is *oikonomos*, household management, and this etymology underlies his incensed and unwavering claim in *Unto This Last* (1860) that "all true economy is 'Law of the house.'"[43] In *Goblin Market,* Laura and Lizzie's self-contained domestic economy high-lights the historical and metaphorical connection between the household and the economy. The poem represents their home life as a busy but cozy scene of production utterly divorced from a sense of the market; they even "produce food for their own consumption, enacting on an economic level the hermetic-ism of their domestic scene."[44] In sharp contrast to the home-based economy that sustains them, and apparently antithetical to it, is the foreign influence of the "queer" and outlandish merchant men (94). Once Laura realizes that the goblin market has closed to her, she can no longer perform her work in the domestic sphere:

> She no more swept the house,
> Tended the fowls or cows,
> Fetched honey, kneaded cakes of wheat,
> Brought water from the brook:
> But sat down listless in the chimney-nook
> And would not eat. (293–98)[45]

Later, the poem treats the goblins' assault on the indomitable Lizzie as the siege of a coastal town, in terms that partially reverse its pairing of the goblins and the colonial in order to show the domestic and the feminine heroically resisting an attack from outside:

> Like a royal virgin town
> Topped with gilded dome and spire
> Close beleaguered by a fleet
> Mad to tug her standard down. (418-21)

The vagaries of the wandering goblins and their market threaten Lizzie and Laura's previously isolated domestic (and, as critics have long observed, sexual) economy. And no wonder: the noisy, male, highly mobile goblins—clear analogues of the itinerant costermongers who so fascinate Mayhew in the first volume of *London Labour and the London Poor*—are presented as the menacing opposite of Lizzie and Laura in their quiet "nest" (198). Whereas the two women prepare simple country fare that requires some physical labor to produce (butter, cream, wheat cakes, honey), the goblins offer goods that promise instant gratification but seem to exist only on the market, fruits without roots, pure commodities. Both the merchant men and their merchandise appear mysteriously, if selectively, foreign and perhaps southern, but the precise roots of neither are at all clear. The occluded origins of the goblin men and their goblin fruit are part of the puzzle, and part of the danger, they present.

SERMON, FAIRY TALE, PARABLE

Near the end of the Sermon on the Mount, one of several biblical texts informing *Goblin Market*,[46] Jesus expresses a similar concern with the origins of fruit:

> Beware of false prophets, which come to you in sheep's clothing, but inwardly they are ravening wolves. Ye shall know them by their fruits. Do men gather grapes of thorns, or figs of thistles? Even so every good fruit tree bringeth forth good fruit; but a corrupt tree bringeth forth evil fruit. A good tree cannot bring forth evil fruit, neither can a corrupt tree bring forth good fruit. Every tree that bringeth not forth good fruit is hewn down, and cast into the fire. Wherefore by their fruits ye shall know them. (Matt. 7:15-20)

His logic is simple; good fruit indicates good roots, and bad fruit reveals evil ones. And, obviously, Christ's fruit is not literal fruit but metaphorical fruit, fruit in the "biblical" sense, fruit as consequence or as issue, productive or reproductive.

This is the level on which the fruit in *Goblin Market* has most frequently been interpreted. In these readings, the fruit is only incidentally fruit; since so much of the poem's criticism "treats its story of buying and selling, like its rhymes and goblins, as the figurative dress for a narrative of spiritual temptation, fall, and redemption," the goblin fruit tends immediately to resolve into something else.[47] Usually (and quite credibly) it becomes sexual temptation, sexual knowledge, heterosexuality, or—more recently—sexual difference.[48] Or it is the male, public sphere, the sphere that includes economic life, in which women only have one available position, that of prostitute; after all, Laura must indeed sell part of her body, "a precious golden lock," in order to receive the fruit (126). And before her there was poor, etiolated Jeanie, who "for joys brides hope to have / Fell sick and died / In her gay prime" (314-16). "For" is ambiguous here (it may denote a cause in the past or regrets for a future that will never come), and "gay," applied to a young woman, carried for the Victorians an implication of prostitution.[49] Or the fruit is simply the temptation of the world for the Christian who forgets the nature of attractive surfaces, the relationship of roots to fruits.

In connection with Christina Rossetti's dismissal of *Goblin Market* as merely a fairy tale, Elizabeth Helsinger has noted the preoccupation of many fairy tales with buying and selling.[50] She could just as easily have noted that many of the famous New Testament parables use economic situations to represent spiritual ones: the parable of the talents, the parable of the two debtors, the parable of the lost silver coin, the parable of the merchant and the great pearl, and the parable of the workers in the vineyard, which would become the central example of "true" political economy for John Ruskin in *Unto This Last* (*UTL*, pp. 34-36). Christina Rossetti knew Ruskin through her brother Dante, and without a doubt the dozen or so years surrounding *Goblin Market* represented the high point of the friendship between Ruskin and the Rossettis; as unlikely as it may seem, at one time, Christina's still more pious elder sister Maria even wrongly imagined herself the object of Ruskin's romantic admiration.[51] While Rossetti was composing *Goblin Market,* Ruskin was doing work that highlighted issues of interpretation and economics, that is, for Ruskin, the relationship between aesthetic perception and ethical economic action. And in Ruskin's work, the expression of this relationship centered around biblical parable.

As an art critic, Ruskin is known for the unparalleled acuity of his sight, and his belief in the moral necessity of clear vision underwrites his social criticism as well; in both strains of Ruskinian criticism he tries to teach his readers how and what to see. In the famous "Nature of Gothic" chapter from *The Stones of Venice* (1851–53), Ruskin reads social and economic relations in Gothic architecture and uses his visual abilities to reach moral conclusions about medieval society. Later, in *The Political Economy of Art,*[52] a two-part lecture given in 1857, and still more explicitly in *Unto This Last,* a collection of essays serialized in the *Cornhill Magazine* in 1860, he encourages a similar practice with regard to consumption. As Ruskin examines the consumable object, he claims that "consumption absolute is the end, crown, and perfection of production" (*UTL,* p. 98) and, in truth, stops scarcely short of Marx's contemporary recognition that "consumption [is] thus . . . a moment of production."[53] "In all buying," Ruskin writes, "consider, first, what condition of existence you cause in the producers of what you buy" (*UTL,* p. 113). *Look* at what you buy, urges Ruskin, "Raise the veil boldly" (*UTL,* p. 114); and elsewhere he elaborates: "if the veil could be lifted not only from your thoughts, but from human sight, you would see—the angels do see—on those gay white dresses of yours, strange dark spots, and crimson patterns . . . and among the pleasant flowers that crown your fair heads . . . the grass that grows on graves" (*PE,* pp. 51–52). However, as even Ruskin admits, because it can be so devilishly difficult to see the ethical implications embedded in consumable objects, "wise consumption is a far more difficult art than wise production" (*UTL,* p. 98). Ruskin's criticism amounts to an early formulation of "moral consumption," the idea that a consumer's market behavior necessarily includes ethical choices. Toward the end of the century, tactics based on this concept were widely adopted by such groups as woman-suffragists, labor organizers, and Irish nationalists, adding new strategies for activist groups in market society and even a new word to the English language: *boycott.*

Ruskin's belief in the power of seeing what is really there informs his choice of a foundation for his critiques. In place of the defining scientism of the "modern *soi-disant* science of political economy" (*UTL,* p. 25), Ruskin—even as he is losing some component of his religious faith, becoming what he later called "*un*-converted"[54]—chooses New Testament parables as a model for his very different economic vision. And, again, it is a vision based on sight; Ruskin insists on seeing what is there, and he reads the biblical parables literally, as expressions of economic truth. If he carefully over-reads economic goods (splendid white dresses with cut glass beads) and artistic productions

(Greek temples or Gothic cathedrals), Ruskin studiously *under*-reads the New Testament parables. For Ruskin in *Unto This Last,* the parable of the vineyard in which every laborer receives the same wage, even those who arrive late and perform less work, expresses not the availability of salvation to tardy converts but the necessity of paying everyone what she or he needs to live a good life. In *The Political Economy of Art,* Ruskin offers a similar analysis of the parable of the talents:

> [I]s it not a strange thing, that while we more or less accept the meaning of that saying, so long as it is considered metaphorical, we never accept its meaning in its own terms? You know the lesson is given us under the form of a story about money. Money was given to the servants to make use of: the unprofitable servant dug in the earth, and hid his lord's money. Well, we, in our political and spiritual application of this, say, that of course money doesn't mean money: it means wit, it means intellect, it means influence in high quarters, it means everything in the world except itself. And do you not see what a pretty and pleasant come-off there is for most of us, in this spiritual application? . . . we have no talents entrusted to *us* of any sort or kind. It is true we have a little money, but the parable can't possibly mean anything so vulgar as money; our money's our own. (*PE,* pp. 98–99)

Ruskin under-reads the parable, or for him the parable indeed ultimately proves parabolic, moving from the material through the metaphorical or allegorical and then emphatically back to the material. The motion parallels that of *Goblin Market,* which itself seems rather like a parable, only one curiously detached from its ground. But, despite their comparable appropriations of the classic gospel genre and some of its familiar imagery, there is an important difference between Ruskin's parables and Rossetti's, and between his critique of political economy and hers.

MARKETPLACE ETHICS AND GOBLIN POETICS

In early 1861, Dante Gabriel Rossetti gave John Ruskin manuscript copies of several poems by his sister Christina, hoping that Ruskin would commend them to William Thackeray, who was then publishing *Unto This Last* in the *Cornhill.* As Ruskin's reaction hints, the collection almost certainly included

Goblin Market, which would subsequently figure as the first, longest, and title poem of *Goblin Market and Other Poems* (1862), Christina Rossetti's first commercially published book of poetry. After receiving some of the poetry that would soon compose this critically successful collection, Ruskin assessed it in a letter to her brother:

DEAR ROSSETTI,

I sate up till late last night reading poems. They are full of beauty and power. But no publisher—I am deeply grieved to know this—would take them, so full are they of quaintnesses and offences. Irregular measure (introduced to my great regret, in its chief wilfulness, by Coleridge) is the calamity of modern poetry. The *Iliad,* the *Divina Commedia,* the *Æneid,* the whole of Spenser, Milton, Keats, are written without taking a single license or violating the common ear for metre; your sister should exercise herself in the severest commonplace of metre until she can write as the public like. Then if she puts in her observation and passion all will become precious. But she must have the Form first. *All* love to you and reverent love to Ida.

Ever affectionately yours,
J. RUSKIN[55]

Ironically, at a time when much of his own criticism was becoming decidedly social, Ruskin criticized Christina Rossetti's poetry formally, for its unabashed and sometimes jarring metrical irregularity. Simultaneously he seems to have dismissed or, much more probably, to have completely missed the economic dimensions of the poetry, perhaps because he did not expect to find such themes in the work of a young lady, or perhaps because these dimensions, while broadly similar to his own critique, differ in a crucial way.

Goblin Market is indeed a parable without the necessary allegorical parallel to its deceptively simple story, insistently material but illimitably metaphorical: thus the endless interpretations of its plot, its eroticism, its goblin men, its fruit; and thus Christina Rossetti's ability to dismiss it, with some plausibility, as only a fairy story. But maybe the poem only "cultivates the appearance of inconsequence partly to conceal its own pretensions to a consequence far greater than most of the poetry then being produced" in spaces closer to the ideological heart of Victorian England.[56] In this case, a modest and subtle Christina Rossetti might well claim to retreat precisely because the stakes are so high. If this withdrawal seems suspect, it is not simply because it is Rossetti who has raised the stakes in the first place but also because it may be precisely the unresolvable thematic and formal contradictions of *Goblin Market* itself that render such retreat necessary.

In a crucial way, *Goblin Market* is even more insistently critical than *The Political Economy of Art* or *Unto This Last*. In those works, Ruskin articulates his criticism of Victorian society through his confidence in the power of sight to "raise the veil" and descry the conditions of production beneath the rough carvings on a Gothic cathedral or the shiny surface of a glass bead, even though he admits that the task may be difficult. For Ruskin, the transparency of the parable is the corollary to his valorization of vision. But Christina Rossetti shows no such confidence in sight; it can reveal neither the origins of the goblin fruit nor the allegory of the poem, for its shiny surfaces are impossible to pierce without the threat of being poisoned, as Laura is, by desire.[57] Rossetti's skepticism would be entirely appropriate for a Londoner who would have known Covent Garden Market and heard the cries of Mayhew's costermongers.[58] After all, even when natural "orchard fruits" are blighted by frost, there will soon be fruit in the market again, courtesy of mysterious industrial or imperial "bowers / Where summer ripens at all hours," although it may be impossible to tell where the fruit is from and how it has been produced. Indeed, a blight on homegrown orchard fruit may well end up expanding the trade in goblin fruit, as seems likely to have happened in 1859, when commentators urged the refinement of horticultural technology, and British imports of foreign fruit increased dramatically.[59]

Rossetti seems to understand, as Ruskin desperately tries not to, one of the essential qualities of commodities in the marketplace: "Once products enter a capitalist market, it is notoriously difficult to figure out how, when, or where they were made."[60] In the famous section on commodity fetishism in *Capital* (1867), Marx also makes the connection between visual perception and commodification, but his treatment of vision is far less sanguine than Ruskin's:

> A commodity is therefore a mysterious thing, simply because in it the social character of men's labour appears to them as an objective character stamped upon the product of that labour; because the relation of the producers to the sum total of their own labour is presented to them as a social relation, existing not between themselves, but between the products of their labour. This is the reason why the products of labour become commodities, social things whose qualities are at the same time

perceptible and imperceptible by the senses. In the same way the light from an object is perceived by us not as the subjective excitation of an optic nerve, but as the objective form of something outside the eye itself. But, in the act of seeing, there is at all events, an actual passage of light from one thing to another, from the external object to the eye. There is a physical relation between physical things. But it is different with commodities.[61]

Our experience of apparently unmediated vision is itself misleading, *pace* Ruskin; what hope can there be then for vision alone, no matter how keen, to deal adequately with the "metaphysical subtleties and theological niceties" (*C*, p. 319) of the commodity?

Classical political economy sets out to examine the commodity but becomes tangled in attempts to reconcile the different (but possibly related) sources and standards of its value: (1) value in use, (2) value in exchange, (3) the value in the labor that has produced an object, and (4) the value in the labor necessary in order to purchase it (the difference between these last two values is more or less the "surplus value" that constitutes profit in capitalist production). Although Adam Smith seems to vacillate, in one passage he offers a measure of value apparently based on the last of these standards. Responding to Smith's inconsistencies, Ricardo attempts to formulate a labor theory of value based on the third of these measures, the differing amounts of productive labor embedded in different commodities, admitting that "from no source do so many errors, and so much difference of opinion in [political economy] proceed, as from the vague ideas which are attached to the word value."[62]

In his economic criticism, Ruskin modifies the labor theories of value of classical political economy. "THERE IS NO WEALTH BUT LIFE," he claims, and the organization and wages of labor should be based upon what workers need in order to live good lives (*UTL*, p. 105). In essence, Ruskin argues for a moral standard of value based on the social conditions entailed by a commodity's production. As he insists that consumers see the labor enshrouded in the product, Ruskin echoes the orthodox political economists' treatment of the secret of the commodity, and their concern for its hidden wellspring of value. Marx too builds upon classical economic theories of value, but he recognizes that political economy has become so mesmerized by the secret *behind* the commodity, so concerned with locating and debating its mysterious source of value, that it has not been able to recognize the significance of the commodity as form:

> Whence, then, arises the enigmatical character of the product of labour, so soon as it assumes the form of commodities? Clearly from this form itself. Political Economy has indeed analysed, however incompletely, value and its magnitude, and has discovered what lies beneath these forms. But it has never once asked the question why labour is represented by the value of its product and labour-time by the magnitude of that value. These formulæ . . . bear it stamped upon them in unmistakable letters that they belong to a state of society, in which the process of production has the mastery over man, instead of being controlled by him. (*C*, pp. 320, 327)

Marx describes the product of this phenomenon as commodity "fetishism," the way in which capitalism seems to endow objects of exchange with the importance and attributes of living things (*C*, p. 321).

Goblin Market may not offer an analysis of the commodity form as Marx does, but it incisively locates the play of surface and secret in the commodity and suggests the perils presented by its inarguable allure. The goblins' fruit, initially so palpable and so palpably tempting, stands revealed as pure exchange value, pure commodity. As the poem obscures the roots of the goblin fruit, frustrates attempts to pin down its own allegory, and demonstrates the curious attraction of such obscurity and frustration, it seems implicitly to recognize the mystified character of the commodity, and the way in which it simultaneously acquiesces to—indeed, seduces—and thwarts vision.

This critical awareness is exactly what makes *Goblin Market* so alive to the workings of a commodity culture that might have been particularly seductive to Victorian middle-class women, raised to appreciate attractive little things like goblin fruit, glass beads, wombats, or even albums of poetry, to become lost in the material, so that aesthetic pleasure may lead to a dangerous implication in the market—or, in the case of Laura and her "golden curl," to the possibility of selling herself as a commodity on the market (126). From its swart-headed mulberries and bloom-down-cheeked peaches to its comparisons of Lizzie to "a fruit-crowned orange-tree" and Laura to a "wind-uprooted tree," the poem raises the possibility that women may closely correspond to fruit, as far as the goblin market is concerned (415, 517). The correspondence may even underlie the goblins' attempts to "force" Lizzie and the ability of their fruit to cause premature maturity (or, more precisely, senescence). The market itself, like the goblin merchant men and the imperial merchantmen, like the industrial and imperial roots that nourish goblin fruit, is at once everywhere and nowhere on earth. It may inhabit Covent Garden Market or the streets of London or a parlor in Cranford, but more importantly, it enters and organizes human relationships and transforms the subject of the market, she who is both a potential consumer and a potential object of consumption—for instance, Laura. In *Goblin Market*, Laura's relationship with the market is an all-consuming one, both because it may threaten to make the market's subject into its object and because it engenders desires that can by definition never be satisfied. In the familiar geometric representation of the market, the curve representing consumer demand intersects supply and yet continues.

Insofar as *Goblin Market* offers a sense of consumer ethics in any way analogous to Ruskin's, it implies a canny, skeptical approach not dependent upon the aesthetic relationship of sensory life to ethical action. Welcomed by the goblins, Laura seeks to participate in their market but seems unprepared; she eyes their fruit but admits that she has no money: "Good folk, I have no coin; / To take were to purloin" (116-17). When the goblins suggest that she offer a "golden curl" in exchange for their fruit, she agrees, allowing them to set the terms of the bargain. Savvy Lizzie is a far better shopper. First of all, she arrives armed with "a silver penny in her purse" (324); how she acquired it may ultimately be the central mystery of the poem—presumably by a sort of primitive accumulation beyond the purview of *Goblin Market,* with its determined separation of the domestic and commercial economies.[63] "Mindful of Jeanie," Lizzie then insists that the goblins trade on her terms: a penny in exchange for goblin fruit, to be taken *home* to one who waits (364). After the goblins demur, Lizzie moves from exercising her power of voice to trying her power of exit:

> "So without further parleying,
> If you will not sell me any
> Of your fruits tho' much and many,
> Give me back my silver penny
> I tossed you for a fee." (385-89)

The goblins attempt to force-feed her, but Lizzie resists, clamping her mouth resolutely shut. She "laugh[s] in heart to feel the drip / Of juice that syrup[s] all her face," until the merchant men relent, fling back her coin, and leave (433-34).

Lizzie's triumph in fact contradicts Laura's approach to the market completely; to take without paying is to purloin, but Lizzie manages to escape with a free sample, as it were. Lizzie saves: she saves her pennies, she saves herself, she saves her fruit juice, and at last she saves her sister.[64] Lizzie saves but never spends, never consummates an exchange. *Contra* Helsinger, it is *not* the case that "for once, sisterhood intervenes so that women can successfully buy in markets run by men,"[65] but instead that sisterhood manages to shut down the shop. As she has *taken* (or been forced to take) the juice, so Lizzie *gives* it to Laura—a courageous act and the poem's supreme example of an ethical one. Lizzie, after all, does not find the fruit tempting; "her story has not to do with temptation resisted . . . but with danger braved and overcome."[66]

In political economic terms, Lizzie performs a miraculous feat, and if the poem describes a transubstantiation, it is precisely this: without becoming either the subject or the object of exchange, Lizzie transforms pure exchange-value (the commodity of goblin fruit) into pure use-value (the "fiery antidote" that saves Laura). *Goblin Market,* through its ethics of renunciation, rejects consumer desire and exchange-value itself. Yet the poem does not amount to crystal-clear Ruskinian parable nor Marxian analysis nor call to action. Instead, *Goblin Market* remains after all something like a fairy tale, a story about surviving the perils and deceptions of the market through love for a sister and the ethical action that arises from this domestic tie. If the poem is a fairy tale, however, it is a remarkably political economic one, not only mindful with Ruskin that the marketplace compels but conceals ethical choices and moments of self-constitution, but also crucially aware that looking into the commodity, eyeing the fruit, may not help reveal them.

This is also the situation when it comes to a text as self-consciously mysterious as *Goblin Market.* Several recent critics have ascribed to Christina Rossetti a keen (if conflicted) awareness of the commercial status of her work; Jan Marsh has pointed out that as her brother was showing her poetry to Ruskin, Christina Rossetti was "on her own initiative" sending a selection of poems to David Masson at *Macmillan's Magazine,* with far more success.[67] Even beyond such biographical evidence, Rossetti's recognition of the commercial possibilities of her work seems clear, for *Goblin Market* evinces an awareness of its own status as commodity, as itself something like a species of literary goblin fruit. As an inheritor of not only the irregular metrics of "Christabel" (as Ruskin notes) but also the poetic stance of Coleridgean Romanticism, *Goblin Market* offers an allegory of its artistic origins that is more oblique but just as untrustworthy as those offered by "Kubla Khan" or "The Eolian Harp."

Thus the disjunctions noted earlier: London versus the countryside, specific dates versus timelessness, a real fruit shortage versus imagined surfeit and mystical scarcity. If beyond this Romantic obscuring of poetic labor intrudes an additional level of complexity, even of duplicity, in Rossetti's poem, this has everything to do with the poem's fraught relationships to both the marketplace it was to enter and the commodity form it seeks to treat imaginatively—that is, to the fruit that it finds alluring, dreams of domesticating, and in some measure turns out to be.

Goblin Market is deliciously mystifying, and this is precisely because it deals with its own status as a commodity, as goblin fruit, by mystifying deliciously. It maps out not only a movement from material object to commodity, from physical goblin fruit to political economic fruit, but also its own trajectory from poem to commodity in the literary marketplace, complete—like goblin fruit, like the commodity form—with unknown roots and tantalizing meaning. Yet it is this final movement that Rossetti must obscure, because of the poem's endorsement of an ethical stance that rejects and reforms the commodity. When after entering the literary marketplace the poem attracted an audience of fascinated Lauras eager to explicate it, no wonder Rossetti could only hedge and call it a fairy story. In doing so, she naturalized its production and obscured its roots just as surely as the goblins with their promises of "[w]ild free-born cranberries." Ironically, the simultaneous openness and opacity of *Goblin Market,* borne of its ambivalent recognition of itself as goblin fruit and commodity and its fraught pre-emptive self-commodification, may in fact have assisted its success in the literary marketplace even in the face of Ruskin's fear that Rossetti was not writing "as the public like," or as Spenser, Milton, or Keats did.

As *Goblin Market* attempts to reject economics, so it rejects one dominant mode of aesthetics, a rejection that Ruskin recognized even before its publication. This broad, male, and largely secular tradition includes thinkers with a variety of influences and interests, from Kant to Ruskin and later even—in his own compellingly self-contradictory way—to Oscar Wilde. In various manners and with varying degrees of success, this tradition attempts to harmonize the life of the senses with life of the individual subject as ethical actor (Kant), ethical consumer (Ruskin), or ethical stylist (Wilde). In contrast, Rossetti's religious faith and, arguably, her gender, compel her to regard the world of sense perceptions with mistrust, even when she might like what she sees.

Like Ruskin, Gilbert and Gubar recognize the poem's disavowal of conventional poetics, but they can only consider the rejection of Miltonic or Keatsian aesthetics as a form of artistic suicide and conclude that "Rossetti, banqueting on bitterness, must bury herself alive in a coffin of resentment."[68] Yet the poem's relationship to prevailing strains of political economy and aesthetics, and even to the missing fruit of the spring of 1859, suggests a rather different conclusion. Instead of simply offering a diagnosis of anorectic claustrophobia, one might separate the poem's "renunciatory aesthetics" into an aesthetics of plenitude which helps render goblin fruit so palpable and so tempting, coupled with an ethics of renunciation and self-sacrifice. Such an ethics becomes necessary because *Goblin Market,* in contrast to Ruskin's economic writing, treats aesthetics not as a corrective to the economics of the market but as a corollary to it.

In *Goblin Market,* Christina Rossetti suggests archly that various traditions of both nineteenth-century aesthetics and Victorian political economy depend on a commodity fetishism as dangerous as Laura's fruit fetish. With its renunciatory ethics or aesthetics, the poem not only renounces the political economy of market capitalism but finally threatens to renounce even aesthetics itself, recognizing their twin goblin fascinations; moreover, the poem imagines that such renunciation may be a heroic and selfless act of resistance, not a passive withdrawal but a feat that creates a space outside the masculine and the mercantile, a locus for the domestic economies of sisterhood and motherhood. Might such a heroic negation be possible, at least in art? Even Ruskin, after all, must admit the curious "power" of Rossetti's work. But the poem's simultaneous recognition and rejection of its own status as commodity suggest that, at least within the economy of Romantic poetry, even a renunciatory strategy may land a consumer, or an author, in a trap from which the only escape is nostalgia or fantasy.

In the poem's coda, as it turns to the utopian and enters a place of fantasized female self-sufficiency, a mother's story suffices to warn against the "wicked, quaint fruit-merchant men"; ethics pass directly from parent to child, unmediated by aesthetics, uncorrupted by economics—but still transferred by telling a story. Clearly, the tale the women tell their children must be *Goblin Market* itself, represented in this instance not as an object of exchange (or, for that matter, as an object of production) but one of pure use. After reading *Goblin Market,* even as Lizzie's and Laura's children might hear the story, after encountering the poem's skepticism about pleasant appearances and recognizing its brilliant and ambivalent exposure of itself as goblin fruit and commodity, we cannot quite believe that possible.[69]

NOTES

1. Bell, p. 230. William Michael Rossetti recalls similar professions in his notes to *PW.*

2. Sandra M. Gilbert and Susan Gubar, *The Madwoman in the Attic: The Woman Writer and the Nineteenth-Century Literary Imagination* (New Haven and London: Yale University Press, 1979), pp. 564-75.

3. Karl Marx, "Economic and Philosophical Manuscripts of 1844," in *The Marx-Engels Reader,* ed. Robert C. Tucker (New York: Norton, 1978), p. 95. The "true ideal" of political economy, Marx claims, is on the one hand the capitalist, an *"ascetic* but *extortionate* miser" and on the other the laborer, an *"ascetic* but *productive* slave."

4. Terrence Holt, "'Men Sell Not Such in Any Town': Exchange in *Goblin Market,"* VP 28 (1990): 51. The title *Goblin Market* was suggested by Dante Gabriel Rossetti, and immediately embraced by his sister as superior to her initial choice, "A Peep at the Goblins."

5. Elizabeth Campbell, "Of Mothers and Merchants: Female Economics in Christina Rossetti's 'Goblin Market,'" VS 33 (1990): 393-410; Mary Wilson Carpenter, "'Eat Me, Drink Me, Love Me': The Consumable Female Body in Christina Rossetti's *Goblin Market,"* VP 29 (1991): 415-34; Elizabeth K. Helsinger, "Consumer Power and the Utopia of Desire: Christina Rossetti's 'Goblin Market,'" *English Literary History* 58 (1991): 903-33.

6. On the "antithetical relation" between "the primal scene, as it were, of all of Rossetti's poetry" and her "immediate experience," see Jerome J. McGann, "The Religious Poetry of Christina Rossetti," *Critical Inquiry* 10 (1983): 138-39.

7. See *CP,* 1:11-26, line 234. Subsequent citations of *Goblin Market* are from this source and will be cited parenthetically by line number.

D. M. R. Bentley seizes upon a passage in L. M. Packer's biography of Christina Rossetti ("It is of course impossible to know whether the poem was written out first and then copied or whether Christina wrote it out exactly as it appears in the Dennis Notebook [March 21, 1859, to Dec. 31, 1860, pp. 3-38]") and argues for a later date of composition—but only in order to propose, unconvincingly it seems to me, that *Goblin Market* was written for and read to "an audience of fallen women . . . at the St. Mary Magdalene Home for Fallen Women" in Highgate, where Rossetti worked beginning in 1860, according to L. M. Packer and other biographers. Bentley speculates that the line "There is no friend like a sister" refers to the "Anglican Sisters" of the home. See "The Meretricious and the Meritorious in 'Goblin Market': A Conjecture and an Analysis," in Kent, pp. 59, 58, 71.

The more recent work of Jan Marsh, however, has demonstrated that Rossetti began her work at Highgate during 1859, although the exact date remains uncertain. Consequently, Bentley's "conjecture" about the poem no longer necessitates rejecting the date on its manuscript. Marsh's hypothesis, which seems more probable to me than Bentley's, is that *"Goblin Market* was not written explicitly for the girls or Sisters at Highgate, but was prompted by the prospect or challenge of working there, and was perhaps composed, or at least begun, during the period between Christina's initial approach and formal induction" at the Home. See "Christina Rossetti's Vocation: The Importance of *Goblin Market*," *VP* 32 (1994): 244, and Marsh, *CR,* pp. 218–38.

8. "Climate in Respect to Fruit Growing," *Turner and Spencer's Florist, Fruitist, and Garden Miscellany,* May 1859; reprinted in *Gardeners' Chronicle and Agricultural Gazette,* 14 May 1859, p. 424.

9. Shirley Hibberd, "The Late Snowfall and Frost," *Gardeners' Chronicle and Agricultural Gazette,* 9 April 1859, p. 314.

10. "Climate in Respect to Fruit Growing," p. 424.

11. "The Frost on the Morning of the 1st inst," *Gardeners' Chronicle and Agricultural Gazette,* 16 April 1859, p. 338.

12. "The [fruit] crop of 1857. . . was a very heavy one . . . [and] the crop of 1858 in this country was one of the most abundant ever known." M. Saul, "Fruit Prospects," *Gardeners' Chronicle and Agricultural Gazette,* 14 May 1859, p. 424. In a report on the abundance of dried fruit in the market (written several months before the spring frosts), the *Times* reports that "the low prices this season are causing a large consumption of all kinds" of fruit. "Trade Report," *Times* (London), 11 December 1858, p. 5.

13. J. B., "Fruit Prospects," *Gardeners' Chronicle and Agricultural Gazette,* 28 May 1859, p. 466.

14. Saul, p. 424.

15. In mid-April, issues of *Punch* include two cartoons and a poem commenting on the weather: ". . . 'Tis strange / In a few days what a change! / Here we were, a week ago, / Walking ancle-deep in snow, / Now we have to ice our wine, / And with perspiration shine." At this point, before the final April frost, the verse claims that there are fruit trees in bloom. See *Punch, or the London Charivari,* 16 April 1859, p. 161.

16. "Colonial and Foreign Produce Markets: Transactions of the Week," *Economist,* 23 April 1859, pp. 463–64; 30 April 1859, pp. 491–92; 7 May 1859, pp. 520–21.

17. Mary Arseneau, "Incarnation and Interpretation: Christina Rossetti, the Oxford Movement, and *Goblin Market*," *VP* 31 (1993): 84.

18. John Stuart Mill, *On Liberty,* ed. Alburey Castell (Northbrook, Ill.: AHM, 1947), p. 68.

19. Mill contributed many short notes to the *Phytologist: A Botanical Journal* and at least one letter to the *Gardeners' Chronicle.* Biographers have even speculated that a typically vigorous episode of botanical fieldwork may have led to Mill's death in 1873. See John M. Robson, introduction to *Miscellaneous Writings,* vol. 31 of *Collected Works of John Stuart Mill,* ed. John M. Robson (Toronto: University of Toronto Press, 1969; London: Routledge, 1989), pp. xlii–xliii.

20. "Forcing," *Gardeners' Chronicle and Agricultural Gazette,* 24 July 1858, p. 574.

21. "Horticulture. Chapter IV," *Imperial Journal of the Arts and Sciences,* ed. W. J. Macquorn Rankine et al., 2 vols. (Glasgow: William Mackenzie, [1858-66]), 2:84.

22. "Climate in Respect to Fruit Growing," p. 424.

23. "Forcing," p. 574.

24. J. Sheppard, "Heating," *Gardeners' Chronicle and Agricultural Gazette,* 1 December 1860, p. 1062.

25. P. Wallace, "On the Cultivation of Exotic Fruits," *Journal of the Royal Horticultural Society of London,* o.s., 3 (1853): 47.

26. "The grapes grown in Great Britain in the open air are much smaller, and by no means *so luscious,* as those of foreign countries; but those raised in hot-houses are quite equal, if not superior, to the latter" (emphasis added). The pineapple, "though a tropical fruit, is now extensively cultivated in hothouses in this country, and is well known to every one. When of a good sort and healthy, it is the most luscious, and, perhaps, the best fruit that this country produces; and when carefully cultivated, is superior in point of quality to that produced in the West Indies." J. R. McCulloch, *A Dictionary, Practical, Theoretical, and Historical, of Commerce and Commercial Navigation,* new ed. (London: Longman, 1850), pp. 639, 1023.

27. "Calendar of Operations: Forcing Department," *Gardeners' Chronicle and Agricultural Gazette,* 1 January 1859, p. 8.

28. Max Weber, *The Protestant Ethic and the Spirit of Capitalism,* trans. Talcott Parsons (New York: Scribners, 1958), pp. 24-27.

29. Eric Roll, *A History of Economic Thought,* 4th ed. (London: Faber and Faber, 1973), pp. 190-91, 201-2. As Roll notes, Ricardo largely accepted Say's law but rejected its corollary that the increased use of machinery in production would not reduce the demand for labor. See his well-known chapter "On Machinery" in *The Principles of Political Economy and Taxation,* 3d ed. (Homewood, Ill.: Irwin, 1963 [1821]), pp. 228-35.

30. "Notices to Correspondents," *Gardeners' Chronicle and Agricultural Gazette,* 31 December 1859, p. 1056.

31. McCulloch, pp. 944, 804, 290, 639, 1027.

32. "Currants" are actually two different kinds of fruit: the berry grown in England primarily for jam, and the small Mediterranean grape often dried and imported into England.

33. Carpenter, p. 427.

34. McCulloch, p. 45; *Encyclopædia Britannica,* 9th ed. (New York: Scribners, 1878-89), s.v. "Plum"; Mrs. [J. W.] Loudon, et al., eds., *Loudon's Encyclopædia of Plants* (London: Longmans, 1872), p. 423; McCulloch, p. 467.

35. In an 1888 lecture (later published in *Nineteenth Century*), Matthew Arnold compares the class-linked consumption of fruit in England and America: in the United States, "[e]ven luxuries of a certain kind are within a labouring man's easy reach. . . . The abundance and cheapness of fruit is a great boon to people of small

incomes in America. . . . what [English] labourer, or artisan, or small clerk, ever gets hot-house peaches, or Newtown pippins, or Marie Louise pears? Not such good pears, apples, and peaches as those, but pears, apples, and peaches by no means to be despised, such people and their families in America get in plenty." See "Civilisation in the United States," in *The Last Word,* vol. 11 of *The Complete Prose Works of Matthew Arnold,* ed. R. H. Super (Ann Arbor: University of Michigan Press, 1977), p. 354. Arnold was himself an amateur fruit grower (pp. 488–89 n. 354:25–28).

36. Henry Mayhew, *London Labour and the London Poor,* vol. 1 (New York: Dover, 1968), p. 120; see also p. 83.

37. Elizabeth Gaskell, *Cranford* (New York: Oxford University Press, 1972). On the expanding consumption of tea, sugar, and jam (the combination of sugar and fruit) in eighteenth- and nineteenth-century Britain see Sidney W. Mintz, *Sweetness and Power: The Place of Sugar in Modern History* (New York: Sifton-Viking, 1985), pp. 114–50.

38. *A Naval Encyclopædia* (Philadelphia: L. R. Hammersly, 1881), p. 493.

39. Adam Smith, *The Wealth of Nations* (New York: Everyman-Knopf, 1991 [1776]), vol. 1, bk. 3:373.

40. "Pomeloes or Forbidden Fruit," *Gardeners' Chronicle and Agricultural Gazette,* 15 January 1859, p. 39. Almost as tantalizing, the claim, attributed to "Dr. Sickler," appears in the context of a letter about a "fruit sold in Covent Garden market under the name of Pomeloes, or Forbidden Fruit" (pomelos, sometimes indeed referred to as "forbidden fruit," are actually a type of shaddock or grapefruit); just months before Rossetti composed *Goblin Market,* then, someone at Covent Garden Market was hawking "Forbidden Fruit."

41. See William Michael Rossetti, ed., *Ruskin: Rossetti: Preraphaelitism: Papers 1854 to 1862* (New York: Dodd, Mead; London: George Allen, 1899), p. 207; Georgina Battiscombe, *Christina Rossetti: A Divided Life* (New York: Holt, Rinehart and Winston, 1981), p. 102.

42. Carpenter discusses "In the Round Tower at Jhansi, June 8, 1857," the poem that follows *Goblin Market* in *Goblin Market and Other Poems,* in order to argue that the second poem makes explicit what remains hidden in the first, namely, that sisterly gender solidarity only goes so far, and that its limits have to do with "class or racial differences" (p. 430).

Written in response to inaccurate reports during the 1857 "Indian Mutiny" that a white officer had shot first his "pale young wife" and then himself in order to prevent her rape by the "swarming howling wretches down below," "In the Round Tower at Jhansi" demonstrates an obvious historical and ideological specificity absent in *Goblin Market*'s gestures toward fairy-tale timelessness (*CP,* 1:26, lines 5, 3). I would simply point out that the colonial subtext of *Goblin Market,* with its quasi-exotic goblins, citrons from the South, and defense of the domestic against the foreign, is actually expressed in the poem, not merely displaced retroactively onto a work composed a year and a half earlier. See also Jan Marsh, "The Indian Mutiny and Christina Rossetti's First Appearance in *Once a Week,*" *Journal of Pre-Raphaelite Studies,* n.s., 1 (1992): 17-18.

43. John Ruskin, *Unto This Last,* in *The Works of John Ruskin,* ed. E. T. Cook and Alexander Wedderburn, 39 vols. (London: George Allen, 1903-12), 17:113. Subsequently cited in the text as *UTL.*

44. Holt, p. 53.

45. For two divergent critical accounts of the poem's relationship to eating disorders, see Paula Marantz Cohen, "Christina Rossetti's 'Goblin Market': A Paradigm for Nineteenth-Century Anorexia Nervosa," *University of Hartford Studies in Literature* 17 (1985): 1-18; and Deborah Ann Thompson, "Anorexia as a Lived Trope: Christina Rossetti's 'Goblin Market,'" *Mosaic* 24, nos. 3-4 (1991): 89-106. While Cohen simply "diagnoses" the poem as dealing with a "pathology" (pp. 1, 13), Thompson explores the way in which "'Goblin Market' dramatizes the deep link between 'free' market economics, the commodification of women, and consumption disorders" (p. 105).

46. See Jerome J. McGann, "Christina Rossetti's Poems: A New Edition and a Revaluation," *VS* 23 (1980): 247.

47. Helsinger, p. 903.

48. See Helena Michie, "'There Is No Friend Like a Sister': Sisterhood as Sexual Difference," *English Literary History* 56 (1989): 401-21.

49. Helsinger suggests that Jeanie is a version of the eponymous prostitute in Dante Gabriel Rossetti's "Jenny" (pp. 919ff.).

50. Helsinger, pp. 903, 929 n. 1.

51. Marsh, *CR,* pp. 171-72.

52. Published as *A Joy Forever* [originally titled *The Political Economy of Art*], in *Works of John Ruskin* 16:51-52. Subsequently cited as *PE* in the text.

53. Karl Marx, "*Grundrisse,*" in *The Marx-Engels Reader,* p. 232.

54. See Tim Hilton, *John Ruskin: The Early Years, 1819-1859* (New Haven: Yale University Press, 1985), pp. 254-57; John Dixon Hunt, *The Wider Sea: A Life of John Ruskin* (London: J. M. Dent, 1982), pp. 262-64.

55. W. M. Rossetti, *Ruskin: Rossetti,* pp. 258-59.

56. McGann, "Christina Rossetti's Poems," p. 252.

57. Compare Rossetti's playful "Winter: My Secret," in which the "secret" of the poem is that the speaker's unverifiable claim to have a secret occasions a poem that presumes and evokes the reader/addressee's desire to know without satisfying it—and, in the process, creates a fully satisfying short poem (*CP,* 1:47).

58. An early study of *Goblin Market* by B. Ifor Evans goes beyond the obvious step of connecting the goblin men's cries to those of street merchants by noting the

literary sources for Rossetti's representation of their poetic sales pitch. See "The Sources of Christina Rossetti's 'Goblin Market,'" *Modern Language Review* 28 (1933): 161–63.

59. The *Economist* records the importation of 674,061 bushels of lemons and oranges into Britain during the first eleven months of 1857, and *over a million* bushels of them during all twelve months of 1859. After a lag in the spring, then, the destruction of the British fruit crop seems to have helped expand the trade in imported fruit. See "Supplement to the *Economist*," *Economist* 25 Dec. 1858, p. 66; 18 Feb. 1860, p. 90.

60. Thomas Richards, *The Commodity Culture of Victorian England: Advertising and Spectacle, 1851–1914* (Stanford, Calif.: Stanford University Press, 1990), p. 4.

61. Karl Marx, *Capital, Volume One,* in *The Marx-Engels Reader,* pp. 320–21. Subsequently cited as *C* in the text.

62. Ricardo, p. 6. Smith claims that "[t]he value of any commodity . . . to the person who possesses it, and who means not to use it or consume it himself, but to exchange it for other commodities, is equal to the quantity of labour which it enables him to purchase or command. Labour, therefore, is the real measure of the exchangeable value of all commodities" (vol. 1, bk. 1:26). Ricardo considers labor the measure of the value of commodities in a different sense from Smith's; he treats the "relative quantity of labour [that has already gone into the production of commodities] as almost exclusively determining the relative value of commodities" (p. 10).

63. On primitive accumulation see Marx, *Capital,* pp. 431–34. Marx claims that the mysterious "so-called primitive accumulation" (which, according to writers such as Smith, preceded and paved the way for the capitalist economy) "plays in Political Economy about the same part as original sin in theology" (*C,* p. 431).

64. Given this pattern, Helsinger is surely justified in suspecting that "[p]erhaps the fantasy of withdrawal from exchange relations played out in 'Goblin Market' may conceal the desire, not to give and nurture, but to hoard—goods, words, sex, children, and even money" (p. 928).

65. Helsinger, p. 919.

66. Dorothy Mermin, "Heroic Sisterhood in *Goblin Market,*" *VP* 21 (1983): 112.

67. Helsinger, pp. 908–10; Campbell, pp. 393ff.; Marsh, "Christina Rossetti's Vocation," p. 246; see also Marsh, *CR,* pp. 267–79.

68. Gilbert and Gubar, p. 575.

69. I would like to thank everyone who has offered comments and suggestions on this essay, especially Regenia Gagnier (who inspired and guided it), Barbara Gelpi, Donald Gray, Antony H. Harrison, Sujata Iyengar (who, like D. G. Rossetti, supplied the title), and Lorraine Janzen Kooistra (who provided the accompanying illustration). The appearance of E. H. Shepard's cartoon, "Gobbling Market," in *Punch* (March 11, 1942) during World War II suggests how resonant Rossetti's fable about "missing fruit" continued to be in the twentieth-century marketplace (fig. 5.1).

CHAPTER 6

Visualizing the Fantastic Subject

Goblin Market *and the Gaze*

LORRAINE JANZEN KOOISTRA

hristina Rossetti's best-known poetic fantasy, *Goblin Market,* is a
work of immense visual power, employing a figural language both
richly evocative and suggestively vague. With its mixture of the
erotic and the religious, the social and the moral, the childlike and the
profound, *Goblin Market* has always been a potent inspiration for illustrators.
From 1862 to the present, *Goblin Market* has sparked the imaginations of at
least eighteen artists, each of whom has responded to the poem's intriguing
indeterminacies with pictorial representations designed to fix Rossetti's fantastic subject by reifying her metaphors. These illustrated editions offer us a
range of "visual 'positions'"[1] for Rossetti's fantasy in cultural contexts extending from the Pre-Raphaelite to the postmodern. The interaction between
Rossetti's Victorian text and the images that have been produced to accompany it provides a fruitful study in cultural poetics, for visual depiction, as
Gordon Fyfe and John Law observe, "is never just an illustration. . . . [I]t is
the site for the construction and depiction of social difference. To understand
a visualisation is thus to inquire into its provenance and into the social work
that it does . . . to note its principles of exclusion and inclusion, to detect the
roles that it makes available, to understand the way in which they are distributed, and to decode the hierarchies and differences that it naturalises. And

it is also to analyse the ways in which authorship is constructed or concealed and the sense of audience is realised."[2]

Illustrations have the power to visualize Rossetti's poetic fantasy for a variety of audiences in a range of historical times and places. The implications of this power extend well beyond a single poem's history of production and reception to include the larger question of the role of visual culture in identity formation generally[3]; as W. J. T. Mitchell demonstrates in *Picture Theory,* "the tensions between visual and verbal representations are inseparable from struggles in cultural politics and political culture."[4] Thus, in order to understand the "social work" performed by illustration, it is indeed necessary, as Fyfe and Law suggest, to interrogate the ways in which roles are constructed, hierarchies and differences established, and audiences realized. My focus in this study of *Goblin Market's* cultural production from the mid-nineteenth century to the present is on the ways in which feminine subjectivity has been visualized in contexts ranging from fine art books to children's picture books to pornographic magazines. "What is at stake" here, as Rosemary Betterton argues in *Looking On: Images of Femininity in the Visual Arts and Media,* "is the power of images to produce and to define the feminine in specific ways."[5] Indeed, visual culture demands investigation because it is one of the "defining and regulatory practice[s]" by which sexualities are represented, produced, mediated, and transformed.[6] In a work such as *Goblin Market,* whose subject matter turns on the pleasures and transgressions of looking as they relate to the formation of female subjectivity and identity, pictures of women and goblins present spectacles of fantasy and femininity that are neither passive nor innocent. Rather, they have the power to compete with the text for the dominant representation of the story. By visualizing metaphor, artists construct critical lenses through which readers view Rossetti's fantasy. Thus image and text are engaged in a dialogue in which two ways of looking at femininity, and two ways of encoding that vision, are presented to the reader.[7] The dialogic relations between picture and word enact a struggle between spectatorship and spectacle which mirrors *Goblin Market's* own engagement with the conflicting (and conflicted) positions of looking and being looked at.

In illustrated versions of *Goblin Market* the identity of the subject is constructed along a split axis of visual and verbal images in a way that parallels both the conflicted consciousness of Rossetti herself and the split subjectivity of her female subjects, Lizzie and Laura.[8] As feminists from Simone de Beauvoir onward have noted, feminine subjectivity entails a divided consciousness: a woman is simultaneously aware of her self as an independent ego and her self as object. A woman's awareness of her self as "Other" is constructed both through the gaze of the male subject who has the power to perceive and manipulate objects, and through the reciprocal, coopted consent of the woman who "must pretend to be an object."[9] Following feminist theories of the gaze, Dolores Rosenblum has written powerfully about Rossetti's own double awareness of herself as active creative agent and passive artistic model, noting that in *Goblin Market* Rossetti overcomes "the dualism between the 'active' see-er and the 'passive' seen" to the extent that "the model transcends the artist, and the spectacle for all eyes becomes the witness" of Lizzie's restorative actions of watching and rescuing.[10] The transcendence Rosenblum assigns to Rossetti's text, however, is part of the poet's utopian fable, and is limited to her own production of the poem as verbal narrative. When her text is reproduced in illustrated editions, the poet loses authorial control, and the fantasy becomes a collaborative enterprise—a cultural commodity whose production and reception are determined by the imaginative vision of artists and the audiences for whom their images are constructed.

Rossetti's poem contests the traditional paradigm whereby "pleasure in looking . . . [is] split between active/male and passive/female"[11] with her recuperation and celebration of not only the female spectator, but also the redemptive function of woman *as* spectacle. However, many of the visual images that have been produced to illustrate *Goblin Market*'s themes have offered the more familiar story of feminine subjectivity in relation to visual pleasure. Some of these visualizations redirect the subversive energy of the poem by representing Lizzie and Laura as passive objects of the gaze; others comment critically on the text by providing images of female resistance and struggle; all construct the feminine when they compose their fantastic subjects. If Rossetti's poem asserts the need for women to be engaged with their world as lookers and doers, the illustrations have the power to transform these active female heroes into objects to be looked at, still images of beautiful otherness. Readers of illustrated *Goblin Market*s are thus frequently faced with two ways of looking at the same story, and their reading of Rossetti's narrative is mediated by the dialogue between the poetic fantasy and the visual object. For this reason, I will begin by examining the text's attitude to looking before moving on to investigate the ways in which Rossetti's fantasy has been offered to the gaze of its readers in illustrated editions.

LOOKING AT ROSSETTI'S POETIC FANTASY

Goblin Market is a poem that turns on women's relation to looking and being looked at. Rossetti's initial title for the poem—"A Peep at the Goblins"—focuses on its scopophilic themes. While at first blush the word "peep" may evoke the innocent playfulness of her cousin Eliza Bray's *A Peep at the Pixies*,[12] in the context of the narrative itself "peep" becomes overlaid with the connotations of furtive looking, stolen glances at the forbidden, clandestine curiosity. Both the feminine desire to look at the world and the prohibitions against it are established in the sisters' opening speeches. "We must not look at goblin men," says Laura, even as she is "pricking up her golden head" to get a better view. "You should not peep at goblin men," replies Lizzie, as she "cover[s] up her eyes, / . . . lest they should look."[13] Throughout the first half of the poem, Laura maintains her curiosity—her desire to see and experience—while Lizzie keeps her eyes deliberately closed to the wonders of the world: Laura "stare[s]," but Lizzie "dare[s] not look" (105, 243). The goblins and their luscious fruit become objects of Laura's gaze, sensuous emblems of her desire. She succumbs to temptation first because of what she sees and imagines and only secondarily because of what she tastes. When she can no longer hear the goblins' cries and is prohibited from buying more fruit, her first reaction is to feel "blind," not hungry (259). Her "sunk eyes" mirror her wasting subjectivity as she begins to see false mirages of her desire (288–92). At last Lizzie, who "watch[es] her sister's cankerous care" (300), becomes impelled to action, leaves her cottage for the haunted glen, "And for the first time in her life / [Begins] to listen and look" (327–28).

Venturing into the outside world means that Lizzie becomes a spectacle as well as a spectator: the goblins "spy" her at the very moment that she begins her furtive "peeping" (330) and immediately begin their visual seduction as they hold up dishes laden with fruit: "Look at our apples," they tell her, describing their wares in beautiful detail (352–62). Unlike Laura, however, Lizzie looks without succumbing to temptation; for her, the goblins and their fruits are not objects of desire, but means to an end. With her clear-sighted vision, Lizzie is able to recognize, as Laura was not, that the goblins' "looks were evil" (397). Thus, although the goblins viciously pummel her with their fruit, Lizzie resists them and triumphantly brings home the restorative juices in syrupy streaks upon her face. When Laura kisses her, tastes the goblin juices, and falls into a fit that looks like death, Lizzie watches over her until Laura revives at dawn with her eyes clear and full of light, ready to see the world in new ways and to picture her experience for others in the language of story.

One of the lessons of *Goblin Market* is the visual/spiritual one of learning how to look and interpret correctly—to know that what seems fair may be foul: attractive goblin men betray; delectable fruits poison.[14] This is certainly the lesson that Laura learns, and the one she passes on to the children at the end of the narrative. But Lizzie, too, learns something. She learns that a woman cannot live in the world without looking and being looked at. And she learns that, while these activities are paradoxically both destructive and redemptive, they are also essential to life, to love, to creativity. As a result of Lizzie's actions, Laura regains control over her selfhood; the sisters' relationship achieves a more intense level of love through their painfully acquired knowledge and power; and their experience is affirmed through the continuity of children and storytelling. In the course of their goblin encounters, Lizzie and Laura learn to look at themselves and each other in new ways, and to formulate alternate visions of female subjectivity.

Similarly, Rossetti invites her readers to contemplate the ways in which her hero, Lizzie, has the power to be both spectator and spectacle without forfeiting her individual subjectivity. In Christian terms, she can be "in the world but not of it"; in feminist terms, she can see men looking at her without becoming alienated from her own selfhood. In this way, the dynamics of looking in *Goblin Market* radically challenge the binary opposition between active male "see-er" and passive female "seen." Rossetti's fantasy posits a world in which women can take pleasure in looking and survive the ordeals of being looked at to emerge triumphant as storytellers who deliberately display themselves to the gaze of others as part of an exemplary spectacle—a redemptive image of feminine power and Christian virtue to be seen, understood, and imitated. Such a spectacle takes on special significance if we imagine Rossetti's ideal audience to be, as Jan Marsh posits, the girls and sisters at the Highgate Penitentiary for Fallen Women, where Rossetti was working as a lay sister when she wrote her poem.[15]

Goblin Market is one of the many Victorian fairy tales whose alternate visions staged a social protest against the status quo by expressing a utopian desire for a better world. As Jack Zipes's groundbreaking work in the field suggests, these utopian tales had a characteristically "feminine, if not feminist" slant, not only because of their strong female protagonists, but also because of their emphatic suggestion "that utopia will not be just another men's world." The feminism of these fantasies—and Zipes specifically cites

Goblin Market in this instance—involves "an intense quest for the female self."[16] Many other readers of *Goblin Market* have seen precisely this kind of quest in the poem.[17] Yet at the same time that Rossetti struggled to envision a female subjectivity encompassing action, desire, knowledge, and power, she was also constrained by the conventions of Victorian society, which constructed the feminine as passive, innocent, beautiful, and helpless.[18] These were certainly the feminine virtues Rossetti herself conveyed when she modeled for the mother of God in two of her brother Gabriel's early works, *The Girlhood of Mary Virgin* and *Ecce Ancilla Domini.*[19] As Rosenblum points out, Rossetti's dual experience as artist and model produced a split consciousness that is enacted in her poetry itself in "a range of seeing acts and visual 'positions.'"[20] In trying to envision new ways of looking at women in *Goblin Market,* Rossetti both exploits and subverts the notion that women are objects of the gaze. Drawing on a religious rather than a carnal iconic tradition, Rossetti attempts to revision femininity by offering the story of Laura and Lizzie as an exemplary spectacle of strong and active womanhood.

LOOKING AT PICTURES

When Rossetti's poetic images are illustrated, however, she loses control over her female subjects, her feminist fantasy, and her religious iconography. Illustrated editions of the poem tend to position the reader/viewer outside a picture frame in which Lizzie and Laura become passive objects of the gaze, particularly in scenes depicting the girls' encounters with the goblins or relations with each other. What is at issue here is not so much the objectification as the positioning. All images, of course, objectify. Indeed, as Kate Myers reminds us, "There is a sense in which the process of sight and perception necessarily entails objectification in order to conceptualize and give meaning to the object of our gaze."[21] Objectification, then, is part of the imaging process: verbal imagery evokes pictures in our mind; visual imagery displays pictures to our sight. The difference is that in illustration the process of composition fixes the subject and positions the viewer according to a preset paradigm of perception. In illustrated editions of *Goblin Market,* the reader has been situated in a number of ways vis à vis the text, each one related not only to a particular way of looking at women, but also to an ideology of femininity implicit in the conventional formations of fantasy. For this reason, Rossetti's attempt to construct alternate images of

GOBLIN MARKET
and other poems
by Chriſtina Roſſetti

"Golden head by golden head"

London and Cambridge
Macmillan and Co. 1862

Fig. 6.1. Dante Gabriel Rossetti, "Golden head by golden head." Title-page design for Christina Rossetti, *Goblin Market and Other Poems* (London: Macmillan, 1862). Reproduced with the kind permission of the Osborne Collection of Early Children's Books, Toronto Public Library.

femininity in her fable of female heroism is often counteracted by traditional representations of sexual difference.

The reader/viewer's position as sexual voyeur was established by the poet's brother, Gabriel Rossetti, in the title-page plate he designed for the first edition of the poem (fig. 6.1).[22] "Golden head by golden head" is composed as a window into the feminine boudoir in which the audience is situated as voyeurs who "peep," not at the goblins, but at the girls. A vignette set into a delicate framework of roses, the picture is a close-up of the sisters wrapped in each others' arms, dreaming together in a bed hung about by exotic draperies. This image of female innocence and beauty is tinged with eroticism, suggested by the women's close embrace, the luxurious hangings, and the closely framed, but clandestine, view of a moment both private and vulnerable. Lizzie and Laura are pictured at their most passive, and in a way that makes them subject to every Peeping Tom's fantasies. Indeed, the dream balloon in the upper left corner provides a telescopic opening into the bedroom through which the goblins can view the unconscious sleepers. It is not clear which woman is dreaming of the goblins and their fruit, though it is presumably Laura, who has, by this point in the poem, already succumbed to temptation and exchanged a lock of hair for the goblins' enticing wares. One sister—perhaps the one who dreams of goblins—clutches the other's golden hair as she sleeps, thus subtly intensifying the erotic charge of the scene. Since the sisters are so nearly identical as to be indistinguishable, "Golden head by golden head" pictures a male fantasy in which female sexuality is both passively available and pleasurably doubled.

Few illustrators have followed Gabriel Rossetti's lead in visualizing this evocative scene.[23] However, both the position of sexual voyeur and the framing of feminine passivity established by his vignette have been repeated in the work of a number of other artists, especially in the scene in which Lizzie is attacked by the goblins, usually titled "White and Golden Lizzie Stood." In the early years of this century, when the Victorian tradition of fairy painting survived in the colored plates of gift books and children's fairy tales, illustrations of *Goblin Market*'s climactic scene often followed a well-established iconography. As Barbara Garlick describes the genre, "the female figure is positioned in relation to hobgoblins, sprites, strange creatures and grotesque apparitions as a beautiful centre in the world of faery, a world which is full of activity and variety in contrast to the blandness of this central figure." Such "visual encoding of the feminine" within the fairy picture worked to emphasize "passive otherness and chastity," often by using the

They trod and hustled her,
Elbowed and jostled her,
Clawed with their nails.

Fig. 6.2. Dion Clayton Calthrop, "They trod and hustled her / Elbowed and jostled her, / Clawed with their nails." Illustration for Christina Rossetti, *Goblin Market* (London and Edinburgh: T. C. and E. C. Jack, [1906]), facing p. 22. Reproduced with the kind permission of The British Library (Shelf Mark 11646.de.51).

diminution of scale to render discordant features innocuous.[24] This strategy is especially evident in the illustrated versions of *Goblin Market* as a fairy tale for children that began to emerge at the turn of the century.[25]

Children's book artists who depict scenes of dramatic encounter, temptation, and attack in Rossetti's poem have the special problem of not making such moments either too violent or too sexy. One way that the frightening aspect of *Goblin Market* has been muted to make it appropriate children's fare is by diminishing the goblins to tiny little elfish folk no more annoying than insects. This technique is evident in the work of one of the first artists to illustrate the poem for a juvenile audience, Dion Clayton Calthrop (1906).[26] Calthrop was a commercial artist so active in Edwardian fantasy illustration that he confessed he had "made rather a corner in fairies."[27] His goblins are tiny spider-like creatures with long limbs who do not seem to be at all threatening (fig. 6.2). Lizzie withstands their attack not by standing "White and golden . . . // Like a beacon left alone / In a hoary roaring sea" (408, 412–13), but by sitting in a recumbent posture looking as if she is asleep. Such a representation transforms Rossetti's active and resilient hero into a passive victim whose virtue is natural to her, not an enacted choice. A similar representation of Lizzie standing "white and golden" amid diminutive grotesques was produced in 1912 by Margaret Tarrant, the well-known illustrator who dominated the children's book field in the domain of the fanciful and the sentimental until well into this century (fig. 6.3).[28] Tarrant positions Lizzie on a grassy knoll surrounded by goblins. Drawing on the iconography of the fairy painting genre, Tarrant represents the goblins as winged creatures who hover in the air holding out gigantic fruit. Lizzie stands centrally positioned directly facing the viewer, apparently unhurt by the assault: her neat attire is not even disarrayed. The composition works to reinforce the notion of female sexuality as passive or sleeping, while at the same time emphasizing the inviolability of the pure woman.

Perhaps the most influential of children's book artists to depict this scene is Arthur Rackham, who illustrated *Goblin Market* in 1933.[29] Along with Edmund Dulac, Rackham helped both to popularize and to domesticate Victorian fairy painting in the twentieth century although, as Jeremy Maas points out, "somehow the fairies have lost their transparency and become opaque" in his work.[30] The fleshliness of Rackham's fairies added an eroticism to his illustrations, enhancing their appeal for the collectors who were his best customers. By the thirties, Rackham's ordinary trade editions were no longer selling as well, but his limited de luxe editions were "vastly over-applied for."[31]

Fig. 6.3. Margaret W. Tarrant, "White and golden Lizzie stood." Illustration for Christina Rossetti, *Goblin Market* (London: George Routledge and Sons, [1912]), facing p. 33. Reproduced with the kind permission of The British Library (Shelf Mark 011651.h94) and The Medici Society Limited, London.

As hot collectors' items, Rackham's books always had a dual drawing room/nursery audience. Indeed, Rackham's *Goblin Market* dramatically demonstrates what Jacqueline Rose has called "the impossibility of children's fiction."[32] Arthur Rackham's illustrated gift books were not only produced *by* adults, but also, in part at least, *for* adults. In these de luxe editions the child exists only as a transparent category useful for invoking a particular kind of innocence and beauty in a fantasy world.

Rackham's "White and golden Lizzie stood" draws on the fairy painting tradition by positioning the female figure as the luminous center in a dark world of feral activity (fig. 6.4). The spindly-limbed woodland creatures behind Lizzie appear to be so much a part of the tree that the forest itself, in true nightmare fashion, seems to be coming alive. All the activity of the composition emanates from the goblins and the haunted glen they inhabit. Lizzie is a passive figure in the center but, unlike earlier representations of this scene for children (such as Calthrop's or Tarrant's), she is not blandly innocent. On the contrary, Lizzie seems to be enjoying her goblin experience. Her eyes have a come-hither look and the positioning of her body suggests pleasure rather than protest. If, as some critics have argued, there is a rape fantasy submerged in Rossetti's *Goblin Market*,[33] Rackham's "White and golden Lizzie stood" makes that darkness visible. The sexual associations are acceptable within the context of a children's book because the illustration draws on the fairy painting convention of domesticating fantasy by visually encoding the feminine as passive otherness and chaste purity. At the same time, however, Lizzie's frontal position, in a taut posture with her head thrown back—a figure set off by the concentric patterning of the surrounding goblin grotesques—draws on what Martha Kingsbury has identified as a characteristic configuration for the *femme fatale* in visual representations.[34] As a *femme fatale* in a fantasy world, Lizzie is presented as an image of a feminine sexuality that is both pure and damned—dangerous to herself but delightful to others—to add titillation to the consumer's voyeuristic experience. Positioned to provoke the pleasure of possession in the viewer, Rackham's female figure panders to the male fantasy that even nice women want it, and that innocence is merely a dress that can be stripped off—like Lizzie's missing gown—to reveal aberrant female desire.

In the only fully nude representation of Lizzie in all illustrated versions of *Goblin Market,* the female figure is again positioned frontally, with her head turned away but her eyes exchanging a sidelong look with the goblins who surround her (fig. 6.5). With its sophisticated citation of many strands from

Fig. 6.4. Arthur Rackham, "White and golden Lizzie stood." Illustration for Christina Rossetti, *Goblin Market* (London: George G. Harrap, 1933), p. 36. Reproduced with the kind permission of the Osborne Collection of Early Children's Books, Toronto Public Library.

Western art's tradition of visual fantasy, Kinuko Craft's illustration of "White and golden Lizzie stood" for *Playboy* magazine (1973) parodically plays with centuries of sexual imagery.[35] To begin with, Craft capitalizes on what Linda Nochlin calls "one of the prime topoi of erotic imagery: comparison of the desirable body with ripe fruit."[36] Lizzie is pictured in the midst of a veritable cornucopia of erotic pleasure, surrounded by an array of genital fruit representative of both sexes. Craft's composition also evokes other images drawn from the erotic tradition in visual art. By parodying Rackham's earlier illustration of the same scene, Craft not only plays up the scene's possibilities as a rape fantasy, but also reaches back to the nineteenth-century tradition of fairy painting. At the same time, with her demonic goblins eerily reminiscent of the unsettling fantasies of Hieronymus Bosch, Craft clarifies the sexual sadism underlying the deceptively innocent surface of the fairy genre.[37] This Boschian underworld provides the nightmare setting for Craft's pastiche of Botticelli's *The Birth of Venus* as an image of seductive eros and innocent beauty in the process of corruption. With her half-turned face and serpentine hair, her right hand held up against her breasts in a manner that highlights rather than disguises their beauty, and her left hand positioned over her pudenda, Lizzie is clearly a perverse stand-in for Botticelli's famous Goddess of Love. The effect of Craft's visual references, of course, is to overlay putatively "innocent" representations with sexually explicit themes. At the same time, Craft exploits the positioning of the viewer for whom Western art has traditionally produced the nude. As John Berger puts it, "the 'ideal' spectator is always assumed to be male and the image of the woman is designed to flatter him" as one whose gaze denotes ownership, power, control.[38] Certainly in *Playboy*, which markets itself as "Entertainment for Men," the sex of Craft's audience may be understood as relatively hegemonic.

Because Craft's illustrations for *Goblin Market* appear in the context of a set of images marketed and distributed by the pornography industry, the positioning of the viewer and the object of the gaze are more sexually defined than in any other depiction of Rossetti's poem. However, while Craft's representation of female sexuality may be more explicit than other illustrations we have viewed thus far, it is, nevertheless, on a continuum with, rather than opposed to, many children's book versions of "White and golden Lizzie stood." Theories of spectatorship and the gaze are based too rigidly on a binary model in which, as Laura Mulvey claims, "The determining male gaze projects its phantasy onto the female figure which is styled accordingly."[39] While it is true that in illustrations like Craft's "White and golden Lizzie stood" Lizzie

Fig. 6.5. Kinuko Craft, "White and golden Lizzie stood." Illustration for Christina Rossetti, *"Goblin Market:* A Ribald Classic," *Playboy* 20 (September 1973), p. 117. Reproduced by Special Permission of *Playboy* magazine. Copyright © 1973 by *Playboy* magazine.

loses the power and control ascribed to her by the verbal narrative to become an erotic icon projecting both desire and sexual availability, it is also true that many visualizations of this scene, regardless of the sex of the artist or the age of the audience, construct similar images of femininity. Indeed, it is not accidental that Craft's pornographic illustration parodies Rackham's children's book version of the same scene, for her purposes are much the same: to capitalize on traditional views of feminine innocence and purity, while simultaneously offering a contradictory message of female sexual desire.

Not all illustrators of this scene, however, position the viewer as voyeur and the female subject as passive erotic icon. On the contrary, some artists respond to Rossetti's suggestive metaphors by depicting the struggle between the girl and the goblins in such a way as to emphasize womanly sacrifice, strength, and resistance. In this way, Rossetti's poem is envisioned as a spiritual, rather than a carnal, spectacle to be contemplated by the viewer, while the femininity of her subject is presented in terms of martyrdom and self-sacrifice rather than sexuality and desire. Such illustrations respond both to the religious implications of the text's imagery and to a long tradition of viewing the essential feminine nature as sacrificial and altruistic.

In 1893 Laurence Housman became the first artist to illustrate "White and golden Lizzie stood," in the lavishly decorated edition he designed for Macmillan.[40] He is also one of the few artists to focus on the religious significance of Rossetti's metaphors. Housman's version of "White and golden Lizzie stood" is a double-page spread (fig. 6.6). On the verso, the cloaked goblins are hawking their wares. The recto depicts their violent assault on Lizzie. The goblins are not diminutive fairy folk but full-sized demonic creatures, part man, part beast, drawn from some surreal underworld. Housman interprets the scene as a religious allegory. In this crowded composition, the woman, the tempters, and the tree unite in a richly allusive symbolism simultaneously pointing backward to the Fall and forward to Redemption. The goblins who pull and tug at Lizzie are both a demon crew wishing to bring about Eve's certain death by forcing her to eat the forbidden fruit and, at the same time, a host of revilers abusing the patiently suffering Christ. Putting the tree and the cross in the same place, Housman's composition not only draws on a long tradition of biblical typology, but also presents a radical feminist iconography characteristic of his work.[41] With her feet locked together and her upraised arms hung from the branch of the tree, Lizzie becomes a suffering female Christ who redeems the sinful Eve. This complex illustration asks the viewer to experience and interpret the composition, not to stand outside its frame and visually possess it.

Other illustrations of this scene that refuse to construct a position of voyeurism for the reader/viewer and demand instead an active engagement with the image are found in two contemporary *Goblin Markets* for children. George Gershinowitz's "White and golden Lizzie stood" is unique in that his is the only depiction to exclude the goblins from the scene (fig. 6.7).[42] This elimination of the narrative's details of male violence and abuse allows him to focus instead on female strength and resistance. Gershinowitz's *Goblin Market* is not the story of women's victimization, but rather the story of women's choices, actions, and consequences. On the other hand, Martin Ware's four-frame design for this scene focuses squarely on violence and its

Fig. 6.6. Laurence Housman, "White and golden Lizzie stood." Double-page illustration for Christina Rossetti, *Goblin Market* (London: Macmillan, 1893), pp. 44–45. Reproduced with the kind permission of the Osborne Collection of Early Children's Books, Toronto Public Library.

effects by fragmenting Lizzie's experience of abuse into its component parts (fig. 6.8).[43] Rather than depicting the chain of metaphors beginning with "White and golden Lizzie stood," which, when visualized, can have the effect of iconicizing Lizzie, Ware chooses instead to illustrate the sequence describing her physical experience as the goblins

> Elbowed and jostled her,
> Clawed with their nails,
> . . . .
> Tore her gown and soiled her stocking,
> Twitched her hair out by the roots,
> Stamped upon her tender feet. . . . (399–405)

Ware's first frame includes a goblin man, but the other frames show only human hands with sharp nails and a bestial, clawed foot. Ware also captures the dual animal/human nature of these strange "fruit-merchant men" by picturing the goblin with a rat's head and a naked male torso. Lizzie herself looks out at the viewer directly. The exchange of looks locks the viewer into the scene as a complicit participant in her suffering. In the second frame, Lizzie's pain is focused on more directly as the goblin moves out of the picture to allow Lizzie's screaming face and ripped dress to articulate the intensity of her experience. The last two frames cut up her body into parts, so that her suffering is both itemized and prolonged. Ware's etching, designed for a book marketed for children aged nine to eleven, is a challenging and unsettlingly literal account of Rossetti's language of violence.

But the etching is also challenging for another reason. One of the feminist arguments against the spectatorship implicit in pornography is that it denies women wholeness by fragmenting their bodies, reducing them to fetishized parts to be visually consumed. Many representations of women, however— including this illustration designed for a juvenile audience—fragment the female figure, just as children's picture books may also depict women as passive victims of male violence. Pornography does not have a monopoly on such images, nor is it the only form of representation that "objectifies" women. It is precisely because femininity is constructed in the visual images which are part of Western culture's sexual discourse that all representations of the feminine demand scrutiny and analysis. Clearly, it is not the act of representation itself that automatically degrades women by reducing them to the status of objects; meanings do not inhere in pictures any more than they do in words. Rather, meanings take shape at the moment of viewing as well as during the act of production. As Rosalind Coward comments, "Meaning is given to a representation by its context, use and the arrangement of elements in it. The meanings of an image are decided by how it is lit, framed, the position of the subject, where the look is directed, and so on."[44] In Ware's illustration of Lizzie's attack by the goblins, the fragmented pictorial narrative prevents the viewer from controlling and visually possessing the scene. The viewer is not given a detached position of power but is required to work at putting the pieces together in order to understand the represented experience.

This is less true of a sequence of four pictures Ware designed to illustrate the moment in the text when Lizzie returns from the haunted glen calling to Laura to "Hug me, kiss me, suck my juices / Squeezed from goblin fruits for you" (468-69) (fig. 6.9). The pictorial sequence begins by illustrating the lines

Fig. 6.7. George Gershinowitz, "Lizzie." Illustration for Christina Rossetti, *Goblin Market* (Boston: David R. Godine, 1981), p. 27. Reproduced with the kind permission of David R. Godine, Publisher. Illustration copyright © 1981 by George Gershinowitz.

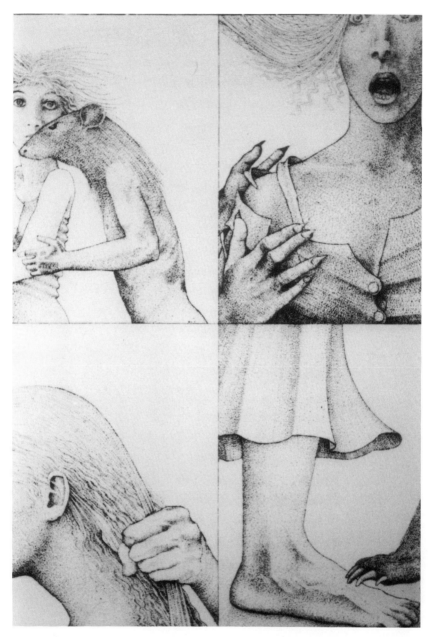

Fig. 6.8. Martin Ware, "Elbowed and jostled her . . ." Etching for *Goblin Market* (London: Victor Gollancz, 1980), p. 34. Reproduced with the kind permission of the artist.

"Laura started from her chair, / Flung her arms up in the air, / Clutched her hair" (475–77). The initial two pictures depict Laura's reaction to Lizzie's sacrifice. In the first frame, an empty chair is tipped up against the wall, dramatically conveying her impulsive haste and anxiety; the second gives a view of Laura in profile, her hands gripping her head, her shadow dark against the wall. The effect is to make the viewer the source of light in the composition, a powerful position. The next two pictures remove the shadows and place Lizzie and Laura in undifferentiated white space. Illustrating the lines "She clung about her sister, / Kissed and kissed and kissed her" (485–86), the final two pictures show Lizzie and Laura in a close embrace. The first depicts Lizzie with her back to the viewer as Laura kisses her. The second moves the viewer in on a close-up of Lizzie, with her head cut off by the picture frame so that her mouth, expressive of pleasure, becomes the main focus. Laura is in profile beside her, sucking her face as a displaced symbol for the breast which is also removed from view, but which Laura's fingers are clearly stroking.

Despite the juvenile audience,[45] this is an erotic sequence that interprets the love between the sisters in much the same way that Mary Wilson Carpenter does when she claims Rossetti's poem is about the kind of "'sisterhood' which . . . permits the female gaze to feast on the female form," substituting the desire for phallic goblin fruit with the desire for the maternal body. Carpenter claims that in the exchange of female gazes, feminine subjectivity is confirmed and hierarchies of sexual difference denied.[46] But within the poem itself there is, in fact, no "exchange of female gazes": the eyes of Lizzie and Laura are directed only toward the male goblins and their fruit. Moreover, Laura's feasting on Lizzie is a gustatory rather than a visual experience for her. Only for the reader does this scene become a visual feast for the imaginative eye. Rossetti's evocative language deliberately sets out to make the encounter between the sisters a spectacle to be contemplated, perhaps even an object to be consumed at the moment that Laura consumes Lizzie. Like Laura, the reader is being taught to look and interpret correctly. In witnessing this moment of all-consuming love, Rossetti's reader is invited to contemplate caritas and agape rather than eros—to consume the offered body eucharistically rather than erotically.

But the offered spectacle, of course, cannot be contained once the poem is reproduced and received in other contexts. Meaning is not single, but multiple, and Rossetti's metaphors are notoriously multivalent. Moreover, if the poem's metaphors seem to require a redirection of desire from physical to spiritual, they do so in particularly physical ways. For this reason, Rossetti's

Fig. 6.9. Martin Ware, "Laura started from her chair. . . ." Etching for *Goblin Market* (London: Victor Gollancz, 1980), p. 42. Reproduced with the kind permission of the artist.

figurative language in the scene in which Laura kisses Lizzie has been read sexually at least as often as it has been interpreted spiritually. For this reason, too, *Goblin Market*'s "Hug me, kiss me, suck my juices" scene has always been a popular one with illustrators, whose visualizations of the love between the sisters have explored the full range of sacred and secular possibilities.

Sexually explicit versions of the sisters' love have appeared in two fantasy publications directed at predominately male audiences: the adult fantasy comic *Pacific Comics* (1984) and *Playboy* magazine (1973). Mixing erotic fantasy with the horror genre, the comic-book artist, John Bolton, depicts a ravaged Lizzie running home to embrace Laura (fig. 6.10).[47] In the next scene, the wasted Laura reaches out of the shadows like a ghoul. Beside her, the overturned chair speaks of her anxious desire. The final strip shows Laura feasting on Lizzie in a scene that evokes vampirism as much as it does lesbianism, thus adding the thrill of horror to erotic pleasure. The feminine here is defined as both seductive and dangerous, sacrificial and insatiable. Similarly, in Kinuko Craft's *Playboy* illustration, the "Love me" scene is presented as a specifically sexual relationship between the two sisters, who are depicted engaged in oral sex in an idyllic pastoral setting (fig. 6.11). Here the feminine is defined almost exclusively in terms of beauty, desire, and pleasure. While the focus of the scene appears to be female pleasure, however, the context of this illustration in a men's magazine makes it clear that this is a spectacle addressed to a protagonist who does not appear in the composition itself but is nevertheless artfully positioned in front of the picture: the male consumer who has purchased the image for his enjoyment.[48] Craft's illustration of Lizzie's and Laura's sexual embrace participates in what John Ellis describes as the pornography industry's promotion of female sexual pleasure "to the status of a fetish in order to provide representations of sexuality which are more 'explicit' for an audience conceived of as male." Lesbian activities are staged for the pleasure of the man who owns and thus controls the image.[49] Such stagings of women's pleasure, as Luce Irigaray suggests in her speculations on the significance of woman as a fetishized object of the gaze in pornographic images, actually function to demonstrate masculine power.[50]

But feminine sexuality constructed for the pleasure of the male gaze is not the only way in which this scene from Rossetti's fantasy has been visualized. Other illustrations of this climactic meeting between the sisters construct the feminine in images that draw out both the religious and the feminist meanings of Rossetti's metaphors. In George Gershinowitz's illustration, for example (fig. 6.12), the glowing colors, rich detail, and positioning of the sisters

Fig. 6.10. John Bolton, "She cried 'Laura' up the garden. . . ." Illustration for Christina Rosetti [*sic*], *Goblin Market* (*Pacific Comics* 1, no. 1 [1984]), p. 17. Reproduced with the kind permission of the artist. Artwork © John Bolton.

Fig. 6.11. Kinuko Craft, "She kissed and kissed her with a hungry mouth." Illustration for Christina Rossetti, "*Goblin Market:* A Ribald Classic," *Playboy* 20 (September 1973), pp. 118-19. Reproduced by Special Permission of *Playboy* magazine. Copyright © 1973 by *Playboy* magazine.

develop the sensuality, even the passion of the scene, but the sexual element is downplayed. Lizzie's offering of herself is sacrificial rather than erotic. To emphasize the point, Gershinowitz draws the viewer's attention to an enormous Rose of Sharon bloom in the foreground, from which a hummingbird is sucking nectar. The implied analogy links the girls to a natural world of nurture and restoration. At the same time, the image introduces a biblical typology that associates Lizzie with the mother of Christ, making her a type of Mary to redeem the sinful Eve. The Rose of Sharon is, after all, Mary's flower. Lizzie's redemptive power is highlighted, moreover, by the fact that Laura ignores the fruit escaping from her sister's golden hair to feed instead on the juices that form like drops of sacrificial blood on Lizzie's throat.

While most artists have produced erotic or religious meanings for this scene, others, like the late Pre-Raphaelite artist Florence Harrison,[51] have elaborated the text's feminist vision. As we have seen, erotic iconography often works by situating the viewer outside the frame of the picture in a position of power and control; religious iconography, on the other hand, frequently directs the viewer to contemplate the spiritual significance of the scene by reading and interpreting its symbols. Florence Harrison's composition asks her viewers to contemplate the relationship between the sisters by creating, as Carpenter does in her interpretation of the poem, an exchange of looks as Laura learns of Lizzie's sacrifice (fig. 6.13). Harrison's version of the encounter between the sisters is remarkable for the passion of that interlocked gaze, from which the viewer seems excluded. By illustrating the moment before the kiss, Harrison refuses to construct a position of voyeurism for her viewer, thereby focusing on female relationship rather than sexual exchange.

Goblin Market is, of course, a poem about both female relationship and sexual exchange. Indeed, Rossetti's change in title from "A Peep at the Goblins" to "Goblin Market" draws attention precisely to the exchange value of women in the sexual marketplace.[52] In Marxist terms, *Goblin Market* is about commodity fetishism—about how, in capitalist, patriarchal society, the production of women as objects of exchange and as objects of the look alienates them from their own bodies.[53] When Jeanie, "Who should have been a bride" (313), subjects herself to the goblins' gaze and falls prey to their enticing wares, she suffers the ultimate alienation of death. Laura also becomes estranged from her body in her wasting sickness, refusing food until she too almost dies. Even Lizzie seems to go out of her body in her martyred rapture when she displaces her pain and laughs "in heart to feel the drip / Of juice that syrupped all her face" (433–34). Lizzie's experience, however, stages a

Fig. 6.12. George Gershinowitz, "She kissed and kissed her with a hungry mouth." Illustration for Christina Rossetti, *Goblin Market* (Boston: David R. Godine, 1981), p. 35. Reproduced with the kind permission of David R. Godine, Publisher. Illustration copyright © 1981 by George Gershinowitz.

Fig. 6.13. Florence Harrison, "'For your sake I have braved the glen / And had to do with goblin merchant men.'" Illustration for *Poems by Christina Rossetti* (London, Glasgow, and Bombay: Blackie and Son, 1910), p. 20. Reproduced with the kind permission of The British Library (Shelf Mark KTC.11.b.11).

spectacular reversal in which she can both redeem her sister's looks and preserve her own identity. For this reason *Goblin Market* is not, as Garlick claims, "an angry poem in which woman is both active subject, and fetishised object of the gaze,"[54] but rather a subversive narrative which celebrates a femininity that can recuperate the spectacle and educate the spectator. On the other hand, *Goblin Market*'s illustrations have often undermined this exemplary representation of female power and returned Rossetti's hero to her cultural position as erotic icon. What a century and more of *Goblin Market* illustrations indicate is that the visual language for representing images of women that are both powerful and positive is extremely limited. Despite women's ability to imagine a subjectivity for themselves that moves beyond the proscriptions of gender, visual culture has the power to regulate and define femininity in particularly inhibiting ways. If *Goblin Market* is, indeed, a feminist fable of an imagined utopia in which women can subject themselves to the gaze and survive with their selfhoods intact, then few artists have been able to construct images equal to its vision.[55]

NOTES

1. I borrow the phrase from Rosenblum. In her chapter on "The Female Pose: Model and Artist, Spectacle and Witness," Rosenblum elaborates on the "visual metaphor . . . involved in issues of identity," and discusses how "the awareness of self as other . . . is represented in Rossetti's poems by a range of seeing acts and visual 'positions,'" most notably in *Goblin Market* (p. 110). This paper investigates how the "seeing acts and visual 'positions'" in Rossetti's *Goblin Market* are reproduced, reinterpreted, and revised in the illustrations that have been produced for the poem, and discusses the ways in which visual culture contributes to the formation of female identity.

2. Gordon Fyfe and John Law, introduction to *Picturing Power: Visual Depiction and Social Relations: The Sociological Review, Monograph #35* (New York and London: Routledge, 1988), p. 1. Qtd. in Julie Codell, "The Aura of Mechanical Reproduction: Victorian Art and the Press," *Victorian Periodicals Review* 24, no. 1 (1991): 4-10.

3. I have argued elsewhere about the impact of illustrations on *Goblin Market*'s history of production and reception. See "Modern Markets for *Goblin Market*," VP 32 (1994): 249-77.

4. W. J. T. Mitchell, *Picture Theory: Essays on Verbal and Visual Representation* (Chicago and London: University of Chicago Press, 1994), p. 3.

5. Rosemary Betterton, ed., *Looking On: Images of Femininity in the Visual Arts and Media* (London and New York: Pandora, 1987), p. 5.

6. Lynda Nead, *Myths of Sexuality: Representations of Women in Victorian Britain* (Oxford: Basil Blackwell, 1988), p. 8.

7. Throughout this paper, I adapt the notion of dialogism in the novel that M. M. Bakhtin elaborates in *The Dialogic Imagination: Four Essays by M. M. Bakhtin,* ed. Michael Holquist, trans. Caryl Emerson and Michael Holquist (Austin: University of Texas Press, 1981) to the specific relations of image and word as they interact with their own verbal and visual "languages." For a detailed explication of the dialogics of illustrated books, see Lorraine Janzen Kooistra, *The Artist as Critic: Bitextuality in Fin-de-Siècle Illustrated Books* (Aldershot: Scolar, 1995).

8. Many critics have noted that Lizzie and Laura may be viewed as two aspects of a single female subjectivity. See especially Winston Weathers, "Christina Rossetti: The Sisterhood of Self," *VP* 3 (1965): 81-89.

9. Simone de Beauvoir, *The Second Sex,* trans. H. M. Parshley (New York: Vintage Books, 1989), pp. 297, 371, 357.

10. Rosenblum, p. 113.

11. Laura Mulvey, "Visual Pleasure and Narrative Cinema," in *The Sexual Subject: A Screen Reader in Sexuality,* ed. John Caughie and Annette Kuhn (London and New York: Routledge, 1992), p. 27. Following Jacques Lacan's notion of the split female subject, Mulvey pioneered a theory of spectatorship in visual cinema, which I am adapting here for the relationship of viewer and image in illustrations. See also Jacques Lacan, *Feminine Sexuality: Jacques Lacan and the école freudienne,* ed. Juliet Mitchell and Jacqueline Rose, trans. Jacqueline Rose (New York and London: Norton, 1985).

12. In an 1893 edition of *Goblin Market* (illustrated by Laurence Housman), Rossetti wrote that the poem was first named "'A Peep at the Goblins' in imitation of my cousin Mrs. Bray's 'A Peep at the Pixies' but my brother Dante Gabriel Rossetti substituted the greatly improved title as it now stands" (R. W. Crump's textual note in *CP,* 1:234). See Marsh, *CR* for a discussion of the influence of Eliza Bray's book on *Goblin Market* (pp. 230-31).

13. Christina Rossetti, *Goblin Market,* in *CP,* 1:11-26, lines 41-42 and 49-51. Unless otherwise indicated, all citations of *Goblin Market* are taken from this source and will be cited parenthetically by line number.

14. For detailed discussions of *Goblin Market* as a poem about interpreting the visible world in spiritual and moral terms, see Mary Arseneau, "Incarnation and Interpretation: Christina Rossetti, the Oxford Movement, and *Goblin Market,*" *VP* 31 (1993): 79-93; and Katherine J. Mayberry, *Christina Rossetti and the Poetry of Discovery* (Baton Rouge: Louisiana State University Press, 1989).

15. Marsh, *CR,* p. 235. D. M. R. Bentley first posited this audience in "The Meretricious and the Meritorious in *Goblin Market*: A Conjecture and an Analysis," in Kent, pp. 57-81.

16. Jack Zipes, ed., *Victorian Fairy Tales: The Revolt of the Fairies and Elves* (New

York: Methuen, 1987), pp. xxv-xxvi. See also Charlotte Spivack, "'The Hidden World Below': Victorian Women Fantasy Poets," in *The Poetic Fantastic: Studies in an Evolving Genre,* ed. Patrick D. Murphy and Vernon Hyles (New York: Greenwood, 1989), pp. 53-64.

17. See especially Rosenblum, p. 70.

18. See Nead for a good overview of the ways in which feminine sexuality was constructed by cultural discourses in Victorian society.

19. For an analysis of how Christina Rossetti's poetry engages with, and revises, the biblical typology and sexual stereotyping found in D. G. Rossetti's early paintings, see Linda H. Peterson, "Restoring the Book: The Typological Hermeneutics of Christina Rossetti and the PRB," *VP* 32 (1994): 209-32.

20. Rosenblum, p. 110.

21. Kate Myers, "Towards a Feminist Erotica," in Betterton, p. 198.

22. Christina Rossetti, *Goblin Market and Other Poems,* illus. D. G. Rossetti (London and Cambridge: Macmillan, 1862).

23. I am aware of only three other artists who have illustrated "Golden head by golden head" in their depictions of Rossetti's *Goblin Market;* all of these are recent productions: Martin Ware (Victor Gollancz, 1980); George Gershinowitz (David R. Godine, 1981); and John Bolton (*Pacific Comics,* 1984).

24. Barbara Garlick, "Christina Rossetti and the Gender Politics of Fantasy," in *The Victorian Fantasists,* ed. Kath Filmer (New York: St. Martin's Press, 1991), pp. 137, 133, 140.

25. Although *Goblin Market* is often referred to as a Victorian children's classic, it was not, in fact, produced for the juvenile market until the twentieth century. See Kooistra, "Modern Markets for *Goblin Market.*"

26. Christina Rossetti, *Goblin Market,* illus. Dion Clayton Calthrop (London and Edinburgh: T. C. and E. C. Jack, [1906]).

27. Dion Clayton Calthrop, *My Own Trumpet: Being the Story of My Life* (London: Hutchinson, 1935), p. 108.

28. Christina Rossetti, *Goblin Market,* illus. Margaret W. Tarrant (London: Routledge, [1912]).

29. Christina Rossetti, *Goblin Market,* illus. Arthur Rackham (London: George G. Harrap, 1933).

30. Jeremy Maas, *Victorian Painters* (London: Barrie and Rockliff, 1969), p. 161.

31. James Hamilton, *Arthur Rackham: A Life with Illustration* (London: Pavilion Books, 1990), p. 142.

32. Jacqueline Rose, *The Case of Peter Pan, or The Impossibility of Children's Fiction* (London: Macmillan, 1984).

33. See especially Cora Kaplan, "The Indefinite Disclosed: Christina Rossetti and Emily Dickinson," in *Women Writing and Writing about Women,* ed. Mary Jacobus (London: Croom Helm, 1979), p. 69.

34. Martha Kingsbury, "The Femme Fatale and her Sisters," in Thomas B. Hess and Linda Nochlin, eds., *Woman as Sex Object: Studies in Erotic Art, 1730-1970* (London: Allen Lane, 1973), p. 182.

35. Christina Rossetti, *"Goblin Market:* A Ribald Classic," illus. Kinuko Craft, *Playboy* 20 (September 1973): 115-19.

36. Linda Nochlin, "Eroticism and Female Imagery in Nineteenth-Century Art," in Hess and Nochlin, p. 11.

37. For discussions of the sadism underlying Victorian fairy painting see Maureen Duffy, *The Erotic World of Faery* (London: Hodder and Stoughton, 1972), p. 294; and Maas, p. 154.

38. John Berger, *Ways of Seeing* (London: Penguin, 1988), p. 64.

39. Mulvey in Caughie and Kuhn, p. 27.

40. Christina Rossetti, *Goblin Market,* illus. Laurence Housman (London: Macmillan, 1893).

41. Laurence Housman was drawn to the notion of a female deity. He illustrated *Goblin Market* immediately after completing his illustrations for George Meredith's *Jump-to-Glory Jane* (London: Swan, Sonnenschein, 1892), in which he also focuses on the image of the female Christ in his representation of Jane. For an analysis of Housman's illustrations for that text, see Kooistra, *Artist as Critic,* pp. 149-52.

42. Christina Rossetti, *Goblin Market,* illus. George Gershinowitz (Boston: David R. Godine, 1981).

43. Christina Rossetti, *Goblin Market,* illus. Martin Ware (London: Victor Gollancz, 1980).

44. Rosalind Coward, "What Is Pornography? Two Opposing Feminist Viewpoints," in Betterton, p. 176.

45. In a personal correspondence to the author dated 3 July 1993, Martin Ware claims that the target audience was never made clear to him by his publisher, and that he merely produced good images in the belief that "children were at least as receptive to good illustrations as adults." The book was, however, marketed and distributed by Victor Gollancz for nine- to eleven-year-olds. For a discussion of the contested boundaries of adult and child audiences in illustrated editions of the poem, see Lorraine Janzen Kooistra, *"Goblin Market* as a Cross-Audienced Poem: Children's Fairy Tale, Adult Erotic Fantasy," *Children's Literature* 25, special issue on Cross-Writing Child and Adult, guest ed. by Mitzi Myers and U. C. Knoepflmacher (New Haven and London: Yale University Press, 1997), pp. 181-204.

46. Mary Wilson Carpenter, "'Eat Me, Drink Me, Love Me': The Consumable Female Body in Christina Rossetti's *Goblin Market,"* VP 29 (1991): 425. For a different view of *Goblin Market* as a poem which privileges the female gaze so that, as I argue, Lizzie and Laura (and their audience) learn about the dangers and rewards of looking, see Catherine Maxwell, "Tasting the 'Fruit Forbidden': Gender, Intertextuality, and Christina Rossetti's *Goblin Market,"* chapter 4 in this collection.

47. Christina Rosetti [*sic*], *Goblin Market,* illus. John Bolton, in *Pacific Comics: Pathways to Fantasy* 1, no. 1 (1984): 9–18.

48. A similar point is made about European oil paintings of the nude by Berger, p. 54.

49. John Ellis, "On Pornography," in Caughie and Kuhn, p. 164

50. Luce Irigaray, *This Sex Which Is Not One,* trans. Catherine Porter (Ithaca and London: Cornell University Press, 1990), p. 183.

51. A children's book author and illustrator in the late Pre-Raphaelite style, Florence Harrison produced a sumptuous Edwardian gift book, *Poems by Christina Rossetti* (London, Glasgow, and Bombay: Blackie and Son, 1910). Later, selections from this text were included in *Shorter Poems by Christina Rossetti* and in *Goblin Market and Other Poems,* both of which were part of Blackie's "Beautiful Poems" series (1923). Harrison also illustrated Tennyson's *Dream of Fair Women and Other Poems* and *Guinevere and Other Poems* for this series.

52. See Terence Holt, "'Men Sell Not Such in Any Town': Exchange in *Goblin Market,*" VP 28 (1990): 51–67, for an analysis of *Goblin Market* in terms of the economic, sexual, and linguistic exchanges incorporated in the poem. Holt also employs spectator theory in his discussion of Laura as object of the goblins' gaze, arguing that the children who surround her at the end of the tale are goblin progeny, and that the larger audience of readers is also positioned as goblins and voyeurs of sexual exchange. Holt's argument, however, assumes that the poem's audience is male, whereas I have argued that Rossetti's poem is constructed principally for women who are to be taught new images of femininity and new ways of looking at themselves.

53. Irigaray, pp. 176–83.

54. Garlick, p. 144.

55. I am grateful to the Social Sciences and Humanities Research Council of Canada, and to Nipissing University, for their support of my research.

CHAPTER 7

"Frogs and Fat Toads"

Christina Rossetti and the Significance of the Nonhuman

KATHRYN BURLINSON

In his Memoir of Christina Rossetti, William Michael Rossetti writes that his sister's poetry shows "A Love of Animals, and more especially such animals as are frequently regarded as odd or uncouth, rather than obviously attractive."[1] Although not taken seriously by critics, tending to be dismissed as "quaint whimsy,"[2] Christina Rossetti's representations of nonhuman life are both poetically and culturally significant. A letter to William Michael, written during a stay at Longleat in 1850, reveals how central to Rossetti's overall poetic perception is her attraction to uncouth creatures:

> The other day I met a splendid frog. He was of a sort of *sere yellow* spotted with black, and very large. Were you in this lovely country, you could hardly fail to gush poetry; with me the case is altogether different. The trees, the deer, the scenery, and indeed everything here, seems to influence me but little, with two exceptions, the cold, and the frog. The cold can never fail to interest a well brought-up Englishwoman; and the frog possesses every claim on my sympathy. He appeared to be leading a calm and secluded life.[3]

Rossetti is not only inspired by "meeting" frogs. Her representations of other animals, insects, and amphibians, as well as her prose defenses of their rights, amount to a challenge to contemporary scientific models and offer an alternative conception of the significance of the nonhuman. The directly political implications of Rossetti's treatment of primitive nature may have been overlooked, but her impassioned protests against the exploitation of animals along with her humanitarian ethical stance locate her not as the withdrawn and conservative religious poet of popular belief, but as a dissident Victorian, contributing to a counterculture by speaking out against prevalent socio-scientific practices and ideologies.

"Ask Now the Beasts, and They Shall Teach Thee"

As well as marking politically resistant tendencies, Rossetti's nonhuman world also becomes a repository for fantasy. The "birds and the bees" are used, quite conventionally, as a discourse of sexuality, but Rossetti is often idiosyncratic and surprising in her choice of sentient objects. *Goblin Market* provides ample evidence of Rossetti's fascination with zoological diversity; the yoking of sexuality and the marketplace so prominent in that poem also reappears in others, in which the world of primitive nature and the sphere of sexual and economic reproduction are rhetorically linked. Not all texts propose the connection with the energetic insistence and libidinous charge of *Goblin Market,* but a poem such as "Summer" ("Winter is cold-hearted," *CP,* 1:142– 43) neatly illustrates Rossetti's attraction to primitive life-forms. The poem seems at first simply to privilege the warmest season over all others for conventional enough reasons, registering summer's abundance and joyousness:

> Summer days for me
> When every leaf is on its tree;
> When Robin's not a beggar,
>   And Jenny Wren's a bride,
> And larks hang singing, singing, singing,
>   Over the wheat-fields wide . . . (5–10)

What is subsequently revealed to render summer especially appealing, however, is the multitude and activity of insect life. Maurice Bowra's observation upon the Pre-Raphaelite love of "odd and captivating details"[4] is thus extended to the unlikely stratum of insect low-life. The rhetorical energy of the poem is most prominent when the speaker turns her attention to invertebrates, and it is at this point too that the economic and sexual are conjoined in a flurry of winged activity:

> And blue-black beetles transact business,
>   And gnats fly in a host,
> And furry caterpillars hasten
>   That no time be lost,
> And moths grow fat and thrive,
> And ladybirds arrive. (14–19)

The insect communities are depicted as urgently trading, consuming, and traveling. In this economic ecology time is pressured: the caterpillars must be efficient if they are to equal the fat moths, whose prosperity is the result of successful consumption. The economic metaphor in this stanza doubles as a sexual metaphor, for the beetles' business with one another is reproductive, and the relationship between the moths and the caterpillars inevitably invokes cycle, even if they are not identical breeds. Reference to sexuality and reproduction appeared in the description of "Jenny Wren" as a "bride" earlier in the poem, but this is developed only in the subsequent representation of insects.

The speaker's attraction to this scene of activity is endorsed in the final stanza as she articulates her preference for this "one day in the country" (22) over "a day and a year / Of the dusty, musty, lag-last fashion / That days drone elsewhere" (24–26). The rural/urban division registered here needs to be interpreted specifically, for while "elsewhere" points to the town or city, it is not the industrialized urban space, but the enclosed domestic space of middle-class femininity that is evoked by "dusty, musty," and "lag-last." Time drags and dust collects in the enclosed space of "elsewhere." It is in contrast, then, with this restricted location that release into an environment of free sexual and market exchange seems appealing. To grow fat and thrive is an activity that takes place not in the legitimized feminine domestic space, but in a fantasized environment of the wild and free-born.

A text that may bear comparison with "Summer" is "Twilight Calm" (*CP*, 1:52–54), where an initial reliance on cliché and sentiment grades into more idiosyncratic territory. The reader is drawn into a world of gnats and slugs by way of five preceding stanzas that provide comforting and conventional views of natural environment. As the poem proceeds it constructs an image of pastoral harmony complete with lowing cattle (21–22), a squirrel (8), and a dormouse who "squats and eats / Choice little dainty bits" (16–17). This

cloying, greeting-card depiction of nature gives way, in the sixth stanza, to a
literal portrayal of primitive life as the nocturnal creatures begin to emerge:

> The gnats whirl in the air,
>   The evening gnats; and there
> The owl opes broad his eyes and wings to sail
> For prey; the bat wakes; and the shell-less snail
>   Comes forth, clammy and bare. (26–30)

It is only in this stanza, where the viscous fleshy nudity of the slug and
the predatory power of the owl are figured, that the text surrenders comfort
for verisimilitude. This is potentially a witches' brew, with its bats, eyes, and
wings, yet the tone of the stanza is calm and matter-of-fact. Rossetti is not
aiming for gothic creepiness, however strong the links are between her chosen
tropes and occult traditions. The representation here bears out William
Michael's summary of her attitude toward animals, for there is no repulsion
or recoil registered towards the "uncouth"—the bat simply wakes up and the
slug simply "comes forth, clammy and bare." Such untroubled, unambitious
acceptance is a recurrent feature of Rossetti's writings on sentient nature.[5]
Christabel Coleridge likened this appreciation of the "smallest and tenderest
creatures of earth"[6] to her grandfather's similar propensity, but Rossetti goes
further than Coleridge in integrating this attitude into her poetry.

Such integration may be seen in her strange poem of earthly renunciation,
"From House to Home" (CP, 1:82–88), where the uncivilized world plays a
vital role in fantasies of plenitude. This is in many ways a more obviously
introspective text than either "Summer" or "Twilight Calm." At the start of
the poem, the speaker recalls her now-relinquished "pleasure place within my
soul" (6), yet while the image echoes "Kubla Khan," and the architectural
structures Rossetti proceeds to describe evoke Tennyson's "Palace of Art," the
description of lost pleasures focuses ever-increasingly on the wildlife that feed,
breed, and thrive in her garden.

Two distinct physical areas are represented—firstly the cultivated, "undu-
lating green" (17), where familiar animals and birds eat and sing, and beyond
this, the wild heath:

> My heath lay farther off, where lizards lived
>   In strange metallic mail, just spied and gone;
> Like darted lightnings here and there perceived
>   But no where dwelt upon.

Frogs and fat toads were there to hop or plod
    And propagate in peace, an uncouth crew,
Where velvet-headed rushes rustling nod
    And spill the morning dew.

All caterpillars throve beneath my rule,
    With snails and slugs in corners out of sight;
I never marred the curious sudden stool
    That perfects in a night.

Safe in his excavated gallery
    The burrowing mole groped on from year to year;
No harmless hedgehog curled because of me
    His prickly back for fear. (29–44)

As in "Summer" and "Twilight Calm," it is when Rossetti is representing not the lambs and squirrels of pastoral but insects, invertebrates, and amphibians that the text departs from convention and figures a vital and energetic scene. The transition from garden to heath precipitates the appearance of elusive, brilliant lizards—flashes of corporeal energy, just spied and gone. Easier to perceive are the ungainly and peculiar "frogs and fat toads" enjoying undisturbed sex among the bulrushes. Propagation is significantly permissible in this heath or heathen space, and not just for the frogs—even the bulrushes seem to reach orgasm.

Yet for all this teeming activity, there is a marked emphasis on safety and security in this environment—lambs are "safe from the unfeared knife" (22), amphibians breed in peace, moles and hedgehogs are safe and fearless, and even the sudden erection of the mushroom is nurtured and facilitated. In this fantasized space, where the female speaker rules the land and owns the property, nature is depicted as physical matter not to be exploited, conquered, or destroyed, but rather nurtured and protected.[7] Feminine government encourages harmonious ecology, as it does also in Elizabeth Barrett Browning's dream of "An Island" where a multitude of animals and insects, free from the threat of "guns and springes" remain "glad and safe."[8]

Rossetti's poem may have been influenced by Barrett Browning's, but neither text reproduces conventional Victorian anxieties about the natural world. "From House to Home" was written the year before Darwin published *The Origin of Species,* and it reveals no conflict or struggle in nature. Absent, too, is the Tennysonian view that nature "is one with rapine" and "red in tooth and claw."[9] Rossetti's work seems to be unaffected by the radical scientific challenges to theologies of nature that other Victorian poets felt compelled to address in their poetry. This does not simply indicate a sentimental avoidance of the cruelties of the natural world, for Rossetti acknowledges and accepts predatory and destructive animal instincts elsewhere in her writings.[10] In fantasy representations, however, where a feminine order is in place, a combination of freedom and security seems to generate peaceable and sensual nonhuman relations. Rossetti's heath abounds with sexual energy, but this does not create the same problems as it does elsewhere in the poet's work. Furthermore, the teeming heath includes and embraces what is often rejected as revolting, not least in the case of the slimy frogs and, in particular, the fat toads.

Historically toads have rarely been figured with such equanimity. By the seventeenth century their ugliness was proverbial, and toads are "loathed" in a number of Shakespeare plays, most notably *Othello,* where the toad forms part of a tropological network that circumscribes women as secretive, untrustworthy, and disgusting.[11] Spenser, too, depicts the amphibian negatively in *The Faerie Queene,* while Milton has Satan "Squat like a toad, close at the ear of Eve" in *Paradise Lost.*[12] The association of toads and female sexuality is unmistakable in Bosch's and Breugel's paintings, where toads appear on women's breasts and genitals in paintings of hell and the Last Judgment.[13] Even Dante Gabriel uses the toad as a figure of enduring lust in "Jenny."[14] Toads are traditionally the accomplices of witches—according to Robert Degraaff, a woman with a pet toad in the seventeenth century was likely to be accused of witchcraft, and as late as 1857, a year before Rossetti wrote "From House to Home," a woman from Shropshire was murdered, possibly for keeping a box of live toads.[15] However cosy and even whimsical Rossetti's representation of amphibians appears, then, it also amounts to a rejection of conventional aesthetic codes and associations. Rossetti refuses to conform to a cultural tradition that locates both toad and woman as "other," as sexually polluted and polluting.[16] Looking again at the fantasized "pleasure-place" of the speaker in "From House to Home," the reptiles, amphibians, invertebrates, and mammals that inhabit the heath are all potentially or conventionally repellent, yet all are accepted in their otherness and not despised for it. Unlike Goethe's Mephistopheles, Rossetti's speaker is not a spirit who always negates the pullulating fertility of nature, but rather "always allows."[17]

The element of acceptance in Rossetti's writings is generated as much by her faith as her femininity, notwithstanding biblical complicity in constructing women, toads, lizards, and frogs as evil and rapacious. There is no question in Rossetti's mind that God created all things, nor that humans can learn from the creatures that surround them. She writes that all creatures possess "in a more or less degree a resemblance of Himself"[18] and this perspective fundamentally affects her attitude toward nonhuman life. Her efforts to appreciate the unappealing are recorded in *Seek and Find*:

> Which of us, even supposing such a chance to occur,—which of us would feel drawn to fondle a scaly slippery person? Beholding fishes so cold, so clean, so compact, one might fancy them destitute not of souls only but of hearts also. Yet have they an abundance of good gifts whereby to honour God and cheer man. Gold or silver or a humming-bird does not surpass the vivid lustre and delicacy of their changeable tints; their motions are replete with strength and grace; their swiftness is a sort of beauty. (*SF,* p. 113)

The beauty and grace of fish are a direct reflection of the divine, for "all the good which resides in any creature (be that creature great or small, lofty or lowly) is an outcome of Himself" (*SF,* p. 260). Rossetti's theology also, however, has substantial implications for human contexts, since to reject "scaly slippery" persons is to deny them their "heart" and their share of divinity. As is often the case in Rossetti's devotional writings on nature, indirect criticism of the social order appears within a predominantly orthodox discourse.

The connections between Rossetti's theological views on nature and wider political ideologies will be explored further, but it is also necessary to point to two literary traditions, one predominantly male, the other female, which Rossetti inherited and worked within. The poet's view of creation places her in a masculine literary/religious tradition that dates back to the seventeenth century. Such a theology is represented in the writings of George Herbert and continues in a modified form through the eighteenth century in the work of James Thomson, William Cowper, and Christopher Smart. Common to this tradition is the perception of "man" as the most significant creature on earth, and of "nature" as existing for the benefit of humans. Creation declares the glory of God, and the Bible assists humans in discerning the significance of the natural world. Reading nature for the lessons it offers is suggested in Job 12:7–8, which Rossetti quotes in *Seek and Find:* "Ask now the beasts, and they shall teach thee; and the fowls of the air, and they shall tell thee: or speak to the earth, and it shall teach thee: and the fishes of the sea shall declare unto thee" (p. 110).

Parabolic interpretations abound in Rossetti's devotional prose works, revealing her commitment to traditional and typological theologies of nature.[19] An example of parabolic reading as well as of Rossetti's circumspect and respectful treatment of an insect is revealed in an autobiographical entry in *Time Flies,* where she recounts an event that occurred during a stay at Penkill Castle in Ayrshire:

> Once in Scotland, while staying at a hospitable friend's castle, I observed, crossing the floor of my bedroom, a rural insect. I will call it, though I daresay it was not one in strictness, a pill millepede.
>
> Towards my co-tenant I felt a sort of good will not inconsistent with an impulse to eject it through the window.
>
> I stooped and took it up, when in a moment a swarm of baby millepedes occupied my hand in their parent's company.
>
> Surprised, but resolute, I hurried on, and carried out my scheme successfully; observing the juniors retire into cracks outside the window as adroitly as if they had been centenarians.
>
> Pondering over this trifle, it seems to me a parable setting forth visibly and vividly the incalculable element in all our actions. I thought to pick up one millepede, and behold! I was transporting a numerous family.
>
> If thus we cannot estimate the full bearing of action, how shall we hope to estimate the full extent of influence? I thought to catch one millepede, and an entire family lay at my mercy![20]

In this passage, the metamorphosis of one millepede into a multitude prompts Rossetti to speculate upon and call for an expansion of human consciousness so that the multiple resonances of every action may be more fully apprehended. What she does not call particular attention to is her decision to relocate rather than crush the insect, but again Rossetti facilitates rather than destroys. Her attitude toward earthly existence is not only devout but also conservationist and tends towards egalitarianism. In this she departs from seventeenth-century influences such as Herbert, who insists on the supremacy of Man, "the worlds high Priest," in texts such as "Providence." She does, however, inherit the tradition of eighteenth-century women poets such as Anna Seward, Ann Yearsley, Anne Finch, and Anna Barbauld who, as Margaret Anne Doody has suggested, challenge hierarchical Enlightenment models of the relation between human and animal.[21] Without entirely abandoning the conception of hierarchy within the animal world, Rossetti draws on feminine traditions in emphasizing that since both the "lofty" and the "lowly" resemble God, all creatures have a right to space in the world and humans have a responsibility to protect them. In *The Face of the Deep,* Rossetti interprets parabolically an incident concerning "Three frogs and three newts":

> Of the three frogs, one on being taken in hand croaked, moving to sympathy the heart of its captor. . . . the risk of being laughed at [shall not] prevent my remarking that the croak of the helpless frog, yet not helpless because of that very faculty of helpless appeal lodged in it, sets before me much higher images.
>
>   We know on the highest Authority that not one sparrow is over-looked.[23]

The humble croak of a helpless frog thus suggests to Rossetti the boundless compassion of the Almighty, while it also illustrates the spiritual importance of protecting the vulnerable. Rossetti is concerned with all links in the Great Chain of Being and, like her eighteenth-century sister poets, asserts a fellow-ship of sense that promotes identification with, rather than separation from, the objects of perception.

A protectionist impulse toward the lowly but sentient appears clearly in one of the instructional texts included in *Sing-Song:*

> Hurt no living thing:
>   Ladybird, nor butterfly,
> Nor moth with dusty wing,
>   Nor cricket chirping cheerily,
> Nor grasshopper so light of leap,
>   Nor dancing gnat, nor beetle fat,
> Nor harmless worms that creep. (*CP,* 2:43–44, 1–7)

Rossetti's catalogue of insects is full of particular distinguishing features, which, it is implied, deserve attention and appreciation. An expansion of human con-sciousness enables us to admire and desire to protect the "harmless," while a lack of identification may result in the unthinking and cruel human action depicted in another *Sing-Song* poem, "Hear what the mournful linnets say" (*CP,* 2:22), which illustrates, in conjunction with Arthur Hughes's highly anthropo-morphized portrayal of the linnets, the cruelty of egg-stealing (fig. 7.1). While these poems reproduce the conventional socializing ethics of Victorian children's literature, such considerate conduct and protective action do not concur with the dominant ideology of mid-to-late Victorian culture. Rossetti's theological and feminine inheritance sets her at odds with cultural trends, for all that her fascination with natural history may bind her to her historical moment. Darwin's monumentally influential model of nature as a struggle for survival of the fittest is not easily reconcilable with Rossetti's nurturing impulses or her visions of harmonious ecology.

It is unlikely that Rossetti read Darwin—there is no direct evidence in her writings or correspondence to indicate that she did—but the impact of his work was so widespread that exposure to his ideas was virtually unavoidable. What is perhaps more surprising than the differences between Darwin and Rossetti are the points at which they overlap. It has been observed that Darwin retains a modified version of the Great Chain of Being in his system.[24] His theory also insists on animal-human continuity—a perspective indubitably present in Rossetti's writings. Darwin states in *The Descent of Man* that "no-one with an unbiased mind can study any living creature, however humble, without being struck with enthusiasm at its marvellous structure and properties."[25] Rossetti expresses similar appreciation of "humble" creatures throughout her poetry and prose. Both writers celebrate the human intellect, but both also think that sympathy with "lower" animals is morally important (despite Darwin's laissez-faire attitude toward powerless humans).[26]

Such overlaps are hardly startling, though they illustrate that theological and scientific discourses are rarely absolutely separable. Darwin was a product of, as well as a prime contributor to, a culture enchanted by the "marvellous structure and properties" of the natural world at home and abroad, and his scientific writings are inevitably infused with contemporary religious, ethical, and moral discourses as well as zoological argument. As is increasingly noted by historians of science, Darwin's theories reproduce a host of powerful Victorian ideologies. His hierarchical model of evolution places the white Western male at its zenith, while his emphasis on struggle, as he himself admits, is heavily influenced by Malthus's theory of population, and reproduces capitalist notions of competition. The evolutionary model is also adopted by Victorian progressivist ideologies, and contributes to the perception of Victorian England as the most highly evolved and therefore "highest" civilization.[27] As Karl Marx perceived, Darwin's theories are saturated with the values and structures of Victorian England: "Darwin recognises among brutes and plants his English Society with its division of labour, competition, opening up of new markets, 'inventions' and Malthusian 'struggle for existence'. . . . with Darwin the animal kingdom figures as bourgeois society."[28]

Hear what the mournful linnets say:
  "We built our nest compact and warm,
But cruel boys came round our way
  And took our summerhouse by storm.

"They crushed the eggs so neatly laid;
  So now we sit with drooping wing,
And watch the ruin they have made,
  Too late to build, too sad to sing."

14

Fig. 7.1. Arthur Hughes, "Hear what the mournful linnets say." Illustration for Christina Rossetti, *Sing-Song* (London: Macmillan, 1893), p. 14.

Such perceptions of human and animal social organization conflict with Rossetti's views. In common with other critics of Darwin who contest the universality of competition and point out the importance of mutual aid and interspecific symbiosis in animal communities, she emphasizes the interrelatedness of natural species.[29] Her High Anglican perspective will not allow her to see nature as amoral and purposeless, dependent upon chance rather than design, and although her view of nature as the creation of a beneficent God may be anachronistic, her perception of animal-human continuity aligns her to an ecological tradition of thought that, as Carolyn Merchant has shown, has strong affinities with the women's movement past and present.[30] The imaginative connection between humans and animals also fuelled Rossetti's antivivisectionist politics, and it is in this context that her dissident voice is heard at its most vociferous.

"NERVES WITHOUT PITY AGONISED"

[M]ay not life wantonly destroyed and nerves without pity agonised enter a prevalent appeal against men who do such things or take pleasure in them? . . . if we honestly weigh up the claims of all our sentient fellow-creatures, I think we shall forbear to adopt some pretty fashions in dress, and to follow up some scientific problems. . . . Alas for us, if when the fashion of this world passes away . . . and partial knowledge is done away . . . the groans of a harmless race sacrificed to our vanity or our curiosity should rise up in the judgment with us and condemn us. (SF, pp. 115–16)[31]

Rossetti's appeal here is ethical. She is urging her readers to reflect upon human responsibility at the end of two centuries that had witnessed the progressive erosion of theologies of nature in favor of scientific experimentation, explanation, and exploitation. But Rossetti is also arguing very specifically against vivisection. Antivivisection societies and pressure groups proliferated in the 1870s and 1880s—a period when scientific disciplines were becoming increasingly specialized and when science as discourse seemed to wield more power than ever before.[32] Although there was no uniformity of political persuasion within anti-vivisection groups, the movement was dominated by middle-class women. As Mary Ann Elston observes, press reports often describe meetings as being full of women; when large groups of men were present they were usually hostile medical students.[33]

The ideological association of women with nature and the construction of femininity as tender, caring, and sentimental no doubt contributed to the movement's gender bias, while this in turn attracted predictable ridicule: antivivisectionists were ugly old maids ignorant of the need for scientific progress.[34] Men in the movement exhibited anxieties regarding its "female" image and resented the visibility of women such as Frances Power Cobbe.[35] George Jesse, Honorary Secretary of the Society Abolition Vivisection [sic], complained in a letter to Darwin that the *Times,* "a partisan in this Controversy, is, cunningly, ready to give notoriety to a *Woman* as the professed exponent of the Anti-Vivisectionists on a great Ethical and Scientific Question. . . ."[36] Darwin, for his part, reportedly delighted his staunch supporter Thomas Huxley by "the most beautiful double-barrelled score" when Darwin said of the antivivisectionist and *Spectator* editor Richard Hutton, "he seems to be a kind of *female Miss Cobbe.*"[37]

Misogyny may have existed both within and outside the antivivisection societies, but the female-dominated movement increasingly aligned itself to other campaigns affecting oppressed groups. Just as the antivivisection societies had drawn on antislavery rhetoric to bolster their cause,[38] so too they forged links with the Campaign Against the Contagious Diseases Acts and with the campaign for sexual purity which attracted many late nineteenth-century feminists. The connection was resistance to the power of science: as Elston summarizes, "All three were campaigns against the increasing claims of science and medicine to the right to dictate morality and personal behaviour."[39] Particular concern was focused on the treatment of poor women in hospitals, who, like animals in scientific experiments, were said to be subjected to painful and offensive treatment at the hands of medical men. Anxieties around gynaecological issues and antivivisectionist politics went hand in hand for many of the women involved.

For a woman writer to take an antivivisectionist position, then, potentially implicates her in wider political debates. We know that Rossetti was a sufficiently motivated opponent of vivisection to persuade Dante Gabriel to sign Cobbe's petition in 1875, but do her writings reflect the broader ideological connections antivivisectionists established? Rossetti makes a specific connection between animals and women in her famous letter to Augusta Webster on the subject of women's suffrage, where she speaks of "that mighty maternal love which makes little birds and little beasts as well as little women matches for very big adversaries."[40] This is a letter declining support for suffrage, but in it Rossetti speculates on expanding Parliament to include women M.P.'s, and resists the suffragists' support for a franchise that excludes married women. Such views are, paradoxically, commensurate with her desire for fair representation for all.

In *Time Flies,* Rossetti uses the threat of an ultimate judgment day to jolt her readers into reflection:

> Two frogs I met in early childhood have lingered in my memory: I frightened one frog, and the other frog frightened me.
>
> The frightened frog evinced fear by placing its two hands on its head: at least, I have since understood that a frog assumes this attitude when in danger, and my frog assumed it.
>
> The alarming frog startled me, "gave me quite a turn," as people say, by jumping when I did not know it was near me.
>
> My fright was altogether without justifying cause. Not so the first frog's: for presumably my warm finger made the cool creature uncomfortable. Besides, how could it tell what was coming next? although in truth I meant it no harm.
>
> I wish that as regards their intention as much could nowadays be certified for some of the wisest of this world, and that every scared frog were like my scared self, unreasonable.
>
> But seeing that matters are as they are—because frogs and such like cannot in reason frighten us now,—is it quite certain that no day will ever come when even the smallest, weakest, most grotesque, *wronged* creature will not in some fashion rise up in the Judgment with us to condemn us, and so frighten us effectually once and for all? (*TF,* pp. 128–29)

Rossetti draws here upon the egalitarian politics of some Christian teachings to mount her critique of oppression. Her championing of the small, weak, and grotesque challenges to the point of near threat those who condone or ignore the sufferings of others. She is not directing her remarks solely at scientists, but at any person who frightens, endangers, or harms a frog, or "such like." (Perhaps Rossetti had in mind George Henry Lewes, who in the course of his scientific forays in the 1860s and 1870s set up a home laboratory "where hundreds of frogs had their brains experimented with.")[41] The abhorrence Rossetti feels toward the torture of innocents is mirrored by the disgust at social inequality which she also reveals. Writing to Ellen Proctor during the last year of her life, she protested: "The contrast between London luxury and London destitution is really appalling. All sorts of gaieties advertised, and deaths by exposure or starvation recorded in the same newspaper."[42]

In private letters and in published texts, Rossetti speaks out against inequality and on behalf of the silent, wronged creatures of the world. Her inclusion of the smallest and weakest living things in her poetic texts is a politically significant gesture, since it is precisely *exclusion* from representation and from cultural space and self-determination that is the experience of subordinated groups. In her depiction of biological nature a feminine critique of dominant nineteenth-century ideologies and cultural practices emerges, as the author marks out a space for and calls attention to the unrepresented or negatively depicted, and voices fierce objection to exploitative treatment of the oppressed.

Rossetti also put her politics into action throughout her life. Her work at Highgate Penitentiary is one example, while her efforts to secure signatories for various petitions is another. Her later letters contain numerous requests for support for "the cause of the helpless," whosoever they may be.[43] This practice extended beyond the immediate family circle: Mackenzie Bell quotes a letter Rossetti wrote to Frederick Shields in April 1883 in which she mentions her efforts to collect signatures for "Petitions to Parliament" on the protection of minors.[44] A subsequent letter to Shields in 1885 indicates her involvement in the antivaccination lobby (another campaign that established links with the Campaign Against the Contagious Diseases Acts): she is "procuring a few signatures" for a "Memorial . . . for Presentation to the Home Secretary beseeching him not to licence a so called 'Institute of Preventive Medicine' which will establish Pasteur's treatment and I suppose other horrors in our midst."[45]

Although Rossetti's prose writings reveal her involvement in contemporary social issues, she did not publish much that is directly related to antivivisectionism. She would have known Dora Greenwell's "Fidelity Rewarded" and Mary Howitt's "The Cry of the Animals," but her own poetic protests against contemporary discourses of science are, perhaps characteristically, oblique.[46] Nevertheless, even in apparently humorous and playful allegorical poems that take animal victims as their anthropomorphized subjects, leveling political impulses and critiques of scientific and technological developments may be discerned. Rossetti included both "Contemptuous of his home beyond" (*CP*, 3:51) and "A handy Mole who plied no shovel" (*CP*, 3:50) in *Time Flies*—a context that suggests that while they may be comical they are not simply frivolous. They may even be barbed. "A handy Mole who plied no shovel" concerns a mole who meets an earthworm in a tunnel but ignores it, ostensibly because he is not hungry. Thus "Each wrought his own exclusive tunnel / To reach his own exclusive funnel" (13–14). Such insular strategies prove futile, however, as both dominant and subordinate are subsequently annihilated by the "impartial ploughshare of extinction" (19) which "Annulled them all without distinction" (20).[47] Thus the social, physical, or intellectual superiority of the mole is rendered irrelevant, the rigidities of social structure absurd, and bourgeois snobberies futile. Since we are all equal in death, it is implied, anything other than egalitarian relations on earth are erroneous.

The message that death is a great leveler is one that provides a measure of comfort for Victorian women: Emily Dickinson makes a similar point in a poem that also uses both toad and gnat as figures:

> A Toad, can die of Light—
> Death is the Common Right
> Of Toads and Men—
> Of Earl and Midge
> The privilege—
> Why swagger, then?
> The Gnat's supremacy is large as Thine—[48]

Dickinson's sarcastic undercutting of pomposity finds a parallel in Rossetti's "Contemptuous of his home beyond," where, unfortunately for the frog, "swaggering" leads him to destruction.[49] This comical, violent, and unsentimental text highlights the absurdity of pride and isolationism in the quotidian world, as the frog's hubris and recklessness lead it to abandon safe enclosures and hop off down "the *imperial* highway" (4, my emphasis). Supremely confident in personal as well as national identity and power, the masculine frog comes to grief, run down by a "broadwheeled waggon" (13). Addressing his kin, or countrymen, in personal pronouns that appeal sentimentally to history and national tradition, too late the frog realizes his fallibility: "'Ye buoyant Frogs, ye great and small, / Even I am mortal after all'" (17–18). At this point in the poem a new dimension appears. Rossetti not only figures the difference between dying frog and "unconscious" waggoner (24), again marking the incalculable element in all our actions, but she also adds an ironic sting. In suggesting brutally that the waggoner may have been whistling "'A Froggy would a-wooing go'" (27), she calls attention to the separation of the massacred object from its rhetorical representation.

In the final part of the poem, the narrator echoes the frog's address:

> O rich and poor, O great and small,
> Such oversights beset us all:
> The mangled frog abides incog,
> The uninteresting actual frog;
> The hypothetic frog alone
> Is the one frog we dwell upon. (30–35)

Rossetti uses cliché to signal irony in the first line above, for the realities of exploitation and destruction are not equitable. The point she ultimately makes offers a critique of human abstraction where it blinds us to material realities. The waggoner is absorbed in his own discourse and the mangled frog remains invisible, but this signifies beyond the immediate. While an ethical critique of human behavior emerges unequivocally, this has repercussions in specific discursive fields, since hypothesis is figured as that which obscures the experiential reality of the object under scrutiny. This bears not only upon the issue of vivisection (where a parallel situation might be a scientist singing "Three Blind Mice" or, as actually happened, Lewes naming an amphibian "Froggie" and observing it live for several months without most of its brain, before it finally died of starvation),[50] but also upon human contexts, with their extreme power relations operating between "great" and "small." Notwithstanding the critique that is presented of the proud male frog, its ultimate powerlessness aligns it to other oppressed groups whose bodies and bodily functions were the source of many a hypothesis, while they were simultaneously excluded from access to scientific professions. Rossetti's darkly comic intervention, then, has a special resonance.

Rossetti's attitude toward science and subhuman nature is comparable to the ecological politics of the late twentieth century and strikingly close to that expressed by the present-day feminist theologian, Rosemary Radford Ruether:

> An ecological-feminist theology of nature must rethink the whole Western theological tradition of the hierarchical chain of being and chain of command. This theology must question the hierarchy of human over nonhuman nature as a relationship of ontological and moral value. It must challenge the right of the human to treat the nonhuman as private property and material wealth to be exploited.[51]

Ruether, like Rossetti, is part of a long tradition of women writers and activists positing alternative conceptions of ethics and responsibility toward the nonhuman. Three centuries of women writers, drawing upon theological paradigms or the Enlightenment rhetoric of rights, challenge the dominant discourses of scientific rationalism and, like Rossetti, insist on saying "A Word for the Dumb" (*CP*, 3:52): "Spare *all* the harmless tenants of the earth: / Spare, and be spared:—or who shall plead for thee?" (7–8, my emphasis).

It would be limiting, however, for us to construct Rossetti as "Perfectly pure and good" according to late-twentieth-century formulations, for she is not *always* a sensitive champion of the helpless.[52] Her parabolic reading of nature, her invocation of an interpretive frame beyond the biological, sometimes renders her as dismissive of the consequences of her own actions as any Victorian vivisectionist. In the following entry in *Time Flies,* Rossetti describes an event which she perceives as especially emblematic:

> If ever I deciphered a "Parable of Nature" surely I did so one summer night at Meads.
> The gas was alight in my little room with its paperless bare wall.
> On that wall appeared a spider, himself dark and defined, his shadow no less dark and scarcely if at all less defined.
> They jerked, zigzagged, advanced, retreated, he and his shadow posturing in ungainly indissoluble harmony. He seemed exasperated, fascinated, desperately endeavouring and utterly helpless.
> What could it all mean? One meaning and one only suggested itself. That spider saw without recognising his black double, and was mad to disengage himself from the horrible pursuing inalienable presence.
> I stood watching him awhile. (Presumably when I turned off the gas he composed himself.)
> To me this self-haunted spider appears a figure of each obstinate impenitent sinner, who having outlived enjoyment remains isolated irretrievably with his own horrible loathsome self.
> And if thus in time, how throughout eternity? (*TF,* pp. 121–22)

Immediately noticeable here is Rossetti's insistence that "One meaning and one only" can be gleaned from the spider's mad dance. While readers may not want to dispute the idea that the spider was attempting to escape its own shadow, Rossetti's theological reading nevertheless forecloses other possibilities. In the first place, she is indirectly responsible for what amounts to an act of torture, since it is the light from the gas lamp that creates both the shadow and the consequent madness. Despite the speaker's emphasis on the wall, the wall is irrelevant, and this is subsequently half-acknowledged as Rossetti reveals the real cause of distress in the parenthetical statement later in the passage: "(Presumably when I turned off the gas he composed himself)." The speaker's power is total, even God-like. She makes the spider insane with her combination of light and heat, which renders visible not only self but shadow, not only self but self-as-other.

The spider is sent mad by its own representation, the reproduction of its image. It cannot become one with itself, nor can it cope with the existence of a simulacrum, for all that it is "fascinated" as well as "exasperated." The splitting that takes place does indeed create a double—that staple figure of Victorian literary culture—yet to suggest, as does Rossetti, that the "self-haunted" are reducible to "obstinate impenitent sinner[s]" is too easy and too special a moral line. Her own part in the creation of the double problematizes this perspective, and although her "deciphering" of the incident refuses any immediately self-referential dimension, the frightful double, the split self, the self-haunted subject is not confined to those who have "outlived enjoyment."

The penultimate sentence of this passage constructs the spider/sinner as a Dorian Gray figure, attracted and repulsed by self and by its representation. Self-division in fact pervades the entire passage—not least since this is an event recalled, re-presented, drawn from memory and anchored anew. The speaker is representing herself, her own actions, responses, conclusions. She is casting light upon a shadowy past, drawing past and present selves together. These are never made identical, however, for the tense shift toward the end of the passage separates past experience from present interpretation, creating a shadow self as well as a speaking one. Thus is the text ruptured as well as joined, divided as well as connected. Rossetti's theological reading of the event limits and reduces, disallowing the energies that erupt in the spider's desperate dance.

Rossetti's imposition of a theological frame, then, comes at the cost of attention to other possibilities: the author has not recognized, any more than she was able to in the millipede episode, "the full extent" of her own "influence." Nevertheless, while the spider passage has much in common with other Rossetti texts similarly marked by self-haunting and split by self-division, it is more anomalous than typical of the poet's writings on nonhuman nature. Ordinarily, as we have seen, her theological perceptions and broadly egalitarian, conservationist politics are closely connected with one another and at odds with the dominant scientific perspectives of her culture. Taken as a whole, Rossetti's treatment of nonhuman nature provides us with a fuller understanding of the poet's ideological position vis à vis her culture and shows us how committed she was to attending to, and speaking for, the silent.

NOTES

1. *PW,* p. ix.

2. Lionel Stevenson, *The Pre-Raphaelite Poets* (Chapel Hill: University of North Carolina Press, 1972), p. 121.

3. Qtd. in Antony H. Harrison, "Eighteen Early Letters by Christina Rossetti," in Kent, p. 204. The inspiration offered by frogs reappears in *Speaking Likenesses* (in *Christina Rossetti: Poems and Prose,* ed. Jan Marsh [London: Dent, 1994], pp. 324-53), where the tale of Edith is prompted by the cry: "Aunt, do tell us the story of the frog who couldn't boil the kettle" (p. 339). In the event, the frog does not play a particularly large part, but he always excites: "A frog—[*The* frog, Aunt?—Yes, Laura,]—*the* frog hopped at a leisurely pace" (p. 342).

4. Maurice Bowra, *The Romantic Imagination* (Cambridge, Mass.: Harvard University Press, 1949), p. 254.

5. It was also characteristic of her behavior. Grace Gilchrist Frend recalls that Rossetti would "take in her hand cold little frogs and furry, many-legged caterpillars" ("Great Victorians: Some Recollections of Tennyson, George Eliot and the Rossettis," *Bookman* 77 [1929]: 10).

6. Christabel Coleridge, "The Poetry of Christina Rossetti," *Monthly Packet* 89 (1895): 278.

7. The same harmonious depiction of animals occurs in the story of Edith in *Speaking Likenesses.* Edith sits in a wood surrounded by a dog, a cat, a cockatoo, a squirrel, several birds, a mole, two hedgehogs, a frog, and a toad. The narrator declares that it is a "wonder" that the pets [the dog, cat, and cockatoo] "let this small fry come and go at pleasure and unmolested; but, whatever their motive may have been, they did so" (p. 342). Even when a fox comes by there is no disruption of the peace.

8. Elizabeth Barrett Browning, "An Island," in *The Poetical Works of Elizabeth Barrett Browning,* ed. Frederick G. Kenyon (London: Smith, Elder, 1897), pp. 112–14, lines 83-84.

9. Alfred Tennyson, *Maud* (1.123) and *In Memoriam* (56.15) in *The Poems of Tennyson,* ed. Christopher Ricks (London: Longmans, Green, 1969), pp. 1037-93 and 853-988.

10. In a letter to her nephew Arthur, written in 1889, Rossetti refers to a cat that "Takes in its mouth some white mice . . . without injuring them. I hope instinct

will not suddenly assert itself to the dire detriment of mousey." In Lona Mosk Packer, "Christina Rossetti's Correspondence with Her Nephew: Some Unpublished Letters," *Notes and Queries* 204 (1959): 431.

11. William Shakespeare, *Othello,* in *The Riverside Shakespeare,* ed. E. Blakemore Evans et al. (Boston: Houghton Mifflin, 1974), 3.3.268–73.

12. Edmund Spenser, *The Fairie Queene,* 1.4.30–31; and John Milton, *Paradise Lost,* in *The Poetical Works of John Milton,* ed. David Masson (London: Macmillan, 1890), vol. 2, 4.800.

13. According to Richard Barber and Juliet Barker, thirteenth-century preachers chastised miscreant knights with the threat that in hell, rather than enjoying the advances of young women, they would be sexually molested by toads (*Tournaments* [Woodbridge: Boydell, 1989], p. 144). I am grateful to Bella Millett for this reference. The association of feminine sexuality and toads continues in contemporary erotic iconography, as evident in the illustration for *Goblin Market* by Kinuko Craft for *Playboy* in 1973. (See fig. 6.5 in Lorraine Janzen Kooistra's essay in chapter 6 of this collection: a small toad in the lower right hand corner of the composition applauds the sexual activity of the scene it witnesses.)

14. Dante Gabriel Rossetti, "Jenny," in *The Works of Dante Gabriel Rossetti,* ed. W. M. Rossetti (London: Ellis, 1911), lines 282–97. In contrast with "Jenny," the toad in Edith's story in *Speaking Likenesses* is appealing—"his eye like a jewel" (p. 342)—and wise: "[How came the toad to be so much cleverer than his neighbours, Aunt?—. . . because toads so often live inside stones . . . And suppose his father, grandfather and great-grandfather all inhabited stones, the idea of doing everything inside something may well have come naturally to him]" (p. 344).

15. Robert M. Degraaff, *The Book of the Toad: A Natural and Magical History of Toad-Human Relations* (Cambridge: Lutterworth, 1991), p. 147.

16. Rossetti's *Sing-Song* poem, "Hopping frog, hop here and be seen" (*CP,* 2:32) is another text that depicts amphibians positively. In the second stanza, the cultural hostility toward toads is registered but rejected: "Plodding toad, plod here and be looked at, / You the finger of scorn is crooked at: / But though you're lumpish, you're harmless too; / You won't hurt me, and I won't hurt you" (5–8).

17. See Johann Wolfgang Goethe: "Ich bin der Geist, der stets verneint!" in *Faust,* ed. R. M. S. Heffner, Helmut Rehder, and W. F. Twaddell (Madison: University of Wisconsin Press, 1975), 1:1338.

18. *SF,* p. 260. Subsequent citations from *Seek and Find* will be noted parenthetically in the text.

19. Rossetti maintained the traditional Christian view that nature is the work of the Creator and that, while it may reveal His glory, it is not coincident with God. The distinction between believing (as did Deists) that knowledge of God may be ascertained through nature, and believing (as did Tractarians) that knowledge of nature may be established in the light of God, sets "natural theology" apart from

"theology of nature." For further analysis of these distinctions and a history of theological interpretation of nature, see George S. Hendry, *Theology of Nature* (Philadelphia: Westminster, 1980).

20. *TF,* pp. 61–62. Subsequent citations from *Time Flies* will be noted parenthetically in the text.

21. George Herbert, "Providence," in *The English Poems of George Herbert,* ed. C. A. Patrides (London: J. M. Dent, 1974), pp. 129–33.

22. Margaret Anne Doody, "The Sensuous Eighteenth Century," plenary address, Rethinking Women's Poetry Conference, Birkbeck College, University of London, 20 July 1995.

23. *FD,* 162–63. I am grateful to Mary Arseneau for bringing this passage to my attention.

24. Lynda Birke, *Women, Feminism, and Biology* (Brighton: Harvester, 1986), p. 129.

25. Charles Darwin, *The Origin of Species by Means of Natural Selection and The Descent of Man and Selection in Relation to Sex* (Chicago: University of Chicago Great Books of the Western World Series, 1990), p. 341.

26. For a discussion of Darwin's ambivalent and sometimes contradictory attitudes toward oppressed groups, including his controversial statements regarding state systems that allow weak members of society to propagate, see Brian Easlea, *Science and Sexual Oppression* (London: Weidenfeld and Nicolson, 1981), pp. 154–57; and Barbara Noske, *Humans and Other Animals* (London: Pluto, 1989), p. 70.

27. Gillian Beer points out that evolutionary theory does not privilege the present, but that it is persistently recast as doing so. See *Darwin's Plots* (London: Routledge and Kegan Paul, 1983), p. 13. She also observes that the evolutionary metaphor confirms the sense of Victorian culture representing the pinnacle of civilization, an idea already central to eighteenth-century rationalist and Enlightenment ideologies of progress (p. 18).

28. Karl Marx, *Marx and Engels on Malthus,* trans. D. L. and R. L. Meek, ed. R. L. Meek (London: Lawrence and Wishart, 1953), p. 173.

29. The anarchist Peter Kropotkin articulated his resistance to Darwin in *Mutual Aid* (1902): "how false is the view of those who speak of the animal world as if nothing were to be seen in it but lions and hyenas plunging their bleeding teeth into the flesh of their victims. One might as well imagine that the whole of human life is nothing but a succession of war massacres. Association and mutual aid are the rule with mammals." Qtd. in Birke, p. 130. See also Noske, pp. 66–78 for critiques of Darwin's model.

30. Carolyn Merchant, *The Death of Nature* (London: Wildwood House, 1982).

31. Rossetti also protests against the use of animals for fashionable decoration in a letter to Arthur Rossetti, in which she refers to a "Poor harmless happy swallow, sacrificed to a fashion" (qtd. in Packer, p. 431).

32. In *Victims of Science* (London: National Anti-Vivisection Society, 1983),

Richard Dyder notes that the issue of vivisection first came to public notice in the 1860s, when pictures of experiments taking place in France appeared in British newspapers (p. 132).

33. Mary Ann Elston, "Women and Anti-Vivisection in Victorian England, 1870-1900," in *Vivisection in Historical Perspective,* ed. Nicolaas A. Rupke (London: Croom Helm, 1987), p. 264.

34. Easlea quotes Herbert Spencer, writing in *Popular Science Monthly* in 1873 of the social danger of female compassion, which Spencer sees as having anti-individualist tendencies, possibly resulting in individual rights being overridden in the pursuit of beneficent ends (pp. 152-53).

35. As early as 1863 Frances Power Cobbe had written against vivisection in an essay entitled "The Rights of Man and the Claims of Brutes," *Fraser's Magazine* 68 (July-December 1863): 586-602. Cobbe founded the Victorian Society for the Protection of Animals liable to Vivisection, and was an active campaigner for many years.

36. George Jesse, *Correspondence with Charles Darwin on Experimenting upon Live Animals* (London: Pickering, 1881).

37. Qtd. in Easlea, p. 264.

38. The Manifesto of the Society Abolition Vivisection proclaims: "The wrongs perpetrated by man on Animals are even more dire than those inflicted on his own species. The Abolition of Slavery was an act of high Christian philanthropy. It is no less noble or less Christian to stop the sufferings of other helpless creatures of our God." See George Jesse, *History of the Foundation and Operations of the Society Abolition Vivisection* (London: Pickering, 1877), p. 5.

39. Elston, p. 274.

40. Bell, p. 112.

41. Robin Gilmour, *The Victorian Period* (London: Longman, 1993), p. 143. Kathleen Jones details the hostility of the Rossettis toward Lewes, whose wife they knew. See *Learning Not to Be First: The Life of Christina Rossetti* (Moreton-in-Marsh: Windrush, 1991), pp. 91-92.

42. Ellen Proctor, *A Brief Memoir of Christina Rossetti* (London: SPCK, 1895), p. 66.

43. The phrase comes from a letter Rossetti wrote to Edmund McClure at the SPCK, 21 March 1894 (forthcoming in *The Letters of Christina Rossetti,* ed. Antony H. Harrison, vol. 4: 1887-94).

44. Bell, p. 94. For further information on Rossetti's involvement in Minors' Protection, see Marsh, *CR,* pp. 514-22.

45. Bell, p. 110. The practice of vaccination (where a person is inoculated with a virus as a protection against the same disease) was objected to by many Victorians, who felt it was dangerous and morally questionable. Pasteur was a well-known supporter of vaccination.

46. According to Marsh's biography, Rossetti sent a poem entitled "Hope Deferred" to an antivivisection annual (*CR,* p. 516). I have been unable to trace this poem.

47. Rossetti's lines recall two of Blake's aphoristic "Proverbs of Hell" in *The Marriage of Heaven and Hell:* "Drive your cart and your plough over the bones of the dead" (2) and "The cut worm forgives the plough" (6), although Rossetti emphasizes mechanistic indifference rather than hellish energy.

48. Emily Dickinson, "A Toad, can die of Light—" in *The Complete Poems of Emily Dickinson,* ed. Thomas H. Johnson (London: Faber and Faber, 1987), no. 583, p. 285.

49. Rossetti's poem may have been influenced by Robert Rockliff's "The Frog and the Frogling" in his *Literary Fables* (London, 1851). Rossetti owned a copy of this work, now in the Troxell Collection at Princeton.

50. Gilmour, pp. 143-44.

51. Rosemary Radford Ruether, *Sexism and God-Talk* (London: SCM Press, 1983), p. 85.

52. The quotation is from Robert Browning's "Porphyria's Lover," in *Robert Browning: The Poems,* ed. John Pettigrew and Thomas J. Collins (New Haven: Yale University Press, 1981) 1.37.380-81.

CHAPTER 8

Astronomy of the Invisible

Contexts for Christina Rossetti's Heavenly Parables

LINDA E. MARSHALL

A s a topographical context for Christina Rossetti, that area of London taking in St. Marylebone and Regent's Park would include some of the main points of interest in her life and writings. Besides various Anglo-Catholic landmarks like Christ Church, Albany Street, and the home of the first Anglican Sisterhood in Park Village West, there could be found Madame Tussaud's equivalent of "The Dead City" in Marylebone Road as well as a livelier "Processional of Creation" at the Zoo.[1] But along with the wombats and crocodiles in Regent's Park, there were stars on view—at Mr. Bishop's observatory, in operation near his residence at South Villa, Inner Circle, from 1836 until his death in 1861. This near-at-hand base of sidereal investigation helps situate Christina Rossetti's own heavenly research, a devotional and poetic undertaking that nonetheless was informed by the new astronomy of the nineteenth century, founded, as its historian Agnes Mary Clerke recounts, on Sir William Herschel's verification, in 1802, of the "*physical* existence of double stars," kept together by mutual attraction. This overture made what was "entirely unfamiliar" and "incredible" incontestable, and proved that "the fundamental quality of attractive power" was "common to matter so far as the telescope was capable of exploring."[2] Not only the telescope, but eventually the spectroscope and the camera probed the physical qualities of heavenly bodies in the foundation of a science by which, as Clerke says, "the nature of the earth can be made better known by the study of the stars." Yet at the same time the new astronomy—"astronomical or cosmical physics," as it was termed—"finds its best opportunities in unlooked-for disclosures; for it deals with transcendental conditions, and what is strange to terrestrial experience [such as double stars] may serve admirably to expound what is normal in the skies."[3] At the Regent's Park observatory, the Reverend William Dawes investigated and catalogued double stars, a work continued by John Russell Hind;[4] comets and new planets there hove into view; in 1848 Hind discovered a temporary star in Ophiuchus on a day otherwise always notable to Christina Rossetti—April 27, her mother's birthday. There is no evidence that Rossetti had particular knowledge of these local astronomical pursuits, but her interest in such developments of sidereal science clearly manifests itself in her devotional prose and memorably glimmers here and there in her verse—both of which, it need scarcely be said, are concerned with terrestrial analogies of heaven as well as with the strangeness of "transcendental conditions."

P. G. Stanwood notes in his study of Rossetti's devotional prose the "rare glimpses of her intellectual leanings" afforded by her musings about the stars in *Seek and Find,* but her allusions to the new astronomy are neither as rare nor as distinctly "intellectual" as Stanwood implies.[5] Rather, her numerous and reasonably well-informed references to such matters as lunar thermal energy, solar physics, eclipses, celestial spectroscopy, planetary discovery, double stars, variable stars, nebulae, external galaxies, and theories about the structure of the universe, are all made parabolically and poetically to conduce to what for her was "the true end of all contemplation," as she says at the conclusion of *Seek and Find,* "to 'see Jesus.'"[6] Science provided Rossetti with parables not "for scientific experts," as she explains apropos her discussion of the chemistry of sulphur in *The Face of the Deep,* but "for verbal dabblers like myself,"[7] that is, for herself both as interpreter of scripture and as poetic transmitter of the "symbolic analogies" of the kingdom of heaven found in scripture and the natural world (*SF,* p. 65). For Rossetti, the new astronomy, like contemporary advances in science and technology generally, was an additional source of those parables and analogies that by means of the visible unearth the invisible and thus speak of a future world through terrestrial apperceptions of it.[8] While she would not have supported Coventry Patmore's "hard saying" that "[t]he greatest and perhaps the only real use of natural science is to supply similes and parables for poets and theologians,"[9] Rossetti's interest in science was, as she says, experimentally "verbal," and directed towards signifiers of the invisible; she was especially drawn to new ways of envisioning what St. Paul in 1 Corinthians 15:49 calls "the image of the heavenly," the image that those raised up through Christ's resurrection will bear. The tremendous developments in astronomy lent themselves with singular felicity to Rossetti's belief that "[a] Greater than Solomon is with us, and has deigned to instruct us by things new and old," and that "[b]y analogy of things visible He has shown us things invisible" (*SF*, p. 273).

Particularly suggestive for Rossetti's devotional appropriation of sidereal science was the so-called Astronomy of the Invisible, founded by the German astronomer F. W. Bessel (1784–1846). Arguing that "'[t]here is no reason to suppose luminosity an essential quality of cosmical bodies'," he proposed in 1844 that the irregular motions of the two Dog-Stars, Sirius and Procyon, were due to the presence of obscure bodies with which they formed "real binary systems, consisting of a visible and an invisible star."[10] By the same token he suspected that anomalies in the movements of Uranus were caused by the presence of an unknown body, but he died only months before the position of that body, eventually named Neptune, was calculated by a Cambridge senior wrangler, John Couch Adams, the "master-mind" to whom Rossetti may refer in *Seek and Find* as exemplifying the "wonderful" and "awful . . . intellectual faculties . . . shrined within mortal man," faculties which "track out the invisible by clue of the visible." Though she does not name Adams, nor the planet he helped locate, she unmistakably represents the means by which the Astronomy of the Invisible led to Neptune's discovery: "a certain master-mind by the aberration of one celestial body from the line of its independent orbit, argued the influential neighborhood of a second luminary till then undiscerned" (*SF*, p. 27). Given the attention to argument rather than to calculation, it is possible that Rossetti actually refers to that celebrated master-mind, Mary Somerville, whom Adams acknowledged as having inspired his mathematical undertaking by her suggestion, in the 1842 edition of *On the Connexion of the Physical Sciences,* that discrepancies in the motions of Uranus "may reveal the existence . . . of a body placed for ever beyond the sphere of vision."[11] Not only the master-mind, however, but to some degree "every one of us inherits this awful birthright of intellectual power," whose only legitimacy, Rossetti cautions, is in the seeking out of "the kingdom of God and His righteousness"; consequently, we must not "exercise ourselves in matters beyond our present powers of estimate, lest amid the shallows (not the depths) of science we make shipwreck of our faith" (*SF*, pp. 27–29). Nevertheless, Rossetti's parenthesis allows that those who do ply "the depths" of science—those regions where master-minds may track out the invisible by clue of the visible—offer no threat to faith, and perhaps help underwrite its security. Rossetti shares with Agnes Mary Clerke this reverent view of the astronomer's mission. In her *Popular History of Astronomy during the Nineteenth Century,* first published in 1885 and reaching its fourth edition in 1902, Clerke writes that the patient toil of astronomers "is its own reward, if pursued in the lofty spirit which alone becomes it. For it leads through the abysses of space and the unending vistas of time to the very threshold of that infinity and eternity of which the disclosure is reserved for a life to come."[12]

In *Time Flies,* the Astronomy of the Invisible provides Rossetti with a "physical hypothesis" from which to work out "a spiritual analogy." She notes that "science, endeavouring to account for certain recurrent obscurations of one or more . . . [stars], suggests that among them and with them may be revolving other non-luminous bodies; which interposing periodically between individuals of the bright host and our planet, diminish from time to time the light proceeding from one or other; and again, by advancing along an assigned orbit, reveal their original brightness" (*TF,* pp. 208, 207). Rossetti apparently refers to the phenomenon of "eclipse-stars," of which the best-known is Algol in the Head of Medusa, investigated in 1880 by the American physicist and astronomer, Edward Charles Pickering, who theorized that the periodic dimming of the star's light was due to the revolving of "an obscure body" around it.[13] Such variable white stars, as those like Algol were termed, have without exception "proved also to be compound," Clerke points out in another of her popularizing works, *The System of the Stars.*[14] Though Rossetti, quoting Psalm 139:6, would have it that "[s]uch knowledge is too wonderful and excellent for me: I cannot attain unto it," she is prompt to educe a charitable lesson from astronomy's recently catalogued variables and their dark companions: "If certain stars which present mere dimness and obstruction to our eyes are notwithstanding genuine celestial bodies fulfilling their proper revolution in their legitimate orbit, may not some human fellow creatures who to us exhibit no sign of grace, yet be numbered among the children of God, and have their lot among the saints?" (*TF,* p. 208).

Actual observation of "star-combinations" suggests another "heavenly parable" in *Called to Be Saints,* where Rossetti recounts that when she peers at "the lesser light" associated with "a brilliant luminary" she usually fails to discern it, "while if I fix my eye on its more refulgent neighbour, then I become vividly conscious of the presence of the second also, which again eludes me when I revert to it." From this she draws the passionate lesson of *"Monna Innominata"* concerning "that supreme love of God which includes and involves all secondary affections: though these must dwindle, disappear, and as it were come to nothing, if we fix on them exclusively or primarily the eye of the heart."[15] A parable made of her own predilection for sky-watching occurs in *The Face of the Deep,* where, confessing that "I once grieved and grudged because I could not betake myself to a vantage point whence to watch an eclipse," she uncovers the darker side of her disappointment: "the grief might have been simply blameless, but the grudge proved that I was in a double sense loving darkness rather than light" (*FD,* p. 231).

Parables and analogies concerning heavenly light and darkness abound in Rossetti's writings, some acquiring through "scientific" allusion a certain edge. Proposing in *Letter and Spirit* that "an infringement exclusively of the First Commandment . . . cannot be discernible except by God Omniscient, and possibly by the individual culprit," she brings light-years to bear on the apparent radiance of the dark culprit, who "even as a star extinct for a thousand years past, may still when gazed at from earth appear luminous."[16] Perhaps the most original of her reflections on heavenly luminosity can be found in her Creation study of Sun and Moon in *Seek and Find,* where, proclaiming her intention as a woman to glorify the subordinate entity in the pairs Sun and Moon, man and woman, she alludes to the "careful observation" which now makes doubtful the popular supposition that the moon "is no more than a mirror reflecting the sun's radiance," and instead "leads towards the hypothesis that she may also exhibit inherent luminosity" (*SF,* pp. 30–31). Rossetti here refers rather optimistically to the observations of lunar radiation made by the Earl of Rosse during the years 1869–72, which seemed to prove that the moon acted, Clerke reports, "as a direct radiator no less than as a reflector of heat."[17] That is, Lord Rosse determined that the greater portion of lunar thermal energy was not transmitted with the solar light reflected by the moon's surface, but instead was radiated from the moon after it had first absorbed the solar heat falling upon it. Rossetti may have encountered (and misread) these findings in an essay published in *Fraser's Magazine,* which, like most literary and topical magazines of the day, kept close track of astronomical research.[18] In any case, Rossetti's skewed bulletin on science's latest collection of moon data is accompanied by a scriptural elucidation of the lambency of "the feminine lot," which "copies very closely the voluntarily assumed position" of Christ, nor does she hesitate to draw St. Paul's reminder that there is "one glory of the sun, and another glory of the moon" (1 Cor.

15:41) into her celestial argument on behalf of woman's special Christ-like-ness and proper "luminosity" (*SF*, pp. 30–31).

In some striking revisions or adjustments of symbolic values traditionally associated with heavenly bodies, Rossetti took note of recent solar as well as lunar observations. Christ as the irradiating "Sun of Love" in such poems as "From House to Home" (*CP*, 1:87, 181–84) and "An Old-World Thicket" (*CP*, 2:127–28, 148–60) is a time-honored figure, but elsewhere Rossetti recasts it in accord with new developments in solar physics. For example, in *Time Flies* her thoughts for June 3 about "the bottomless pit" as a symbol of the "everlasting recoil" by which the sinner may elude "the pursuing love of God" are complemented in the entry for June 4 with an allusion to spectro-scopic observations, carried out in the 1870s and early 1880s, of the formation and dispersal of stupendous solar projections:

> I have read how matter can be exploded, or at the least can be conceived of as exploded, from the sun, with such tremendous force as to carry it beyond the radius of solar attraction.
>
> That attraction which unifies and sways a whole harmony of depen-dent planets, recalls not one atom which has passed beyond the pale. (*TF*, pp. 105–6)[19]

Rossetti's parable of the sinner's passing irretrievably beyond the gravitational force of the Sun of Love is likely based on widely-published accounts of huge uprushes from the sun, which, judged in some cases to be traveling four to five hundred miles a second, would thus "escape for ever from [the sun's] control."[20]

Other developments in solar physics, notably the investigation of sunspots and calculations of the relative insignificance of our sun in a vast cosmos, are involved in Rossetti's occasional depreciations of the sun's figurative divinity. Characterizing Envy in *Letter and Spirit*, she finds "congenial parables" of its blight in nature: "Spots in the sun, thorns to the rose" (*LS*, p. 99). In "Mirrors of Life and Death," a poem included in the 1881 *Pageant* volume, "the Sun with glory and grace / In his face" is nevertheless "Not without spot, / Not even the Sun" (*CP*, 2:75, 14–15 and 19–20). In *Seek and Find*, Rossetti variously suggests that the stars beyond our sun shine with more numinous significance. "It is merely to our sight that the sun obliterates the stars, the sun being in truth of inconsiderable bulk when compared with many of them," she writes in her Creation series, "yet by reason of its nearness to our eyes it fairly puts them all out, until only an act of recollection can during the daylight hours summon before our consciousness the ever-present, ever-luminous multitudinous lights of the sky." We must recollect Christ's presence even as we recollect the stars, and the ever-increasing telescopic and spectroscopic knowledge we have of them as our conception of the universe expands to make our sun "no more than a sub-centre" among further and further sub-centers all "revolving round some point of overruling attraction" must help constitute our "stepping-stones towards heaven" (*SF*, pp. 33, 35–37).[21] Again, in the Redemption series, Rossetti reiterates that "the starry host" best "represents to our apprehension the Divine Omnipresence and Omniscience," since sun and moon are both periodically shut out from us by the earth's and moon's proper rotations, but "from all stars simultaneously no man is ever excluded, except by such merely apparent exclusions as may be brought about by daylight or by mist: be our hemisphere and our zone which it may, be the stars at a given moment discernible or indiscernible by our vision, yet seen or unseen a multitude of their celestial host abides ever above every horizon; our planet poised as a very small thing amid their magnitudes, as a very obscure thing amid their splendours." Though various writers "moved by the Holy Ghost" have figuratively designated Christ as sun, "or compared Him as with a similitude," Christ did not call himself the sun, but rather "the bright and morning star" (*SF*, pp. 192–93).

If the stars best represent divinity, they also represent ourselves bearing "the image of the heavenly." The epigraph from 1 Corinthians 15:41 heading the Redemption study of "Stars"—"One star differeth from another star in glory"—is the key to Rossetti's identification of the individually human with the individually stellar: "As in the future glory, so in the present grace, stars are of unequal magnitudes and lustres; but the least is no less than a star precious to Him Who made it, and the greatest is no more than a star whose splendour is His free gift" (*SF*, pp. 192, 196). Amongst the brightest stars Rossetti no doubt would include the Christian martyrs, whom in *The Face of the Deep* she names the "alphas of constellations" (*FD*, p. 465).

"One Star differeth from another Star" was the original title of Sonnet 9, "Star Sirius and the Pole Star dwell afar," in *Later Life: A Double Sonnet of Sonnets* (*CP*, 2:142, 388).[22] This tremendously poised sonnet, itself a kind of perfectly-articulated orrery, supposes a communion between Sirius, emblemizing our own short summer's blaze, and Polaris, the enthroned, "unchangeable," and solitary guide to wandering and suffering humanity, even though the two stars are so celestially divided that

> They own no drawings each of other's strength,
>> Nor vibrate in a visible sympathy,
>>> Nor veer along their courses each toward each. (9.9-11)

Their lines of communication, as set forth in the last tercet, may be spiritually resonant, but they are also astronomically intelligible:

> Yet are their orbits pitched in harmony
>> Of one dear heaven, across whose depth and length
>>> Mayhap they talk together without speech. (9.12-14)

The proposition depends upon our earthly perception of the movements of Sirius in relation to the "fixed" Pole Star: Sirius appears to move, as do all stars in the northern hemisphere, in a daily orbit around Polaris, never approaching it nor withdrawing from it, but rotating always in relation to it across "one dear heaven." From the observation that the two stars are thus geometrically "pitched in harmony," the poet infers a musical or transcendentally sonic accord, a conversing "without speech."

   To the idea of speechless stellar communication Rossetti returns in *Time Flies*, a work otherwise filled with reflections on the speaking and singing voice, variously and individually human, whether on earth or in the heavenly choir (*TF*, pp. 29-31). "Christians are called to be like stars," she writes for January 2, and "[s]tars, like Christians, utter their silent voice to all lands and their speechless words to the ends of the world" (*TF*, p. 2). Commenting for September 5 on human affection, which "illustrates and certifies to us . . . the corresponding Divine Affection," she compares it to "the celestial luminaries which discourse without speech: its sound is gone out into all lands, and its words unto the ends of the world, declaring the Glory of God" (*TF*, p. 172). Echoed in both passages are Psalm 19:1-4 and Romans 10:18 harmonized: "The heavens declare the glory of God" with "no speech nor language," the Davidic psalmist sings, yet their voice is heard everywhere, and their words are gone out "to the end of the world"; St. Paul insists that Israel has heard the gospel from preachers whose "sound went out into all the earth, . . . their words unto the ends of the world." Stars, Christians, human affection preach the tacit but reverberant gospel of divine love, the word of God made audible in that love from which faith proceeds, as St. Paul says in Romans 10:17: "So then faith cometh by hearing, and hearing by the word of God." What the stars say, however, depends upon who hears them, Rossetti writes elsewhere in *Time Flies*: "The starry heavens are so far like their (and our) Maker, that they answer and instruct each man according to his honest intention, his tolerated stumbling-block, his bosom-idol, as the case may be," and therefore "[t]o some they say nothing," "[s]ome they address through the intellect exclusively," "[w]hile to Magi (that is, to Wise Men) they declare the Glory of God, and show His handiwork" (*TF,* p. 7). Celestial beacons of the invisible, Rossetti's stars also signal a divine language silently communicating between God and man, a language falling on deaf ears or only partly intelligible, "as the case may be," but broadcast "to the ends of the world" for reception according to what astronomers might call the "personal equation"—the phenomenon, to which Bessel first drew attention, of each individual's different *"rate of perception"* in making celestial observations.[23] In imagining such transmissions from the stars, it is as if Rossetti, often drawing for her devotional prose and verse on the astrophysics of the nineteenth century, here scripturally preempts the radio astronomy of the twentieth.

Stars, along with Galaxies and Nebulae, Comets and Meteors, declare the glory of God in "'All Thy works praise Thee, O Lord.' A Processional of Creation" (*CP,* 2:129–38), Rossetti's poetic reworking of the *Benedicite,* the canticle to which she devotes a double series of studies in *Seek and Find.* In thus updating the astronomical phenomena of the *Benedicite* by drawing into its ranks of praise-givers celestial subjects addressed by nineteenth-century science, Rossetti lays claim to them as signifiers of divine presence. Just as the Heavens declare that they "float before the Presence Infinite" and "cluster round the Throne in [their] delight, / Revolving and rejoicing in God's sight" (13–15), the Galaxies and Nebulae affirm their choreographing of divine omnipresence:

> No thing is far or near; and therefore we
> Float neither far nor near; but where we be
> Weave dances round the Throne perpetually. (31–3)

In negating the perspectives of distance and proximity, and in identifying themselves with movements of limitless duration, the Galaxies and Nebulae set forth spiritual analogies of "the Presence Infinite" which have some basis in actual telescopic observation of the heavens and in speculation about the significance—physical and metaphysical—of the "vista unmeasured, incalculable," opened by advances in astronomical research (*SF,* pp. 35–36). Plotting the structure and extent of the universe and determining the status of nebulae were related problems tackled by nineteenth-century astronomers, who debated whether nebulae were remote galaxies or star-making mists within our sidereal system, a question bound up with the difficulty of gauging celestial distances. With regard to surveying our own Galaxy, "[o]ur situation . . . close to the galactic plane is the most disadvantageous possible," as Clerke points out, since "[g]roups behind groups, systems upon systems, streams, sheets, lines, knots of stars, indefinitely far apart in space, may all be projected without distinction upon the same sky-ground," and "[w]e are thus presented with a flat picture totally devoid of perspective-indications."[24] What was a stumbling-block for the surveying astronomer, however, could be a godsend to the devout poet, who can make our perception of the Galaxy and its attendant nebulae configurations "neither far nor near" of infinite presence.

But Galaxies, rather than the Galaxy, are collocutors with Nebulae in Rossetti's poem, and the plural goes against the "practical certainty," in the view of late-nineteenth-century astronomers, that there were no galaxies beyond our own.[25] In the eighteenth century, Immanuel Kant, taking up the religiously burnished ideas of Thomas Wright, had theorized that nebulae were external galaxies, and Sir William Herschel (1738-1822) initially had determined through telescopic observation that all nebulae were milky ways probably larger than ours; nevertheless, Herschel later gave up this belief, conjecturing in the light of perplexing new evidence that nebulae were sites of stars in various phases of formation, and that they were all contained within our Galaxy, the bounded universe whose size and shape might well elude our calculations. Though Lord Rosse's great reflecting telescope resolved some hitherto misty nebulae into starry points, reviving in midcentury the theory of external galaxies, Herschel's revisions of nebulae, complementary to Laplace's nebular hypothesis concerning the development of the solar system, held sway until the century's end.[26] "No competent thinker, with the whole of the available evidence before him," Clerke reported in 1890, "can now, it is safe to say, maintain any single nebula to be a star system of co-ordinate rank with the Milky Way." The universe, moreover, is "finite" and "measurable," according to competent thinkers, and all its contents "stand in ordered mutual relations within the limits of one all-embracing scheme."[27] Unable to attain unto this wonderful and excellent knowledge, Rossetti counted the telescopic discovery of external galaxies among the achievements of nineteenth-century astronomy, listing it with spectrum analysis in *Seek and Find* as one of the advances in science that even those occupying the "comparative shallows of intelligence" can appreciate: "we can realise mentally how galaxies, which by reason of remoteness present to our eyes a mere modification of sky-colour, are truly a host of distinct luminaries" (*SF*, pp. 36–37). Ironically, Rossetti's trust in the telescopic unveiling of remote galaxies disqualifies her as a competent thinker with regard to the available evidence of her own day, but aligns her with twentieth-century astronomers who confirmed that those discredited "luminaries" indeed exist, and in a cosmos infinitely expanded beyond the galactic limits of the "single scheme" Clerke had confidently descried.[28] Our heavens, like Rossetti's "Processional of Creation," include both galaxies and nebulae, differentiated groups rather than reductive alternatives, and a distinctive pairing few of her scientific contemporaries countenanced.

In 1867, when Rossetti's friend Anne Gilchrist read Herbert Spencer's essay on "The Nebular Hypothesis," which combated the "idea, rashly espoused by sundry astronomers, that the nebulae are extremely remote galaxies," she found it utterly convincing; so did Tennyson, with whom she discussed the essay, its emphasis on the mysterious but provable evolution of heavenly bodies no doubt appealing to both.[29] According to Clerke, Spencer's arguments about the coexistence of nebulae and stars in the same region of space helped disprove "the conception of the nebulae as remote galaxies, which Lord Rosse's resolution of many into stellar points had appeared to support," banishing it to the realm "of discarded and half-forgotten speculations."[30] It is tempting to imagine Anne Gilchrist broaching "The Nebular Hypothesis" with another of her poet-visitors, Christina Rossetti; but whether or not Rossetti was aware that the distant galaxies discovered by Lord Rosse's telescope had given way to evolutionary glimmerings nearer home, her persistent envisioning of Galaxies makes apparent the metaphysical appeal of those "host[s] of distinct luminaries," which, perspectivelessly resolved and mirrored in the reflector's eye, emblemize "the Presence Infinite." Although "[t]he telescope which has revealed to us a thousand galaxies of suns has failed to show us that Heaven which we once believed was close overhead," as Frances Power Cobbe acknowledged in 1869, it has "admitted [us] to a spectacle for which angels might envy the sons of men."[31] That spectacle could as much oppress as rejoice its beholder thus exalted. Contemplating the "immeasurable worlds" reflected in the Rosse telescope, Thomas De Quincey had darkly refurbished Jean Paul's "Dream-vision of the Infinite as it reveals itself in the Chambers of Space," re-echoing in a universe now terrifyingly abysmal the dreamer's angel-guide: "'End is there none to the universe of God? Lo! also THERE IS NO BEGINNING'."[32] In contrast, the astronomer Richard A. Proctor (1837–1888) reverently heard that same angel as Science proclaiming, in the Newtonian law of attraction and the Darwinian law of evolution, the proven infinity of space and time.[33] Even though Proctor argued on the grounds of spectroscopic evidence that none of the nebulae could be external galaxies, he did not relinquish galaxies, but placed them forever beyond our field of vision in an infinite universe "watched over and controlled by an omnipresent, omnipotent, and omniscient Being."[34] For some, extinguishing far galaxies might keep Heaven near, "close overhead,"[35] and for others make the universe potentially measurable in its finitude; for Proctor, as for Christina Rossetti, the physical hypothesis of an infinite universe invisibly illumined by myriad galaxies could produce a spiritual analogy figuring a Being neither far nor near, but infinitely present.

In 1881, the same year that Rossetti's "Processional of Creation" was published in *A Pageant and Other Poems,* Agnes Mary Clerke's older sister, Ellen Mary, placed her own volume, *The Flying Dutchman and Other Poems,* before the public. Like her sister, Ellen wrote popularizing works on astronomy and "an immense number of magazine articles" on a wide range of subjects, scientific and literary; moreover, her versified translations of Italian poetry appeared in Garnett's *History of Italian Literature,* in her own study of *Fable and Song in Italy,* and in her 1881 volume of poems; in 1902 she published a novel, *Flowers of Fire.*[36] Though Agnes, awarded the Actonian prize in 1892 and elected an honorary member of the Royal Astronomical Society in 1903, won more distinction in her scientific pursuits than did Ellen, this was not at the expense of creditable literary undertakings; Agnes's *Familiar Studies in Homer* is a book that might well have been attempted by the Homer-stung sister in Rossetti's "The Lowest Room."[37] Born in Skibbereen, County Cork, Agnes and Ellen spent many winters in Italy, finally settling in London, and into their productive writing careers, in 1877. The Clerke sisters, star-lovers and devoted Catholics, suggest a particularly appropriate context for Rossetti's devout astropoetics. One of Ellen's poems, "Night's Soliloquy," conveys their shared admiration for astronomy's tracking out the invisible by clue of the visible, upon which it fixes its searching gaze:

> Who calls me secret? are not hidden things
>   Revealed to science when with piercing sight
> She looks beneath the shadow of my wings,
>   To fathom space and sound the infinite?[38]

That feminine "science" which looks into the obscurities of a feminine Night to sound the infinite evokes a certain gender-conscious delight in the Astronomy

206 LINDA E. MARSHALL

of the Invisible. Night's soliloquy, however, gives but a faint echo of that celestial discourse to which Christina Rossetti was attuned, and to which she gave voice in heavenly parables and spiritual analogies of the invisible.

NOTES

1. Born and raised in the vicinity of Regent's Park, Rossetti lived from 1854 to 1867 in an Albany Street house close to Christ Church, where she began attending services in 1843. In "The Dead City," written in 1847 (*CP,* 3:63-71), the visionary speaker encounters vivid but "statue-cold" banqueters reminiscent of the "waxen crowd which put [Rossetti] out of countenance" when in her youth she visited Madame Tussaud's (*TF,* p. 36). From childhood Rossetti delighted in the Regent's Park Zoo, especially in some of its more uncouth denizens; in "'All Thy works praise Thee, O Lord.' A Processional of Creation," published in *A Pageant and Other Poems,* 1881 (*CP,* 2:129-38), various groups of animals join in the praise-giving.

2. Agnes M. Clerke, *The System of the Stars* [1890], 2d ed. (London: Adam and Charles Black, 1905), p. 151; Agnes M. Clerke, *A Popular History of Astronomy during the Nineteenth Century* [1885], 4th ed. (London: Adam and Charles Black, 1902), p. 19.

3. Clerke, *Popular History,* pp. 142, v.

4. George Bishop (1785-1861) gives a detailed account of the work carried out by Dawes and Hind in *Astronomical Observations Taken at the Observatory, South Villa, Inner Circle, Regent's Park, London, during the Years 1839-1851* (London: Taylor, Walton, and Maberly, 1852). The "principal objects of attention" were double stars (pp. 1-173), new planets (pp. 176-98, 250-51), comets (pp. 200-238), and the "new or variable star in Ophiuchus" (pp. 242-48).

5. P. G. Stanwood, "Christina Rossetti's Devotional Prose," in Kent, p. 234.

6. *SF,* p. 325. All subsequent citations of *Seek and Find* will be cited parenthetically in the text.

7. *FD,* p. 456. All subsequent citations of *The Face of the Deep* will be cited parenthetically in the text.

8. Thus Rossetti assigns to Judgment Day certain phonographic and photographic revelations: the playing of a recording on which all the groans of animals we have injured are registered (*SF,* p. 116), and the opening of the Book of Works to reveal one's own page therein so detailed "[i]t is as if all along one had walked in a world of invisible photographic cameras charged with instantaneous plates" (*FD,* p. 473).

9. Coventry Patmore, "Love and Poetry," in *Principle in Art, Religio Poetae, and Other Essays* (London: Duckworth, 1913), p. 336; the essay was first published in the *St. James Gazette,* 31 December 1886. In a letter to Patmore (20 Jan. 1887), Gerard Manley Hopkins calls Patmore's dictum on the use of natural science a "hard saying," and queries, "who can hear it?" (*cf.* John 6:60). See *Further Letters of Gerard Manley*

Hopkins, Including His Correspondence with Coventry Patmore, ed. Claude Colleer Abbott, 2d ed. (London: Oxford University Press, 1956), p. 377.

10. Qtd. in Clerke, *Popular History,* pp. 41–42.

11. Mary Somerville, *On the Connexion of the Physical Sciences,* 7th ed. (London: John Murray, 1846), p. 68. The 1846 edition retained the provocative sentence from the 1842 edition, in the very year of Neptune's discovery.

12. Clerke, *Popular History,* p. 123.

13. Clerke, *Popular History,* p. 390.

14. Clerke, *System,* p. 180.

15. Christina G. Rossetti, *Called to Be Saints: The Minor Festivals Devotionally Studied* (London: SPCK, 1881), p. 503. A similar view of "that supreme love of God which includes and involves all secondary affections" may be found in *SF,* pp. 52–53. In *"Monna Innominata": A Sonnet of Sonnets* (*CP,* 2:86–93), the "unnamed lady" designated in the title explains to her lover the comprehensive dynamic of loving God the most:

> Yet while I love my God the most, I deem
> That I can never love you overmuch;
> I love Him more, so let me love you too;
> Yea, as I apprehend it, love is such
> I cannot love you if I love not Him,
> I cannot love Him if I love not you. (6.9–14)

16. *LS,* p. 25. All subsequent citations of *Letter and Spirit* will be cited parenthetically in the text.

17. Clerke, *Popular History,* p. 269.

18. "Lunar Warmth and Stellar Heat," *Fraser's Magazine* 81 (January 1870): 36–43. This anonymous essay is quoted extensively by Richard A. Proctor, *The Moon: Her Motions, Aspect, Scenery, and Physical Condition* (London: Longmans, Green, 1873), pp. 273–81. *Fraser's Magazine,* for which Christina's brother William wrote art reviews during the 1860s, and which hired their friend William Allingham as subeditor in 1870, was apt to have been read in the Rossetti household.

19. In *The Face of the Deep,* the fallen star given "the key of the bottomless pit" in Revelation 9:11 is identified with the "self-blasted" outcast from heaven, who falls "Beyond return, beyond far sight / Of outmost glimmering nebular" (*FD,* pp. 257–58).

20. Clerke, *Popular History,* p. 205. Possibly Rossetti had read Richard A. Proctor's essay, " What, Then, Is the Corona?," *Fraser's Magazine* 83 (April 1871): 515–28, an earlier account of such solar "explosions," which includes a discussion of the velocity required to send a projectile beyond the sun's attractive domain.

21. Rossetti's reference to spectrum analysis typically shows her grasp of the significance of scientific procedures despite her inability to apprehend their technical bases: "we [i.e., "we who occupy comparative shallows of intelligence"] can understand,

though we cannot follow the process by which the analysis of a ray certifies various components as existing in the orb which emits it" (*SF*, pp. 36–37). The devotional opportunities offered by science's "noble contemplations" (*SF*, p. 36) were perhaps recognized by the publishers of Rossetti's devotional prose, the SPCK (Society for Promoting Christian Knowledge), who in 1877 published Richard A. Proctor's *The Spectroscope and Its Work*. In Rossetti's contemplation of our sun as "sub-centre" in a vast aggregation of star systems, she reproduces the dizzying speculations of Johann Heinrich Lambert's *The System of the World* (*Cosmologische Briefe*, translated into English in 1800): "Thus everything revolves—the earth round the sun; the sun round the centre of his system; this system round a centre common to it with other systems; this group, this assemblage of systems, round a centre which is common to it with other groups of the same kind; and where shall we have done?" (qtd. in Clerke, *Popular History*, p. 14).

22. I wonder if this sonnet prompted Robert S. Ball (Royal Astronomer of Ireland and subsequently Lowdean Professor of Astronomy and Geometry at Cambridge University, as well as a successful popularizer of astronomy) to formulate the question, "Does Sirius, for instance, attract the pole star?" in his essay "The Boundaries of Astronomy," *Contemporary Review* 41 (June 1882): 923–41, which came out in the year following publication of *Later Life* in *A Pageant and Other Poems*. Ball asks the question in order to indicate the limits of astronomical knowledge: "We really do not know," he replies, "[n]or can we ever expect to know. If Sirius and the pole star do attract each other, and if the law of their attraction be the same as the law of attraction in the solar system, it will then be easy to show that the effect of this attraction is so minute that it would be entirely outside the range of our instruments even to detect it" (p. 927). In writing that Sirius and the Pole Star "own no drawings each of other's strength" (*CP*, 2:142. Sonnet 9.9), Rossetti seemingly represents a contemporary view of the matter, and also, in her particular choice of stars, may have provided Ball with a likely pair with which to illustrate his point. My thanks to Dr. Jim Hunt, Professor of Physics, University of Guelph, for helping me to picture the "orbits pitched in harmony" (Sonnet 9.12).

23. Clerke, *Popular History*, p. 123.

24. Clerke, *System*, p. 333.

25. Clerke, *System*, p. 349.

26. Richard Berendzen, Richard Hart, and Daniel Seeley, *Man Discovers the Galaxies* (New York: Science History Publications, 1976), pp. 7–14; Clerke, *Popular History*, pp. 19–26, 422. The great Rosse telescope (the so-called "Leviathan of Parsonstown") was completed at Birr Castle by the third Earl of Rosse, William Parsons; it was his son Lawrence, the fourth earl, who conducted the observations of lunar heat mentioned above.

27. Clerke, *System*, pp. 349, 361. Although I quote from the second edition (1905), these passages are unchanged from the first (1890).

28. Clerke, *Popular History*, p. 422. However, the "Great Debate" about external galaxies (a debate complicated by differing estimations of the size of our galaxy and of the distance of spiral nebulae) was not resolved until 1935, when Edwin Powell Hubble's work in the 1920s—the discovery of Cepheids (pulsating variable stars) in spiral nebulae—was eventually found decisive.

29. Herbert Spencer, "The Nebular Hypothesis," *Essays Scientific, Political, and Speculative* (New York: Appleton, 1896), 1:118; the essay was first published as "Recent Astronomy, and the Nebular Hypothesis," in *Westminster Review* 70 (July 1858): 185-225. For Gilchrist's and Tennyson's view of it, see *Anne Gilchrist: Her Life and Writings,* ed. Herbert Harlakenden Gilchrist, with a Prefatory Notice by William Michael Rossetti (London: Unwin, 1887), pp. 166, 170. Anne Gilchrist, with whom Christina Rossetti exchanged visits and letters after their first meeting in 1864, found in the recently formulated law of the conservation of energy arguments for a spiritualized conception of matter (the poetic annunciation of which she was to recognize in the poetry of Walt Whitman), and for science as a God-given means of contemplating the undiminished mystery of God's works. In her essay "The Indestructibility of Force," *Macmillan's Magazine* 6 (August 1862): 337-44, Gilchrist deprecates the distrust of and contempt for science evident "in the minds of the religious" and "in our highest literature," arguing that "if [physical science] have one decided tendency at the present day, it is to exalt and spiritualize our idea of matter, and, far from destroying, to enhance the sense of mystery" (p. 344). Though by no means as orthodox in her profession of faith as Christina Rossetti, Gilchrist shared (and indeed may have helped foster) Rossetti's conviction that science was no enemy to faith, but (at least in its "depths") its ally and supporter. For Anne Gilchrist, "Nature's great laws of Continuity and Indestructibility" applied to souls as well as to "atoms and forces," and proved there was a future life: so she said to Tennyson in 1867, and wrote the same to William Michael Rossetti in 1882, after Dante Gabriel Rossetti's death (*Life and Writings,* pp. 170, 265). Such was the view of the devout Scottish physicist, Balfour Stewart, who with Professor P. G. Tait argued that the Law of Continuity made science Christianity's "most efficient supporter," in their controversial treatise, *The Unseen Universe, or Physical Speculations on a Future State,* 7th ed. (London: Macmillan, 1886), pp. 270-73; the work was first published anonymously in 1875.

30. Clerke, *Popular History*, p. 422.

31. Frances Power Cobbe, "To Know, or Not to Know?," *Fraser's Magazine* 80 (December 1869): 786-87. The "spectacle" is produced not only by the recent "surveys" of the astronomer, but by those of the geologist and botanist as well; though such increased knowledge increases sorrow, Cobbe concludes, "nothing can dim its triumphant and inalienable joy" (p. 787). Cobbe's essay appears in the same issue as Richard A. Proctor's "The Rosse Telescope Set to New Work" (pp. 754-60), which contains a preliminary report on Lord Rosse's observations of lunar heat, and which

also rehearses what the giant telescope had famously accomplished, the resolution of nebulae "into glorious galaxies of stars" (p. 755). Here Proctor does not call into question the resolution of nebulae, as he was presently to do.

32. Thomas De Quincey, "System of the Heavens as Revealed by Lord Rosse's Telescopes," in *The Collected Writings of Thomas De Quincey,* ed. David Masson (London: A. and C. Black, 1890), 8:23, 33–34. The essay was originally published in *Tait's Edinburgh Magazine* 17 (September 1846): 566–79. De Quincey, along with Thomas Carlyle, introduced Jean Paul (Johann Paul Friedrich Richter, 1763–1825) to English readers through translations and appreciations; Jean Paul's "Dream upon the Universe" is one of the "Analects from Richter" accompanying De Quincey's "Jean Paul Frederick Richter" (*Collected Writings,* 11:290–93). On De Quincey's "System of the Heavens" and his remaking of Richter's "Dream," see V. A. De Luca, *Thomas De Quincey: The Prose of Vision* (Toronto: University of Toronto Press, 1980), pp. 90–96.

33. Richard A. Proctor, "Newton and Darwin," *Contemporary Review* 41 (June 1882): 1002. From the mid-1860s through the 1880s, a steady stream of Proctor's popularizing essays on various aspects of contemporary astronomy appeared in such magazines as *Fraser's, Cornhill, Contemporary Review, Nineteenth Century, St. Paul's,* and *Temple Bar.*

34. Richard A. Proctor, *Other Worlds Than Ours: The Plurality of Worlds Studied under the Light of Recent Scientific Researches,* 2d ed. (London: Longmans, Green, 1870), p. 337. The first edition of this work, published in May 1870, was sold out in less than three months, prompting a second edition in October. In the preface to the second edition, Proctor notes that he has omitted some passages from the last chapter ("Supervision and Control") because "they touched too closely on the subject of revealed religion," and insists that "the chapter is a *chapter of fancies*—nothing more; though haply the fancies are such as may invite profitable reflection. What I know respecting the manner in which the Almighty watches over and controls this universe is about what other men know,—ABSOLUTELY NOTHING" (p. xx).

35. A finite universe keeps Earth more confidently at the center of God's attention, a point enforced by William Whewell's *Of the Plurality of Worlds* (1853), which Clerke cites along with Spencer's work as influential in discrediting the idea of external galaxies (*Popular History,* p. 422).

36. Lady [Margaret Lindsay (Murray)] Huggins, *Agnes Mary Clerke and Ellen Mary Clerke: An Appreciation* (printed for private circulation, 1907), pp. 52–53. Lady Huggins's memoir and Henry Park Hollis's article on the Clerke sisters in the *DNB* (*Supplement* [1901–1911], 1:371–72) are the sources for the biographical material in this paragraph. Lady Huggins, elected an honorary member of the Royal Astronomical Society, assisted her husband, recognized as Britain's foremost expert in spectroscopy from the 1860s onwards, in carrying out various research projects. E. M. Clerke's *Flowers of Fire: A Novel* (London: Hutchinson, 1902), set in Naples at the time of the 1872 eruption of Mt. Vesuvius (which Clerke, a member of the Manchester Geo-

graphical Society, describes in compelling detail), tells the story of an exiled Polish family harried by Russian agents, and contains interesting vignettes of Neapolitan and gypsy life. An incidental story about an Englishwoman's suffering because her Neapolitan husband forbids her to walk out alone, as she insists she has a right to do (p. 112), may well have lent something to E. M. Forster's first novel, *Where Angels Fear to Tread* (1905).

37. Agnes Mary Clerke, *Familiar Studies in Homer* (London: Longmans, Green, 1892). Clerke's topics at any rate would have appealed to Rossetti: besides Homeric astronomy, Clerke discusses such things as Homeric dogs, trees and flowers, meals, magic herbs, and metals, and concludes with a chapter on "Amber, Ivory, and Ultramarine." Rossetti's "The Lowest Room" may be found in *CP*, 1:200–207.

38. E. M. Clerke, *The Flying Dutchman and Other Poems* (London: W. Satchell, 1881), p. 54.

Speaking Likenesses

Hearing the Lesson

JULIA BRIGGS

In *A Room of One's Own,* Virginia Woolf refers to Christina Rossetti only as the author of "My heart is like a singing bird," whose verses "women hummed at luncheon parties before the [first world] war." She characterizes Charlotte Brontë, on the other hand, as angry, starved, indignant— adjectives that recall Matthew Arnold's impression of the author of *Villette* as driven by "hunger, rebellion, and rage."[1] It is precisely these qualities that critics have recognized in *Speaking Likenesses* (1874), and have found offensive. In this, her longest work for children, Rossetti transforms the celebratory note of "A Birthday" into "hunger, rebellion, and rage," emotions peculiarly characteristic of childhood (although notes of joy are usually considered more appropriate for child-readers). *Speaking Likenesses* has seemed to its critics a harsh, judgmental, and moralizing story in the tradition of Day's *Sandford and Merton* or Mrs. Sherwood's *Fairchild Family,* books that the young Rossettis are said to have rejected.[2] With inexplicable sourness, Rossetti (or her narrator) attacks the new child as exemplified in Carroll's *Alice's Adventures in Wonderland* (1865) and *Through the Looking-Glass* (1871),[3] the arbiter in a world of delightful play. She criticizes the middle-class child, encouraged to play in the walled rose garden and protected from any knowledge of the poverty and deprivation beyond. Such anger distressed her former admirers: writing to F. S. Ellis in January 1875, Ruskin expressed his dislike of *Speaking Likenesses,* condemning it as the worst of that year's Christmas books for children. He had looked forward with pleasure to a sequel to *Sing-Song,* the book of nursery poems that Rossetti had published with illustrations by Arthur Hughes two years earlier: "The *worst* [of the books] I consider Christina Rossetti's. I've kept that for the mere wonder of it. How could she or Arthur Hughes sink so low after their pretty nursery rhymes?"[4]

Writing a few days later to her publisher, Alexander Macmillan, Rossetti acknowledged the poor reviews, but was relieved that these had not adversely affected her sales figures: "I am pleased to hear of more than 1000 'Speaking Likenesses' having been disposed of: truth to tell, I had feared the reviews might this time have done me a very real injury with the buying public; but, for me, such a sale is certainly not bad."[5] *Speaking Likenesses* has never achieved popularity, and it is only in the last few years that it has once more been reprinted in full, in U. C. Knoepflmacher and Nina Auerbach's anthology *Forbidden Journeys* (1992), in Jan Marsh's selection of Rossetti's *Poems and Prose* (Dent, 1994), and more recently in David A. Kent and P. G. Stanwood's *Selected Prose of Christina Rossetti* (1998). Earlier reprints often truncated it, reproducing only the first of its three inset stories, as, for example, does Patricia Demers in *A Garland for the Golden Age* (1983),[6] or else omitting the frame and interruptions that hold the stories together. And while editors have carved it up according to one set of expectations, critics have shown a comparable reluctance to see it steadily and see it whole: the explicitly sexual nature of the monster children in Flora's dream — the prickly little boys (erect Quills, sharp Angles and Hooks), and the slithery girls (Sticky and Slime) — has attracted disproportionate attention, as have the punitive games they play — "Hunt the Pincushion" and "Self-Help" (pp. 28, 32, 35).[7] Parallels between their harassment of Flora and the goblins' persecution of Lizzie are conspicuous. Deterred, however, by the narrator/Aunt's evident exasperation with her nieces and other difficulties, critics have not generated a range of feminist readings for *Speaking Likenesses* as they have for *Goblin Market*.

Two articles published in the eighties established the grounds for a serious consideration of *Speaking Likenesses* by exploring its relationship to contemporary children's fiction, and in particular to Carroll's two *Alices*, as well as to the rest of Rossetti's work, in which context it had previously been treated as anomalous or ignored altogether. Wendy A. Katz in "Muse from Nowhere: Christina Rossetti's Fantasy World in *Speaking Likenesses*"[8] made good use of these approaches, concluding that the book's combination of fantasy and moralizing allowed Rossetti to articulate both the more imaginative and the more mundane aspects of her spirituality simultaneously. U. C. Knoepflmacher in "Avenging Alice: Christina Rossetti and Lewis Carroll" also read

Speaking Likenesses back into Rossetti's career as a whole, while regarding its intertextual relationship with the *Alice*s as a reaction not merely to Carroll's text but to the man behind the texts who, as Charles Dodgson, had met, photographed, and corresponded with the Rossetti family, including Christina herself. Knoepflmacher argues that her book constitutes part of an uneasy dialogue between them.

Writing to her brother Gabriel, Rossetti herself indicated her debt to Lewis Carroll in *Speaking Likenesses:* "The story is merely a Christmas trifle, would-be in the *Alice* style, with an eye to the market."[9] Knoepflmacher persuasively argues that it is "an antagonistic work," a conscious response to the commercial success of the *Alice*s, and a repudiation of it, and he locates the narrative's shortcomings in its critique of Carroll's fantasy world, a critique that paradoxically "only managed to reinforce her rival's originality," since it denies and rejects the powers of imagination, thus exposing her own unsuccessful attempt at correction. The many allusions to the *Alice*s and the form they take strongly suggest that Rossetti was indeed attempting to address and even to counter what she found there. Carroll's stature as a writer for children, however, need not invalidate her grounds for dissent or her implicit criticism of his work. At the same time, Knoepflmacher's biographical context for Rossetti's reaction to "the powerful blend of gentleness and sadism that she recognised in Carroll" is bound to be speculative in some measure.[10]

Here and in the introduction to *Speaking Likenesses* in his anthology *Forbidden Journeys,* Knoepflmacher worries away at its many structural inconsistencies: the contrasts in tone and form between the three stories—the first a fantasy indebted to *Alice,* the second a nursery tale, "a nonstory describing a nonaction,"[11] and the third a traditional fairy tale on "Red Riding Hood" lines; and, in the framework within which the tales are narrated, the contrast between the child-listeners' desire for "wonder" and their Aunt's reluctance to meet their demand. Knoepflmacher suggests that the stories record a spiritual journey from the hell of Flora's nightmare to the purgatory in which Edith so signally fails to light a fire, to the paradise signified by Maggie's attainment of home, sleep, and peace. Yet this interpretation undercuts or is at odds with the settings Rossetti has employed: the first two stories take place in the safe enclaves of garden and grove, while the third, a "winter" story, offers a far more explicit representation of a spiritual journey, and is set largely in an icy wilderness. The difficulty of interpreting *Speaking Likenesses* lies not in any shortage of signification but rather in establishing the order, relation, and subordination of its different elements, one to another. As a reviewer for the *Academy* observed, the book induced "an uncomfortable feeling that a great deal more is meant than appears on the surface, and that every part of it ought to mean something, if only we knew what it was."[12]

While Rossetti herself left little in the way of comments on *Speaking Likenesses,* those that she did make suggest that she was clear in her own mind as to the book's structure and meaning. Writing to Alexander Macmillan in the summer of 1874, she insisted that he accept her proposed change of title from "Nowhere," as she had originally planned to call it:

> And then I really must adopt "Speaking Likenesses" as my title, this having met with some approval in my circle. Very likely you did not so deeply ponder upon my text as to remark that my small heroines perpetually encounter "speaking (literally *speaking*) likenesses" or embodiments or caricatures of themselves or their faults. This premised, I think the title boasts of some point & neatness.[13]

As the book went to press, she found herself unhappy with the wording of the title page and the inappropriate captions provided in the list of illustrations, and she wrote to Macmillan asking him to cancel both of them, though in the event he failed to do so. The captions referred to the book's various visionary figures as "fairies." Rossetti objected: "the word 'fairy' I should altogether have excluded as not appropriate to my story."[14] Her point is reinforced by a comparison of *Speaking Likenesses* with two earlier "fairy" tales of granted wishes, "Nick" and "Hero" in *Commonplace and Other Short Stories* (1870), stories far more consciously indebted to Hans Andersen and the brothers Grimm.

While the title Rossetti chose, "Speaking Likenesses," implies a dualism, the similarity and/or opposition of self and antiself, the book itself is constructed as a trilogy, figured at its own center, as Knoepflmacher has observed,[15] as the tripod on which Edith's kettle is hung: "Three sticks, Maude, are the fewest that can stand up by themselves; two would tumble down and four are not needed" (p. 57), and perhaps also in the plain sewing that the Aunt imposes on her nieces in exchange for the second story: "these breadths must be run together, three and three" (p. 50). Within the stories, too, there are many structural parallels and echoes. All three are concerned with food, but the buttered toast that is Maggie's reward for her labors in the third is contrasted with the elaborately described feasts in the first two: Flora's disappointing birthday dinner of meat, potatoes, beans, and jam tart (pp. 8-9) is in turn further contrasted with the strawberry tea and fantasy supper of

"Cold turkey, lobster salad, stewed mushrooms, raspberry tart, cream cheese, a bumper of champagne, a meringue, a strawberry ice, sugared pine apple, some greengages" (pp. 38–39), while Edith's gypsy feast will consist of "Cold fowls, and a syllabub, and champagne, and tea and coffee, and potato-rolls, and lunns, and tongue, and I can't say what besides" (p. 53). As with the Water-Rat's picnic in *The Wind in the Willows,* the author counts on childish greed to confer imaginative life on such menus. In Flora's dream, however, the listed delicacies are all forbidden to her just as she is about to eat them, and she "was too honest a little girl to eat strawberries that were not given her" (p. 25). Her self-restraint is echoed in the third story where Maggie refuses to give away the chocolate she is delivering: "'I'm hungry enough myself, but I wouldn't be a thief'" (p. 86).

Both the listing of delicious food (the "drink me" bottle in *Alice* has "a mixed flavour of cherry-tart, custard, pine-apple, roast turkey, toffy and hot buttered toast")[16] and its withholding recall moments from the *Alice* books, where food and drink either change Alice's size or else, as the perquisites of being grown-up, are physically out of reach: the empty marmalade jar as she falls down the rabbit-hole (p. 27), the Mad Hatter's tea-party (p. 93), the stolen tarts (p. 146), the division of the plum-cake (p. 290), and Alice's final feast in her own honor (pp. 331–32) are all characterized by the withholding of food. It occasions annoyance rather than hunger in Alice, just as the consumption of food is qualified by prudence, rather than by any property ethic. She hesitates to drink the bottle labelled "drink me" in case it is also marked "poison" (p. 31), but she doesn't question her right to drink it. Alice's charm lies in her security and self-confidence, her optimistic sense of her own centrality, though Carroll's narratives also explore the anomalies of the emancipated child, at once her own subject and in control of her world, while also being object and victim, only a child in a world of grown-ups. The alternation or opposition of these positions is figured as Alice's changing size in *Wonderland,* and by the image of mirror reversal in *Through the Looking-Glass.*

The mirror image had always been a powerful one for Rossetti, who borrowed it from Carroll, but drew on its more traditional function, as a "moral-reflective device," as Wendy A. Katz has pointed out,[17] a reminder of the need for reflection in its other sense of self-examination. In Flora's dream she finds herself in a peculiarly accommodating middle-class drawing room in which "both ceiling and walls were lined throughout with looking-glasses: but at first this did not strike Flora as any disadvantage; indeed she thought it quite delightful, and took a long look at her little self full length" (pp.

18–21). When her speaking likeness appears, however, "The birthday Queen, reflected over and over again in five hundred mirrors, looked frightful, I do assure you: and for one minute I am sorry to say that Flora's fifty million-fold face appeared flushed and angry too" (p. 26). The mirrors multiply only too precisely what the child does not want to see, leading her eye into the infinite horror of a *mis-en-abîme*: "in such a number of mirrors there were not merely simple reflections, but reflections of reflections, and reflections of reflections of reflections, and so on and on and on, over and over again" (p. 26). A pool in the second story "mirrored in its still depths the lights, shadows, and many greens of beech-tree, birch-tree and vine" (pp. 56–57), with its unattainable grapes. There are no corresponding reflections in the third story because its heroine is happily free from the illusions that possess Flora and Edith.

Whichever group of images is examined, the first two stories are continually contrasted with the third, so that the triadic structure is reduced once again to a binary opposition, an opposition that some Victorian children, though by no means all, were carefully protected from: this is the contrast between Disraeli's two nations, the haves and have nots, the rich and the poor. The first two stories of Flora and Edith can be compared at every stage: both are surrounded by loving parents and siblings, nurses, pets, toys, good food, comfortable homes with gardens and private woods at hand; they occupy the kind of middle-class paradise that is felt to be every child's birthright. At every point their situations are contrasted with that of Maggie, the orphan of the third story, shut out alone in the cold at Christmastime, like Andersen's "Little Match Girl."[18] If the working-class child is in danger of exposure, the middle-class child is in danger of being overprotected, of being shut in, of finding, as does the speaker of "A Royal Princess," "All my walls are lost in mirrors." Beyond such enclaves, the world looks very different: here men, women, and children are "clamouring to be fed."[19] The third story differs crucially from, yet also recapitulates, the other two, and the narrative as a whole acknowledges that while Flora and Edith exist in a warmth and abundance they take for granted, there are certain basic needs common to all children, which must somehow be met if the child is to prosper. These needs are figured as the dog, cat, and bird who appear at the beginning of the first story and reappear in each of the others, and whose significance helps to determine the development of each story.

Arthur Hughes's opening illustration for *Speaking Likenesses* shows Flora's mother kissing her awake, while a dog, a cat, and a cock strut or stretch themselves around her (fig. 9.1). These animals correspond to the threefold repetition of "Wagga the dog was up and about, Muff the cat was up and about, chirping birds were up and about" (p. 2); and the pattern is later echoed by the trio of Edith's pets, "Frisk, the Newfoundland dog, and Cosy, the Persian cat . . . Crest, the cockatoo" (p. 55), who accompany her to the grove where the gypsy tea will take place (fig. 9.2). But the significance of the three animals becomes fully apparent only in the third story, where they are associated with the spiritual, physical, and social needs of the child. Maggie comes upon a dove, a kitten, and a puppy, on her return journey from the doctor's house, at just those points where she had previously encountered the temptations to sleep (and thus to die, as the Aunt makes explicit in an aside to her listeners), to eat, and to play; the dove thus corresponds to the child's need for spiritual sustenance, the kitten to her need for food and physical nurture, and the puppy to her need for companionship and play (fig. 9.3).

This sequence of needs, epitomized in Maggie's journey and her discoveries, also corresponds to the structure of *Speaking Likenesses* as a whole: the first story focuses on children at play and in social relationships, and is briefly recapitulated in the reappearance of the monstrous children who tempt Maggie to play with them. The second focuses on a family feast, and Edith's eagerness to help provide for it, and is recapitulated as Maggie's experience of hunger personified as a boy who is all mouth. The third is Maggie's own story, a story of spiritual needs figured both as the mysterious sleepers and as the heavenly wonder of the Northern Lights. While Edith and Flora can take their pets for granted, Maggie must rescue from the dark and the cold the animals that embody her own needs. Since the structure of the book is progressive, the lessons of the first two stories have now been learned, and the deprived child finds companionship, food, and even spiritual joy, as in a fairy story, through her own good actions. If Flora, in the birthday Queen, and Edith, in the forest animals, met their own speaking likenesses, bullying or ineffectual, Maggie is already sufficiently in control of her needs for them to take two different forms: first as visionary temptations to be overcome, and subsequently as the abandoned animals whose plight reflects her own orphaned state. In an act of vicarious nurture, she cares for herself by caring for them. The binary oppositions of likenesses in the first two stories become triadic once more in the third, where Maggie remains independent of both the bad likenesses (or temptations) and the good ones, though we can also see how, in a further patterning, Maggie's tempting playmates are identical with the monstrous children of Flora's nightmare, while the abandoned pets she rescues correspond to Edith's animal friends.

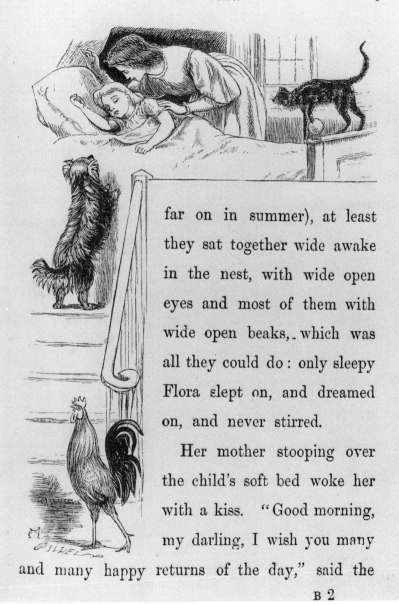

far on in summer), at least they sat together wide awake in the nest, with wide open eyes and most of them with wide open beaks, which was all they could do : only sleepy Flora slept on, and dreamed on, and never stirred.

Her mother stooping over the child's soft bed woke her with a kiss. "Good morning, my darling, I wish you many and many happy returns of the day," said the

Fig. 9.1. Arthur Hughes, "Her mother, stooping over the child's soft bed, awoke her with a kiss." Illustration for Christina Rossetti, *Speaking Likenesses* (London: Macmillan, 1874), p. 3. Reproduced with the kind permission of the English Faculty Library, University of Oxford (Shelf mark XN65.76[Spe]).

Fig. 9.2. Arthur Hughes, "Edith, with her dog Frisk, her cat Cosy, and Crest the cockatoo."
Illustration for Christina Rossetti, *Speaking Likenesses* (London: Macmillan, 1874), p. 56.
Reproduced with the kind permission of the English Faculty Library, University of Oxford
(Shelf mark XN65.76[Spe]).

The first two stories exemplify childish anger and pride, aspects of her own
childhood that Rossetti retrospectively acknowledged. The primal nature of
such feelings is suggested when the Aunt says of the quarreling at Flora's
birthday party, that the children "tossed the apple of discord to and fro as if
it had been a pretty plaything" (p. 10), an allusion further underlined by her
listeners' incomprehension: "What apple, Aunt?" Arthur Hughes's facing
illustration of the scene is dominated by a personification of Discord with
snaky Medusan locks (fig. 9.4). When Flora falls asleep in the yew alley, her
dream begins in a recognizably Victorian interior, a world where at first even
the furniture—stuffed armchairs, sofas, footstools and tea-trays—respond
obediently to her wishes, until her evil double and speaking likeness, the
birthday Queen, appears. Echoing Flora's own cry of "It's my birthday" (pp.
13, 25), she appropriates everything in sight, and Flora herself is displaced
from the center to the periphery, no longer the ruler but her persecuted

Fig. 9.3. Arthur Hughes, "Maggie Drinks Tea and Eats Buttered Toast with Grannie." Illustration for Christina Rossetti, *Speaking Likenesses* (London: Macmillan, 1874), p. 95. Reproduced with the kind permission of the English Faculty Library, University of Oxford (Shelf mark XN65.76[Spe]).

victim, pursued and tormented by prickly or slimy playmates, and excluded from their feast. In the even more nightmarish aftermath, she finds herself walled up with the Queen inside a glowing house of glass that seems to signify the vulnerable self. Here extreme horror and distress overcome her, as the children begin a game of throwing stones: "'Oh don't, don't, don't,' cried out Flora again, almost choking with sobs . . . Half mad with fear" (p. 46). She wakes at the point her dream becomes intolerable.

The violent alternations of power within Flora's dream, as she moves from controlling the compliant furniture to becoming the victim of the children's games and the Queen's dangerous whims, recall similar sudden shifts in *Through the Looking Glass,* where Alice's status as dreamer and later Queen does not exempt her from mockery, exploitation, and helplessness as the subject of the dreams of the Red King, whose waking might extinguish her completely (Carroll, pp. 238-40). As in *Through the Looking Glass,* Flora's

Fig. 9.4. Arthur Hughes, "The Apple of Discord." Illustration for Christina Rossetti, *Speaking Likenesses* (London: Macmillan, 1874), p. 11. Reproduced with the kind permission of the English Faculty Library, University of Oxford (Shelf mark XN65.76[Spe]).

Fig. 9.5. Arthur Hughes, "Maggie and the sleepers in the wood." Illustration for Christina Rossetti, *Speaking Likenesses* (London: Macmillan, 1874), p. 89. Reproduced with the kind permission of the English Faculty Library, University of Oxford (Shelf mark XN65.76[Spe]).

dream begins in a comfortably upholstered Victorian parlor and ends in a rough waking from threatened chaos. Edith's situation, on the other hand—surrounded by animals ready to offer her advice—is more reminiscent of *Alice's Adventures in Wonderland.* Hughes's illustrations, influenced, as Knoepflmacher has shown, by Tenniel's,[20] give both Flora and Edith long, loose hair in the manner of Alice's, but Edith's resemblance is the closer: she wears bar-shoes, has stripes on her dress where Alice has tucks, and has a hair-ribbon such as Alice has in *Through the Looking Glass* (see fig. 9.2). Maggie in the third story wears the boots of the poor child, and a cape and hood that point to Little Red Riding Hood as her main precursor (fig. 9.5). Edith's story functions as an antithesis to Flora's, ostensibly by taking us inside it: the listening nieces ask for the rest of the story begun by Flora's older sister Susan at her party, of which they have heard no more than an intriguing snatch: "—So the frog did not know how to boil the kettle; but he only replied: I can't bear hot water" (pp. 15-16, 49). The children's demand, like their later request for a winter story, serves to camouflage the schematic development of the inset stories.

The relation of a second story already supposed to have been told within the first story involves a regression, and accordingly Edith is significantly younger than Flora. The world of her story is that of a very young child; it has a suitably simple action as its center, and is concerned with the provision of food, among the child's earliest and most urgent needs. It is characterized by the child's animistic vision: Edith imagines herself as all-powerful, and in untroubled communication with the world around her, whether inhabited by grown-ups or by animals. The world of the wood with its delightful small creatures—toad, frog, fox, and mole—is that of the earthly paradise in Rossetti's poem, "From House to Home,"[21] and may have had its origins in memories of her grandfather's cottage at Holmer Green. She remembered its grounds—in reality "quite small and on the simplest scale but in those days *to me* they were vast, varied, worth exploring,"[22] just as, to Edith's eyes, the wood "looked no less than a forest" (p. 51). She also remembered the small child's utter self-absorption and sense of her own autonomy. If Flora wants to control her little world on the occasion of her birthday, Edith has not yet learned to question her right to do so: she "thought herself by no means such a very little girl, and at any rate as wise as her elder brother, sister, and nurse. I should be afraid to assert that she did not reckon herself as wise as her parents: but we must hope not, for her own sake" (p. 51).

After lunch, Edith dresses her doll (as surrogate child) in its best clothes, ready for the afternoon's planned treat, the gypsy tea. The household is fully occupied in making preparations, and no one has any time for Edith. Eager to assist, she "fetched a kettle large and new" which she carries, with some matches, to the wood, accompanied by her dog, cat, and the cockatoo—a little like Christopher Robin, surrounded by his retinue of toys (as in fig. 9.2). But there is an element of Promethean hubris in this small girl's assumption that she can make a fire and boil the kettle single-handed. She drops all but six of the matches on her way, forgets to fill the kettle with water, and finds that the remaining matches blow out before she can get the fire to light. Various animals gather round and offer suggestions, rather as they had gathered round Alice as the pool of tears receded. Charming but ineffectual, these gentle speaking likenesses are unable to advise on such a peculiarly human activity as lighting a fire. Edith makes minimal progress, and, when the fire finally goes out, sits down to cry. Edith is a child so young that she cannot yet distinguish between fact and fantasy, between toys, pets, or animals that talk, who has not yet realized that she cannot do everything that adults can, or identified the skills and experiences that distinguish them from her. It is a very small incident, but on its own terms it offers a graphic fable of pride followed by a fall, a warning of the strict limitations of the child's control over her fragile world.

In providing a winter story to offset these two summer stories, Rossetti moved decisively away from Carroll's stories of "'happy summer days' gone by" (Carroll, p. 174) as he designated them in the poem that introduces *Through the Looking Glass*. Instead she found her starting point in an almost Marxist contemplation of the means of distribution and consumption: the final story begins in the toy shop that has supplied the dolls, playthings, and sweetmeats so unreflectively enjoyed by Flora and Edith. The orphan Maggie works here; her nickname is that of Rossetti's older sister Maria, but also suggests a lower class than those of the other girls named so far. This is the first time, of course, that we have seen a child other than at play: Maggie helps her grandmother in the shop, fetching toys for children luckier than herself. It is Christmas Eve, and when Dame Margaret notices the parcels forgotten by "the doctor's young ladies" (p. 74), Maggie volunteers to deliver them. The presents themselves—a bouncing ball, chocolate, candles for the Christmas tree, and crackers—stand in for the consumer goods that Maggie herself lacks, yet cheerfully distributes to others. They also recapitulate the triadic structure of the book in their figuring of play, food, and the special lights of Christmas that celebrate the birth of the saviour. On her journey,

Maggie undergoes three temptations—to play, to eat, and to fall asleep, each one heralded by her own desire. The first of these sets the ball bouncing in her basket, while in the second, the blind, huge-mouthed boy somehow knows of the chocolate she is carrying and demands it of her. In the third (shown in fig. 9.5), the mysterious night-capped sleepers, dozing before a gypsy fire that recalls Edith's struggles to light one in the previous tale, are soon left behind as Maggie runs on to the doctor's house and delivers the parcels, hoping to be "asked indoors, warmed by a fire, regaled with something nice, and indulged in a glimpse of the Christmas tree bending under its crop of wonderful fruit" (p. 91). Instead, she is turned away from the door, with only the most perfunctory of thanks.

It seems that the doctor's children, like Flora and Edith, have no sense of the labor of a world beyond, through which their toys, sweetmeats, and Christmas candles reach them. Maggie's summary exclusion recalls Rossetti's poem, "Behold, I stand at the door and knock,"[23] in which an old woman, an old man, and a stunted child are successively turned away from a rich woman's doorstep, to be replaced by a judging Christ-figure. Maggie, buoyed up on her outward journey by the hope of being invited in, now shares the disappointment previously experienced by Flora and Edith; yet tired, cold, and hungry though she is, she stops to rescue three creatures as wretched as herself, and, in nurturing them, provides for her own needs. The dove, kitten, and puppy at once symbolize and solace her need for warmth, food, and company. Finally, as she reaches home, she sees something far more wonderful (and it was "wonder" that Laura had specifically requested at the story's outset) than the Christmas tree with all its lights burning. Indeed the Christmas Eve setting suggests Rossetti's unease with the secularization of this religious festival, its becoming an occasion to indulge childish greed by loading children with presents—bouncing balls, chocolate, and crackers. To compensate her for the drawing-room pleasures she has lost, Maggie is shown a natural wonder in the form of the Aurora Borealis, the Northern Lights, illuminating the clouds and the landscape, and turning the forest trees a more beautiful pink than any number of candles could have done: "Every oak-tree seemed turned to coral, and the road itself to a pavement of dusky carnelian" (p. 94). The lights further signify the spiritual illumination that lies open to those who have accepted worldly deprivation. Once home with her Granny (as in fig. 9.3), Maggie and the animals she has rescued find the warmth, food, and comfort that she had denied herself in order to complete her quest and fulfill her promise.

In an article mainly concerned with Mrs. Molesworth's *The Cuckoo Clock,*

Sanjay Sircar has described *Speaking Likenesses* as "The most striking instance of an explicitly auntly narrative voice. . . . This long dramatic monologue gradually reveals that the speaker is indeed an aunt; the text inscribes the nature, number, and responses of her listeners, as well as her own character and relationships with them."[24] It is this narrator, characterized as moralizing, reluctant, and gloomy, who is felt to embody the most offensive aspects of the text. She has been directly identified with Rossetti herself, who, after her brother William's marriage in 1874, could anticipate aunthood; but also as her own "speaking likeness," that is, her own least attractive aspect; or else as the traditional "mentoria" of children's fiction who might draw moral lessons from all occasions, preside over a framework of inset tales, and prefer rationalism above fairy stories: "one of those didactic anti-fantasists that abounded in children's literature."[25] It is true that Flora's experiences in the yew alley are explained as a dream (as are Alice's), while Maggie's might be considered the result of a bang on the head when she slips on some ice (p. 76). Only the second story, with its very young protagonist, is unambiguously supernatural, though the Aunt dismisses the animals speaking as "a marvel scarcely worth mentioning after Flora's experience" (p. 50). But the harshest charge against the aunt's rationalism is that, in purporting "to put down the childish fantasies of power that were given such a free range by Lewis Carroll . . . she reveals her own hunger for domination."[26]

Such a reading seems to accept the fictional standing of the tales while treating their teller as if she were "a real person," somehow located outside the fiction altogether, or, just as problematically, a transparent mouthpiece for Rossetti herself.[27] The narrative framework is, of course, as much an invented and deliberate fiction as that of the inset stories. Its naturalism creates a sense of stories spontaneously unfolding that is designed to camouflage their schematic organization and to establish a link with the familiar world, functioning as the equivalent frames had done in the work of Lewis Carroll. But while the stories themselves move from a Carrollean state of innocence to a world of experience, so the Aunt increasingly comes to resemble Blake's green-faced nurse, lamenting "Your spring and your day are wasted in play."[28] Her resentment is directed against the self-centered world of childhood that cannot look beyond itself, or imagine the sufferings of others, but it may also point up her own insecurities—"All eyes on occupations, not on me lest I should feel shy!" (p. 2)—and a limited tolerance of children. In compensation, she also attempts fair-mindedness, admitting the justice of her nieces' claim upon her:

"You know, Aunt, you are always telling *us* to try."

"Fairly put, Jane, and I will try, on condition that you all help me with my sewing." (p. 49)

In the tradition of such frame stories (which goes back through Mrs. Sherwood and Mary Wollstonecraft's *Original Stories* to Sarah Fielding's *The Governess, or the Little Female Academy* of 1749), an older woman addresses a group of young girls.[29] Typically, she emphasizes moral teaching and sets her stories in a context of harsher lives whose presence is evoked by the sewing tasks Rossetti's Aunt imposes, pointing out "I have too many poor friends ever to get through *my* work" (p. 50). Thus at one level her storytelling sessions are a children's version of the "sewing circles" that Victorian ladies regularly participated in, where someone read aloud or told stories to the rest as they worked at hemming and plain-sewing clothes and sheets for the poor. One function of the Aunt within the story is thus to bring into her narratives some question of what her nieces, like Flora and Edith within their respective tales, have taken for granted, their own privileged and untroubled existence; to introduce to them what the enclaves of middle-class childhood might otherwise have rendered invisible, the existence of the poor beyond the gates, and of transience beyond apparent security: "to every one of you a day will most likely come when sunshine, hope, presents and pleasure will be worth nothing to you in comparison with the unattainable gift of your mother's kiss" (p. 4), she warns her nieces at the beginning of the book. To modern sensibilities, the idea of reminding children to value their parents' love because one day they will die is distasteful; for Rossetti it was merely an acknowledgment of the uncertain human condition.

But while Rossetti would have sympathized with the sources of the Aunt's anger, the text as a whole views both the spoilt nieces and their irritable Aunt with a balanced irony. The childless Aunt, but not her creator, has forgotten the urgency of childhood feelings; she blames her nieces for a lack of perspective that they, like Flora and Edith, have not yet had time to acquire. The narrative itself is altogether gentler, recognizing Flora's horror at the self she had begun to become, and her eagerness to make amends: "Before tea was over, she had nestled close up to Anne, and whispered how sorry she was to have been so cross" (p. 48). Edith, too, is rescued from her impasse by her nurse and sent back to safety within the family who have missed her and have been searching for her. It is the best and most optimistic feature of childhood that the young can learn from having their feelings exercised, and it is precisely this quality in her young readers that Rossetti consciously addressed.

According to this interpretation, *Speaking Likenesses* should take its place not beside Carroll's *Alice,* whose world of play without learning it criticizes, but rather beside those other central Victorian classics whose fantasies were associated with social conscience: Charles Kingsley's *The Water-Babies* (1863), which juxtaposes the lifestyles of rich little Ellie and poor Tom the chimney sweep, and which acts out the logic of the ethical imperatives of Doasyouwouldbedoneby and celebrates the wonders of the maritime world; or George MacDonald's *At the Back of the North Wind* (1871), another book illustrated by Arthur Hughes, in which little Diamond is taken by North Wind to meet Nanny the crossing-sweeper, and is himself ultimately carried to the country "at the back of the north wind." Or it should be set beside less canonical and more popular texts such as Maria Charlesworth's *Ministering Children* (1854), where every child of whatever class "ministers," that is, makes a contribution of her own to the needs of others, within a closely networked community of children.[30] *Speaking Likenesses* has consistently posed problems to its readers because of its elaborate construction and its delicate and rapidly changing tones, but it shares with a great deal of Victorian writing for children the aim of encouraging its readers not only to look inward at their own behavior, but also to look outward, at those children who knew nothing of toys, parents, nurseries, or gardens—children who, in Mrs. Castle Smith's powerful if sentimental formulation, "have immortal souls, and . . . are our brothers and sisters, though we may not own them." Her peroration continues with an unconscious echo of Rossetti's poem, "Behold I stand at the door and knock":

> As we hope to partake of the same citizenship in the one Everlasting City, let us take care how we disregard our pastor's pleading, for when we are arraigned at the Last Day before the Judgement seat of Christ, and Christ asks us, "What have you done for my little ones?" the excuse, "Lord, we never knew any!" will avail us little with Him, who made His Kingdom above all a children's Kingdom, and who will hold us responsible.[31]

NOTES

1. Virginia Woolf, *A Room of One's Own* (London: Hogarth, 1929), pp. 20, 110; Arnold in a letter to Mrs. Forster, 14 April 185, in *Matthew Arnold: Poetry and Prose,* ed. John Bryson (London: Rupert Hart-Davis, 1954), p. 743.

2. Packer, p. 13; Georgina Battiscombe, *Christina Rossetti: A Divided Life* (London: Constable, 1981), p. 21; and Wendy A. Katz, "Muse from Nowhere: Christina Rossetti's Fantasy World in *Speaking Likenesses*," *The Journal of Pre-Raphaelite and Aesthetic Studies* 5, no. 1 (November 1984): 14-15.

3. Lewis Carroll, *The Annotated Alice: Alice's Adventures in Wonderland and Through the Looking Glass*, ed. Martin Gardner (Harmondsworth: Penguin, 1970).

4. Ruskin to F. S. Ellis, 21 January 1875, in *The Works of John Ruskin*, ed. E. T. Cook and A. Wedderburn, 39 vols. (London: George Allen, 1903-12), 37:155; qtd. by U. C. Knoepflmacher in "Avenging Alice: Christina Rossetti and Lewis Carroll," *Nineteenth-Century Literature* 41 (1986): 310-11.

5. Christina Rossetti to Alexander Macmillan, 26 January 1875, in *The Rossetti-Macmillan Letters*, ed. Lona Mosk Packer (Berkeley and Los Angeles: University of California Press, 1963), p. 105.

6. Nina Auerbach and U. C. Knoepflmacher, *Forbidden Journeys: Fairy Tales and Fantasies by Victorian Women Writers* (Chicago and London: University of Chicago Press, 1992); *Christina Rossetti: Poems and Prose*, ed. Jan Marsh (London: J. M. Dent, 1994); Patricia Demers, ed., *A Garland from the Golden Age: An Anthology of Children's Literature from 1850 to 1900* (Toronto: Oxford University Press, 1983).

7. This and subsequent references in the text to Christina Rossetti, *Speaking Likenesses* (London: Macmillan, 1874) will be noted parenthetically.

8. For details of this and Knoepflmacher's article, see above, notes 2, 4. See also Roderick McGillis, "Simple Surfaces; Christina Rossetti's Work for Children," in Kent, pp. 208-30.

9. Christina Rossetti to Dante Gabriel Rossetti, 4 May 1874, in *FL*, p. 44.

10. Knoepflmacher, "Avenging Alice," pp. 311, 324, 301.

11. In Auerbach and Knoepflmacher, *Forbidden Journeys*, p. 319.

12. *Academy*, 6 December 1874, qtd. in Packer, *The Rossetti-Macmillan Letters*, pp. 106-7 n. 1. Roderick McGillis comments that "it deserves attention because of its intricate form" (in Kent, p. 29).

13. Christina Rossetti to Alexander Macmillan, 27 July 1874, in Packer, *The Rossetti-Macmillan Letters*, p. 101. In May 1874, Dante Gabriel wrote to William Michael Rossetti that Christina's earlier title, "Nowhere," "seems unlucky because of that free-thinking book called *Erewhon*, which is 'Nowhere' inverted. The title would seem a little stale; I should change it." *Dante Gabriel Rossetti: His Family Letters* (London: Ellis and Elvey, 1895), 2:310.

14. Christina Rossetti to Alexander Macmillan, Friday evening [Autumn 1874], in Packer, *The Rossetti-Macmillan Letters*, p. 103. The list of illustrations includes "Maggie meets the fairies in the wood" (frontispiece), where "fairies" refers to the visionary children; and "The cross fairy deprives Flora of her strawberry feast" (p. 24), where "the cross fairy" is in fact the birthday Queen.

15. Auerbach and Knoepflmacher, *Forbidden Journeys*, pp. 321-22.

16. Carroll, *The Annotated Alice,* p. 31. Subsequent page references in the text are to this edition.

17. Katz, p. 21.

18. Hans Christian Andersen, "The Little Match Girl," *Fairy Tales and Legends,* illus. Rex Whistler (London: Bodley Head, 1935).

19. "A Royal Princess," in *The Prince's Progress and Other Poems* (1866), *CP,* 1:149–52, lines 10 and 56.

20. Knoepflmacher, "Avenging Alice," pp. 318–19.

21. "From House to Home," in *Goblin Market and Other Poems* (1862), *CP,* 1:82–88, esp. pp. 82–83.

22. Letter from Christina Rossetti to Edmund Gosse, 26 March 1884, qtd. by Marsh, *CR,* p. 9. Marsh suggests that Rossetti used Holmer Green as the setting for Edith's story (pp. 9–10).

23. Composed 1 December 1851; *CP,* 3:27–28.

24. Sanjay Sircar, "The Victorian Auntly Narrative Voice and Mrs. Molesworth's *Cuckoo Clock," Children's Literature* 17, ed. Francelia Butler (New Haven and London: Yale University Press, 1989), p. 16.

25. These last two suggestions are made by Knoepflmacher, in Auerbach and Knoepflmacher, *Forbidden Journeys,* pp. 318–19; and in "Avenging Alice," p. 313. According to McGillis, "Rossetti, through her narrator, expresses a distrust of fantasy, of make-believe, of story for its own sake" (in Kent, p. 225).

26. Knoepflmacher, "Avenging Alice," p. 315.

27. "[W]e should be careful not to conclude that this 'aunt' speaks for Christina Rossetti." McGillis in Kent, p. 225.

28. "Nurse's Song" from *Songs of Experience,* in *The Poems of William Blake,* ed. W. H. Stevenson and David V. Erdman (London: Longman, 1971), p. 214.

29. Mrs. Sherwood, *The History of the Fairchild Family* (Wellington, Salop: F. Houlston, 1820); Mary Wollstonecraft, *Original Stories from Real Life* (London: J. Johnson, 1791); Sarah Fielding, *The Governess; Or, The Little Female Academy* (London: Sold by A. Miller, 1749).

30. Charles Kingsley, *The Water-Babies: A Fairy Tale for a Land-Baby* (London and Cambridge: Macmillan, 1863); George MacDonald, *At the Back of the North Wind* (London: Strahan, 1871); Maria Louisa Charlesworth, *Ministering Children: A Tale Dedicated to Childhood* (London: Seeley, 1854, 1895).

31. "Brenda" (i.e., Mrs. G. Castle Smith), *Froggy's Little Brother* (London: John F. Shaw, 1875), p. 198. On the last page of this children's novel about "street Arabs," Mrs. Castle Smith appealed to "Parents and little children" to heed their clergymen and "send money and relief to the poor East End."

III. FEMALE POETICS

CHAPTER 10

Father's Place,
Mother's Space

*Identity, Italy, and the Maternal
in Christina Rossetti's Poetry*

ALISON CHAPMAN

> We cannot fathom these mysteries of transplantation.
> —Edmund Gosse on Christina Rossetti's Italian extraction[1]

In the nineteenth century Italy functions as a privileged trope, as the metaphorical site where issues of the past, political revolution, and the exotic coalesce.[2] For Victorian women poets, however, Italy is also invested with particularly acute and gender-inflected questions of identity and homeland. Angela Leighton reads this concern as the reaction of female poets both to the post-Romantic formulation of the home as a stable feminine sphere and to the associated feminization and interiorization of poetry. Summarizing Felicia Hemans's reaction to this discourse of Italy as homeland, Leighton argues that "In many of her poems, home is either empty of its main figurehead, the father, or else home is somewhere else: in Italy, in the south— paradoxically, in one of those places still subject to the convulsions of political change."[3] Leighton's anthology of Victorian women poets, edited with Margaret Reynolds, demonstrates the fascination with and importance of Italy as a reclaimed alternative feminine home. Elizabeth Barrett Browning's conception of Italy as a homeland in *Aurora Leigh* and *Casa Guidi Windows* is well documented, but other poets pursue the connection further and in different ways. Poems such as Alice Meynell's "The Watershed," for example, testify to the transformative and enabling potential of this trope to forge a replenishing sense of feminine place and belonging as an alternative to the patriarchy of Victorian Britain:

> But O the unfolding South! the burst
>   Of Summer! O to see
> Of all the southward brooks the first!
>   The travelling heart went free
> With endless streams; that strife was stopped;
>   And down a thousand vales I dropped,
> I flowed to Italy.[4]

The images of warmth, fluidity, and *jouissance* occasioned by travel into Italy here connote the maternal, an association also made by other writers of the period. Mary Elizabeth Coleridge declares of her journey to Italy "I feel as if I'd come not to a Fatherland but to a Motherland that I had always longed for and had never known."[5]

For Christina Rossetti, however, Italy proves a more problematic trope. Her poetry conceptualizes Italy as a homeland, but it is a homeland from which she is estranged. This double figure of home and exile provides a focal point for explorations of identity and heritage that emerge in multiple configurations of loss.[6] Of special interest here is the relationship between the dominant figures that signify loss: the connection of the maternal and the beloved to Italy.

In the Freudian narrative of sexuality, the mother represents the original experience of loss, for the child must relinquish the pre-Oedipal identity with the mother in order to take up a position in the Symbolic Order. As a result, the mother is the point to which all intimations of lost homelands, of absence and of exile, return.[7] By positioning her mother as a Muse, Rossetti speaks from the position of celebration and mourning as she remembers the "homeliness" of the maternal body and marks her estrangement from it. But, in addition, her mother is also the primal love object, and Rossetti's sequence of Italian love poems to Charles Bagot Cayley, *Il Rosseggiar dell'Oriente* (*The Reddening Dawn, CP*, 3:301-12), suggests that the Italian language itself is a vehicle that signifies not a familiar and homely "mother tongue," but the loss of a maternal homeland remembered and rehearsed in her relationship with the beloved.

Rossetti's poetry, however, does not endlessly rehearse the painful trauma of loss. In the multiple configurations of absence and exile, she forges a personal space that signifies the paradisal by repressing the memory of separation from the mother. Such a space is both maternal and recuperative and gestures to the utopian possibilities of paradise as a refound homeland. Elisabeth Bronfen, in *Over Her Dead Body: Death, Femininity, and the Aesthetic*, persuasively argues that femininity is the metonym for death, absence, grief, and loss, for, in the dominant representational scheme, the feminine signifies both the ground and vanishing point of the Symbolic Order.[8] But, in her thematic concern with the mother, the beloved, and Italy, Rossetti's poetry does not merely reinscribe the aesthetic's metonymical collapse of femininity with death. Rather, she gestures to alternative representational axioms that promise the restoration of the afterlife as a lost and refound maternal homeland, of which Italy is the imperfect earthly precursor.

Italy and the Italian language enjoyed priority for the Rossetti family by virtue of the father Gabriele Rossetti, a political exile and Dante Alighieri scholar. Frances Rossetti, Gabriele's wife, was herself half Italian through her paternal line, the Polidoris. Christina, Dante Gabriel, William Michael, and Maria Rossetti were all bilingual, and the family therefore had a double literary, cultural, and linguistic identity. In the biographies, however, Gabriele is represented as quintessentially foreign and Frances as quintessentially English: he is eccentric, odd, and flamboyant; she is modest, correct, and "full of commonsense." Marsh summarizes the comparison thus: "fatherly exuberance was balanced by maternal steadiness, and her firmness softened by his generosity." Although Christina Rossetti's Italian literary heritage is mediated by the paternal association with Dante Alighieri, in Rossetti's poetry Italy is conceived as maternal.[9]

Christina Rossetti's close association with her mother is circulated in the biographies as the distinguishing feature of her identity. Rossetti is depicted as the ideal daughter and is constantly equated with her mother. In the seminal biographical text, the Memoir prefixed to his edition of the poems, William Michael Rossetti comments that "for all her kith and kin, but for her mother beyond all the rest, her love was as deep as it was often silent. . . . To the latter (Frances Rossetti) it may be said that her whole life was devoted: they were seldom severed, even for a few days."[10] The first biographer, Mackenzie Bell, tells how Rossetti's doctor remembers her most for her love for her mother, which was "a feeling shown in every word and look. In the whole course of his life he had never known an instance of affection

more absorbing in itself or more touchingly evinced."[11] This excessive identification with her mother marks Rossetti as an eternal daughter, forever identified securely as feminine. As her mother's companion, and after her mother's
death the companion of her aunts, Rossetti is always socially dependent,
never independent. The ideal domestic, feminine sphere she inhabited with
her mother secures and refines her spinsterly status into the reflection of the
highest love, maternal love, and also enables Rossetti's asexuality, in line
with her saintly persona, to be sustained.[12] As Deborah Gorham asserts, the
contradiction inherent in the Victorian notion of female sexuality—the ideal
of asexual feminine purity and the active sexuality required for motherhood—is resolved by the emphasis upon the daughter and her childlike
dependency, transposed from the mother.[13] In fact, Bell quotes from Watts-
Dunton's review in *The Athenaeum*, 15 February 1896, of the posthumously
published *New Poems:* "All that is noblest in Christina Rossetti's poetry, an
ever-present sense of the beauty and power of goodness, must surely have
come from the mother."[14]

Christina Rossetti believed that the maternal love was the highest of
earthly love, the ideal to which all other love recurs. In a famously contradictory letter to Augusta Webster, she responds to the question of women's
suffrage with a statement of the value of maternal love:

> I take exception to the exclusion of married women from the suffrage—
> for who so apt as Mothers—to protect the interests of themselves and of
> their offspring? I do think if anything ever does sweep away the barrier
> of sex, and make the female not a giantess or a heroine but at once and
> full grown into a hero and a giant, it is that mighty maternal love which
> makes little birds and little beasts as well as little women matches for
> very big adversaries.[15]

In a letter to Caroline Jenner, dated 26 January 1875, Rossetti states her belief
that "the Maternal Type is to me one of the dear and beautiful things which
on earth help towards realizing that Archetype which is beyond all conception
dear and beautiful." The "Maternal Type," she asserts, typifies divine love.[16]
In *Seek and Find: A Double Series of Short Studies of the Benedicite,* Rossetti
develops her conception of the ideal love by exploring her belief that Christ's
love is maternal.[17]

As well as her reiterated assertion that maternal love is the ideal, Rossetti
also spoke from the position of the mother in what can be seen as an exper-

imental subject position, suggesting the possibility of a total identification with the maternal. Along with *Sing-Song,* the volume of nursery rhymes that adopt the mother's voice, there is also another, more autobiographical instance. As an appendix to her *Family Letters,* William Michael Rossetti gives extracts from a diary she kept on behalf of her mother between 1881 and 1886, and he notes that "This, as the wording shows, purports to be the diary of Mrs. Rossetti, our mother; but my sister, acting on her behalf, was, with a few exceptions in the earlier dates, the real writer of the diary, so far as handwriting is concerned, and no doubt the composition or diction is often hers as well."[18] In the act of writing this diary, Rossetti adopts her mother's subject position and enacts discursively her close relationship with the maternal. Significantly, she continues speaking in her mother's voice while giving an account of Frances Rossetti's death: "The night over, no rally: unconsciousness at last. . . . Mr. Nash prayed beside my bed-side, but I knew it not (?)." The parenthetical question mark exposes Rossetti's own subject position here as she speaks from and through the uncertainty of her mother's consciousness, literally (if tentatively) refiguring the maternal at the mother's death. Only in an afterword to the diary after Frances Rossetti's death does she assume her own voice as a daughter: "I, Christina G. Rossetti, happy and unhappy daughter of so dear a saint, write the last words."[19] The ventriloquized, and, in the final entries, prosopopoeic, diary illustrates Christina Rossetti's ability to transpose subject positions between her own signature and that of her mother's. This dialectic translation from self to maternal and back again suggests a subject discursively engaged with the mother as Other. Rossetti's diary entries adopt a subject-in-process that enjoys an intersubjectivity which questions the stability of identity, for the stability is established at the expense of exile from the mother necessitated by the entry into the Symbolic Order.

Despite Rossetti's close identification with her mother, the attempt to forge an intersubjective dialogue between the subject and (m)Other in the poetry cannot completely free itself from androcentric axioms. Indeed, according to the Freudian masculinist definition of ego formation as separation, identity is established at the painful expense of a union with the mother. Instead of total identification, tropes of exchange disclose both difference from and sameness with the maternal. In Rossetti's poetic language, the mother is depicted as the origin of love, the perfect precursor, to whom all heterosexual love recurs. *A Pageant and Other Poems* contains a dedicatory poem which celebrates maternal love in a love sonnet:

> Sonnets are full of love, and this my tome
>   Has many sonnets: so here now shall be
>   One sonnet more, a love sonnet, from me
> To her whose heart is my heart's quiet home,
>   To my first Love, my Mother, on whose knee
> I learnt love-lore that is not troublesome . . . (*CP*, 2:59)

The poem both supplements the oeuvre of love poems and refers back to their origin. The speaker associates her mother with requited and restful love, whose heart is the resting place of the speaker's heart. In later lines the mother is the "loadstar while I come and go," the point of a stability to be returned to, a guide. The reciprocity of the love means that the speaker will dedicate the volume to her mother: "I have woven a wreath / Of rhymes wherewith to crown your honoured name." And, in the final couplet, the maternal love is seen to transcend all that is changeable: the flame of love's "blessed glow transcends the laws / Of time and change and mortal life and death." Along with the idealized picture, the speaker's emphatic insistence on her position as a daughter responding to the mother's love associates her with the passive. The first maternal love is the ideal: all future love is imperfect and there is always a return to the perfection of the origin, to the mother.

Rossetti also wrote Valentines to her mother for each year between 1877 and 1886. The Valentines represent a sequence of love poems that celebrate the relation between mother and daughter as a pure and refined version of heterosexual love and that attempt to redefine the relation of subject to Other on these lines. As a note in the manuscript explains,

> These *Valentines* had their origin from my dearest Mother's remarking that she had never received one. I, her CGR, ever after supplied one on the day= & so far as I recollect it was a *surprise* every time, she having forgotten all about it in the interim. (*CP*, 3:487)

This note adds a narrative to the poems that attaches them through the anecdote to an origin, to the mother as the primal experience of love. The anecdote also suggests how the Valentines themselves form a repetitive pattern, as they are written for the same day each year and each year surprise Frances Rossetti. In fact, the theme of the poems establishes a repetition attached to seasonal repetition, while depicting maternal love as the superlative earthly love, pure and constant. The feast of St. Valentine is associated with the proximity of spring, with all its typical symbolic overtones for Rossetti: "More shower than shine / Brings sweet St. Valentine" (1880; *CP*, 3:316), "Too cold almost for hope of Spring" (1881), and the feast day comes at Winter's first sign of Spring, "When life reawakens and hope in everything" (1886). The topos of repetition is also evident in the Valentine for 1877, which describes the transformative effect of familial love:

> Own Mother dear
> We all rejoicing here
> Wait for each other.
> . . . .
> Till each dear face appear
> Transfigured by Love's flame
> Yet still the same,—
> The same yet new,—
> My face to you,
> Your face to me,
> Made lovelier by Love's flame,
> But still the same . . . (*CP*, 3:314-15)

The iteration of sameness despite the transfiguration tells of more than the retention of an individual's identity; for daughter and mother, sister and brother, are mirrored onto each other as the same and yet difference is retained between them, emphasized by the personal pronouns "you" and "me."

The mother, as "embodied Love," is the ideal precursor to which all subsequent love refers but cannot equal: "A better sort of Venus with an air / Angelic from thoughts that dwell above" (1882). She represents domesticated asexual love to which the subject always returns. This suggests what Bronfen terms "an economy of love based on repetition," for it endlessly repeats the experience of maternal love. This is, however, a repetition that hinges on a paradox: as well as returning to the primordial loss of the maternal body, the repeated act of return attempts to supplement and cover up the loss with a new love object. Repetition, according to this model, is the conflation of loss and addition, and "describes a longing for an identity between two terms, even as it stages the impossibility of literal identity."[20] The wish to return to a full pre-Oedipal union with the mother is frustrated at the very point at which it is desired.[21]

The inability to sustain a total identification with the mother leads to the double figure of the maternal space as both homeland and exile that also emerges in the poetic treatment of Italy. The poem "En Route" is paradigmatic of this double figure. W. M. Rossetti's note to "En Route" links his sister's relation to Italy with Gabriele Rossetti and suggests that, for both of them, the country is not wholly foreign: "the passionate delight in Italy to which *En Route* bears witness suggests that she was almost alien—or, like her father, an exile—in the North."[22] W. M. Rossetti's insistence that his sister's sense of partial exile from Italy identifies her with her father is part of the biographical insistence that the father represents all that is foreign in the Rossetti household. But, in "En Route," Italy is associated with the mother. The speaker in the poem addresses Italy:

> Wherefore art thou strange, and not my mother?
> Thou hast stolen my heart and broken it:
> Would that I might call thy sons "My brother,"
>   Call thy daughters "Sister sweet;"
> Lying in thy lap not in another,
>   Dying at thy feet. (*CP,* 2:382–83)

The speaker expects Italy to be familiar and maternal; instead, it is "strange." The poem also, however, insists upon the familiarity of Italy, for "With mine own feet I have trodden thee, / Have seen with mine own eyes." In fact, the first line of the stanza cited above encapsulates the disturbingly double nature of the speaker's relation to Italy as both familiar home and unfamiliar exile. "Wherefore art thou strange, and not my mother" has a peculiar logic. It suggests Italy's association with a maternal homeland, for the speaker expects the country to be familiar and therefore to be her mother. But by virtue of the zeugma, "strange" refers to the mother as well as to Italy; the "strange" homeland is not maternal, because the speaker is herself estranged from the mother. The zeugma, working here as the rhetorical figure of the repressed (the adjective "strange" in the second clause of the line) marks the maternal as the trope *par excellence* of homeland, as well as of exile and loss. Freud, in his essay "The Uncanny," suggests that the process by which the familiar becomes unfamiliar marks an uncanny moment, when the homely *(heimlich)* signifies the unhomely *(unheimlich)*.[23] This poem marks an uncanny moment when Italy and the maternal are rhetorically acknowledged as both known and unknown.

In the following stanza, the departure from Italy, the "land of love," prompts intense and excessive "yearnings without gain." Rather than simply a yearning for a return to that country, however, the desire is for something *never* possessed:

> Why should I seek and never find
> > That something which I have not had?
> > Fair and unutterably sad
> The world hath sought time out of mind, . . .
> Our words have been already said,
> > Our deeds have been already done:
> > There's nothing new beneath the sun
> But there is peace among the dead. (*CP,* 2:120–21)

If the analogy of Italy to the maternal is pursued, this stanza suggests that the original and total identification with the mother has been repressed as "That something which I have not had" because the fact of loss is so painful. Although the sense of loss in this stanza is provoked by the departure from Italy, the excessiveness of the loss and its lack of a referent ("that something") intimates an additional cause of grief. Earlier in the poem, the speaker suggests that her gender is the cause of her grief:

> Men work and think, but women feel;
> > And so (for I'm a woman, I)
> > And so I should be glad to die
> And cease from impotence of zeal,
> And cease from hope, and cease from dread,
> > And cease from yearning without gain,
> > And cease from all this world of pain,
> And be at peace amongst the dead. (*CP,* 2:120)

The feminine is here equated with yearning, passivity, and loss, and death gives the only relief. The emphatically feminine speaker is estranged from a maternal homeland and her sense of loss will be appeased only with death, suggesting that death is the speaker's true homeland.

Part of the unpublished stanzas of "En Route" is included in *A Pageant and Other Poems* (1881) as "An 'Immurata' Sister" (*CP,* 2:120–21). In this revised version, the three stanzas that refer to Italy are deleted and new lines are added that seem to resolve the disturbing nature of the other, for they suggest that death brings a renewal and a mystical purification reminiscent of Vaughan's *Silex Scintillans* (1650):[24]

Hearts that die, by death renew their youth,
   Lightened of this life that doubts and dies;
Silent and contented, while the Truth
   Unveiled makes them wise. (*CP,* 2:120-21, 13-16)

Sparks fly upward toward their fount of fire,
   Kindling, flashing, hovering:—
Kindle, flash, my soul; mount higher and higher,
   Thou whole burnt-offering! (*CP,* 2:120-21, 25-28)

The addition of these lines, along with the deletion of those referring to Italy, resolves the sense of loss by portraying death as rejuvenation in a realm *beyond* language and *beyond* loss. The title of this version, furthermore, suggests a speaker removed, or literally walled off, from earthly concerns whilst awaiting a spiritual release in death. In this way, the sense of exile from a maternal homeland is deleted and replaced with the intimation of Paradise as a replenishing utopian space.

   The revisions that produce "An 'Immurata' Sister" imply that desire for the homeland of Italy translates into, or substitutes for, a desire for the paradisal. This shift of longing is commensurate with the repression of loss from the maternal body, for paradise is enjoyed as a utopian and feminine space of union between speaker and (m)Other that recalls the primary and pre-Oedipal relationship of the child with the mother. In fact, the repression of loss is refigured in this poem as sisterhood, another feminine relationship. In the deleted section of "Seeking Rest" (*CP,* 3:429), the space of the grave, the home for the sleeper who awaits the Resurrection, is also portrayed as a feminine space—but here it is maternal:

She knocked at the Earth's greeny door:
   O Mother, let me in;
For I am weary of this life
   That is so full of sin.

As the site for spiritual rebirth, the grave is here analogous to the womb. The implication is that these spaces "outside" the Symbolic Order—the pre-Oedipal and death—are both feminine versions of the paradisal.

   The desire of the feminine subject to align itself with the maternal testifies to a yearning for an original perfect wholeness, prior to separation, that becomes the projected paradigm for all love. This is, however, also the utopian condition upon which the afterlife is desired; both origin and end, death and life, converge in the association of the maternal unity with a feminine paradise. The fullest statement of this is found in "Mother Country" (*CP*, 1:222–24), published in *Macmillan's Magazine* in March 1868 and then added to *Goblin Market, The Prince's Progress and Other Poems* (1875). The poem begins with the question:

> Oh what is that country
> And where can it be,
> Not mine own country,
> But dearer far to me? (1–4)

Only the title identifies this land as firmly maternal and also a land of origin. The speaker does not belong to the place, and possession of it is deferred, "If one day I may see" (5). The attributes listed, however, suggest an exotic place, with spices, cedars, gold, and ivory; but these are only intimated in a transitory and fleeting vision:

> As I lie dreaming
> It rises, that land;
> There rises before me
> Its green golden strand,
> With the bowing cedars
> And the shining sand;
> It sparkles and flashes
> Like a shaken brand. (9–16)

The speaker now positions herself as dreaming and perceiving the land in glimpses. In the next stanza it becomes clear that she imagines herself as a sleeper in Hades who can catch the "windy song" (20) of the angels and understand their nonverbal communication, "Like the rise of a high tide / Sweeping full and strong" (21–22).[25] The subject is involved in a double projection: she positions herself as dead and, as a sleeper who dreams of the Resurrection, she anticipates the time when the dreams become real. The following stanzas emphasize the space of the grave as a social leveler and as a separation from the material world: "Gone out of sight of all / Except our God" (47–48). And then, in the final three verses, the subject depicts herself in a semiotic or pre-Oedipal retreat from language and at a point of repetition, as the afterlife is both an end and a beginning:

> Shut into silence
>> From the accustomed song,
> Shut into solitude
>> From all earth's throng
>
> . . . .
>
> Life made an end of,
>> Life but just begun,
> Life finished yesterday,
>> Its last sand run;
> Life new-born with the morrow,
>> Fresh as the sun:
> While done is done for ever;
>> Undone, undone. (49-53, 57-64)

The repetition in the language mimics the theme that life and death coalesce. The final stanza, however, reverses the repetition: if the afterlife is life then it is also real, and the material world is a dream:

> And if that life is life,
>> This is but a breath,
> The passage of a dream
>> And the shadow of death . . . (65-68)

The poem works on the principle of repetition as a recurrence to a point of origin and, by imagining the afterlife as a utopia accessible through dream and nonverbal communication that juxtaposes life and death, also associates that land with the semiotic maternal body.

The utopian vision of a maternal, feminine paradise as homeland can be imagined only on the condition that loss is repressed. In "Italia, io ti saluto" (*CP*, 2:74-75; also published in the *Pageant* volume), however, the speaker refuses to repress her difference from Italy and the Italian language. Italy is imagined as only a partial identification and the result is a statement of Italy's difference from and sameness to the speaker. The speaker is resigned to leaving Italy: "To see no more the country half my own, / Nor hear the half familiar speech, / Amen, I say" (6-8). The south and the north are firmly differentiated and set up as opposites: "I turn to that bleak North / Whence I came forth— / The South lies out of reach" (8-10). The distance and loss are negotiated by swallows, whose migration back to the south reminds the speaker of "the sweet South" and "the sweet name." As with Swinburne's "Itylus," the swallows mediate between the two opposites, north and south, but the prevailing sense of Rossetti's poem is that of both assimilation and isolation from the "half familiar" country and language (made more immediate when we remember that the all members of the Rossetti family were bilingual).[26]

To posit Italy as partially identifiable, as "half familiar," suggests the conjugation of both loss and union, difference and sameness, which is the condition of the speaking subject predicated on the loss of the mother. But Rossetti, through the reiteration of the phrase "cor mio" in her poetry, attempts to forge a space of intersubjective exchange where difference and loss are expelled. "Cor mio" (my heart) signifies both the speaker's love *and* the beloved.[27] The phrase is a common platitude in the Italian language, but in Rossetti's poetry it is transformed to figure the intensely private space of the heart and, in fact, is used only in poems that remained unpublished during Rossetti's lifetime, probably because of their personal nature and because of fears that her non-native Italian would be criticized.[28] The concept of a private interior space that is both a physical reality and yet also beyond interpretation and language is to be found in much of her poetry (for example, in "Winter: My Secret"). But the special significance of the Italian phrase "cor mio" is that it denotes *both* the speaker's heart *and* her beloved, and so suggests that the concept of Italy and the Italian language that the phrase represents are part of the subject and Other. In fact, the rhetorical function of this Italian phrase indicates a movement of translation (literally, of course, carrying over) and exchange between subject and Other, for it is a space of mediation. Further, this translation is an anticipation and an intimation of the utopian and paradisal union of subject and Other that rehearses the pre-Oedipal intersubjective relationship with the mother that occurs in a space prior to the knowledge of difference.

In a posthumously published sonnet that takes the Italian phrase as its title, the speaker addresses a beloved from her past as "cor mio."[29] This phrase denotes the speaker of the poem as well as the beloved; as a result "cor mio" functions as part of the movement of exchange between subject and the beloved. By the articulation of "cor mio," the "two divided parts" of the subject's heart are brought together:

> Still sometimes in my secret heart of hearts
> I say "Cor mio" when I remember you,
> And thus I yield us both one tender due,
> Wielding one whole of two divided parts. (*CP*, 3:346, 1–4)

The naming of the beloved is located firmly within the subject's "secret heart of hearts," within the interior security of a self-reflexive doubling prompted by memory. The ambiguous unity of subject and beloved is immediately suggested by "one tender due," "due" implying that the union is not actual but owed to them both, and also implying monetary value, which the following lines emphasize in images of exchange. The union between subject and Other becomes, in fact, not a union but an exchange between them. But the Other is again already part of the subject, representing both the loss and re-finding of the primary love object, the mother. "Would you have given me roses for the rue / For which I bartered roses in love's marts?" (7–8): in this rhetorical question, exchange works back on itself as the speaker posits the reversal of an earlier transference, figured, significantly, as occurring in the marketplace. The beloved is asked whether he would have *replaced* the roses that the speaker exchanged for rueful love, but this questions if the beloved would have *accepted* roses from the speaker in return for rue. The uncertainty as to what type of exchange is meant ensures that neither the beloved nor the speaker is given a secure marketplace position, as producer or consumer of a commodity, and heightens the sense that exchange itself is not a transferal of equivalents, of roses for rue, love for pain, but a type of substitution of the subject for the Other.[30]

The sestet, however, increases the speaker's alienation from the beloved as the emphasis moves back to memory, upon which the sonnet is predicated. Despite being her "heart," the beloved forgets the speaker's sacrifice just as "late in autumn one forgets the spring" (9). The previous octave, which had told of exchange, gives way to a sense of loss, of impasse and of the speaker's powerlessness:

> So late in summer one forgets the spring,
>   Forgets the summer with its opulence,
> The callow birds that long have found a wing,
>   The swallows that more lately got them hence:
> Will anything like spring, will anything
>   Like summer, rouse one day the slumbering sense? (9–14)

The memory of the act of exchange leads to a rhetorical question that doubts the inevitability of the cycle of the seasons, the eventual substitution of autumn for spring.[31] Exchange between subject and beloved is entirely retrospective and intransigent. The final line suggests a fruitless anticipation that the "slumbering sense" might awaken; the passive speaker's loss is heightened by the absence of the addressee, for the question is rhetorical.

As a figure for the relation between subject and beloved, the phrase "cor mio" does not work rhetorically as a metaphor, as a similarity of things not normally contiguous. Instead, there is a metonymical substitution of the attribute of the beloved for the beloved himself, of heart ("cor") for Other. This substitution is a type of translation (or, in Julia Kristeva's terms, transposition) that dramatizes less the assimilation of the subject with the Other than a repression of the difference between them.[32] By the sonnet's sestet, however, the act of translation gives way to the acknowledgment of difference. Significantly, the structure of the sestet sets up an analogy (an expression of the same subject with a difference) between itself and the octave by the word "So" (9) that admits the inability to maintain the incorporation of subject and Other, for the difference repressed in metonymy returns.[33] The poem suggests that a metonymical identity between subject and Other can be sustained only in retrospect and memory. Such an intersubjective exchange is, however, the condition of the pre-Oedipal child's relation to the mother, which in this poem is posited as the imaginary (if unsustainable) union of speaker and beloved. The use of analogy is here a rhetorical figure based upon the primal loss of the maternal, when the same subjects (to adapt Coleridge's expression) become inscribed with difference. In the poem, the sestet's analogical structure suggests that the memory of the union between the speaker and the beloved cannot repress the difference between them.[34]

Absence of the beloved also predominates in the Italian sequence *Il Rosseggiar dell'Oriente* (*The Reddening Dawn; CP,* 3:301-12), which is similarly concerned with a type of exchange between the subject and beloved utilizing the phrase "cor mio," but the exchange is here superseded by a looking forward rather than back in a proleptic desire for the afterlife. As in the sonnet "Cor Mio," reciprocity is stressed and "cor mio" is the space that enables this, for it connotes both the subject and the beloved:

> Possibil non sarebbe
> > Ch'io non t'amassi, o caro:
> Chi mai si scorderebbe
> > Del proprio core?
> Se amaro il dolce fai,
> > Dolce mi fai l'amoro;
> Se qualche amor mi dài,
> > Ti do l'amore. (Poem 16)

> *{It would not be possible for me not to love you, oh*
> *darling: whoever would forget their own heart? If you*
> *make bitter the sweet, sweet you make the bitter; if you give*
> *me a little love, I give you love.}*[35]

The sense of a secretive locale, the "cor mio" and the more amorphous concept of the afterlife, is especially emphatic in this sequence, for it is loaded with personal references, presumably to Charles Bagot Cayley whom the sequence is traditionally taken to address.[36] W. M. Rossetti names Cayley as the addressee of the sequence in the Memoir to the *Poetical Works* of 1904 and suggests that, although his sister apparently rejected his proposal of marriage on religious grounds, "she loved the scholarly recluse to the last day of his life, 5 December 1883, and, to the last day of her own, his memory." He asserts that much of the relationship was very private, for "Christina was extremely reticent in all matters in which her affections were deeply engaged." The suggestion that the relationship has a wholly private and interior existence, especially after Cayley's death when it was located in her memory, is again repeated in his notes to the sequence with reference to the manuscript itself:

> For any quasi-explanation as to these singularly pathetic verses — "Love's very vesture and elect disguise," the inborn idiom of a pure and impassioned heart — I refer the reader to the Memoir. The verses were kept by Christina in the jealous seclusion of her writing-desk, and I suppose no human eye had looked upon them until I found them there after her death.[37]

In *Il Rosseggiar,* there is a constant emphasis upon reciprocity between the subject and the beloved within the secret space of the subject's heart. In poem 4 the speaker posits possible reunions independent of material time, and concludes

> E perciò "Fuggi" io dico al tempo, e omai
> "Passa pur" dico al vanitoso mondo:
> Mentre mi sogno quel che dici e fai
> Ripeto in me "Doman sarà giocondo,
> "Doman sarem" — mai s'ami tu lo sai,
> E se non ami a che mostrarti il fondo? —

> {*And therefore to time I say "flee," and now "please pass by" I say to the vain world. While I dream what which you say and do, I say to myself again and again "tomorrow will be joyful, tomorrow we will be . . ." — but if you love me you know, and if you don't love, why show you the depths of my heart?*}

Exchange is located in anticipation, memory, and dreams; but, significantly, the reverie is broken off with an assertion that the beloved does not, or should not, know her thoughts, for the gesture of showing the heart to the beloved is deemed unnecessary if he loves her and superfluous if he does not. The interplay of subject and other is thus grounded in retrospect, expectation, and gesture.

The exchange is made possible by the separation of subject from beloved — in fact, the sequence's subtitle translates "To my distant friend."[38] His absence incites the desire for presence, as in poem 13, where the speaker looks out from her "eastern window" in the direction where the beloved lives, and yearns for him. Unlike Barrett Browning's *Sonnets From the Portuguese*, which was an important influence upon Rossetti, the sequence does not seem to be based upon a linear narrative, for interspersed amongst poems that imply that the beloved is alive there are lyrics based upon his death. The first suggestion of this is in poem 5, where the speaker laments "Dolce cor mio perduto e non perduto, / Dolce mia vita che mi lasci in morte" [my sweet heart lost and not lost, my sweet life that left me on dying]. The following poem seems placed before the beloved's death, when the speaker imagines meeting the beloved in his house; but the death of the beloved does not impede communion and exchange, for he is both "lost and not lost" (poem 5). The physical separation through death of the Other, however, signals another type of exchange in which the beloved is bargained for by the speaker, who urges God to allow them a union in the afterlife:

> Che Ti darò Gesù Signor mio buono?
> Ah quello ch'amo più, quello Ti dono:
> Accettalo Signor Gesù mio Dio,
> Il sol mio dolce amor, anzi il cor mio;
> Accettalo per Te, siati prezioso;
> Accettalo per me, salva il mio sposo. (Poem 12)

> *{What shall I give You, Jesus my good Lord? Ah that*
> *which I love the most I will give You: accept it, Lord*
> *Jesus, my God, my only sweet love, indeed my heart; accept*
> *it for Yourself, may it be precious to you; accept it for me,*
> *save my groom.}*

The gesturing toward the afterlife that allows glimpses of paradise is by virtue of the "cor mio." In the secret space of the heart, a movement is signaled toward an intersubjective exchange and translation between subject and Other. In the sonnet "Cor Mio," the metonymical identity of subject and Other could not repress the difference between them. Poem 12, however, sustains the translation through God, who acts rhetorically as a supplement to the binary pair subject/Other. In poem 19, the speaker describes the transformative effect of the separation caused by death in Dantesque terms:

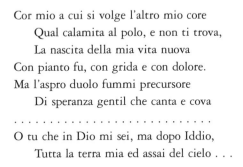

> Cor mio a cui si volge l'altro mio core
> > Qual calamita al polo, e non ti trova,
> > La nascita della mia vita nuova
> Con pianto fu, con grida e con dolore.
> Ma l'aspro duolo fummi precursore
> > Di speranza gentil che canta e cova
>
> . . . .
>
> O tu che in Dio mi sei, ma dopo Iddio,
> > Tutta la terra mia ed assai del cielo . . .

> {My heart toward which the other heart of mine turns like
> a magnet to the pole, and can't find you: the birth of my
> new life was with crying, with shouting and with pain.
> But the bitter grief was the precursor of a gracious hope
> that sings and broods . . . oh you who are in God for me,
> but after God, all of my world and much of my sky}

The doubleness of "cor mio" and "l'altro cor mio" suggests a mutual identification frustrated by separation; the "new life," however, intimates a mystical communion that is now possible, if painful, because of the separation. The semantic twists—"O tu che in Dio mi sei, ma dopo Iddio"—place, again painfully, the beloved as secondary to God. The very last poem in the sequence also suggests that there is hope for reunion in the afterlife through the speaker's mediation and negotiation with God: "Tu che moristi per virtù d'amor, / Nel altro mondo donami quel cor / Che tanto amai" [You who died for love, in the other world give me that heart I loved so much].

The ability to glimpse the afterlife that sustains hope of a reunion occurs through the deployment of the phrase "cor mio," in which language is manipulated so that it exceeds its denotation as a platitude. As a cliché, "cor mio" includes and exceeds its own semantic limitations and, by virtue of its almost mystical reiteration, enables the afterlife to be connoted through its metonymical repression of difference between subject and (m)Other. W. David Shaw discusses Rossetti's creation of "elusive contextual definitions for the dictionary meaning of so apparently simple a word as 'heart.'" He suggests that the gesturing beyond accepted meanings is a "crisis of representation," an attempt "to cross the divide that separates knowledge from belief." Her reserve and obliqueness are skeptical, self-protective, and yet rooted in her faith, for "rather than saying less about God than she means to say, she prefers to say nothing."[39] The "cor mio" signifies less a crisis of representation than the impossibility of representing the crisis; it gestures toward the afterlife which is *beyond* direct representation, for it is nonreferential and can only be intimated in fragmentary visions. As such, it refers to the original, semiotic union of mother and child prior to the acquisition of language and prior to the child's entry into the Symbolic Order.

These brief mystical glimpses of the afterlife are themselves uncannily half-familiar. Paradise is "the other life" (1), "the other world" (21), "up there" (5):

> . . . "Con lui discerno
> "Giorno che spunta da gelata sera,
> "Lungo cielo al di là di breve inferno,
> "Al di là dell'inverno primavera." (Poem 5)

> *{With him I discern the day that breaks from the icy*
> *evening, the long heaven beyond the brief hell, beyond*
> *winter, spring}*

In poem 10, the afterlife is both known and unknown as "the day of love," but it is an eternal day without moon or sun:

> . . . venga poi, ma non con luna o sole,
> Giorno d'amor, giorno di gran delizia,
> Giorno che spunta non per tramontare.

> *{then let the day of love come, but not with moon or sun,*
> *day of love, day of great delight, day which breaks never*
> *to set.}*

The speaker in poem 13, "Finestra mia orientale" (My eastern window), seems to give the land in which the lovers are imagined together Italian traits, which correspond *almost* to paradise:

Fossiamo insieme in bel paese aprico!
   Fossiamo insieme!
      Che importerebbe
   U'si facesse
      Il nostro nido?
   Cielo sarebbe
      Quasi quel lido.

*{If only we were together in the sunny land! If we were
together! What would it matter where we had made our
nest? It would almost be paradise, that shore.}*

The south, Italy, is seen as the counterpart of the colder north in "Italy, io ti
saluto" and "Enrica." The latter, published in *Goblin Market, The Prince's
Progress and Other Poems* (1875) maintains such a stereotype and finds it
manifest in the character of an Italian visitor to England: "She summer-like
and we like snow" (*CP*, 1:194).

The construction of the paradisal as both known and unknown marks, in
Freudian terms, an uncanny moment. As the speaker in "En Route" declares,
Italy is "Sister-land of Paradise," for the familiarity of Italy and the paradisal
recalls the primal union with the maternal body in alternative feminine terms
(here as sisterhood). The poetical transformation of Italy into a paradisal
homeland thus reworks the memory of the separation from the maternal body,
to recur to the maternal prior to the painful experience of loss. The exchange
between subject and beloved that the phrase "cor mio" initiates represses the
difference between them, allowing perfect earthly love to be envisioned in a
re-membering of the semiotic plenitude of the maternal body.[40] The utopian
love envisaged in *"Monna Innominata"* — "With separate 'I' and 'Thou' free
love has done / For one is both and both are one in love" (*CP*, 2:88) — is both
anticipated and intimated rhetorically. But when, as in *Il Rosseggiar*, the
beloved is transposed and depicted as absent, the anticipation of a meeting
in the afterlife heightens the pressure of memory on the Symbolic Order. Such
retrospection combines with anticipation: effectively in Freudian terms a
maternal trope, the conjugation of birth with death that intimates, for
Kristeva, the maternal space of the *chora* (the Greek for receptacle, womb).
The *chora* is the place prior to a knowledge of sexual difference where the
drives of the pre-Oedipal child gather and, after the entry into the Symbolic
Order, allow a disruptive pressure to be exerted on language: "the *chora*
precedes and underlies figuration and thus specularization, and is analogous

only to vocal or kinetic rhythm."[41] The afterlife, in such moments, is glimpsed in dreams and nonverbal language, a type of nonsignificatory practice that is associated with the semiotic and the maternal. The "cor mio" signals the analogous secret space of the grave where the sleeping soul dreams of Paradise. The pulsations of the "core," suggesting the pulsations of the *chora* upon the Symbolic,[42] intimate a movement of retrospection as well as a longing for death that would release the subject from the Symbolic Order. Both constructs are spatial and amorphous, physical and spiritual, embedded in but also positioned beyond the significatory practice that they interrupt.

Rossetti's poetry can thus gesture to the paradisal through a revision of the primary separation from the maternal body. *Il Rosseggiar dell'Oriente* imagines a new relation between subject and Other that is predicated on this revision, and which suggests a mode of figuration based, not on the repression of difference, but on the disruptive memory of the semiotic union between mother and child. The paradisal is a utopian homeland accessible through the Italian language as an alternative "mother tongue" whose intimation suggests the possibilities of an alternative aesthetic that reimagines the relation between the feminine and death, and that might provide us with a way of refiguring not just maternity in Christina Rossetti's poetry, but sisterhood as well.

NOTES

1. Edmund Gosse, *Critical Kit-Kats* (London: Heinemann, 1896), p. 139.

2. Hilary Fraser argues that the metaphorical colonization of Italy in this period is part of a wider concern to reappropriate the past. See *The Victorians and Renaissance Italy* (Oxford: Blackwell, 1992), p. 4.

3. Angela Leighton and Margaret Reynolds, eds., *Victorian Women Poets: An Anthology* (Oxford: Blackwell, 1995), pp. xxxv–xxxvi.

4. Alice Meynell, "The Watershed," in Leighton and Reynolds, p. 522.

5. Qtd. in Leighton and Reynolds, pp. 610–11.

6. Rossetti made only one brief visit to Italy, between 22 May and 26 June 1865, with her mother and William Michael Rossetti. The trip encompassed Paris, Langres, Lucerne, and an Alpine journey via St. Gotthard into Italy. Once there, they visited Lake Como, Verona, and Milan (Marsh, *CR,* pp. 334–40). Rosenblum notes the importance of Italy as a metaphor for identity, the mother country, and the afterlife, but assumes the relation is stable and unproblematic (pp. 49–50); see also Sandra M. Gilbert, "From *Patria* to *Matria:* Elizabeth Barrett Browning's Risorgimento," *PMLA* 99 (1984): 194–209.

7. See Sigmund Freud, "Three Essays on the Theory of Sexuality" (1905), *Standard Edition of the Complete Psychological Works of Sigmund Freud*, 24 vols., trans. and ed. by James Strachey (London: Hogarth Press and the Institute of Psycho-Analysis, 1953–73), 7:123–245.

8. See Elisabeth Bronfen, *Over Her Dead Body: Death, Femininity, and the Aesthetic* (Manchester: Manchester University Press; New York: Routledge, 1992).

9. Marsh, *CR*, pp. 18, 24. For a discussion of the biographical representation of Christina Rossetti, which emphasizes the construction of her identity as a product of Victorian gender ideology, see my "History, Hysteria, Histrionics: The Biographical Representation of Christina Rossetti," *Victorian Literature and Culture*, vol. 24 (forthcoming); See also Marsh, *CR*, chapters 1 and 2. For an elucidation of Rossetti's varied responses to her Italian literary heritage see Mary Arseneau, "'May My Great Love Avail Me': Christina Rossetti and Dante" and Marjorie Stone, "'*Monna Innominata*' and *Sonnets from the Portuguese*: Sonnet Traditions and Spiritual Trajectories," chapters 2 and 3, respectively, in this collection.

10. *PW*, p. lv.

11. Bell, p. 21.

12. Compare Lynda Nead: "As masculinity and femininity were defined in relation to their different fields of activity — the public and the private — gender identities became organized around the ideology of separate spheres." See *Myths of Sexuality: Representations of Women in Victorian Britain* (Oxford: Blackwell, 1988), pp. 32–33. Nina Auerbach sees Rossetti's spinsterhood as the springboard for her own self-recreation: "The quiet sister's devout, family-bounded existence contained its own divine potential for violent metamorphoses." See *Woman and the Demon: The Life of a Victorian Myth* (Cambridge, Mass.: Harvard University Press, 1982), p. 117.

13. Deborah Gorham, *The Victorian Girl and the Feminine Ideal* (London and Canberra: Croom Hill, 1982), p. 7.

14. Bell, p. 116.

15. Qtd. in *Christina Rossetti: Poetry and Prose,* ed. Jan Marsh (London: J. M. Dent, 1994), pp. 418–19.

16. Qtd. in Marsh, *CR,* p. 436.

17. For an analysis of the implications of Rossetti's maternal conception of Christ, see Sharon Smulders, "Woman's Enfranchisement in Christina Rossetti's Poetry," *Texas Studies in Literature and Language* 34 (1992): 568–88. Perhaps the gendering of Christ as both male and female may also be related to Holman Hunt's use of Christina Rossetti as a model for the face of Christ in the painting *Light of the World* (1853).

18. *FL,* p. xiii.

19. *FL,* p. 232.

20. Bronfen, p. 324.

21. The desire for the maternal should be distinguished from an inability of the subject metaphorically to separate from the mother, which is a psychic necessity

(Bronfen, p. 135). In "And the one doesn't stir without the other" (*Signs* 7, no. 1 [1981]: 60–67), Luce Irigaray identifies the daughter's perception of the mother as one of two categories, the phallic or the castrated mother. For the Victorians the identification of the daughter with the mother and the daughter's struggle to forge a separate identity are complicated by the tendency to conflate, in legal, social, and cultural discourses, femininity and maternity. Lila Hanft relates these issues to *Sing-Song;* see "The Politics of Maternal Ambivalence in Christina Rossetti's *Sing-Song,*" *Victorian Literature and Culture* 19 (1991): 213–32. On Rossetti's language and the use of repetition, see Steven Connor, "'Speaking Likenesses': Language and Repetition in Christina Rossetti's *Goblin Market,*" *VP* 22 (1984): 439–48; and Mary Arseneau, "Incarnation and Interpretation: Christina Rossetti, the Oxford Movement, and *Goblin Market,*" *VP* 31 (1993): 79–93.

22. *PW,* p. 485.

23. Sigmund Freud, "The Uncanny" (1919), in *Standard Edition,* 19:217–56.

24. "I was a flint—deaf and silent . . . / You draw nearer and break that mass which is my rocky heart. . . . / See how it is torn, its fragments at last setting your heavens alight . . . / by dying I live again." *Henry Vaughan: The Complete Poems,* ed. Alan Rudrum (Harmondsworth: Penguin, 1976; repr. 1983), pp. 137–38.

25. Linda E. Marshall's article eloquently describes Rossetti's belief in Hades, "the intermediate state of the soul between death and doomsday." See "What the Dead Are Doing Underground: Hades and Heaven in the Writings of Christina Rossetti," *VN* 72 (1987): 55–60, esp. p. 55.

26. Algernon Charles Swinburne, *Swinburne's Collected Poetical Works,* 2 vols. (London: Heinemann, 1927). In a letter to Lucy Rossetti, her sister-in-law, on 20 March 1892, Christina suggests not a double identity, but a partial one: "perhaps it is enough to be half an Italian, but certainly it is enough to be a Rossetti, to render Dante a fascinating centre of thought" (*FL,* p. 184).

27. The poems in which the phrase, "cor mio," is used are: "Lisetta all'Amante" (*CP,* 3:133); *Il Rosseggiar dell'Oriente* (*CP,* 3:301 ff.); "Cor mio, cor mio" (*CP,* 3:336); and "Cor mio" (*CP,* 3:346). See also "Amore e Dovere" (*CP,* 3:91).

28. In the preface to his edition of her poetical works, W. M. Rossetti quotes an unnamed Italian critic who disparages Rossetti's Italian verses: "they not only do not add anything to her fame as a poet, but rather detract from it, so formless and inept do they seem to me. It might almost be thought that the writer of those verses did not, as we know she did, speak from early childhood her paternal language." W. M. Rossetti declares such a criticism harsh and cites another unnamed literary Italian who values the poems as "not undeserving of commendation, and [they] assimilate to native work more nearly than those of Dante Gabriel Rossetti" (*PW,* pp. vi–vii).

29. See also "Cor mio, cor mio," "Cor del mio core" [heart of my heart] (*CP,* 3:336).

30. Terence Holt suggests that "*Goblin Market* attempts to imagine a position for women outside systems of power, but its language, which cannot escape from gender,

undoes the attempt: the autonomy is an illusion." See "'Men Sell Not Such in Any Town': Exchange in *Goblin Market,*" *VP* 28 (1990): 51–67, esp. p. 51. The separation of Lizzie and Laura from the economics typified by the goblins is unstable; they emerge as embroiled in exchange but their position in this system does not seem to be clearly marked.

31. This octave is used for sonnet 18 of *Later Life: A Double Sonnet of Sonnets,* published in *A Pageant and Other Poems* (*CP,* 2:146), another type of substitution.

32. Julia Kristeva defines transposition as "the passage from one signifying system to another [which] demands a new articulation of the thetic." See *The Kristeva Reader,* ed. Toril Moi (Oxford: Basil Blackwell, 1986), p. 111. The thetic is, significantly, the breaching of the semiotic *chora,* when the subject takes up an identity and position in the Symbolic Order.

33. S. T. Coleridge, in "Aids to Reflection," terms analogy tautologous: "expressing the *same* subject but with a difference." In comparison, he formulates metaphors as "always *all*egorical (i.e. expressing a *different* subject but with a resemblance)." See *The Oxford Authors: Samuel Taylor Coleridge,* ed. H. J. Jackson (Oxford: Oxford University Press, 1985), p. 672. Of course, my deployment of this definition alters the sense of "subject" from subject matter to speaking subject.

34. Interestingly, analogy was the mode of signification favored by the Tractarians, by which material types figured spiritual anti-types. See Arseneau, "Incarnation and Interpretation."

35. This conditional and provisional reciprocity is also to be found in "Lisetta all'Amante": "Se a te fedel son io, / Sarai fedele a me?" [If I am faithful to you, will you be faithful to me?] (*CP,* 3:133). I am indebted to Bob Cummings and Jean Ellis D'Allessandro for checking my translation of *Il Rosseggiar dell'Oriente.*

36. Harrison notes that the afterlife is often depicted as amorphous in Rossetti's poetry (Harrison, *CR,* p. 157). For an exploration of Rossetti's literary relationship to Charles Bagot Cayley, and in particular to his translations, see Kamilla Denman and Sara Smith, "Christina Rossetti's Copy of C. B. Cayley's *Divine Comedy,*" *VP* 32 (1994): 315–37.

37. *PW,* pp. liii, 439.

38. "All' Amico Lontano." Crump's edition gives the last word as "Contano," from Rossetti's manuscript. I use William Michael Rossetti's text which gives "Lontano," assuming an error in the manuscript or in Crump's transcription (*CP,* 3:480).

39. W. David Shaw, *Victorians and Mystery: Crises of Representation* (Ithaca and London: Cornell University Press, 1990), pp. 258, 251, 252.

40. See also *"Monna Innominata,"* where this is a dominant concern: "So shall we stand / As happy equals in the flowering land / Of love, that knows not a dividing sea" (*CP,* 2:89). Later in this sonnet sequence the speaker employs the conventional Petrarchan conceit of giving the beloved up to another love if it makes him happy

(*CP,* 2:92). In the second sonnet of "By way of Remembrance" (*CP,* 3:313), the speaker promises to rejoice if the beloved dies before her and finds another "to share / Your gladness, glowing as a virgin bride." Throughout Rossetti's oeuvre, union with the beloved in the afterlife is not anticipated as a certainty.

41. *Kristeva Reader,* p. 94. The *chora* is controversial in feminist theory: see Judith Butler, *Gender Trouble: Feminism and the Subversion of Identity* (New York and London: Routledge, 1990) and Kelly Oliver, *Reading Kristeva: Unraveling the Double-bind* (Bloomington and Indianapolis: Indiana University Press, 1993) for two different interpretations.

42. Despite the similarity of the two words, they denote separate concepts. Both are related semantically, however, to enclosed bodily space, the womb (as the etymological root of *chora*) and the heart. See *Kristeva Reader,* pp. 93-98.

CHAPTER 11

Rossetti's Cold Women

Irony and Liminal Fantasy in the Death Lyrics

SUSAN CONLEY

> . . . even the best-informed among us are no better instructed
> about death than a spinster is about love.[1]

APHRODITE ACULEATA

At the beginning of 1877, Charles Cayley sent Christina Rossetti a souvenir of his seaside holiday, a small sea creature he had preserved in a bottle of spirits. The creature, he explained in the accompanying note, "is called in Sussex a *seamouse,* but by naturalists more politely Aphrodita aculeata, or needly Venus."[2] The mixture of pleasure and pain conjured by the Latin name of this sea creature was perhaps associated in the mind of this subtle and pedantic scholar and linguist with his old, thorny love, Christina Rossetti. Inspired by Cayley's gift, Rossetti wrote the poem, "My Mouse" (1877),[3] in which she plays upon one half of the sea-mouse's Latin name, alluding to the birth of Venus:

> A Venus seems my Mouse
> Come safe ashore from foaming seas,
> Which in a small way & at ease
> Keeps house. (*CP,* 3:337, 1-4)

In the second stanza, the sea-mouse is compared with Iris, goddess of the rainbow and messenger of the gods. This comparison combines witty allusions to what Cayley's note describes as the sea-mouse's "bright, many-coloured scales" and to its housing in a bottle. The third stanza interprets the "message" of the sea-mouse in terms personal but nonspecific:

> A darling Mouse it is:—
> Part hope not likely to take wing,
> Part memory, part anything
> You please. (9–12)

The retreat into the playful, coy, but self-protective "anything you please" echoes the elusive guessing-games of a poem such as "Winter: My Secret" (1857). While this strategy invites the reader into the interpretive game which is the poem's subject, without the extratextual history it becomes an obscure guessing-game indeed. Appropriately, then, in the final stanza the "message" of the sea-mouse housed in a bottle becomes a "secret" housed in the heart:

> Venus-cum-Iris Mouse
> From shifting tides set safe apart,
> In no mere bottle, in my heart
> Keep house. (13–16)

Although the poem ostensibly addresses only one half of the sea-mouse's Latin name, the turn away from interpretation toward secretiveness suggests the self-protective armor of the "needly Venus." *Aphrodite aculeata* is an apt figure for Rossetti's poetic practice and for her poetic identity as constituted in that practice; an apt figure, that is, for a prickly poetess.

Despite the tone of gentle explanation in Cayley's note, Rossetti was probably already acquainted with the sea-mouse. She and her brother, William, were keen seaside fossickers from early days, as the following letter, written in Seaford to William in Broadstairs, attests:

> I hope your bottled monsters are not less long-lived or more smelly than in the days of our common experiences. I do not discern any symptoms of "monsters" here, but my investigations are carried on from a camp-stool pitched some way from the water's edge,—so are by no means exhaustive.[4]

Even if Rossetti had never seen a sea-mouse before Cayley's gift, she would have learned about them many years earlier in her copy of *The Common Objects of the Sea Shore* (1857), by the Reverend J. G. Wood. Of this volume, William had written to his mother in 1858:

> Will you tell Christina, in answer to a precedent note, that I *did,* shortly after leaving town, think of her *Common Objects of the Seashore* [*sic*] with regret at not having brought it, but that some days ago, finding the book at a shop hereabouts, I purchased a copy for myself. It is sufficiently to the purpose.[5]

Common Objects of the Sea Shore devotes two pages of text to the sea-mouse, plus an illustration (fig. 11.1). Part of the text reads:

> It is a strange thing, and one that shows the lavish beauty of creation, that an animal endowed with such glorious colours, that can only be exhibited by a full supply of light, should have its habitation in the mud. When kept in an aquarium, they generally appear to avoid the light rather than to seek it. . . . Among other offices, [their bristles] seem to play the part of weapons, like the spines of the porcupine. . . . All these lances can be withdrawn into the body of the sea-mouse at the will of their owner.[6]

The *Aphrodite aculeata* is, therefore, a creature whose habits might also describe a poet "tenacious of [her] obscurity";[7] one who with her dread of "self-display" appears to avoid the light rather than to seek it; and one whose self-protectiveness usually expresses itself in reticence and scrupulous politeness, but can also turn prickly. Known for her "piquant" utterances as a temperamental child, as a more self-controlled adult she can still be "gently caustic of tongue."[8] Above all, the sea-mouse's Latin name, with its combination of unlike elements, figures Rossetti's contradictory identity as woman poet, whose gender dictates that she inspire, not author, poetry.[9] Aphrodite is the ruling goddess of Sappho, the representative woman poet for the "poetesses" who precede Rossetti, notably Felicia Hemans and Letitia Elizabeth Landon (who published as L.E.L.), and whose dominant subject is love. Elizabeth Barrett Browning is perhaps the first English "poetess" to treat the subject of woman and love explicitly within the context of contemporary social and political questions. Yet Rossetti is the first English woman poet in whose poetry romantic love becomes an explicitly thorny subject, a subject treated with irony and skepticism.

As well as "needly" or "prickly," *aculeata* when referring to language means "stinging" or "quibbling." The sting in the tail of many of Rossetti's so-called love poems is felt only if the female voice figured in these poems is heard ironically. For Dorothy Mermin, nineteenth-century women poets, unlike their male counterparts, "could not afford irony, for their first task was to show their right to a place in poetry, not their discordance with it."[10] Yet for Rossetti, as surely for Barrett Browning, part of the struggle to show her "right to a place in poetry" involves an interrogation of the poetic discourses with which her work engages, an interrogation which certainly registers "discordances" with those dominant discourses. Irony, says Mermin, "with its doubleness of meaning and emotional detachment, went against everything a woman writer was supposed to be."[11] While this may be so, it is just these features that characterize many of Rossetti's most famous lyrics. That even some contemporary Victorian readers were capable of seeing beyond the decorative, aesthetic charms of these poems is evident in the comment of one early critic who, citing "Song" ("When I am dead, my dearest"), noted that "[c]ertain of her poems are marked by an air of composure, of quiet scorn, of tender trifling,—rare in a woman's poems."[12] Indeed, in such lyrics Rossetti perfected a poetic voice far removed from that found in the verse of the "poetesses," a female voice of cool composure and "quiet scorn." Yet in this century, it is only within the last ten years that critics have begun to hear this ironic poetic voice in Rossetti's work once more and to explore its significance.

The group of poems on which I focus in this essay are mostly the much-anthologized lyrics on which Rossetti's reputation as a ladylike singer of sweet and simple songs was long based. This was in part due to Rossetti's own overdetermined use in these lyrics of a world-renouncing, melancholy subject-speaker and the stylized trappings of the Pre-Raphaelites' medievalizing, Keatsian aesthetic. Yet primarily this reputation was due to the dominant reading practices of literary academe in this century, as Jerome McGann has persuasively argued.[13] The emergence of new discursive communities within the academy over the last twenty-five years has created the conditions for reading Rossetti's work anew. Feminist and new-historicist theories, in particular, have made it possible to read Rossetti's work as, in part, an ironic counter-discourse within Victorian poetry. Dolores Rosenblum was the first feminist critic to suggest the relevance of reading Rossetti's work in terms of

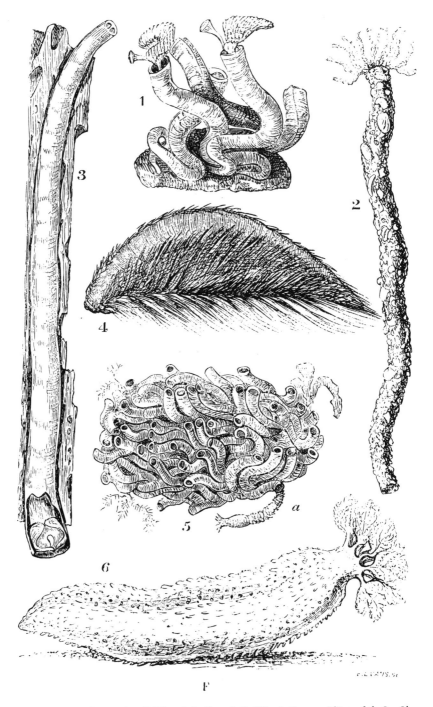

Fig. 11.1. "Aphrodite aculeata" (Fig. 4). In Rev. J. G. Wood, *Common Objects of the Sea Shore* (London: Routledge, 1857). Reproduced with the kind permission of the Fisher Library, University of Sydney.

Irigaray's notion of parodic mimicry,[14] whereby a woman restages or re-presents herself in terms of phallocentric discourse but with an excessiveness which marks her failure to be contained by that discourse. Irony, in its doubleness or duplicity, is one such parodic marker. Many of Rossetti's poems can be read as counter-discursive, working within the ideological, gender-marked language of Victorian poetic discourse in such a way as to destabilize it. Irony is one of the major modes of this destabilization. As Linda Hutcheon writes, "irony's intimacy with the dominant discourses it contests . . . is its very strength, for it allows ironic discourse . . . to buy time (to be permitted and even listened to, even if not understood)" while challenging the authority and appropriating the power of the dominant discourses. Yet, as Hutcheon adds, the "intimacy" of such such irony, its operation from within, risks being read as complicity; in such a mode, irony may not be recognized *as* irony.[15] Such, indeed, has been the fate of lyrics such as "Remember" and "After Death." While in my disscussion of Rossetti's response to Elizabeth Siddal's poetry I establish a partial basis for attributing irony as an intentional effect in Rossetti's own poetry, the "making" of irony in written texts depends as much on the interpretation and intention of the reader as on the intention of the writer.[16] Consequently, my own readings are strategically overdetermined in their effort to read against the apparently simple, decorative surfaces of these poems, and to hear the double voice of irony at work in them.

ROSSETTI'S SENTIENT DEAD

Some of Rossetti's lyrics in which the speaker is a dead or dying woman seem to take the image of the confined or incarcerated woman so prevalent in Victorian literature and art to a logical extreme. Poems such as "Echo" and "The Convent Threshold" depict the grave as the Pre-Raphaelite woman's ultimate nightmare, an entrapment in living hell. In other lyrics death seems the fulfillment of the speaker's wish, offering a potentially liberating liminal space and time. Poems such as "Song" ("When I am dead, my dearest"), "Remember," and "After Death" are melancholy songs of lovers sundered by death, replete with decorative imagery and stylized archaisms; at the same time, however, they perform a sleight of hand, a resistance to the very aesthetics with which they appear complicit. In these poems, death becomes both an indictment of life and the moment of revenge on oppression, an opportunity, paradoxically, for the dead woman to exercise power and control.

Writing of two twentieth-century women poets, Sylvia Plath and Anne Sexton, Elisabeth Bronfen argues that they "cite conventional conceptions of feminine death so as to recode these radically in such a way that death emerges as an act of autonomous self-fashioning."[17] This is, I believe, how many of Rossetti's death lyrics should be read. The living dead, one who speaks from the grave, is as paradoxical a being as the woman poet; both speak from the traditional position of silence and radical otherness. Furthermore, speaking from the liminal space and time of death on the one hand provides a figure for the woman poet's disembodied act of creation; in this figure (the voice of the dead) she escapes her female body—which ideologically circumscribes her as the muse and matter of art—and gives full rein to her "Poet mind."[18] Yet on the other hand, speaking from the place of the body—the deathbed or grave—as these speakers do, refuses that very escape: the cool, self-contained and thus powerful female voice is kept in close, uncanny proximity to the site that confirms her ideological association with mute, corruptible matter.

Some critics have sought to establish the theological bases of Rossetti's poems on the death-state. Jerome McGann argues for the influence of the premillennarian doctrine of "Soul Sleep," claiming it as "the single most important enabling feature of her poetry."[19] Linda E. Marshall explicitly counters McGann, arguing that rather than the minority view of "Soul Sleep," Rossetti's poems embody a range of "typical and traditional" Anglican ideas on the intermediate state of the soul between the death of the body and the Final Resurrection. Crucial here is the concept of Hades. Most commonly, Hades was a place "where the soul between death and doomsday may rest in Paradise . . . or suffer a foretaste of hell"; yet for some Church of England divines, Hades was confined to "the grave," where "the person is extinct; the soul sleeps in profound unconsciousness."[20] Marshall cites many and varying points of contact between these wide-ranging views and the wide-ranging scenarios of Rossetti's death poems. Yet it is precisely this variety of treatments in Rossetti's poems which suggests the limitations of reading them solely or primarily in terms of theological positions. While a revised historicist awareness is valuable here, it does not account for the sometimes radical perspective offered by the dead or dying in Rossetti's poems. Those poems in which we hear the voice of a dead or dying woman frequently show no sign of religious faith of any kind. In such poems, as Angela Leighton argues, the twilight dream-world of the grave is "not a theological resting place, but a restless and skeptical in-between-land where doubt shadows faith."[21] Significantly, those death poems which do have, among other things, an unambiguous Christian-didactic function, usually have a speaker who is living (for example, "Dream-Land," "Rest," "My Friend").[22] It is Rossetti's dead or dying who, when they speak, undermine the optimistic religious faith of the living; who are, in other words, the voice of the repressed in her poems. Furthermore, in many of the poems in which the dead or dying speaker addresses a living lover—such as "Song" ("When I am dead, my dearest"), "Remember," and "After Death"—the death of the body metonymically embraces the death of worldly affections; the place of the body, the grave, is their locus, rather than a spiritual abode; and there is no mention of either eternal love or the immortality of the soul.

"A CASE OF KNIVES": "REMEMBER" AND "AFTER DEATH"

In the sonnet "Remember" (1849) the speaker addresses a lover concerning her imminent death, with the repeated imperative to "remember me" (*CP*, 1:37). Unlike "Song" ("When I am dead, my dearest") (1848), in which the speaker withdraws from the beloved into the indifference of death, "Remember" presents a speaker who at least appears to engage with the beloved and offer remembrance as the possibility of continuity between life and death. However, while adopting a different strategy to that of "Song," in which death renders null and void the terms "remember" and "forget" through an equivocating diction of indifference—"Haply I may remember, / And haply may forget" (*CP*, 1:58)—"Remember" privileges first one term and then the other, until their independent value is eroded.[23]

Death is never named in "Remember," but is invoked in the opening lines through the common conceit of the distant, "silent land" (2), and elaborated in lines 3-6 in a description of a future of loss, of a negation of the lovers' present happiness. Yet what is the nature of their present relationship—why does the speaker vacillate between going and staying (4); why is it "*our* future that *you* planned" (6, my emphasis)? The subtle suggestion through these details of a problematic love relationship retrospectively undermines even the apparently easy intimacy of line 3—"when you can no more hold me by the hand"—until it hints at coercion: unlike the lover, death at least lets her "turn [and] go" (4). As in "Song," the desire for death rather than the beloved speaks loudest in the poem; death as an escape from a life that is enigmatically unsatisfactory, from an intimate relationship that mysteriously falls short.

Why, then, the repeated exhortations to "remember me"? The phrase occurs three times in the octave, becoming urgent in the final repetition, "Only remember me" (7). The addition of the adverb here is further highlighted by its inverted stress, and the phrase as a whole is isolated by the caesura which follows, the only mid-line break in the whole poem. Yet the ambiguous syntax—"remember me alone" or "simply remember me"—undermines the very urgency of her plea; and the value of remembrance itself is in turn made dubious by what follows—"you understand / It will be late to counsel then or pray" (7-8)—which implies that remembrance is what is left when it is too late to do something more effective. So even before we reach the sestet and the sonnet's turn, the rubric "remember me" appears to be virtually emptied of its literal meaning. While in one way a talisman *against* death, the realm of forgetting, its repetition creates a somnolent refrain where sound overwhelms sense, until it proleptically signifies the dissolution of meaning and the speaker's own forgetting in death. Its loss of proper meaning conjures its opposite: the void of forgetting.

Nevertheless, after the entreaties to "remember me," the turn at line 9 is still unsettling, especially due to the ease with which the speaker permits the lover to forget her. Lines 9-10 illustrate the paradoxical nature of the relationship between remembering and forgetting, acknowledging as they do that the lover will grieve only when he remembers he has forgotten; that remembering depends for its meaning on, and is only kept alive by, the possibility of forgetting: "Yet if you should forget me for a while, / And afterwards remember, do not grieve." As the dialectic of remembering and forgetting becomes more intricate, Rossetti takes bold license with the rhyme scheme in the sestet, with a nonsymmetrical pattern, *cddece*. One way in which the subtle and subversive effects of this poem are achieved can be observed by noting that the lines in which the word "forget" appears (once in the first line of the sestet and once in the penultimate line) also contain the most widely spaced of the poem's five end rhymes, forming thus the subtlest of alliances: "while" and "smile" link the passing of time with the passing of grief, suggesting the inevitable passage from remembrance to forgetting.

Such an inevitable progression, or perhaps regression, is suggested more directly in lines 11-12: "For if the darkness and corruption leave / A vestige of the thoughts that once I had." These lines seem to reveal the poem's real interest, which revolves less around whether the lover remembers or forgets, than around the "darkness and corruption" of the grave and the fate of human "thoughts" therein. By projecting the speaker into the grave, rather than into an identifiably Christian afterlife, these lines could be read, like many of

Rossetti's poems on the death-state, as a virtual denial of such an afterlife in their exclusive focus on the grave, the place of the body. The vision of death is especially bleak in these lines, with their metonymic extension of the literal destruction of the dead body to the figurative destruction of her "thoughts" of the lover, and, vice versa, their extension of a figurative, that is, metaphysical "darkness and corruption" to the "thoughts that once I had." Further, the use of the neutral "thoughts," rather than the expected "love," creates an emotional detachment consonant with the speaker's ambivalence toward the lover detected in the octave. As in "Song," the speaker seems to become absorbed into the indifferent world of the dead during the course of the poem. Thus, by the closing lines—"Better by far you should forget and smile / Than that you should remember and be sad"—the poem has achieved a complete *volte-face,* from imploring remembrance, to preferring that the lover forget her. Rossetti has employed the form of the Petrachan sonnet with a sinister logic. The binary thematics of the poem, based on both stated and implicit pairs of terms—living/dead, stay/go, past/future, smile/sad, remember/forget—are completely realigned by the end: life is linked with remembrance and sorrow, while death is linked with the smile of forgetfulness.

As I have suggested, these lyrics are the basis on which Rossetti's work has been characterized solely and often dismissively in terms of a lyric spontaneity and simplicity. Even in a recent critical anthology on Rossetti, a prolific critic of Victorian poetry writes that by the end of "Remember," "tactful concern for the lover . . . displaces any self-centred desire to live on in his memory."[24] Such a reading is clearly overdetermined by the prevalent biographical myth of Rossetti as a meek, deferential Victorian spinster, "tactfully" self-renouncing. By contrast, I am arguing for a reading that hears a skeptical, ironic female voice.

"Remember" and "After Death" (1849) were copied into Rossetti's notebook within three months of each other; and in *Goblin Market and Other Poems* she placed "After Death" immediately following "Remember." This latter fact at least invites comparison between the two; at most, it suggests that "After Death," in which we hear the voice of a woman now dead, may be read as the sequel to "Remember." "After Death," however, establishes an altogether different mood from that of "Remember." This is partly due to its different use of the sonnet form. Unlike the unbroken lines and verbal echoes of "Remember," contributing to its dreamy melodiousness—"gone away / Gone far away"; "turn . . . turning"; "day by day"—"After Death" breaks up the line more often than not with increased punctuation and enjambment. In addition, the octave, consisting of the speaker's description of the scene in the room where she has just died, has less of a lyric and more of a narrative structure than "Remember":

> The curtains were half drawn, the floor was swept
>> And strewn with rushes, rosemary and may
>> Lay thick upon the bed on which I lay,
> Where thro' the lattice ivy-shadows crept.
> He leaned above me, thinking that I slept
>> And could not hear him; but I heard him say:
>> "Poor child, poor child:" and as he turned away
> Came a deep silence, and I knew he wept. (*CP*, 1:37–38)

The first quatrain suggests an archaic, perhaps medieval setting — the rushes, herbs, and flowers, and the ivy-covered lattice window — and this, as part of a deathbed scene, immediately conjures the world of Pre-Raphaelite gothic. Enhancing this is the effect of the uncanny, produced by the contrast between the speaker's straightforward, nonemotive reportage, and the awareness that she is dead.

The next quatrain introduces the would-be mourner of her death, an unnamed "he." The speaker appears at pains to display her superior vantage point over this man; for while "He leaned above me" connotes a figuratively superior position, this is quickly shown to be falsely assumed, both by him and us: "but I heard him say." The speaker's ascendancy over him is heightened here by the simple, monosyllabic diction and balanced syntax of line 6, as she coolly negates his presumption of her deathly insentience. The inclusion of direct speech ("'Poor child, poor child'") is unusual among these death lyrics, in giving the lover a voice, however small, in the poem. Yet it is not a voice in dialogue with the speaker, but a solitary voice on which she eavesdrops; further, his words sound merely patronizing, his pity ironically undercut, placed as it is within her knowing narrative, in which she demonstrates the supreme vantage point of death.

The sestet abandons the narrative mode in which the speaker has quietly established her authority over the living, and offers instead a catalogue of omitted actions through which "he" is judged and found wanting. Here is an ironic variation on the litany of worldly rejection usually uttered by Rossetti's dying speakers ("Sing no sad songs," "Wreathe no more lilies in my hair" ["'The Summer is ended,'" *CP*, 3:204]). Speaking "after death," rather than before, the woman rebukes "his" stance of denial or rejection toward her. The object of the actions listed in lines 9-11 is the dead body, so these are symbolic ministrations, signifying an intense emotional attachment to the physical person of the beloved—the passionate bereavement she would have him feel, if he was the lover she wishes he were. The parallel syntax of lines 9 and 12—"He did not touch," "He did not love"—reinforces the equation offered between these sins of omission and the absence of love.

The final lines of "After Death" have been conventionally read as granting "his" redemption through his pity, the poem ending on a note of self-effacing generosity (not unlike the "tactful" renunciation of "Remember") or, alternatively, of "immature self-pity."[25] Yet to what extent pity redeems him, if at all, depends on the worth assigned it by the poem. Pity is distinguished from love, clearly to its detriment:

> He did not love me living; but once dead
> He pitied me. (12-13)

Firstly, "He pitied me" is isolated by enjambment, to parallel "He did not love me living"; secondly, there is an alignment through alliteration between "love" and "living," and through consonance between "dead" and "pitied."[26] The apparent self-effacement of the closing words—

> . . . and very sweet it is
> To know he still is warm tho' I am cold. (13-14)

—is in one sense real. For when for the first time in the poem the speaker expresses emotion, she effaces herself, as subject, from the utterance. This is in marked contrast to the sprinkling of simple verb phrases in which she has so far presented herself—"I lay," "I slept," "I heard," "I knew"—that collectively emphasize her heightened awareness "after death," even as such emotionally neutral verbs sustain an impression of aloofness and (self-) control. This leads me to suggest that the speaker attaches herself only obliquely to "very sweet" because of the emotional freight of this moment, and instead lends weight to her final words, "I am cold." Abandoning the prose syntax of the rest of the poem, these closing words promote ambiguity, as they simultaneously uncover and obscure the intense feeling they bear. "Sweet" is the only significant term in the last three lines without a companion word: there is "love" and "pitied," "living" and "dead," "warm" and "cold." In such a context, "sweet" invokes "bitter," and indeed *bittersweet* seems to capture precisely the conclusion to this poem.[27]

The words "warm" and "cold" in the final line clearly operate metonymically for "the living" and "the dead." Yet, in addition, their several literal and figurative meanings flicker retrospectively over the poem. The word "cold" is given structural prominence both by being the final word of the poem, and by forming part of a rhyme ("cold"/"fold") that is so widely spaced it is barely heard. This near-dissonance contributes to the unsettling effect of the final line. "Cold" has resonances throughout the poem, from the creeping "ivy shadows," to the dead body whose hand is not held, to "his" tears of chilly pity. "Cold" also is the speaker's voice, a voice that reveals little emotion as she turns a cold, judging eye on the scene of her death and on "him." Such all-pervasive coldness enhances the irony of the final line, in which the epithet "warm" resonates with all that the poem shows to be lacking—life, love, and passionate emotion. And while replete with irony, the final line is, at the same time, sincerely spoken; for, as with almost all of Rossetti's dead or dying, death *is* to be preferred over life, and for this speaker in particular, death is a bittersweet victory over the unloving living.[28]

Elizabeth Siddal and Piquancy

The ironic critique of romantic love ideology I have identified in some of Rossetti's most popular love lyrics can also be found in a poem of Elizabeth Siddal's called "Dead Love." Among the handful of his late wife's poems Dante Gabriel gave Rossetti to read in 1865, she claimed this as her "favourite, piquant as it is with cool, bitter sarcasm."[29] Such a description clearly bears comparison with the "composure" and "quiet scorn" remarked of her own work. While this quality is counted "rare in a woman's poems" by the male critic, it is evidently highly prized by Rossetti. As I mentioned earlier, "piquant" is a word used by William to describe his younger sister's childhood utterances.[30] Now a prickly poetess, she still favors, or savors, what is piquant in others' work as well as her own. Her response to Siddal's poem suggests the relevance of reading her own lyrics in terms of a female voice that is "cool, bitter." To hear such a voice is, essentially, to admit that *irony* is at work in these lyrics, something few critics, now or then, are willing to grant to Victorian women's poetry. Linda Hutcheon, who wants to stress irony's emotional "charge" or "edge," points out that emotional coldness and intellectual detachment have long been seen by theorists as hallmarks of irony, although "many argue that ironists only *appear* cool and restrained on the surface as a way to mask actual hostility and emotional involvement."[31] This seems an apt description of irony's deployment in the lyrics of Rossetti and Siddal.

In "Dead Love," we cannot be sure whether the speaker is male or female, but in either case the "sarcasm" Rossetti detects is female sarcasm; that is, if the speaker is male, then the sarcasm belongs to the woman poet.

> Oh never weep for love that's dead,
>   Since love is seldom true,
> But changes his fashion from blue to red,
>   From brightest red to blue,
> And love was born to an early death
>   And is so seldom true.
>
> Then harbour no smile on your loving face
>   To win the deepest sigh;
> The fairest words on truest lips
>   Pass off and surely die;
> And you will stand alone, my dear,
>   When wintry winds draw nigh.
>
> Sweet, never weep for what cannot be,
>   For this God has not given:
> If the merest dream of love were true,
>   Then, sweet, we should be in heaven;
> And this is only earth, my dear,
>   Where true love is not given.[32]

The melancholy first stanza is still within the orbit of romantic love ideology: love is changeful and "seldom true." Yet, by the final stanza there is a wholesale renunciation of that ideology: it is an incontestable, God-given fact that on earth "true love is not given." In the middle stanza, perhaps the most "sarcastic," the speaker spurns the lover's romantic poses, and makes a certain prediction of their inevitable parting. The word "harbour" seems especially damning; with its connotations of secrecy, the "smile" with which it is coupled becomes potentially duplicitous. It is hardly surprising that this ironic view of romantic love and the naming of "heaven" as the only possible abode of "true" and lasting love struck a chord with Christina Rossetti.

When Rossetti read Siddal's poems, she was preparing a second volume of her own poetry, and suggested to her brother that some of "dear Lizzie's verses" be included in this volume. Dante Gabriel appears to have equivocated over his sister's proposal, and Rossetti herself had second thoughts after she had read them: "I think with you that, between your volume and mine, their due post of honour is in yours. But do you not think that . . . beautiful as they are, they are almost too hopelessly sad for publication *en masse?*" She goes on to cite her own "overstrained fancy" and "excitable imagination" as possible obstructions to a clearer appreciation of Siddal's poems.[33] She thereby communicates to her brother, wittingly or not, the principal case against "publication *en masse*" of his dead wife's poems, which is precisely their reception by the "overstrained fancy" of a prurient public. Dante Gabriel was already censoring the selection: "Meanwhile how odd it seems," his sister continues, "that just III ['Dead Love'], my admiration, is rejected by you as ineligible." Perhaps not so "odd": if Rossetti did not know already, she was about to find out in the course of his editorial interventions in the preparation of *The Prince's Progress and Other Poems* just how little her brother savored piquancy in a woman poet. Siddal's poems appeared in neither Rossetti's volumes.

Two significant deaths thus closely preceded the birth of Rossetti's career: Elizabeth Barrett Browning's and Elizabeth Siddal's. *Goblin Market and Other Poems* was published at the end of March 1862, just six weeks after Siddal's death from a laudanum overdose. Deborah Cherry and Griselda Pollock have explored the way in which as "Siddal" she comes to signify, above all, masculine creativity.[34] Yet with her death, Elizabeth Siddal becomes one of Christina Rossetti's cold women, whose death punishes the unloving living. Like them, her death seems both complicit with and resistant to the ideology of feminine death within a masculine aesthetics. Resistant, because Siddal takes death into her own hands, literalizing and so de-idealizing the figure of female death.

SEX AND DEATH: "A PAUSE" AND "ECHO"

The figure of the woman who speaks from the grave or at its brink is also significant in Rossetti's poetics of obscurity. Situating her in relation to her "poetess" predecessors, Leighton argues that "Rossetti needs a place from which to speak which will not be the over-exposed stage of the Capitol or, its real Victorian equivalent, the admiring family drawing-room, and finds it in the grave."[35] The obscurity of the grave is a figure, therefore, for Rossetti's recoil from "self-display." Yet, in another sense, these death lyrics become exhibitionism under cover of self-effacement. Their speakers are self-composing as well as cool; they carefully construct a scene of which they are the center and focus.[36] The fantasy of "After Death" involves exhibitionism as well as voyeurism on the part of the speaker; the vantage point of death means that she can secretly watch "him," but she also watches herself being watched. Formally, too, obscurity becomes exhibitionist; that is, these sonnets are performances of technical virtuosity that exploit the "besetting vice" of their form, the "obscurity" of conciseness and ambiguity.[37]

Such exhibitionism can also be found in "A Pause" (1853), which displays Rossetti's virtuosity in terms of both the sonnet form and her range within the lyric whose female subject-speaker is dead or dying. While both "A Pause" and "Echo" (discussed below) mark a departure from the cold, ironic modes of voice visible in the earlier death lyrics, these poems offer the irony that those who are cold in death are still warm with desire. Initially, "A Pause" appears similar to "After Death." In both poems, Rossetti manipulates the same elements—sonnet form, floral deathbed, dead woman speaker—but to strikingly different ends. As in "After Death," the speaker in "A Pause" is newly dead on her deathbed. The opening lines, in particular, recall the earlier poem with their retrospective description of the deathbed scene from the perspective of a subject-speaker empowered by her own death; in both poems, the description progressively narrows the focus from room, to bed, to dead body:

> They made the chamber sweet with flowers and leaves
> And the bed sweet with flowers on which I lay . . . (*CP*, 3:215, 1–2)

However, already there is a difference. Unlike "A Pause," the opening lines of "After Death"—"The curtains were half drawn, the floor was swept / And strewn with rushes"—attribute no human agency to the arrangement of the scene, consonant with the speaker's alienated consciousness (not only in death, we feel, but while living). Also in the opening of "A Pause," "sweet" appears twice in as many lines, without the ironic inflection, the burden of untold bitterness, of the closing "sweet" in "After Death"; and while the earlier poem's "rushes, rosemary and may" are redolent of the death in which they ritually participate, the less specific "flowers and leaves" are, conversely, more variously suggestive, even of celebration. The two lines that seem most alike—"Lay thick upon the bed on which I lay" ("After Death" 3) and "And the bed sweet with flowers on which I lay" ("A Pause" 2)—yield their differences most starkly in the context of each poem; yet a comparison between them highlights the subtlety with which Rossetti achieves her effects. In "A Pause," ambiguous syntax allows that, at the very least, the bed is adorned with flowers, with the further suggestion that her deathbed has been made a bed of flowers. In "After Death," we come to hear the connotations of suffocation and burial, when "rushes, rosemary and may / Lay thick," and when syntax and assonance ("Lay thick upon . . . on which I lay") create the claustrophobic layering of flowers, corpse, and bed. Like the sense of alienation that begins with the lack of human agency in the opening lines, this suggestion of the suffocation of burial is felt to pertain as much, if not more, to the conditions of the speaker's life as to her death.

The two poems diverge more obviously after the opening lines. Line 3 of "A Pause" — "While my soul, love-bound, loitered on its way" — introduces two terms rarely encountered in the vocabulary of Rossetti's dead or dying. The "soul" does not enter the worlds of "Song," "Remember," or "After Death," but occurs four times (and "spirit" once) in "A Pause." "Love" is mentioned in "After Death" only to mark its absence, and not at all in "Song" or "Remember." By contrast, "A Pause" is something rare in Rossetti's work, not merely among the poems on the death-state. It is a poem about fulfillment, as complete and utter as she ever imagines in religious terms — "I full of Christ and Christ of me" ("'The heart knoweth its own bitterness,'" *CP* 3:266) — except this is the fulfillment of human love, of lovers united after death. Unlike "After Death"'s eavesdropping loiterer, the speaker in "A Pause" shares the characteristic insentience of Rossetti's dead (4–5), except that her soul remains "love-bound" awaiting an earthly lover who, for once acceptably, "loves . . . remembers, grieves" (8). As in "Echo," the dead still desire, yet here the vigil of a "thirsty soul" (7) is answered by one who experiences a reciprocal lack. Thus the hint of doubt in line 8 — "*Perhaps* he loves" (my emphasis) — is erased in the sestet, which enacts a fulfillment and expansion of the hopes set up in the octave (rather than a movement of negation or reversal, as in "Remember"). In the sestet the lovers are united and the speaker transfigured on the threshold of Paradise:

> At length there came the step upon the stair,
>   Upon the lock the old familiar hand:
> Then first my spirit seemed to scent the air
>   Of Paradise; then first the tardy sand
> Of time ran golden; and I felt my hair
>   Put on a glory, and my soul expand. (9–14)

In the last four lines, her senses return but in a new register, a natural supernaturalism[38] joining "spirit" and "soul" to "scent," "feel," "hand," and "hair." The repetition of "*Then first* my spirit . . . / . . . *then first* the tardy sand" (11–12; my emphases), signifies both the disruption of linear time in a supernatural event, and the sense of a sudden rush. These lines describe the *rapture,* the moment when the soul is conveyed to heaven, a term especially relevant to "A Pause" as it also denotes physical or sensual transport, and so captures the way in which spiritual and sensual seem deliberately blurred in this poem.[39] Dolores Rosenblum persuasively argues that there is an allusion here to the woman clothed in the sun of Revelation, yet the context also suggests sexual climax, for the lover's arrival has made possible her transfigured state. For Rosenblum, the speaker "makes an extraordinary escape from the body," thus abandoning her human lover.[40] Likewise, Angela Leighton argues for a "moment of missed encounter," like that at the end of *The Prince's Progress,* the man's arrival coinciding with the woman's departure, that is, her death.[41] Yet in my reading, the speaker is already dead at the beginning of the poem; "only [her] soul, love-bound, loitered on its way," waiting for the lover. If the "chamber" (1) is read as the grave, which functions as the antechamber to Paradise, then the lover's "step upon the stair" signifies his own death. The speaker's entry into Paradise is predicated on the lover's arrival; consequently, the fulfillment of human, sexual love and spiritual apotheosis is simultaneous.

Such a vision is certainly at variance with that expressed throughout much of Rossetti's work, of the incompatibility between the claims of sexual and divine love; it is perhaps because of this that Rossetti left "A Pause" unpublished in her lifetime. Generally, the most optimistic view of erotic love expressed by Rossetti's poems is the hope of reunion in Paradise, *beyond* the threshold of death. Part II of "Memory" (1865) concludes:

> But often in my worn life's autumn weather
>   I watch there with clear eyes,
> And think how it will be in Paradise
>   When we're together. (*CP,* 1:148, 33–36)

In "The Convent Threshold" the speaker urges her lover to "repent" so that they will one day be in Paradise together:

> How should I rest in Paradise,
> Or sit on steps of heaven alone?
> . . . .
> Should I not turn with yearning eyes,
> Turn earthwards with a pitiful pang? (*CP,* 1:63, 69–70, 75–76)

The poem closes on this hope of reunion in Paradise: "There we shall meet as once we met / And love with old familiar love" (147-48).

"Echo" (1854) offers a more gothic conjoining of sex and death than "A Pause." For the speaker in "Echo," like the speaker in "A Pause," earthly love lives on after death, and she longs to be reunited with her lover. Yet if the premise of these poems is a theological idea of the space-time between the death of the body and the Final Resurrection, then Rossetti here imagines it as a species of nightmare. In "Echo," a poetics of obscurity operates in several ways. First, the poem's foregrounding of the signifier, its overwhelming sound effects—to which an abundance of end and internal rhyme, lexical repetition, anaphora, alliteration, and assonance all contribute—lull and distract from questions of meaning. Second, conciseness is pursued through a radical cutting of an earlier version of the poem, preserved in manuscript, which comprised seven stanzas. Rossetti's editing of her poem completely realigns it, so that the final poem privileges a dreamlike, rather than a coherent, narrative.

The first stanza invokes the lover in a dreamy incantation of repeated "Come"s:

> Come to me in the silence of the night;
>   Come in the speaking silence of a dream;
> Come with soft rounded cheeks and eyes as bright
>   As sunlight on a stream;
>   Come back in tears,
>   O memory, hope, love of finished years. (*CP*, 1:46, 1-6)

"Speaking silence" is an oxymoron that concisely captures the license the dream takes with the logic of the waking world; it also provides one definition of "echo." In counterpoint to the nighttime dream, the image of "sunlight on a stream" allows the speaker access to the daylight world, or life. Indeed, this is the lover's sole function in the poem, to act as a conduit of life, or at least the dream of life, for in this poem, both day and night, life and death, are subsumed by the dream. Similarly, lover and beloved seem subsumed by the dreamer. The syntactic ambiguity of line 5—"Come back in tears"— where it is uncertain whether the tears belong to her lover, or to her, or to both, suggests the blurring of the boundaries of identity.

The second stanza describes a "Paradise" denied the speaker for reasons never explained:

O dream how sweet, too sweet, too bitter sweet,
   Whose wakening should have been in Paradise,
Where souls brimfull of love abide and meet;
    Where thirsting longing eyes
      Watch the slow door
That opening, letting in, lets out no more. (7–12)

Line 7 charts the progress of erotic love, whose "sweet" will always end, at best, on the knife-edge of "bitter sweet." The poem in manuscript has four extra stanzas, which make clear that the speaker is one who watches from Hell with "thirsting longing eyes" (*CP,* 1:247). In the fourth stanza of the manuscript version, she says, "Set my life free that faints upon the rack," and elsewhere speaks of "the sentence time cannot annul." In its original context, the vision of Paradise in the second stanza appears to conform to the common Christian view whereby those in Hell watch with "thirsting longing eyes" the virtuous admitted to Paradise. The early version of the poem, then, would appear to depict that region of Hades which is a foretaste of Hell.[42] Yet in the poem's final form, the position of the speaker is uncertain; she is merely in some twilight realm of dreams. All clues to a coherent theological framework for the poem have been covered over or excised in the published poem. The "thirsting longing eyes" seem to belong to those in Paradise: this is the Paradise of lovers who "sit on steps of heaven alone" ("The Convent Threshold"), awaiting the arrival of their beloveds. To those who wait, Paradise might just as well be Hell. Half of the second stanza is devoted to describing this particular torture of Paradise-which-is-Hell. Its prolonged agony is captured in the present participles used as successive adjectives ("thirsting longing"), and echoed in "opening, letting"; in the division at lines 10–11 of the pentameter line, slowing it down; in the transferred epithet in "slow door," which lends an inanimate object sinister powers; and in the heavy finality of "no more" and its double rhyme with "slow door."

    All that we can be sure of in the final version of the poem is that the speaker has failed to "wake" in Paradise. Thus, there is pathos in her renewed invitation to the lover in the third and final stanza—"Yet come to me in dreams." For this invocation does not produce the union of lover and beloved that enables the transfigured release into Paradise of "A Pause." Rather, the equation of the lover with life is continued more explicitly; dreaming of the lover enables her to "live . . . again":

> Yet come to me in dreams, that I may live
> My very life again tho' cold in death:
> Come back to me in dreams, that I may give
> Pulse for pulse, breath for breath:
> Speak low, lean low,
> As long ago, my love, how long ago. (13-18)

The speaker's tone of intimacy intensifies in this final stanza, yet it is not so much *union* with the lover she seeks, as an *exchange:* "Pulse for pulse, breath for breath." The exchange of "pulse" and "breath" is at once suggestive of sexual intimacy, as well as something more abstract and depersonalized, the rudimentary signs of physical life. As the speaker is bereft of "pulse" and "breath," such an exchange becomes vampiric. Throughout the poem the lover is abstracted—"memory, hope, love"—and atomized—"cheeks," "eyes," "tears," "pulse," "breath." Such fragmentation is consonant with the quality of a dream as well as with death's dehumanization. The poem's macabre conjoining of sex and death is made explicit in the final lines, as "Speak low, lean low" draws attention, for the first time, to the position of the speaker's own body—in its grave.

Rossetti performs a characteristic sleight of hand with this poem. There is in "Echo" the ghost of an orthodox Christian scenario, or the skeleton of its framework, but it too is subsumed by a dream, a dream of transgressive desire: the line between Paradise and Hell blurs because the dead dream; they dream of life and so keep desire alive. The gothic irony that those cold in their graves are still warm with desire is pursued further in Rossetti's ghost poems, written in the late 1850s and early 1860s. These exploit their gothic and ballad features to explore the workings of desire at the margins of those Victorian sexual economies circumscribed by the law, specifically conjugal domesticity, and can fruitfully be read as ironic interrogations of Victorian sexual politics.[43]

All of the lyrics I have discussed in this essay are spoken by a woman from or on the brink of the darkness and corruption of the grave. Despite the range of attitudes displayed by the speakers in Rossetti's death lyrics—whether rejecting of the living or "desirous still"—the liminal space-time of the grave (or the moment of death) enables, in each poem, a fantasy of power that subverts the otherwise disempowering ideological conjunction of woman and death. This liminal site licenses an ideological destabilization registered at syntactic and semantic levels, allowing irony and ambiguity to flourish. In its depiction of a desire that persists into the grave and keeps its speaker bound there, "Echo" looks toward the later ghost poems, while the treatment of this theme in "A Pause" is, as I have suggested, anomalous in Rossetti's work to the extent that it constructs a fantasy of continuity rather than disjunction between living and dead, lover and beloved, earth and heaven. More typical are "Song" ("When I am dead, my dearest"), "Remember," and "After Death." Long regarded as suitably tender and demure "love personals"[44] or, more recently, as wholly complicit with a misogynist aesthetic that eroticizes the figure of female death, these lyrics should be heard as "cool, bitter," ironic commentaries on Victorian sexual and textual politics from the pen of a prickly poetess.[45]

NOTES

1. Margureite Yourcenar, *Coup de Grâce,* trans. Grace Frick. (London: Secker and Warburg, 1957), p. 110.

2. *FL,* p. 65.

3. Although Cayley's letter is dated 2 January 1877, Rossetti dates the fair copy manuscript of the poem 1 January 1877, suggesting that she wanted explicitly to tie her poem to the New Year (*CP,* 3:505). The "hope" and "memory" (10, 11) that the poem's sea-mouse represents are psychologically associated with the New Year.

4. *FL,* p. 80.

5. *Selected Letters of William Michael Rossetti,* ed. Roger W. Peatttie (University Park: Pennsylvania State University Press, 1990), p. 99.

6. J. G. Wood, *The Common Objects of the Sea Shore; Including Hints for an Aquarium* (London: Routledge, 1857), pp. 99–100.

7. In 1893 Rossetti writes to Katherine Tynan Hinkson: "Do come and see me,—only please do not 'interview' me. I own I feel this modern fashion highly distasteful, and am tenacious of my obscurity." Unpublished letter qtd. in Packer, p. 394.

8. W. M. Rossetti, *Some Reminiscences of William Michael Rossetti,* 2 vols. (London: Brown, Langham, 1906), 1:21; and Georgiana Burne-Jones, *Memorials of Edward Burne-Jones,* 2 vols. (London: Macmillan, 1904), 1:293.

9. After Rossetti's death Andrew Lang wrote in *Cosmopolitan Magazine:* "We are now deprived of the greatest English poet of the sex which is made to inspire poetry, rather than to create it." Qtd. in Bell, p. 329.

10. Dorothy Mermin, *Godiva's Ride: Women of Letters in England, 1830–1880* (Bloomington: Indiana University Press, 1993), p. 65.

11. Mermin, p. 65.

12. [John Skelton], "Our Camp in the Woodlands: A Day With the Gentle Poets," *Fraser's Magazine* 70 (1864), p. 210.

13. See Jerome J. McGann, "Christina Rossetti's Poems: A New Edition and a Revaluation," *VS* 23 (1980): 237–54.

14. See Rosenblum, pp. 5–6.

15. Linda Hutcheon, *Irony's Edge: The Theory and Politics of Irony* (London: Routledge, 1995), p. 30.

16. Hutcheon, p. 11.

17. Elisabeth Bronfen, *Over Her Dead Body: Death, Femininity, and the Aesthetic* (New York: Routledge, 1992), p. 401.

18. Rossetti uses this term in an 1865 letter to Dante Gabriel, but see discussion in Harrison, *CR,* pp. 16–17, on its possible origins.

19. Jerome J. McGann, "The Religious Poetry of Christina Rossetti," *Critical Inquiry* 10 (1983): 135.

20. Linda E. Marshall, "What the Dead Are Doing Underground: Hades and Heaven in the Writings of Christina Rossetti," *VN* 72 (1987): 55.

21. Angela Leighton, "'When I Am Dead, My Dearest': The Secret of Christina Rossetti," *Modern Philology* 87 (1990): 375.

22. Rossetti did write some poems in which the dying speaker is a man who addresses a woman, though she chose to leave them unpublished. These include "Song" ("I have loved you for long long years Ellen" [1852]) and "Long Looked For" (1854). Significantly, in these poems coldness and pride are still the preserve of the woman; also, the obscurity of the sonnet is eschewed for longer, narrative ballad forms and, partly in consequence, the attitudes and feelings of the respective players are less ambiguously delineated. Furthermore, the speaker's death in each poem is *explicitly* a form of sexual revenge for the woman's indifference:

> Then to all her coldness
> I also shall be cold,
> Then I also have forgotten
> Our happy love of old.
>
> ("Long Looked For," *CP,* 3:235, 13–16)

23. For a reading of "Song" that highlights its tone of cool irony and indifference, see Leighton, "'When I Am Dead, My Dearest.'"

24. W. David Shaw, "Poet of Mystery: The Art of Christina Rossetti," in Kent, p. 34. Katherine J. Mayberry's reading of "Remember" comes closest to mine, acknowledging "the evolving ambiguity of the five usages of 'remember'" so that it "becomes a desperate request for *separation,* not for lasting remembrance." In *Christina Rossetti and the Poetry of Discovery* (Baton Rouge: Louisiana State University Press, 1989), p. 65.

25. Packer, p. 53. Kathleen Blake remarks that the speaker "is aware of her lover's tears and gratified by them" (*Love and the Woman Question in Victorian Literature* [Brighton: Harvester, 1983], p. 11); and Bram Dijkstra, seeing Rossetti as fully

complicit with a misogynist aesthetic, writes that in "After Death" the poet "tried to convince herself that a good woman should be eager to sacrifice herself for love; the condescending sentiment of pity should be reward enough for any self-effacing female" (*Idols of Perversity: Fantasies of Feminine Evil in Fin-de-Siècle Culture* [New York: Oxford University Press, 1988], p. 61.

26. See also "Brandon's Both": "And pity without love is at best times hard and chilly" (*CP,* 2:103, 11).

27. According to Victorian floral dictionaries the emblematic meaning of may (the flower of the hawthorn tree) is hope (see, for example, Henry Phillips, *Floral Emblems: A Guide to the Language of Flowers* [London: Saunders and Otley, 1831]); yet it is also interesting to note that Charlotte Yonge's *History of Christian Names* (London: Macmillan, 1884) tells us that the name May is derived from the Hebrew meaning "bitter" (pp. 28–29).

28. Constance Hassett acknowledges both the ambiguity of "After Death"'s final lines and the strategic irony at work in the poem as a whole, commenting that it "anticipate[s] its own history in the hands of commentators" who have been reluctant to "lift the fold" on readings more subversive than the "superficial and sentimental." Of the poem's ending, the "possibilities run the gamut from gratitude to magisterial imperturbability"; "vengefulness is . . . possible. . . . Scorn is likely too" ("Christina Rossetti and the Poetry of Reticence," *Philological Quarterly* 65 [1986]: 500).

29. *Rossetti Papers: 1862–1870*, ed. W. M. Rossetti (London: Sands, 1903), p. 76.

30. W. M. Rossetti, *Some Reminiscences,* p. 21.

31. Hutcheon, p. 41.

32. *Ruskin: Rossetti: Preraphaelitism: Papers 1854 to 1862,* ed. W. M. Rossetti (London: George Allen, 1899), p. 152. Siddal's poems are not dated, although William Michael assigns them to the mid-1850s (p. 150).

33. *Rossetti Papers,* p. 78.

34. Deborah Cherry and Griselda Pollock, "Woman as Sign in Pre-Raphaelite Literature: A Study of the Representation of Elizabeth Siddall," *Art History* 7 (1984): 206–27. In a related argument, Elisabeth Bronfen writes: "The cultural conventions and representations of their times seem to have entered literally into the lives of Siddal and [D. G.] Rossetti as they repeatedly enacted a deanimation of the feminine body as engendering an animation of the artist" (p. 177).

35. Leighton, p. 143.

36. Nina Auerbach includes "Song" ("When I am dead, my dearest") in her chapter on "Death Scenes" in *Private Theatricals: The Lives of Victorians* (Cambridge, Mass.: Harvard University Press, 1990). Noting that in contrast to male poets, "female poets tend to play at death with an unself-conscious wish," she says that Rossetti's poem "masks a reverie of power" (p. 99).

37. In his review of Dante Gabriel's *Poems* (1870), William Morris called "obscurity, the besetting vice of sonnets" (*The Academy* 1 [14 May 1870]: 199).

38. Jerome Bump discusses the "natural supernaturalism" that pervades Rossetti's poetic vision of the afterlife, particularly her descriptions of Paradise, distinguishing this from the "supernatural naturalism" of Wordsworth or, in another way, Hopkins ("Christina Rossetti and the Pre-Raphaelite Brotherhood," in Kent, pp. 335-36).

39. I am grateful to Antony H. Harrison for alerting me to the description of the rapture in these lines.

40. Rosenblum, pp. 130-31.

41. Leighton, "'When I Am Dead, My Dearest,'" p. 386. Kathleen Blake's reading concurs with mine when she writes that "Earthly and spiritual consummation are confounded in the poem" (p. 11).

42. See Marshall, p. 55.

43. See especially "The Hour and the Ghost" (1856); "The Poor Ghost" (1863); and "The Ghost's Petition" (1864) (CP, 1:40, 120, and 145).

44. Rossetti expressly wished her poems not to be read as confessional "love personals" (unpublished letter, qtd. in Battiscombe, Christina Rossetti: A Divided Life [London: Constable, 1981], p. 54).

45. I wish to thank Mary Arseneau, Penny Gay, Antony H. Harrison, Lorraine Janzen Kooistra, and Clara Tuite for their helpful suggestions in the preparation of this essay.

CHAPTER 12

Dying to Be a Poetess

The Conundrum of Christina Rossetti

MARGARET LINLEY

Recent anthologies, books of criticism, and collections of essays on poetry by Victorian women writers appear to have arrived at a tacit agreement that the subject that matters is the Woman Poet.[1] This is a conclusion of no small importance given the fact that Victorians themselves chose to organize these same writers—even when they sometimes also called them female poets, gentle poets, or woman poets—around the name of the Poetess. Excluded from title billing in our own canonical lists, the Victorian poetess nevertheless keeps proving every bit as resilient as the obnoxious guest at a dinner party whom no one remembers having invited but who stays until the last glass of wine is empty. In other words, the name that Woman Poet elides remains ineluctably conspicuous.

Resistance to and downright dislike of the word poetess is understandable given that it stands for us today as a reification of a nineteenth-century model of femininity, presumably imposed by men or, if willingly embraced by the writers themselves, exploited as a means of self-protection in a hostile and highly commercialized publishing environment.[2] However, the word poetess was no less contentious, or innocent of the effects of power, for Victorians than it is for us. Located amid the social transfer of authority from the aristocracy to the middle classes that intensified toward the end of the eighteenth century, the emergence of the Victorian poetess can be understood as part of a burgeoning commodity culture that takes gender as one of its primary attributes. Situated, more specifically, at the juncture of popular and exclusive taste, public and private life, gender and sexuality, aesthetics and ascetics, the spectacular icon of the poetess both assists middle-class aspirations to power and unsettles the very nature of that power.

Thus while poetesses are everywhere to be seen in the nineteenth century, the meaning of the term poetess is far from transparent. That meaning cannot be discovered, however, by supplementing the lack of coherence in the category with the names of actual poetesses, such as Felicia Hemans or Letitia Landon. Their self-designation as poetesses and originary position in the rapidly coalescing canon of Victorian women poets currently taking shape appears to provide a stable bedrock against which later women poets can be differentiated. But in place of a resolution, such a historical narrative produces a tautology whereby woman poet and poetess are defined oppositionally: rather than stabilize the meaning of both terms, such a logic raises the question of definition itself.[3] Still, if it is one thing to contextualize earlier women poets as poetesses, it seems quite another to do the same for Christina Rossetti, even though one of the significant determinants of her poetry and career is precisely this controversial gendered space.[4] How, then, might a critical reading of Rossetti's work help to complicate our understanding of the function of the poetess as a cultural category? And how, in turn, might we apply pressure on this category so as to make it a useful instrument of analysis in the study of Victorian women's poetry and of Christina Rossetti's poetry in particular?

Conspicuous Collection

I want to approach these questions by way of Rossetti's *Maude: Prose and Verse*, both a short story and a collection of poems, not only because this text represents her most extended early response to and revision of the image of the poetess, but also because its posthumous publication in 1897 renders it an exemplary instance of the cultural inscription of Rossetti herself into the category of the poetess. Although *Maude* can be, indeed has been, read primarily as veiled autobiography, the extent to which Rossetti formulates this text in relation to a tradition of women's writing as well as to literary canonization processes has been largely overlooked. That she does so by applying pressure to the category of the poetess is one of the main points of my analysis. Before turning to the text, though, I wish to consider some important complications and popularizations of this category that contribute

to the context in which Rossetti began writing *Maude* in the late 1840s. My
purpose is to suggest the extent to which the rules of the poetess were not
fixed or stable, but constantly under revision, and to argue, in addition, that
this shiftiness is what makes the poetess a viable, though vexed, category for
Rossetti and a conundrum for us.

As obsolete as the term poetess may seem to us today, it permeated critical
and cultural representations of nineteenth-century women poets and provided
a crucially volatile theoretical paradigm for both writers and readers. Consequently, the discourse of the poetess offers a complex and discordant field for
analysis of the relationship between gender and genius in the production and
reception of poetry as it was incorporated into national canons of literature.
Such incorporation has a long history, of course. The classification "woman
writer" emerged, according to Paula McDowell, just after the 1730s, making
possible "the formation of the first public 'canons' of British women's literature" and "the consolidation of a sexual division of literary labour that still
remains in evidence today."[5] By the nineteenth century, canonizing processes
of revision, standardization, and sanctification, as Tricia Lootens traces them,
carefully disciplined and dehistoricized women's writing, making Victorian
women poets into "generic feminine saints" while, ironically, guaranteeing
their ultimate disappearance from literary history.[6] No less ironic, though, is
the possibility that while these new norms for female literary activity may
have been, as McDowell argues, "oppressive" in some of their effects, they
also may have enabled women to publish in unprecedented numbers and to
do so in the nineteenth century, as Isobel Armstrong argues, with a respect
unparalleled since.[7] Armstrong's point should not be underestimated, for even
as that respect was highly qualified by gender ideologies that sought to
recuperate women's writing to myths of domestic modesty and essential
femininity, the woman poet's public visibility precisely as poetess acquired a
cultural and ethical force, particularly in the second quarter of the century,
that we have not seen since.

Moreover, just as poetesses were evaluated by constraining and containing
gender politics, they themselves exploited these very conventions to different
ends, turning them back on their culture and judging its prescriptive standards for women generally and for women artists especially. Thus the field of
the poetess that Rossetti inherited became a site not only for the ongoing
interrogation of what it means to write as a woman, but also for the development of strategies that might in fact undo the gender of women's writing,
an undoing which often takes place in Rossetti's writing paradoxically at the

moment it appears most self-consciously and singularly feminine. In addition to this disruptive capacity, the performance of femininity required of a writing woman in the nineteenth century also entailed the constant reformation of authorial image; indeed such reformation, frequently couched in the religious language of redemption and resurrection so central in *Maude,* is vitally constitutive of the category of the poetess itself.

Alexander Dyce's 1825 *Specimens of British Poetesses,* which went into a second edition only two years later, exemplifies the revisionist approach by establishing for the first time in the nineteenth century an explicit link between the term poetess and national literature. Although we now know women poets were publishing in large numbers throughout the Romantic period, Dyce constructs his poetesses out of a model of marginality that renders them both exotic and potentially erotic signifiers of exclusive and cultured taste. He does so by representing his editorial work as a kind of ethnography, involving "a tedious chase through the jungles of forgotten literature" to retrieve lost specimens of the "sensibility," "tenderness," and "grace" that have been "carefully excluded" from the culturally sanctioned canon of male literary history.[8] If the marginalization of literary women, their segregation from the canons of poetry by men, is precisely what makes them exquisite and rare, the quality of "grace" identifies them as simultaneously aristocratic and sacred. "Consecrating" his anthology to women, Dyce anticipates and commodifies that divinity which both Barrett Browning and Rossetti, as I will later discuss, would attempt to abstract in different ways from the poetess as spiritual and political solution to the alienated and dispossessed condition of writing women. Dyce's dislocation of the woman poet from her specific historical context and relocation of her within the serial order of a collection emphatically signals the enormous risks involved for the woman writing as poetess in the commodity culture of Victorian England— artist and art are always potentially mere artifacts.[9]

Almost twenty-five years later when Fredric Rowton published *The Female Poets of Great Britain* (1848), and when Rossetti began composing *Maude,* the paradigm of conspicuous leisure, encouraging middle-class emulation of aristocratic taste, had been emphatically replaced by one based on morality.[10] An "enlightened" society, Rowton argues, should not only be "ashamed" of its cultural neglect of women, but it should also wake up to the consequences of that neglect: a society that abandons women unwittingly punishes itself, and "to tell the truth," Rowton chides, "we have already suffered severely for our folly in this matter."[11] For Rowton, then, moral conscience is of social consequence, a belief which motivates his interest in isolating the historical and material conditions that determine the quantity and quality of women's writing.

Classifying these social constraints as poor education on the one hand and even poorer reception on the other, Rowton nevertheless concedes that the situation for women authors has slightly improved and does so, moreover, by calling attention to the value of the word poetess: "During the last half-century our Poetesses have received a far healthier kind of regard: indeed their claim to distinction has been so far admitted as to make our wise men ask one another whether they should any longer permit such a word Poet*ess* at all?" (p. xlviii). The question here is not whether the word poetess should exist (Rowton does not himself reject the category), but why some "wise *men*" suppose they have the right to censor it.[12] Appearing to interrogate the term poetess, Rowton in fact directs his attack against the authority of "our wise men": literary critics, in other words, who, Rowton implies, are no less patriarchal than Adam in their desire to have supreme authority over which names and categories should be properly recognized in the kingdom of culture. More importantly, their desire for cultural authority has, according to Rowton, a specifically sexual basis. To illustrate the point, he returns the discussion to the social context of sexual discrimination and raises the example of young Female Poets who suffer shameful malice and slander from "critics who could not deny their talents, [but who] have belied their characters" (p. xlviii).

The value of the term poetess is therefore in its *use* for women; they need this cultural category, according to Rowton, precisely because of the nature of masculine desire—a desire he defines as a "coarser spirit" that makes "us" men (self-consciously implicating himself) "too gross, material, sensual, and violent" (p. xxxviii). Although the book announces (in its name) that literary women are entitled to be addressed as Female Poets, the text tells quite another story about the social circumstances compelling continued use of the term poetess. Moreover, because these social circumstances derive from an essential aspect of men, they must be permanently unchangeable. The category of the poetess therefore remains eternally necessary.

As such, *Female Poets* is, in part, a deliberate display of sex calculated to seduce "wise" critics between the covers where, once inside the text, they will learn the lesson that the only thing female poets bare as poetesses is the gendered soul. Whereas for Dyce the poetess's exclusion from the tradition of writings by men paradoxically shapes her into a representative of class exclusivity, a rare specimen of cultural collection and exhibition that perpetuates social status and evinces distinguished taste, for Rowton, biology rather than taxonomy appears to underwrite female cultural distinction. Appearances, however, are deceiving. Despite the reference to biological sex in the title of his anthology, Rowton's argument about the femininity of female poets is logically independent of biology. If the sex of the female poet turns out to be inseparable from material contingencies of gender—poor education and demeaning reception—the female poet's gender can be redeemed through the spiritual category of the poetess whose genius lies in a special ability to manifest, not the body, but the soul. A poetess, by Rowton's definition, may exhibit too much ambition, too much learning, too much passion, but she can never be too rich in soul. Most importantly, soul is the one thing that can go on display without being seen. If the poetess embodies the soul and materializes its effects in her poetry, the soul, as the sign of absolute interiority, dematerializes the image of the poetess and legitimizes her role on the public stage. The poetess is, then, unavoidably a spectacle, but one that is a spectacular contradiction, taking up a "prominent place in the world's esteem" (p. xxxvii) while publicizing the soul in excess of all worldliness.[13]

In a gesture that will prove important in *Maude,* Rowton represents Felicia Hemans as "a perfect embodiment of woman's soul" and her poetry as "*intensely* feminine" (p. 386); he distinguishes Elizabeth Barrett Browning as learned and her poetry as a manifestation of "pure reason" (p. 500), although he would prefer that she give her "soul free unconscious vent" (p. 502); he differentiates Letitia Landon as a much maligned, misrepresented, and, consequently, misanthropic female Byron (p. 424) and her poetry as an expression of a spirit that "is not a true poet's soul" (p. 432). This business of capturing the poetess's soul would eventually discover Rossetti, as Tricia Lootens has demonstrated, with the effect that in seeking to celebrate her "transcendent feminine modesty," critics would "exonerate an artist of the onus of having created art" and attempt "to domesticate a would-be religious saint into a secular one."[14]

As an aspiring female poet Rossetti could not but be concerned with the status of the poetess, and the bulk of her writing points to the conclusion that she was familiar enough with the disparate and contradictory constructions of the poetess to have guessed the secret concealed within such representations of the soul as Rowton's: that they are historically specific. Such depictions of the soul attempt to actualize, maintain, and regulate the shape of female literary production and reception. The result is an image of the soul that can readily be assimilated, as we have seen, to commercial and political ends. However, because the self-sustaining rules informing the poetess, fixing her contours and movements, are always on the move, functioning differently in relation to specific contingencies, the category of the poetess, like a collection of poetesses, can never be complete, indeed must be incomplete. This is part of the category's paradox. Constituted in the mainstream as marginal, the poetess appears always on the verge of extinction, in danger of being left out or forgotten by literary history until an editor chivalrously saves her.

Literary history is not determined by critics and editors alone, of course, and they were not, as I have suggested, the only ones fascinated with the feminine abundance of the erotically charged glorified figure of the abandoned woman writer. Literary women themselves throughout the nineteenth century also manipulated the irreconcilable inconsistencies within the category to display and exploit femininity, to criticize the gender politics of representation, to interpret and shape literary history (and their own location in it), and to protest the social subordination and dispossession of women. In this repository of self-contradiction, Rossetti activates the mechanism of reform that, as mentioned earlier, is vital to the poetess in order to reconstitute the category as the quintessence of a radically disinterested autonomy. Replaying and reviving this moribund figure (simultaneously a figure of moribundity), Rossetti demonstrates that oppressive social and cultural conventions never fully materialize, precisely because they generate more than is consistent with their own normalizing propensities. Given the context out of which her poetic self-fashioning grows, Rossetti's style of excessive restraint and conspicuous asceticism can therefore be understood as an analysis of the category of the poetess oriented toward the gender politics of culture.[15]

AND THEN CAME MAUDE

Begun as early as 1848 and completed in 1850, Christina Rossetti's *Maude* recounts the life of a young poetess during the two years leading up to her death at the age of seventeen from mysterious injuries suffered in a traffic accident. Before taking her final exit, Maude entrusts her cousin Agnes with the responsibility of disposing of her literary property, instructing her to "examine the verses, and destroy what I evidently never intended to be seen."[16] Agnes thus obediently performs the role of literary executor and editor, placing Maude's locked writing book unopened in her coffin and burning all remaining fragments of writing except a small selection for Maude's mother and three poems for herself.

Because Rossetti was unable to procure a publisher for the story at mid-century, *Maude* itself was also a victim of the traffic in literature, a victim of a different sort, however, since Maude implicitly dies of literary ambition while *Maude* remained dormant due to publishers' neglect. William Michael Rossetti selected the manuscript from his sister's literary remains and accelerated it into the new publishing currents perversely made possible by the death of the author herself in 1894. Capitalizing on the commemorative market, the publisher's notice in the *Bookman* advertised *Maude* as a pretext for the mature poetess, "an embryo of poems and ideas afterwards worked out more fully in other books."[17] On actual publication, Rossetti's brother supplied an interpretive framework composed of his own prose sketch of the author in a brief "Prefatory Note" and Dante Gabriel Rossetti's 1848 rough drawing in the frontispiece (fig. 12.1), a portrait of his sister dating from about the time she was writing *Maude*. Taken together, William Michael's prose sketch and Dante Gabriel's drawing further emphasized the nostalgic value of the book and guided reception ever more forcefully toward a conflation of the writer with the text.

Positioning himself as his sister's publicist, William Michael begins by conceding that most of the poems, certainly all of the important ones, have already appeared elsewhere, and that, though competently written, the story is not good enough to be of literary interest. The importance of the text therefore derives from another source: "The literary reputation of Christina Rossetti is now sufficiently established to make what she wrote interesting to many persons—if not for the writing's own sake, then for the writer's. As such, I feel no qualms in giving publicity to *Maude*" (*Maude,* p. 79). Both fittingly and ironically, given that the story is deeply concerned with the relationship between literary and spiritual afterlife, *Maude* enters the authorial canon only after the reputation of the author is confirmed at death, and enters, moreover, as a marginal text, prefatory to a marginal career in a society where poetry is but a minor cause. Gone is the inclusivity of Rowton's soulful poetess, as the value of *Maude* inheres in the ability of the author's personal and private life to appeal to enthusiasts of the aesthetic, and especially of the Rossettis, a point reinforced by the famous signature on the frontispiece drawing. Elsewhere, William Michael describes this "little pencil-head" as "a nice but somewhat slight sketch,"[18] which suggests he perceives complementarity between its incompleteness and the sketchiness of his sister's "juvenile performance" (*Maude,* p. 79). Both are creative exercises illustrating the youthfulness of eventually proven artists and therefore potentially inspiring to the passions of connoisseurs.[19]

Christina G. Rossetti

from a sketch by Dante G. Rossetti

towards 1848.

Fig. 12.1. Dante Gabriel Rossetti, sketch of Christina
Rossetti when she was approximately seventeen years old
(1848). Frontispiece for *Maude: Prose and Verse* (London,
1897). Reproduced with the kind permission of The
Huntington Library, San Marino, California.

In this way, William Michael presents the book as a service to a select group of culturally elite and gender-neutral buyers. His particular emphasis on the enigma of the author (which, as we shall see momentarily, frustrates his own desire for completion) implies, furthermore, that personality is itself a viable subject of book collection. Rather than overexposing the author, the autobiographical work in fact mystifies and sanctifies the poetess and thereby escapes commercialism by transforming consumption into a form of communion as the definitive relationship between memorial text and devout reader. The following year, Mackenzie Bell further publicized the collectibility of Rossetti by allotting almost as much type to details of the manuscript— including size, color, type of paper, and penmanship—as he does to description of the story.[20] None of this is at odds with Rossetti's narrative, though, since the heroine expresses intimacy by giving gifts of her poetry to friends for their own album collections; in addition, Rossetti may have planned *Maude* originally as a vehicle for a small collection of poetry by an aspiring poetess to find its way to market.

Frontispiece and text, however, are apparently in less than complete symbiosis. One of the features William Michael appreciates about his brother's sketch is its "archness of expression," a quality, he adds, "in which the poetess was by no means deficient."[21] Certainly, he is well aware of that archness in stridently dismissing the author's harsh treatment of her heroine, insisting that he "cannot see that the much-reprehended Maude commits a single fault from title-page to finis" (*Maude,* p. 80). Long-standing religious differences between brother and sister prevent any admission into William Michael's biographical sketch of the playfulness that archness also implies and the playfulness that *Maude* actually manifests. The portrait is thus both criticism and corrective directed at author and text alike for failing to conform to a constrained image of the poetess, an image more vivid than ever in 1897.[22] Extending beyond personal differences, this conflict with and over the territory of the poetess exemplifies rifts in the category itself, as its cultural function shifts, turns, divides, and carries resonances of multiple and competing interests.

Such rifts in the category may have motivated Maude to take down the image of the poetess "towering above her sex with horrid height."[23] Three figures in particular preoccupy *Maude:* Letitia Landon, Felicia Hemans, and Elizabeth Barrett Browning, the most famous poetesses at midcentury. Rossetti was likely beginning the story in 1848 when Dante Gabriel Rossetti wrote to his brother: "The only book I have picked up is L.E.L.'s *Improvisatrice,* for which I gave ninepence. By the bye, have you her *Violet* and *Bracelet* with you? I cannot find them in our library."[24] Perhaps he should have asked his sister instead, for in *Maude* the subject of the woman poet, the conflict between ambition and fame, the Sapphic motif, and the fragmentary style are all highly evocative of Landon. That same year, Rowton canonized Felicia Hemans as the saint of femininity and *Blackwood's* noticed that her "reputation has been steadily on the increase" to such a degree that "she has become an English classic."[25] In addition, Elizabeth Barrett Browning's reputation as the leading female poet of the day had been established since her 1844 *Poems,* and she was the only woman to make the 1848 Pre-Raphaelite list of immortals.

Cultural receptiveness has a cost, however, and that cost is what defines Rossetti's own investment in the poetess. Landon exploited the commercial potential of the book market by constituting her poetry ironically as a religion of love beyond the marketplace and by figuring her participation in that marketplace as a form of slavery. Hemans laid the foundation for Rowton's soul-mongering in her sanctification of the feminine soul (as ironically beyond economic exchange) and her figuration of publication as a form of self-sacrifice. Barrett Browning, despite her religious proclivity, marks her radical difference from both of these authors by seeking to have writing recognized in the productive sphere as work and by seizing the material of the world as the proper subject of poetry. Rossetti takes each of these positions to task in *Maude,* examining the poetess and performance in part 1, the poetess and prostitution in part 2, and the poetess and profession in part 3.

Clearly Rossetti was every bit as concerned with distinction as the various collectors we have thus far encountered. Her concern is made all the more pressing because, in the decades between Dyce and Rowton, the gender school of poetry and criticism cultivated by Landon's spiritualizing word paintings, Hemans's martyred femininity, and even Barrett Browning's "modern vicious style" frequently resulted, as we have seen, in a narrowly framed poetess.[26] Moreover, domestic education was teaching young women Maude's age that they were the very embodiment of a spontaneous and natural feminine poetics, making it virtually impossible to distinguish a poetess from any young lady versifier who might be "admired" for her drawing-room accomplishments. This demand for poetic femininity can be seen, along with the supply of collections of poetesses, as a function of class mobility, making it possible for the various and expanding middle classes to distinguish themselves as a group from those above and below and to designate their status in terms of the ability to afford the time and space for leisure. With this kind of democratization

of feminine poetics, that is, with the coding of leisure through signs of femininity, women poets become leveled as women, who are in turn subsumed
within a groundless essence, whether body or soul, of the ideal of woman.
Such an essence could be called upon for convenience, however, as Barrett
Browning points out: expected to express emotion and feeling, women poets
could be condemned for doing just that, for being "mere women, personal and
passionate." [27]

Consequently, the contradictions informing the poetess—that she is different from but exactly like other women, that she is free to choose to write
about love but cannot free herself from being placed in love's plot, that she
spontaneously expresses private feelings but is studious in making them
known, that her writing is from nature but is also a product of ambition and
cultivated femininity—begin to look like dissimulations of art, just as the
critique of materialism, in which all the authors mentioned here are engaged,
acquires the moral taint of hypocrisy when the sign of the poetess comes to
function as a display of the consumer's social status. Rossetti deals with this
proliferation of signs of femininity, which diminishes the cultural value of the
category of the poetess as derivative in direct proportion to the increase in
the social power of the class it serves, by replaying and recycling the inex-
haustible semiotics of that femininity. Stated differently, Rossetti mercilessly
forces Maude to tell the secrets of the poetess, secrets everyone knows, as a
means of working toward a reclamation of the very logic of secrecy on the
one hand and a purification of the image of the poetess on the other.

REPLAYING PERFORMANCE

From the opening scene, when Maude's mother interrupts her in the act of
writing, to the poetry contest at her cousin's birthday party in the country,
part 1 enacts the familiar story of the performing heroine popularized by
Landon's improvising style. Although Maude likes to think of herself as out
of sync with her domestic environs, her oppositional stance could not be more
conventional. Maude's exhibitionism makes a mockery of the notions of sin-
cerity and spontaneity, and her most "natural" tendency is an ambitious desire
for renown. Although Maude outperforms everyone at the party, taking the
prize in the poetry contest, her acting continues; on the following day, she
assumes the renunciatory pose of the poetess, and declares she is "sick of
display and poetry and acting" (*Maude,* p. 41).[28] A formative trope of the

poetess, however, is the rejection of constitutive conventions: she not only abandons poetry, fame, and being itself, but also must be seen as abandoned; she not only displays herself but also must display her rejection of self-display.

Maude's renunciation of display, poetry, and performance cannot therefore be the distinguishing feature of her poetic ambition. Her distinction lies rather in the peculiar way in which she recycles the (Sapphic) poetess, a reconversion, in fact, which is most evident in the lyric she gives to her cousin Agnes at the end of part 1, "She sat and sang alway":

> She sat and sang alway
> By the green margin of a stream,
> Watching the fishes leap and play
> Beneath the glad sun-beam.
>
> I sat and wept alway
> Beneath the moon's most shadowy beam,
> Watching the blossoms of the may
> Weep leaves unto the stream.
>
> I wept for memory;
> She sang for hope that is so fair;—
> My tears were swallowed by the sea;
> Her songs died on the air. (*Maude,* p. 41)

Composed at the end of 1848, this poem crystallizes Rossetti's critique of the poetess. As Dolores Rosenblum argues, the lyric balances mutually exclusive possibilities, presenting a virtual janus-face that simultaneously looks backward, weeping for memory, and forward, singing for hope.[29] Separation exists both within the poem, between weeper and singer, and without, between them and the world, thus multiplying at the structural level, internally and externally, the lyric's emotional disconnection and containment.

A perpetual expression of watching and wanting, "She sat and sang alway" can be called a perfect anatomy of the consuming desire that informs the structure of consumption in a commodity culture. While weeping and singing seem irreconcilable, they are not necessarily contradictory. Rather, the poem articulates the cyclical impulse of consumption in which past and future, new and old, lose their temporal value and become homogeneous in a culture of change that nevertheless keeps everything the same.[30] The difference between "she" and "I," object and subject, is in fact a play of equivalences ("My tears were swallowed by the sea; / Her songs died on the air") that turn the lyric into a self-enclosed tautological riddle. In so doing, "She sat and sang alway" tells the story of productive consumption without revealing anything at all except perhaps that the poem, like the later, more precocious, "Winter: My Secret," may or may not contain a secret.[31]

The lyric's effect hinges in part on a simultaneous denial and revelation of the labor involved in consumption. Rossetti begins, therefore, where Hemans and Landon leave off. In contrast to the monumentality of Hemans's severe and suffering narrators or to the discomposure of Landon's effusive heroines, Rossetti's play of difference and equivalence produces distance rather than empathy, perspective (though often in the form of competing perspectives) rather than proximity. Rossetti abandons the theater of the physical body that brings the gaze up close and threatens to overwhelm with the enlargements of sentiment or the profusion of the spectacle. But her rejection of this favorite mode of self-proclaimed poetesses enables a simultaneous recuperation and reconversion of the very discourse of abandon and renunciation as an ironic recollection, expressing control, completion, and restraint. The pain of consumption continues on display in "She sat and sang alway," but negatively by its very absence, registered everywhere in the very structure of the lyric.

"She sat and sang alway" is therefore a commemoration of the failure of that "sympathy with sorrow" Landon sought to exalt by making an "almost religion" of love's truth.[32] It articulates, in addition, an anticommodity aesthetic. Whereas Hemans and Landon magnify femininity in touching spectacles, Rossetti stresses visibility itself as a barrier to response. Consequently, she exaggerates the bar through which the subject of consumption cannot pass, foregrounding the irrecoverable distance—between subject and object, use value and exchange value, signifier and signified—that the ideology of sympathy naturalizes through the almost tactile illusion of proximity. Most importantly, she reconstitutes the space of disinterest in place of sympathy and thereby purifies the commodified image of the poetess.

Rossetti's anticommodity aesthetic depends, in other words, upon the elimination of need—that essential term in political economy which itself refuses desire that is not organized according to utility. Articulating itself in the past tense, the lyric represents its own disciplined beauty, and the self-sufficiency of its feminine subjects, as that which is "alway" left over from the process of consumption, the surplus of desire that has no need of need, which is to say, no productive value. We therefore recognize the same ineffectuality and inutility in Rossetti's singer and weeper, whose songs were unheard and whose tears were swallowed, that we encounter in Landon's heroines, for example, but we find here neither revenge nor retribution nor even consolation. If Landon's flamboyant performance of the discourse of beauty positivizes the waste of utility, exposing its productive and destructive dependence on objectified femininity and politically exploited women, Rossetti recycles capitalism's excess negatively by refusing to have any interest in it whatsoever. Thus abandon appears to be both beyond and a reflection of the logic of production, defining the very margin of utility.

Not only do renunciation and abandon appear to be a precondition of autonomy, but Rossetti's placement of "She sat and sang alway" at the closing of part 1 further reinforces its status as "left over." Moreover, the poem is integrated into the narrative as a gift from Maude to her cousin Agnes; this private exchange beyond economic exchange appears to circumvent the commercialism that has come to define the poetess. Yet the poem's placement simultaneously breaks the illusion of invulnerable disinterest of the aesthetic artifact by forcing its self-enclosed timelessness into dialogical relation with narrative linearity. The poem therefore also functions both as a monument to the end of Maude's performing-heroine phase (played out at the birthday party mentioned above) and as a prophecy of the mythic, that is ideological, destiny of the poetess she is dying to be.

Soul's Body

It becomes immediately apparent in the next section that Maude is unable to extricate herself from the system of exchange that her poem eschews. Part 2 takes up the thread of Maude's life more than a year after the birthday party, when her cousins come to London to visit. This time Maude is no longer playing the Corinnic heroine, but is bound to domestic duty as one of the Daughters of England.[33] Yet for all Maude's efforts to transform her poetic ambition into the poetry of domestic womanhood, the question of her actual verses continues to haunt her. Hemans, or rather the Victorian construction of Hemans, popularized the notion that one of the constitutive features of woman's "lot" is martyrdom. Not surprisingly, then, Maude is soon called upon to make a Hemansesque self-sacrifice at the domestic altar. This situation transpires when Maude's mother and cousins become "indisposed with colds" (*Maude,* p. 46) and thereby force Maude to venture alone to a tea at Mrs. Strawdy's. Domestic imperative therefore ironically compels Maude in the name of filial duty to go forth and perform as a poetess.

The devaluation and trivialization of Maude's vocational ambitions, already apparent in her mother's opening comment, "a penny for your thoughts" (*Maude,* p. 29), reaches its apotheosis during the scene at Mrs. Strawdy's. Maude finds herself trapped between the appropriately named Miss Savage and another guest who begin to "attack" her with questions about her poetry. When she admits she still writes, a flood of praise follows:

> she was so young, so much admired, and, poor thing, looked delicate. It was quite affecting to think of her lying awake at night meditating those sweet verses—("I sleep like a top," Maude put in drily),—which so delighted her friends, and would so charm the public, if only Miss Foster could be induced to publish. At last bystanders were called upon to intercede for a recitation. (*Maude,* p. 49)

Despite Maude's amused resistance, her body acquires more significance than her poems, and her personal life, much as the posthumous Rossetti's personal image, is plundered for the key to all interpretation. In fact, she finds herself transformed, in much the way the publishing industry transforms literary women into collectible poetesses, into another domestic object, a veritable drawing-room delectable to be consumed with the same "mathematical precision" applied to the dissection of the cake at tea.

Whereas Landon, as mentioned earlier, draws upon the discourse of slavery as a paradigm for the dispossessed condition of women and the commercialization of art, Rossetti looks to that of prostitution. During the 1840s, prostitution, increasingly discussed in sermons and articles, was becoming a central issue in the Victorian social reform movement. Although Rossetti's concern for fallen women, demonstrated in such poems of the 1850s and '60s as "Cousin Kate," "Light Love," "An Apple-Gathering," "Margery," "The Iniquity of the Fathers Upon the Children," and *Goblin Market,* was sustained by her social work in the Anglican church,[34] clearly her interest during her youth was shared and perhaps stimulated by her family. Early versions of Dante Gabriel's "Jenny" date from 1848. In addition, Frances Rossetti's commonplace book contains two poems on fallen women: one is untitled; the other is "Verses for My Tombstone, If Ever I Should Have One," copied in full from Edward Creech's *Fugitive Pieces.*[35] "Verses for My Tombstone" also appears in W. R. Greg's 1850 *Westminster Review* article, "Prostitution," one of the most influential pieces on the topic at midcentury[36] and, given that "good" and "bad" femininity are necessarily defined relationally, a crucial measure of the extent to which the prostitute forms the underbelly, so to speak, of the poetess as defined by Rowton at midcentury.

At the same time that the discourse on prostitution was energizing the gender politics of Victorian social reform, in which Rossetti herself participated, it was also infiltrating the institution of art. In an 1837 review of the annuals for *Fraser's,* William Makepeace Thackeray roundly condemns publishers for forcing painters into producing an art that is "little better than a kind of prostitution." He then goes on to fume that the poetry printed in annuals is no better: "a little sham sentiment is employed to illustrate a little sham art." In his discussion of specific writers, he focuses on Landon in particular as "a woman of genius" who "degrades hers, by producing what is even indifferent."[37] Despite Thackeray's link between commercialism and prostitution, reviewers continued the trend of commodifying women's poetry as a product of the body's beauty, thereby placing the writer before her poems on the market. An 1840 *Quarterly Review* of "Modern English Poetesses" begins by pointing out how "whilst the mind is bent on praise or censure of the [woman's] poem, the eye swims too deep in tears and mist over the poetess herself in the frontispiece."[38] And George Gilfillan, in an 1847 review of Hemans, remarks that "the nature of this poetess is more interesting than her genius" and that her "life was a poem."[39]

Perhaps the most extravagant example of this pattern, though, is William Michael Rossetti's "Memoir," which advertises his sister's posthumous *Poetical Works* in 1904 by devoting over six out of twenty-seven pages to the question of "the amount of good looks with which Christina Rossetti should be credited."[40] William Michael takes the reader on a metaphorical tour of an art gallery display of the author, beginning with his own impressions of his sister's differences from and similarities to other females in the Rossetti family and then continuing with a description of forty-five portraits. In a process of subtle solicitation somewhat reminiscent of Rossetti's own "goblin merchant men," with their famous cry of "Come buy, come buy" (*Goblin Market, CP,* 1:11–26), William Michael's visual biography establishes an equivalence between images of the author's body and the fruits of her art.

The nature of the author as art object is, however, carefully circumscribed. Although William Michael insists that the final portraits, drawn by Dante Gabriel when Christina was forty-six, represent her face in "advanced years," he neither "shows" nor describes the author in the final seventeen years of her life. Focusing on youth rather than on age then, William Michael thus indicates the extent to which the commercial viability of both poetess and poetry depends on feminine beauty. Further reinforcing the connection, he concludes this section of the Memoir by drawing attention to a select group of pictures, roughly one-third of those he has catalogued, for their special ability to convey "a very exact knowledge of what [Christina] was like from the age of seventeen onwards." What differentiates these exclusive portraits is that they share a "true likeness" to their subject, revealing the various ways in which she might be considered beautiful: "exquisitely sweet in contour and expression," "impressive," "chaste," "intellectual," "distinguished," and so on.[41]

Excluded from this select list, though part of the visual biography, is the frontispiece William Michael chose for *Maude* (fig. 12.1). If the portraits settle the matter of Rossetti's looks—teaching the reader how to discern beauty in the author and therefore also in her writing, producing a visual knowledge of her character while also inciting the desire to know and see more—then the choice of frontispiece for the earlier text suggests William Michael thought it uncharacteristic, not of the Rossetti he knew privately but of his public image of her as poetess. Anticipating a small, "indulgent" and "discreet" (*Maude,* p. 80) readership for *Maude,* William Michael displays an image of his sister that intimates a highly personal ("arch") aspect of her character. However, his version of the poetess for the later commercially feasible *Poetical Works* is one which would subordinate all the more forcefully, indeed define itself against, the play which Rossetti herself clearly saw possible in the category.

It is important to notice the degree to which William Michael's marketing strategies inadvertently enact the very problems of literary production and reception that Rossetti analyzes in *Maude.* The heroine's narrative represents a negotiation of the dangers of consumer demand, and, precisely because of her self-positioning as aspiring poetess, Maude is perpetually being induced to visualize herself as art. Even Maude's own mother is more impressed by her daughter's beauty than by her poems, and when copies of her "broken-hearted" verses "were handed about and admired," "some wondered if *she* really had any source of uneasiness" (p. 31, my emphasis). Rossetti's representation of Maude's predicament at Mrs. Strawdy's as that of a victim suffering attack draws on the structural logic that makes bedfellows of poetesses and prostitutes in the marketplace. Both are commodities, one figured as abandoned in literary history, the other in feminine sexuality; each can simultaneously be positioned as object of erotic desire or of social sympathy. Although Maude refuses to allow herself to be seduced by praise and inducements to recite or publish, and always asserts autonomy over sympathetic

identification, the scrutiny she receives at Mrs. Strawdy's nevertheless suggests the drawing room as a significant source of the production of commodified femininity as well as the place of its consumption.

Situated ideologically as separate from the productive sphere, domestic
consumption of feminine objects—poetry and poetesses, for example—is,
Maude's experience at Mrs. Strawdy's implies, a form of productive consumption not the least disinterested and, in fact, indistinguishable from more
public forms of capitalist production. A sphere so thoroughly implicated in
the collapse between public and private can lay no claims, as Rossetti's
ironized narrative makes clear, to moral superiority or cultural autonomy, just
as Rowton's sanctification of the female soul cannot sustain its difference from
other forms of sexual traffic.

DYING TO SURVIVE

Throughout the story, both Maude and her poetic gifts are constantly subject
to the desires of others, frustrating her own longing for literary distinction
and figuring Rossetti's concern (as an aspiring author herself, it must be
remembered, during the writing of *Maude*) with the costs of going public.
However, Maude's self-fashioning as a poetess, her ambitious and renunciatory
disposition, do eventually lead to her most transgressive act: not only a
disavowal of the sacrament of communion but a confession of that denial on
Christmas Eve. As Agnes's "almost indignant" and discouraged response to
Maude's irreverence makes clear (pp. 52–54), from within a religious context
the poetess acquires the shock value which a society, all too familiar with
poetesses, denies her. From this point forward, the story operates on the
principle that if a conventional poetess can alienate religious orthodoxy, then
perhaps religious discourse can estrange the category of the poetess from its
secular confines.

In part 3, Maude puts together her own collection of poems as the series
"Three Nuns," and like the other collections we have considered, hers too is
a revisionist project. Composed as an epithalamium for her cousin Mary's
wedding, "Three Nuns" is more than a little incongruous, perhaps even
"arch," given the occasion. But the poems are less about brides and nuns than
they are about poetesses.[42] Rossetti emphasizes this point in echoes of Elizabeth Barrett Browning that reverberate throughout the poem, from the opening words, "Shadow, shadow on the wall," to the footnoted line "Sweetest

song was ever heard," which draws attention explicitly to the refrain in Barrett Browning's "Catarina to Camoens," "Sweetest eyes were ever seen" (*Maude*, p. 62). With this substitution of a "song" that is "heard" for "eyes" that are "seen," Rossetti intensifies Barrett Browning's structures of visibility precisely by refusing to show them directly. In addition, by transforming the absent lover into a songbird, Rossetti stresses the connection between erotic desire and artistic ambition expressed in Barrett Browning's poem and expands that into a more generalized need for recognition in the world.[43] In so doing, she suggests that the source poem's interest in approval and appreciation, in fact in display, is not just Catarina's but Barrett Browning's as well.

With this Rossetti signals her awareness that the recuperated Catarina represents a vital instance of Barrett Browning's own interventions into the shape of the poetess. If Barrett Browning's dramatic monologue poses as a fictional translation from the sixteenth-century Portuguese,[44] it also dramatically revises Felicia Hemans's 1818 translation of Camoens's sonnets. Hemans devoted much of her career to sounding the voice of women, yet oddly left Catarina silent; Barrett Browning's dramatic monologue thus recovers a crucial record missing from the body of Hemans's own work, and especially her 1828 collection, *Records of Woman.* Although Barrett Browning confessed admiration and respect for Hemans's genius, piety, and high moral tone, she also thought her "a lady rather than a woman, & so, much rather than a poetess."[45] A "poetess in the true sense," she elaborates elsewhere, must possess the "gift" of the "the divineness of poetry" which raises both writer and art above "pride of sex and personal pride."[46] Galvanized by this prophetic potential in the poetess (as Hemans arguably was herself), Rossetti nevertheless appears to have thought Barrett Browning sadly deceived about the weight of circumstance—the gender hierarchy of "sex" and the commodity status of "personality"—that bears upon the Victorian woman author's "gift." This insight may have motivated Rossetti's rigorously literal-minded imitation of Barrett Browning's historiographic strategy. For Rossetti translates Barrett Browning into a role she herself had reserved for Hemans, that of mediator and link to an earlier forgotten female voice.

Just as the first nun hopes her words will make the songbird sing her into memory and just as Catarina hopes her monologue will make Camoens envision her into eternity, Rossetti hopes her translation will make Barrett Browning inspire her into rhapsody with a more originary poetess, *the* poetess Sappho. The first nun's desire for a forgetfulness that might allow her to dream herself "once more a child" (*Maude,* p. 62) recalls Rossetti's "What

Sappho would have said had her leap cured instead of killing her," written two years previously in 1848, and thereby boldly suggests the secondariness of Barrett Browning's Catarina. In that poem, Sappho too is sick at heart, wandering aimlessly through an ethereal pastoral world until she finally cloisters herself in a "narrow bed" beneath a canopy of "thick fragrant leaves" behind curtains a "spider weaves."[47] Initially this poem concluded with Sappho easing into death, but Rossetti eventually added ten more lines, which convert the pagan poetess into a Christian discourse so that she can "go forth and bear [her] pain" (60). Her translation of Sappho through Barrett Browning, in contrast, can, as the final line of the first nun's song indicates, "never be" (*Maude,* p. 63); the first nun "can never be" pure memory; Catarina "can never be" anything more than what she is, Barrett Browning's "unseen" (and dying to be seen) creation.

Rossetti returns to "Catarina to Camoens" all the more vividly in the second nun's poem (actually written first) by way of intensifying the discordant notes that make up the earlier heroine's ambivalence. In other words, this time Rossetti shows all that which Barrett Browning herself refuses to manifest directly. The second nun transforms Catarina's dejection over separation into actual rejection and slides her act of blessing ever closer to a curse. What begins as a dialogue with the self—"I loved him, yes, where was the sin?" and "I prayed for him; was my sin prayer?"—heightens and overflows into threatening tones of vengeance: "I prayed not we may meet again: / I would not let our names ascend, / No, not to Heaven, in the same breath; / Nor will I join the two in death" (*Maude,* p. 64). Because her lover "never bought" her love in the first place, and was therefore never actually a lover at all, the second nun is, moreover, a deeply ironic Catarina, deprived of looking forward to future betrayals or of imagining anything beyond her own earthbound grave. Through this process of ironic inversion, Rossetti recalls Catarina's enormous ambition for "saintly" self-enshrinement: "with saintly / Watch unfaintly / Out of heaven shall o'er you lean / 'Sweetest eyes were ever seen.'"[48] In so doing, Rossetti suggests once again that Catarina's self-sanctification in the hereafter may reflect her author's desire for canonization in the here and now.

However, Rossetti's main concern is less with the scope of Barrett Browning's ambition than with the aesthetic composition of the poetess, a composition which she decomposes under the test of ascetic rigor. The first two poems in "Three Nuns" appear to conclude that, in spite of Barrett Browning's own aims, her representation of the poetess cannot endure. Like

Catarina, both nuns have their minds elsewhere than on religion, but, unlike the Sapphic speaker of "She sat and sang alway," they have nothing in excess of the material structures that produce them. Whereas the convent is for the first two nuns only a metaphor of entrapment, for the third it is definitive. For her, in addition, the cloister is a marginal place for an exclusive poetry in a minor language that vibrates intensely and "flutters, flutters evermore." This third nun's deeply painful consciousness of earthly imprisonment enables an equally vital awareness that her heart is "freeborn" and her soul "a hidden fount" (*Maude,* p. 65). Frustrated desire not only ensures but is a necessary precondition for the "upward moan" that makes up the poetry of the nun's voice, "striving to force its way" toward the guiding celestial "Voice" and the "courts of Heaven" where "my crown" awaits (pp. 66-67). The crowning glory of poetry thus seems unattainable on earth.

Unlike Barrett Browning, however, Rossetti does not write of achieved transcendence, but rather of "hope deferred." The "divineness of poetry" becomes manifest then in the struggle itself for the sacred. Unable to deny entirely those competing voices ringing out the names of "daughter, sister, wife," unable not to see the very rose and sun "I will not look upon," the third nun, reformulated as ascetic poetess, prays in "desperate strife" under the conflicted burden of the call divine (*Maude,* p. 67). Rather than take up a position of opposition, transcendence, or escape, this redeemed poetess composes herself out of the language of the barrier and distills the barrier of language within her own "cruel breast," thereby reconstituting herself out of bounds—sexually, artistically, spiritually, and even commercially—precisely through an erotically charged bondage. With this discourse of cloistered autonomy, Rossetti identifies the revelational, if not revolutionary, conditions of language which make possible the divine sanction of creativity that appears in one of Maude's final poems, "Symbols," a sanction powerfully reinforced by the implied threat of apocalyptic retribution: "And what if God, / Who waiteth for thy fruits in vain, / Should also take the rod?—" (pp. 70-71). Professing her poetry to be for God's eyes only, this poetess takes up her profession not primarily as an economic contract, a personal career, or a national project, but as a vow, a belief, and a sacred calling. The latter authorizes the former, of course, since self-abnegation compels public self-display. But by facilitating visibility in this particular way, the category of the poetess, as the nun's "desperate strife" suggests, offers the woman writer a vivid language through which to express a cultural crisis in vision as well as visuality.

Despite acquiring a Christological significance when she receives a wound to her side in the traffic accident, and a Sapphic resonance when she leaves her poetic fragments behind for Agnes to collect, the fictional author of "Three Nuns," Maude, must die. Rossetti's refusal to deny the worldly constraints upon the poetess while at the same time sanctifying her ambition is precisely what permits the category to survive into literary and spiritual afterlife as both discourse of poetic abandon and gift of renewal. Consequently, Maude's death remains a chastening form of narrative violence, the act of a "cruel breast," directed as much against the reader and the Victorian values that necessitate her story as against the heroine herself.

It is also, however, a vengeance played out with useless pleasure, for Rossetti, unlike Carlyle, never conflated work with poetry, and, unlike Barrett Browning, never confused poetry with work. In fact, it is quite possible that Rossetti thought poetry should *not* "work." Poetry should, rather, purify, not through the domestic affections Hemans represents, not through the romanticized "religion of love" Landon espouses, and not through the conjugal love Barrett Browning chooses, but through the single woman's singular love of the divine. The ascetic renunciation Rossetti's representation of love entails makes possible highly ritualized sacrifices of the productive (and materialistic) value that remains as constitutive of the category of the poetess as of the institution of art itself. By isolating and intensifying the gender politics at work in classifications of the woman writer, Rossetti thus pressures the poetess into disturbing and unsettling the effects of the Victorian heterosexual imperative, thereby releasing a critically aggressive eroticized autonomy only partially recuperable to cultural norms. In *Maude,* therefore, we foresee, on the one hand, a first glimpse of the rough playfulness of *Goblin Market* and, on the other, a prophecy of the "unhappy" poetess in *"Monna Innominata."*

From her earliest writing, then, Rossetti, who published in various annuals, anthologies, and giftbooks throughout her life, develops an anticommodity aesthetic through which to exploit Victorian capitalism's interest in art. In so (re)commodifying the anticommodity, Rossetti guarantees the survival of the category of the poetess well beyond its first commercial exhaustion at midcentury, making it possible for William Michael to claim that his sister thought herself "truly a poetess," and "a good one" at that.[49] Although brother and sister would likely have understood this assertion differently, there can be no doubt that Rossetti's reconstitutions of the category helped inspire the appetite for the ideal poetess toward the end of the century at precisely the moment when critics were virtually unanimous in declaring that poetesses were producing too much material, "hurrying away into oblivion" their best style in a "commercial fervour."[50] In a lifelong process of recollecting, reconverting, and reviving the always dying poetess, Rossetti suggests an ascetic aesthetic for rereading the literary history of the poetess, one which holds out continuing faith in art's critical power of social redemption and which hopes, moreover, that a very different future may materialize in recuperations of our abandoned past.[51]

NOTES

1. See, for example, Angela Leighton's *Victorian Women Poets: Writing Against the Heart* and *Victorian Women Poets: A Critical Reader* (London: Blackwell, 1996); Jennifer Breen's *Victorian Women Poets 1830–1900: An Anthology* (London: Everyman, 1994); Angela Leighton and Margaret Reynolds's *Victorian Women Poets: An Anthology* (London: Blackwell, 1995); and Linda K. Hughes's special issue *Woman Poets: 1830–1894, VP* 33 (1995).

2. The idea that the poetess is imposed by a male-dominated culture is espoused, for instance, by Stuart Curran, who regards it as "a trap enforced by masculine disdain" ("Women Readers, Women Writers," ed. Stuart Curran, *The Cambridge Companion to British Romanticism* [Cambridge: Cambridge University Press, 1993], p. 193), and by Glennis Stephenson, who argues that the poetess was a "marginalized and strictly defined role" ("Letitia Landon and The Victorian Improvisatrice: The Construction of L.E.L.," *VP* 30 [1992]: 1–2). However, Stephenson agrees with Marlon Ross (*The Contours of Masculine Desire* [New York: Oxford University Press, 1989]) and Leighton that the discourse of femininity can be exploited for strategic purposes and that the rigid conventions of the poetess offer possibilities for veiled confrontation, disruption, and subversion. In addition, while critics acknowledge the widespread use of the term in the Victorian period, they limit their own use of it to "a particular type of woman poet" (Stephenson, *Letitia Landon: The Woman Behind L.E.L.* [Manchester: Manchester University Press, 1995], p. 3). Virginia Blain slightly widens the category to include a double-sided tradition: the revered prophetess and the ambivalently regarded improviser ("Letitia Elizabeth Landon, Eliza Mary Hamilton, and the Geneaology of the Victorian Poetess," *VP* 33 [1995]: 415–34). Beyond this tradition, she detects a third strain of self-designated poetesses who do not construct themselves within the popular sense of the term and therefore must be recognized as women poets. Blain's anxiety over the aesthetic value of the poetess (especially the improviser) exemplifies the extent to which the poetess constitutes a battleground for the conflict between popular and high art.

3. As Laurie Langbauer argues, the very process of definition "undoes itself, the articulation of rules calls [those rules] into question." An alternative approach might

highlight, she suggests, "the assumptions that press us into certain definitions and the systems generating those assumptions" (*Women and Romance: The Consolations of Gender in the English Novel* [Ithaca and London: Cornell University Press, 1990], p. 16).

4. Although the existence of the poetess is widely acknowledged in Rossetti criticism, Susan Conley, "'Poet's Right': Christina Rossetti as Anti-Muse and the Legacy of the 'Poetess,'" (*VP* 32 [1994]: 365-86), is the one critic to date who analyzes the category itself. Her argument that Rossetti "most certainly" avoided being seen as a poetess appears to be based on the assumption that the poetess is "marked by various forms of exaggeration and excess" (p. 378). Yet she does acknowledge that Rossetti's characteristic restraint allowed critics to assimilate her within the category. However, restraint and excess are mutually constitutive and, as I will show later in this paper, it is Rossetti's own excessive restraint that defines her relationship to the poetess.

5. Paula McDowell, "Consuming Women: The Life of the 'Literary Lady' as Popular Culture in Eighteenth-Century England," *Genre* 26 (1993): 221. For the view that sexual bifurcation of a nascent "national literary canon encompassing both genders" was a specifically Romantic development, see Greg Kucich, "Gendering the Canons of Romanticism: Past and Present," *The Wordsworth Circle* 27 (1996): 95-102.

6. Tricia Lootens, *Lost Saints: Silence, Gender, and Victorian Literary Canonization* (Charlottesville: University Press of Virginia, 1996), p. 74.

7. Armstrong, p. 321.

8. Alexander Dyce, *Specimens of British Poetesses* (London: T. Rodd, 1825), pp. iii–iv.

9. According to Naomi Schor, "collecting, rather more than *flanerie,* is the activity that most closely approximates that of the author" ("Collecting Paris," in *The Cultures of Collection,* ed. John Elsner and Roger Cardinal [Cambridge, Mass.: Harvard University Press, 1994], p. 253). This is extremely suggestive for an analysis of women consumers and writers, since anyone can be a collector (contrary to Jean Baudrillard's assumptions), whereas the cosmopolitan *flaneur,* usually taken to be the prototype of the modern consumer, requires more freedom of mobility than women usually had in the nineteenth century; see also Baudrillard's "The System of Collecting," in *The Cultures of Collection,* pp. 7-24. On the *flaneur* as the model for the English consumer, see Thomas Richards, *The Commodity Culture of Victorian England: Advertising and Spectacle, 1851-1914* (Stanford: Stanford University Press, 1990). On "eighteenth-century literary history as a mode of collecting," see McDowell, p. 227.

10. Thorstein Veblen, of course, coined the phrases "conspicuous leisure" and "conspicuous consumption" in *The Theory of the Leisure Class: An Economic Study of Institutions* (New York: Random House, [1899] 1931).

11. Frederick Rowton, *The Female Poets of Great Britain, Chronologically Arranged with Copious Selections and Critical Remarks. A Facsimile of the 1853 Edition,* ed. Marilyn L. Williamson (Detroit: Wayne State University Press, 1981), p. xxvii). Hereafter cited parenthetically in the text by page number.

12. For a different interpretation of Rowton's point, see Leighton and Reynolds, *Victorian Women Poets,* p. xxvii. For a contrasting view to Rowton's see Richard Le Gallienne: "To say that Miss Rossetti is the greatest English poet among women is to pay regard to a distinction which, in questions of art, is purely arbitrary—a distinction which has given us the foolish word 'poetess,' a standing witness in our language to the national obtuseness" (*"Poems.* By Christina Rossetti," *The Academy* 979 [February 7, 1891]: 130). While Le Gallienne differs from Rowton in his unequivocal rejection of the term poetess, they both share a conviction that the poetess is linked to national awareness: Rossetti is an "English poet" first; her placement "among women" is an arbitrary distinction, irrelevant to literary merit. Although representations of gender could no longer perform the stabilizing function at the end of the century that they did earlier for Rowton, the artist's, and therefore Rossetti's, sexuality is clearly not irrelevant to Le Gallienne. In his view, the artist is gifted with a pre-gendered "child's imagination," yet gender, despite Le Gallienne's disavowal of the word poetess, perpetually seeps back into his definition of the artist as he describes Rossetti's poetry in such stock feminine terms as "spontaneous," "artless," and "instinctive." Sexuality and national literature thus continue to be expressed in terms of gender.

13. Rowton's motive is ultimately political, of course. His argument is not only directed to an audience of "wise" men, but to middle-class women as well, who were, in 1848, increasingly demanding political, legal, economic, and educational equality. If women keep to their place in the "family of man" as "partners, not rivals" (p. xl), gender, Rowton implies, will do its social work on the national front and bind multiple differences around the single hierarchical difference that makes a man not a woman and vice versa. In marrying a literature of the affections, epitomized by Felicia Hemans, to the Victorian ideal of progress, Rowton thus locates himself in a liberal tradition that promotes the civilizing propensity of the ennobling aesthetics of beauty, and in so doing, anticipates struggles over the politics of representation that would dominate the latter half of the century. Rowton's faith in the female soul is not, finally, so much about saving the poetess as it is about saving the nation from itself.

14. Lootens, p. 182. For an incisive reading of the way in which the idea of the soul and its gender saturated Romantic cultural discourse, and Hemans's writing in particular, see Susan Wolfson, "Gendering the Soul," in *Romantic Women Writers: Voices and Countervoices,* ed. Paula K. Feldman and Theresa M. Kelley (Hanover and London: University Press of New England, 1995), pp. 33–68.

15. Antony H. Harrison argues that Rossetti's secular and religious impulses "enable her to convey ideals and describe idealities that implicitly or explicitly repudiate the *value* (as well as the material and erotic *values*) of the world in which they are initially set" and are "therefore powerfully ideological" (Harrison, *CR,* p. 89). I would add that she not only reacts to the world through an aesthetics of withdrawal and repudiation, but also that this same negativity enables her to share

in Ruskin's, Morris's, and even Pater's faith in art's power of social redemption and linguistic reformation; for a reconsideration of the social impulse in late-Victorian Aestheticism, see Linda Dowling, *The Vulgarization of Art: The Victorians and Aesthetic Democracy* (Charlottesville and London: University Press of Virginia, 1996).

16. Christina Rossetti, *Maude: Prose and Verse*, 1897, ed. R. W. Crump (Hamden, Conn.: Archon Books, 1976), p. 71. Subsequent references to this edition will be noted parenthetically by page number.

17. "Notice of *Maude: Prose and Verse*," *Bookman* 11 (December 1896): 57.

18. *PW*, p. lxiii.

19. The final sentence of the "Prefatory Note" further defines the kind of reader William Michael Rossetti anticipates for *Maude*: "For its prose the 'indulgent reader' (as our great-grandfathers used to phrase it) may be in requisition; for its verse the 'discreet' reader will suffice" (*Maude*, p. 80).

20. Bell, p. 279.

21. *PW*, p. lxiii.

22. With the exception of her first publication, the privately printed *Verses* (1847), Rossetti refrained from showing her face in her books. However, soon after her death in 1894, William Michael and others began to publish portraits of her, especially those by Dante Gabriel, at a rather prodigious rate. In the years following Rossetti's death, reproductions of oil paintings, sketches, and drawings in pencil and chalk appeared in *Dante Gabriel: His Family Letters* (1895), *New Poems* (1896), *Maude* (1897), Bell, *PW*, and *FL*.

23. From Maude's sonnet, "Some ladies dress in muslin full and white" (*Maude*, p. 37), composed during the poetry contest at her cousin's birthday party. While this poem appears to be a critique of people of fashion, it also seems to refer to literary fashion, as indicated in the next two lines: "If all the world were water fit to drown / There are some whom you would not teach to swim" (p. 37). Rossetti may have been thinking of the fashionable Sapphos who filled the pages of the annuals; indeed, she may also have had older women aristocrats in mind, such as Countess Blessington, editor of *Heath's Book of Beauty* for years.

24. *Letters of Dante Gabriel Rossetti*, ed. Oswald Doughty and John Robert Wahl (Oxford: Clarendon, 1967), 1:41. The *Violet* refers to Letitia Elizabeth Landon's *The Golden Violet, with Its Tales of Romance and Chivalry, and Other Poems*, 1827, and the *Bracelet* is short for *The Venetian Bracelet, The Lost Pleiad, A History of the Lyre, and Other Poems*, 1829. See *The Poetical Works of L. E. Landon* (Boston: Phillips, Sampson, 1856).

25. [William Henry Smith and D.M. Moir], "Mrs. Hemans," *Blackwood's Edinburgh Magazine* 64 (Dec. 1848): 658.

26. Dante Gabriel Rossetti told his sister that "The Lowest Room" was derivative of Barrett Browning's "modern vicious style . . . what might be called a falsetto muscularity." *Letters of Dante Gabriel Rossetti*, 2:232.

27. The phrase is Romney Leigh's in Elizabeth Barrett Browning's *Aurora Leigh*

in *The Complete Works of Elizabeth Barrett Browning,* ed. Charlotte Porter and Helen A. Clarke (New York: AMS Press, 1973), 4:45; he invokes it while trying to explain to Aurora why "we shall not get a poet" from women.

28. Jan Marsh argues that, although Maude wins the sonnet contest, "Sister Magdalen's poem is clearly the best" (*Poems and Prose of Christina Rossetti,* p. 251). Rossetti, though, demonstrates in this scene that the rules of the poetry contest (and perhaps, by extension, literary institutions) are not based purely on literary merit. Maude wins not because of her poem only but because she is best able to stage herself as art.

29. Rosenblum, p. 170.

30. For an analysis of the cyclical structure of mass culture, which "speaks to all in order to better return each one to his [*sic*] place," see Jean Baudrillard, *For a Critique of the Political Economy of the Sign,* trans. Charles Levin (St. Louis, Mo.: Telos, 1981), p. 51. In addition, Baudrillard analyzes consumption as a form of production, and shows that the general structure of productivity abstracts desire, in much the same way as it alienates labor, and reduces that desire to the utilitarian function of need (pp. 29-62, 82 ff.). Rossetti not only mystifies the commodity through the logic of secrecy (thereby emphasizing the barrier to revelation), but also attempts to purify desire itself by distinguishing it from the utilitarian logic of political economy. For another discussion of Rossetti's work in relation to commodity culture and political economy, see Richard Menke's "The Political Economy of Fruit: *Goblin Market,*" chapter 5 in this collection.

31. Both Leighton and Armstrong consider "Winter: My Secret" to be paradigmatic of Rossetti's style. Linda M. Shires decisively links the motif of secrecy in this poem with the contradictory structure of commodities: "the *speaker* is erotically stimulated by shutting out her listeners from a putative secret, the *author* upholds the decorum of privacy, and the *poem* ironically deploys the act of withholding, as it demonstrates that withholding contributes to the mystification of commodities" ("The Author as Spectacle and Commodity," in *Victorian Literature and the Victorian Visual Imagination,* ed. Carol T. Christ and John O. Jordan [Berkeley and Los Angeles: University of California Press, 1995], p. 201).

32. Preface to *The Venetian Bracelet,* in Landon, p. 102.

33. The phrase "the daughters of England" alludes to an 1842 domestic conduct manual by Sarah Stickney Ellis in which she effuses over the "poetical associations" of woman (*The Daughters of England, Their Position in Society, Character and Responsibilities* [New York: D. Appleton, 1842], p. 94). Hemans is the most representative of the link between the poetess, domestic feminity, and imperial identity; see especially Lootens, pp. 238-53.

34. Jan Marsh's research indicates that early in 1859 Rossetti "became a voluntary worker at the St. Mary Magdalene Penitentiary in Highgate, supervising young prostitutes" (Marsh, *CR,* pp. 218-19).

35. *Commonplace Book of Frances Rossetti* (University of British Columbia Angeli-Dennis Collection, Box 12, Folder 18, 1816), pp. 30-31 and 35-37. Both poems are briefly alluded to by Diane D'Amico, "'Equal before God': Christina Rossetti and the Fallen Women of Highgate Penitentiary," *Gender and Discourse in Victorian Art and Literature,* ed. Antony H. Harrison and Beverly Taylor (DeKalb: Northern Illinois University Press, 1992), p. 82, n. 28.

36. There are significant differences between Greg's version and that of Frances Rossetti. His changes appear motivated by a desire to neutralize the negative conno- tations of the prostitute and thereby play more forcefully upon the sympathies of the reader. Most importantly, he omits the final twenty lines of the poem in which the speaker emphasizes her experience as a terrible warning for readers. See [W. R. Greg], "Prostitution," *Westminster Review* 52, nos. 1-2 (1850): 448-506.

37. [William Thackeray], "A Word on the Annuals," *Fraser's Magazine* 16 (De- cember 1837): 758 and 763.

38. [H. N. Coleridge], "Modern English Poetesses," *Quarterly Review* 60 (Septem- ber 1840): 375.

39. George Gilfillan, "Female Authors, No. 1—Mrs. Hemans," *Tait's Edinburgh Magazine,* n.s. 14 (1847): 359-63. Reprinted from *The Dublin University Magazine* 56 (Aug. 1837): 127-41.

40. *PW,* p. lx.

41. *PW,* pp. lxv-lxvi and lix-lx.

42. This is not to say that brides and nuns are not important, since Rossetti's engagement to James Collinson ended around this time.

43. As Marjorie Stone has suggested in "Sisters in Art: Christina Rossetti and Elizabeth Barrett Browning," *VP* 32 (1994), Rossetti's echoes of and revisions to this earlier poem extend well beyond the footnoted line (pp. 345 ff.).

44. Barrett Browning's subtitle for "Catarina to Camoens" is "(Dying in his absence abroad, and referring to the poem in which he recorded the sweetness of her eyes)." Camoens, a sixteenth-century Portuguese poet, was exiled from court on account of his love for Catarina de Atalyde, who, being one of the queen's maids of honor, was above his rank; see *Maude,* pp. 92-93 and *The Complete Works of Elizabeth Barrett Browning,* 3:124-29, 374.

45. *The Letters of Elizabeth Barrett Browning to Mary Russell Mitford 1836-1854,* ed. Meredith B. Raymond and Mary Rose Sullivan, 3 vols. (Winfield Kans.: Wedgestone Press, 1983), 2:88. For Felicia Hemans's translation of Camoens's sonnets and her *Records of Woman,* see *The Works of Mrs. Hemans, with a Memoir by her Sister, and an Essay on her Genius,* by Mrs. Sigourney, 7 vols. (Philadelphia: Lea and Blanchard, 1842).

46. *The Letters of Elizabeth Barrett Browning,* ed. Frederic G. Kenyon, 2 vols. (London: Macmillan, 1897) 1:229-33.

47. *CP,* 3:167, 49-52; subsequent references will be noted in the text by line

number. Interestingly, Rossetti published neither "Three Nuns" nor the two Sappho poems (the one mentioned here and "Sappho") during her lifetime. For a reading of this poem in relation to the Sappho poems of Felicia Hemans and Letitia Landon, see my "Sappho's Conversions in Felicia Hemans, Letitia Landon, and Christina Rossetti," *Prism(s): Essays in Romanticism* 4 (1996): 1–35.

48. Barrett Browning, "Catarina to Camoens," in *Complete Works,* p. 125.

49. *PW,* p. lxix.

50. Edmund Gosse, "Christina Rossetti," *The Century Magazine* 46 (June 1893): 211.

51. Research for this paper was supported by the Social Sciences and Humanities Research Council of Canada and by a Simon Fraser University President's Research Grant. I would like to thank the editors of this collection, as well as Miguel Mota, for their careful reading and helpful suggestions.

BIBLIOGRAPHY

Agajanian, Shaakeh. *"Sonnets from the Portuguese" and the Love Sonnet Tradition.* New York: Philosophical Library, 1985.

Alighieri, Dante. *The Divine Comedy.* Trans. Laurence Binyon. In *The Portable Dante,* ed. Paolo Milano. New York: Viking, 1975.

———. *The Divine Comedy of Dante Alighieri with Translation and Comment by John D. Sinclair.* 3 vols. New York: Oxford University Press, 1939.

Andersen, Hans Christian. "The Little Match Girl." In *Fairy Tales and Legends.* Illustrated by Rex Whistler. London: Bodley Head, 1935.

Armstrong, Isobel. "Christina Rossetti: Diary of a Feminist Reading." In *Women Reading Women's Writing,* ed. Sue Roe, pp. 117-37. Brighton: Harvester, 1987.

———. *Victorian Poetry: Poetry, Poetics, and Politics.* London and New York: Routledge, 1993.

Armstrong, Isobel, and Joseph Bristow with Cath Sharrock, eds. *Nineteenth-Century Women Poets.* Oxford: Oxford University Press, 1996.

Arnold, Matthew. "Civilisation in the United States" (1888). *The Last Word.* In *The Complete Prose Works of Matthew Arnold,* ed. R. H. Super, 2:350-69. 11 vols. Ann Arbor: University of Michigan Press, 1960-77.

———. *Poetry and Prose.* Ed. John Bryson. London: Rupert Hart-Davis, 1954.

Arseneau, Mary. "Incarnation and Interpretation: Christina Rossetti, the Oxford Movement, and *Goblin Market.*" *VP* 31 (1993): 79-93.

———. "Pilgrimage and Postponement: Christina Rossetti's *The Prince's Progress.*" *VP* 32 (1994): 279-98.

Auerbach, Nina. *Private Theatricals: The Lives of the Victorians.* Cambridge, Mass.: Harvard University Press, 1990.

———. *Woman and the Demon: The Life of a Victorian Myth.* Cambridge, Mass.: Harvard University Press, 1982.

Auerbach, Nina, and U. C. Knoepflmacher, eds. *Forbidden Journeys: Fairy Tales and Fantasies by Victorian Women.* Chicago and London: University of Chicago Press, 1992.

Austen-Leigh, J. E. "A Memoir of Jane Austen." In *Persuasion,* ed. D. W. Harding. Harmondsworth: Penguin, 1965.

B. J. "Fruit Prospects." *Gardeners' Chronicle and Agricultural Gazette* (28 May 1859): 466.

Bakhtin, M. M. *The Dialogic Imagination: Four Essays by M. M. Bakhtin.* Ed. Michael Holquist. Trans. Caryl Emerson and Michael Holquist. Austin: University of Texas Press, 1981.

Bald, Marjory A. *Women-Writers of the Nineteenth Century.* New York: Russell and Russell, 1923.

Ball, Robert S. "The Boundaries of Astronomy." *Contemporary Review* 41 (1882): 923-41.

Barber, Richard, and Juliet Barker. *Tournaments.* Woodbridge: Boydell, 1989.

Barnes, Warner. *A Bibliography of Elizabeth Barrett Browning.* Austin: University of Texas Press and the Armstrong Browning Library, Baylor University, 1967.

Battiscombe, Georgina. *Christina Rossetti: A Divided Life.* London: Constable; New York: Holt, 1981.

Baudrillard, Jean. *For a Critique of the Political Economy of the Sign.* Trans. Charles Levin. St. Louis, Mo.: Telos, 1981.

Baum, Paull F. "The Bancroft Manuscripts of Dante Gabriel Rossetti." *Modern Philology* 39 (1941): 47-68.

de Beauvoir, Simone. Introduction to *The Second Sex.* Trans. H. M. Parshley. In *New French Feminisms,* ed. Elaine Marks and Isabelle de Courtivron. Brighton: Harvester, 1981.

———. *The Second Sex.* Trans. H. M. Parshley. 1952. Reprint, New York: Vintage Books, 1989.

Beer, Gillian. *Darwin's Plots.* London: Routledge and Kegan Paul, 1983.

Bell, Mackenzie. *Christina Rossetti: A Biographical and Critical Study.* London: Hurst and Blackett; Boston: Roberts Brothers, 1898.

Bentley, D. M. R. "From Allegory to Indeterminacy: Dante Gabriel Rossetti's Positive Agnosticism." *Dalhousie Review* 70 (1990): 70-106; 146-68.

———. "The Meretricious and the Meritorious in *Goblin Market:* A Conjecture and an Analysis." In *The Achievement of Christina Rossetti,* ed. David A. Kent, pp. 57-81. Ithaca and London: Cornell University Press, 1987.

Berendzen, Richard, Richard Hart, and Daniel Seeley. *Man Discovers the Galaxies.* New York: Science History Publications, 1976.

Berger, John. *Ways of Seeing.* London: Penguin, 1988.

Betterton, Rosemary, ed. *Looking On: Images of Femininity in the Visual Arts and Media.* London and New York: Pandora, 1987.

Birke, Lynda. *Women, Feminism, and Biology.* Brighton: Harvester, 1986.

Birkhead, Edith. *Christina Rossetti and her Poetry.* London: Harrap, 1930.

Bishop, George. *Astronomical Observations Taken at the Observatory, South Villa, Inner Circle, Regent's Park, London, during the Years 1839-1851.* London: Taylor, Walton, Maberly, 1852.

Blain, Virginia. "Letitia Elizabeth Landon, Eliza Mary Hamilton, and the Genealogy of the Victorian Poetess." *VP* 33 (1995): 31–52.

Blake, Kathleen. *Love and the Woman Question in Victorian Literature.* Brighton: Harvester, 1983.

Blake, William. *The Poems of William Blake.* Ed. W. H. Stevenson and David V. Erdman. London: Longman, 1971.

Bloom, Harold. *The Anxiety of Influence: A Theory of Poetry.* London, Oxford, and New York: Oxford University Press, 1973.

Bowra, Maurice. *The Romantic Imagination.* Cambridge, Mass.: Harvard University Press, 1949.

Bray, Anna Eliza. *A Peep at the Pixies, or, Legends of the West.* With Illustrations by H. K. Browne. London, 1854.

———. *Traditions, Legends, Superstitions, and Sketches of Devonshire on the Borders of the Tamar and the Tavy.* London: John Murray, 1838.

Breen, Jennifer, ed. *Victorian Women Poets, 1830–1900: An Anthology.* Everyman's Library. London: J. M. Dent, 1994.

"Brenda" [Mrs. G. Castle Smith]. *Froggy's Little Brother.* London: John F. Shaw, 1875.

Briggs, Julia. "Women Writers and Writing for Children: From Sarah Fielding to E. Nesbit." In *Children and Their Books,* ed. Gillian Avery and Julia Briggs. Oxford: Clarendon, 1989.

Bristow, Joseph, ed. *Victorian Women Poets: Emily Brontë, Elizabeth Barrett Browning, Christina Rossetti.* London: Macmillan; New York: St. Martin's, 1995.

Bronfen, Elisabeth. *Over Her Dead Body: Death, Femininity, and the Aesthetic.* Manchester: Manchester University Press; New York: Routledge, 1992.

Browning, Elizabeth Barrett. *Aurora Leigh.* Ed. Margaret Reynolds. Athens, Ohio: Ohio University Press, 1992; New York: Norton, 1996.

———. *The Complete Works of Elizabeth Barrett Browning.* Ed. Charlotte Porter and Helen A. Clarke. 6 vols. 1900. New York: AMS Press, 1973.

———. *Letters of Elizabeth Barrett Browning.* Ed. Frederic G. Kenyon. 2 vols. London: Macmillan, 1897.

———. *The Letters of Elizabeth Barrett Browning to Mary Russell Mitford, 1836–1854.* Ed. Meredith B. Raymond and Mary Rose Sullivan. 3 vols. Winfield, Kansas: Wedgestone, 1983.

———. *The Poetical Works of Elizabeth Barrett Browning.* Ed. Frederick G. Kenyon. London: Smith, Elder, 1897.

Browning, Robert. *Robert Browning: The Poems.* Ed. John Pettigrew and Thomas J. Collins. 2 vols. New Haven: Yale University Press; Harmondsworth: Penguin, 1981.

Bump, Jerome. "Christina Rossetti and the Pre-Raphaelite Brotherhood." In *The Achievement of Christina Rossetti,* ed. David A. Kent, pp. 322–45. Ithaca and London: Cornell University Press, 1987.

———. "Hopkins, Christina Rossetti, and Pre-Raphaelitism." *VN* 57 (1980): 1–6.

Burne-Jones, Georgiana. *Memorials of Edward Burne-Jones.* 2 vols. London: Macmillan, 1904.

Butler, Judith. *Gender Trouble: Feminism and the Subversion of Identity.* New York and London: Routledge, 1990.

Byron, George Gordon, Lord. *The Works of Lord Byron.* Ware: Wordsworth Editions, 1994.

Caesar, Michael, ed. *Dante, The Critical Heritage 1314(?)-1870.* London: Routledge, 1989.

"Calendar of Operations: Forcing Department." *Gardeners' Chronicle and Agricultural Gazette* (1 January 1859): 8.

Calthrop, Dion Clayton. *My Own Trumpet: Being the Story of My Life.* London: Hutchinson, 1935.

Campbell, Elizabeth. "Of Mothers and Merchants: Female Economics in Christina Rossetti's 'Goblin Market.'" *VS* 33 (1990): 393-410.

Carpenter, Mary Wilson. "'Eat Me, Drink Me, Love Me': The Consumable Female Body in Christina Rossetti's *Goblin Market.*" *VP* 29 (1991): 415-34.

Carroll, Lewis. *The Annotated Alice: Alice's Adventures in Wonderland and Through the Looking Glass.* Ed. Martin Gardner. Harmondsworth: Penguin, 1960, 1970.

Caughie, John, and Annette Kuhn, eds. *The Sexual Subject: A Screen Reader in Sexuality.* London and New York: Routledge, 1992.

Chambers, Robert. *Vestiges of the Natural History of Creation.* London, 1844.

Chapman, Alison. "History, Hysteria, Histrionics: The Biographical Representation of Christina Rossetti." *Victorian Literature and Culture* 24 (1996).

Charlesworth, Maria Louisa. *Ministering Children: A Tale Dedicated to Childhood.* London: Seeley, 1854, 1895.

Cherry, Deborah, and Griselda Pollock. "Woman as Sign in Pre-Raphaelite Literature: A Study of the Representation of Elizabeth Siddall." *Art History* 7 (1984): 206-27.

Cixous, Hélène. "The Laugh of the Medusa." Trans. Keith Cohen and Paula Cohen. In *New French Feminisms,* ed. Elaine Marks and Isabelle de Courtivron. Brighton: Harvester, 1981.

———. "Sorties." In *The Newly Born Woman,* trans. Ann Liddle. In *New French Feminisms,* ed. Elaine Marks and Isabelle de Courtivron. Brighton: Harvester, 1981.

Clerke, Agnes M. *Familiar Studies in Homer.* London: Longmans, Green, 1892.

———. *A Popular History of Astronomy during the Nineteenth Century.* 4th ed. London: Black, 1902.

———. *The System of the Stars.* 2d ed. London: Black, 1905.

Clerke, Ellen Mary. *Flowers of Fire: A Novel.* London: Hutchinson, 1902.

———. *The Flying Dutchman and Other Poems.* London: W. Satchell, 1881.

"Climate in Respect to Fruit Growing." *Turner and Spencer's Florist, Fruitist, and Garden Miscellany* May 1859. Reprinted in *Gardeners' Chronicle and Agricultural Gazette* (14 May 1859): 424.

Cobbe, Frances Power. "To Know, or Not to Know?" *Fraser's Magazine* 80 (1869): 776-87.

———. "The Rights of Man and the Claims of Brutes." *Fraser's Magazine* 68 (1863): 586-602.

Cohen, Paula Marantz. "Christina Rossetti's 'Goblin Market': A Paradigm for Nineteenth-Century Anorexia Nervosa." *University of Hartford Studies in Literature* 17, no. 1 (1985): 1-18.

Coleridge, Christabel. "The Poetry of Christina Rossetti." *Monthly Packet* 89 (1895): 276-82.

[Coleridge, H. N.] "Modern English Poetesses." *Quarterly Review* 60 (September 1840): 374-418.

Coleridge, Samuel Taylor. *The Oxford Authors: Samuel Taylor Coleridge.* Ed. H. J. Jackson. Oxford: Oxford University Press, 1985.

———. *Poems.* Ed. John Beer. Everyman's Library. London and Melbourne: J. M. Dent, 1974.

"Colonial and Foreign Produce Markets: Transactions of the Week." *Economist* (23 April 1859): 463-64; (30 April 1859): 491-92; (7 May 1859): 520-21.

Conley, Susan. "'Poet's Right': Christina Rossetti as Anti-Muse and the Legacy of the 'Poetess.'" *VP* 32 (1994): 365-86.

Connor, Steven. "'Speaking Likenesses': Language and Repetition in Christina Rossetti's *Goblin Market.*" *VP* 22 (1984): 439-48.

Cooper, Helen. *Elizabeth Barrett Browning: Woman and Artist.* Chapel Hill: University of North Carolina Press, 1988.

Curran, Stuart. "The Lyric Voice of Christina Rossetti." *VP* 9 (1971): 287-99.

Curran, Stuart. "Women Readers, Women Writers." In *The Cambridge Companion to British Romanticism,* ed. Stuart Curran, pp. 177-195. Cambridge: Cambridge University Press, 1993.

D'Amico, Diane. "Christina Rossetti's *Christian Year:* Comfort for 'the Weary Heart.'" *VN* 71-72 (1987): 36-42.

———. "'Equal before God': Christina Rossetti and the Fallen Women of Highgate Penitentiary." In *Gender and Discourse in Victorian Art and Literature,* ed. Antony H. Harrison and Beverly Taylor, pp. 67-83. DeKalb: Northern Illinois University Press, 1992.

Darwin, Charles. *The Origin of Species by Means of Natural Selection and The Descent of Man and Selection in Relation to Sex.* Chicago: University of Chicago Great Books of the Western World Series, 1990.

Degraaff, Robert M. *The Book of the Toad: A Natural and Magical History of Toad-Human Relations.* Cambridge: Lutterworth, 1991.

De Luca, V. A. *Thomas De Quincey: The Prose of Vision.* Toronto: University of Toronto Press, 1980.

Demers, Patricia, ed. *A Garland from the Golden Age: An Anthology of Children's Literature from 1850 to 1900.* Toronto: Oxford University Press, 1983.

Denman, Kamilla, and Sara Smith. "Christina Rossetti's Copy of C. B. Cayley's *Divine Comedy.*" *VP* 32 (1994): 315-37.

De Quincey, Thomas. *The Collected Writings of Thomas De Quincey.* Ed. David Masson. 14 vols. London: Black, 1890.

DeVane, William Clyde. *A Browning Handbook.* 2d ed. New York: Appleton-Century-Crofts, 1955.

Dickinson, Emily. *The Complete Poems of Emily Dickinson.* Ed. Thomas H. Johnson. London: Faber and Faber, 1987.

Dijkstra, Bram. *Idols of Perversity: Fantasies of Feminine Evil in Fin-de-Siècle Culture.* New York: Oxford University Press, 1988.

Dombrowski, Theo. "Dualism in the Poetry of Christina Rossetti." *VP* 14 (1976): 70-76.

Doody, Margaret Anne. "The Sensuous Eighteenth Century." Plenary Address. Rethinking Women's Poetry Conference. Birkbeck College, University of London, 20 July 1995.

Doughty, Oswald. *A Victorian Romantic: Dante Gabriel Rossetti.* London: Frederick Muller, 1949.

Dowling, Linda. *The Vulgarization of Art: The Victorians and Aesthetic Democracy.* Charlottesville and London: University Press of Virginia, 1996.

Duffy, Maureen. *The Erotic World of Faery.* London: Hodder and Stoughton, 1972.

Dyce, Alexander. *Specimens of British Poetesses.* London: T. Rodd, 1825.

Dyder, Richard. *Victims of Science.* London: National Anti-Vivisection Society, 1983.

Easlea, Brian. *Science and Sexual Oppression.* London: Weidenfeld and Nicolson, 1981.

Eco, Umberto, with Richard Rorty, Jonathan Culler, Christine Brooke-Rose. *Interpretation and Overinterpretation.* Ed. Stefan Collini. Cambridge: Cambridge University Press, 1992.

Ellis, Sarah Stickney. *The Daughters of England, Their Position in Society, Character and Responsibilities.* New York: D. Appleton, 1842.

Ellmann, Maud. *Psychoanalytic Literary Criticism.* London: Longman, 1994.

Elsner, John, and Roger Cardinal, eds. *The Cultures of Collecting.* Cambridge, Mass.: Harvard University Press, 1994.

Elston, Mary Ann. "Women and Anti-Vivisection in Victorian England, 1870-1900." In *Vivisection in Historical Perspective,* ed. N. A. Rupke, pp. 259-94. London: Croom Helm, 1987.

Evans, B. Ifor. "The Sources of Christina Rossetti's 'Goblin Market.'" *Modern Language Review* 28 (1933): 158-65.

Fielding, Sarah. *The Governess; or, The Little Female Academy.* London: Sold by A. Miller, 1749.

Flowers, Betty S. "'Had Such a Lady Spoken For Herself': Christina Rossetti's *'Monna*

Innominata.'" In *Rossetti to Sexton: Six Women Poets at Texas,* ed. Dave Oliphant, pp. 13-29. Austin: Harry Ransom Humanities Research Center, University of Texas at Austin, 1992.

"Forcing." *Gardeners' Chronicle and Agricultural Gazette* (24 July 1858): 574.

Foucault, Michel. *The History of Sexuality, Volume One: An Introduction.* Harmondsworth: Penguin, 1984.

Fraser, Hilary. *The Victorians and Renaissance Italy.* Oxford: Blackwell, 1992.

Fredeman, William E. "Christina Rossetti." In *The Victorian Poets: A Guide to Research,* ed. Frederic E. Faverty, pp. 284-93. 2d ed. Cambridge, Mass: Harvard University Press, 1968.

Frend, Grace Gilchrist. "Great Victorians: Some Recollections of Tennyson, George Eliot, and the Rossettis." *Bookman* 77 (1929): 9-11.

Freud, Sigmund. *The Complete Psychological Works of Sigmund Freud.* Trans. and ed. by James Strachey. 24 vols. London: Hogarth Press and the Institute of Psycho-Analysis, 1953-73.

"The Frost on the Morning of the 1st inst." *Gardeners' Chronicle and Agricultural Gazette* 16 (April 1859): 338.

Garlick, Barbara. "Christina Rossetti and the Gender Politics of Fantasy." In *The Victorian Fantasists,* ed. Kath Filmer. New York: St. Martin's Press, 1991.

Gaskell, Elizabeth. *Cranford.* 1853. New York: Oxford University Press, 1972.

Gelpi, Barbara Charlesworth. "Verses with a Good Deal about Sucking: Percy Bysshe Shelley and Christina Rossetti." In *Influence and Resistance in Nineteenth-Century English Poetry,* ed. G. Kim Blank and Margot K. Louis, pp. 150-165. London and Basingstoke: Macmillan, 1993.

Gilbert, Sandra M. "From *Patria* to *Matria:* Elizabeth Barrett Browning's Risorgimento." *PMLA* 99 (1984): 194-209.

Gilbert, Sandra M., and Susan Gubar,. *The Madwoman in the Attic: The Woman Writer and the Nineteenth-Century Literary Imagination.* New Haven and London: Yale University Press, 1979.

Gilchrist, Anne. "The Indestructibility of Force." *Macmillan's Magazine* 6 (1862): 337-44.

Gilchrist, Herbert Harlakenden, ed. *Anne Gilchrist: Her Life and Writings.* Prefatory Notice by William Michael Rossetti. London: Unwin, 1887.

Gilfillan, George. "Female Authors, No. 1 — Mrs. Hemans." *Tait's Edinburgh Magazine* n.s. 14 (1847): 359-63. Reprinted from *The Dublin University Magazine* 56 (Aug. 1837): 127-41.

Gilmour, Robin. *The Victorian Period.* London: Longman, 1993.

Goethe, Johann Wolfgang von. *Faust.* Ed. R. M. S. Heffner, H. Rehder, and W. F. Twaddell. Madison: University of Wisconsin Press, 1975.

Gorham, Deborah. *The Victorian Girl and the Feminine Ideal.* London and Canberra: Croom Hill, 1982.

Gosse, Edmund. "Christina Rossetti." *The Century Magazine* 46 (June 1893): 211-17.

————. *Critical Kit-Kats.* London: Heinemann, 1896.

————. *English Literature: An Illustrated Record,* vol. 4. New York: Grosset and Dunlap, 1904.

Grahame, Kenneth. *The Wind in the Willows.* London: Methuen, 1908.

Grandgent, C. H. *Companion to the Divine Comedy, as edited by Charles S. Singleton.* Cambridge, Mass.: Harvard University Press, 1975.

[Greg, W. R.] "Prostitution." *Westminster Review* 52, nos. 1-2 (1850): 448-506.

Hallam, Arthur Henry (T.H.E.A.). *Remarks on Professor Rossetti's* Disquisizioni sullo Spirito Antipapale. London: Edward Moxon, 1832.

Hamilton, James. *Arthur Rackham: A Life with Illustration.* London: Pavilion Books, 1990.

Hanft, Lila. "The Politics of Maternal Ambivalence in Christina Rossetti's *Sing-Song.*" *Victorian Literature and Culture* 19 (1991): 213-32.

Harris, Daniel. "D. G. Rossetti's 'Jenny': Sex, Money, and the Interior Monologue." *VP* 22 (1984): 197-215.

Harrison, Antony H. *Christina Rossetti in Context.* Chapel Hill and London: University of North Carolina Press; Brighton: Harvester, 1988.

————. "Christina Rossetti and the Romantics: Influence and Ideology." In *Influence and Resistance in Nineteenth-Century English Poetry,* ed. G. Kim Blank and Margot K. Louis, pp. 131-49. London and Basingstoke: Macmillan, 1993.

————. "Eighteen Early Letters by Christina Rossetti." In *The Achievement of Christina Rossetti,* ed. David A. Kent, pp. 192-207. Ithaca and London: Cornell University Press, 1987.

————. *Victorian Poets and Romantic Poems: Intertextuality and Ideology.* Charlottesville: University Press of Virginia, 1990.

Hassett, Constance. "Christina Rossetti and the Poetry of Reticence." *Philological Quarterly* 65 (1986): 495-514.

Helsinger, Elizabeth K. "Consumer Power and the Utopia of Desire: Christina Rossetti's 'Goblin Market.'" *English Literary History* 58 (1991): 903-33.

Hemans, Felicia. *The Works of Mrs. Hemans, with a Memoir by Her Sister, and an Essay on Her Genius, by Mrs. Sigourney.* 1839. 7 vols. Philadelphia: Lea and Blanchard, 1842.

Hendry, George S. *Theology of Nature.* Philadelphia, Penn.: Westminster, 1980.

Herbert, George. *The English Poems of George Herbert.* Ed. C. A. Patrides. London: J. M. Dent, 1974.

Hess, Thomas B., and Linda Nochlin, eds. *Woman as Sex Object: Studies in Erotic Art, 1730-1970.* London: Allen Lane, 1973.

Hibberd, Shirley. "The Late Snowfall and Frost." *Gardeners' Chronicle and Agricultural Gazette* 9 (April 1859): 314-15.

Hilton, Tim. *John Ruskin: The Early Years, 1819-1859.* New Haven: Yale University Press, 1985.

Hollander, Robert. "Dante and His Commentators." In *The Cambridge Companion to Dante,* ed. Rachel Jacoff, pp. 226-36. Cambridge: Cambridge University Press, 1993.

Holt, Terrence. "'Men Sell Not Such in Any Town': Exchange in *Goblin Market.*" *VP* 28 (1990): 51-67.

Homans, Margaret. *Women Writers and Poetic Identity.* Princeton, N.J.: Princeton University Press, 1980.

Hopkins, Gerard Manley. *Further Letters of Gerard Manley Hopkins, Including His Correspondence with Coventry Patmore.* Ed. Claude Colleer Abbott. 2d ed. London: Oxford University Press, 1956.

"Horticulture. Chapter IV." In *Imperial Journal of the Arts and Sciences*, ed. W. J. Macquorn Rankine et al. 2 vols. Glasgow: William Mackenzie, [1858-66].

House, Humphry. "Pre-Raphaelite Poetry." In *Pre-Raphaelitism: A Collection of Critical Essays,* ed. James Sambrook, pp. 126-32. Chicago and London: Chicago University Press, 1974.

Huggins, Margaret Lindsay (Murray). *Agnes Mary Clerke and Ellen Mary Clerke: An Appreciation.* [London]: n.p., 1907.

Hunt, John Dixon. *The Wider Sea: A Life of John Ruskin.* London: J. M. Dent, 1982.

Hunt, Thornton, ed. *The Correspondence of Leigh Hunt.* London, 1862.

Hutcheon, Linda. *Irony's Edge: The Theory and Politics of Irony.* London: Routledge, 1995.

Irigaray, Luce. "And the One Doesn't Stir without the Other." *Signs* 7 (1981): 60-67.

————. "Sexual Difference." In *The Irigaray Reader,* ed. Margaret Whitford. Oxford: Basil Blackwell, 1991.

————. *This Sex Which Is Not One.* Trans. Catherine Porter. Ithaca and London: Cornell University Press, 1990.

Jarvie, Paul, and Robert Rosenberg. "'Willowwood,' Unity, and *The House of Life.*" *The Pre-Raphaelite Review* 1 (1977-78): 106-20.

Jesse, George. *Correspondence with Charles Darwin on Experimenting upon Live Animals.* London: Pickering, 1881.

————. *History of the Foundation and Operations of the Society Abolition Vivisection.* London: Pickering, 1877.

Jones, Kathleen. *Learning Not to Be First: The Life of Christina Rossetti.* Moreton-in-Marsh: Windrush, 1991.

Kaplan, Cora. "The Indefinite Disclosed: Christina Rossetti and Emily Dickinson." In *Women Writing and Writing about Women,* ed. Mary Jacobus, pp. 61-79. London: Croom Helm, 1979.

Karlin, Daniel. *The Courtship of Robert Browning and Elizabeth Barrett.* Oxford: Clarendon, 1985.

Katz, Wendy A. "Muse from Nowhere: Christina Rossetti's Fantasy World in *Speaking Likenesses.*" *The Journal of Pre-Raphaelite and Aesthetic Studies* 5, no. 1 (1984): 14-35.

Keats, John. *The Poems of John Keats.* Ed. Miriam Allott. Harlow and New York: Longman, 1970.

———. *The Poetical Works and Other Writings of John Keats.* Ed. H. Buxton Forman. Revised by Maurice Buxton Forman. 8 vols. 1939; reprint, New York: Phaeton Press, 1970.

Keightley, Thomas. *The Fairy Mythology.* 2 vols. London, 1828.

———. *The Fairy Mythology, Illustrative of the Romance and Superstition of Various Countries.* Enl. and rev. ed. London, 1850; reprint, New York: Phaeton Press, 1970.

Kelley, Philip, and Betty A. Coley. *The Browning Collections: A Reconstruction with Other Memorabilia.* Winfield, Kan.: Armstrong Browning Library of Baylor University, The Browning Institute, 1984.

Kent, David A., ed. *The Achievement of Christina Rossetti.* Ithaca and London: Cornell University Press, 1987.

Kingsley, Charles. *The Water-Babies: A Fairy Tale for a Land-Baby.* London and Cambridge: Macmillan, 1863.

Knoepflmacher, U. C. "Avenging Alice: Christina Rossetti and Lewis Carroll." *Nineteenth-Century Literature* 41 (1986): 299-328.

Kooistra, Lorraine Janzen. *The Artist as Critic: Bitextuality in Fin-de-Siècle Illustrated Books.* Aldershot: Scolar, 1995.

———. "*Goblin Market* as a Cross-Audienced Poem: Children's Fairy Tale, Adult Erotic Fantasy." *Children's Literature* 25. Special Issue on Cross-Writing Child and Adult, ed. Mitzi Myers and U. C. Knoepflmacher, pp. 181-204. New Haven and London: Yale University Press, 1997.

———. "Modern Markets for *Goblin Market.*" *VP* 32 (1994): 249-77.

Kristeva, Julia. "How Does One Speak to Literature?" In *Desire in Language: A Semiotic Approach to Literature and Art,* ed. Leon S. Roudiez, trans. Thomas Gora, Alice Jardine, and Leon S. Roudiez. Oxford: Basil Blackwell, 1981.

———. *Powers of Horror: An Essay on Abjection.* Trans. Leon S. Roudiez. New York: Columbia University Press, 1982.

———. "Revolution in Poetic Language." Trans. Margaret Waller. In *The Kristeva Reader,* ed. Toril Moi. Oxford: Basil Blackwell, 1986.

Kucich, Greg. "Gendering Canons of Romanticism: Past and Present." *The Wordsworth Circle* 27 (1996): 95-102.

Kuhns, Oscar. *Dante and the English Poets from Chaucer to Tennyson.* New York: Holt, 1904.

Lacan, Jacques. *Ecrits: A Selection.* Trans. Alan Sheridan. London: Tavistock, 1977.

———. *Feminine Sexuality: Jacques Lacan and the école freudienne.* Ed. Juliet Mitchell and Jacqueline Rose. Trans. Jacqueline Rose. New York and London: Norton, 1985.

Landon, Letitia. *The Poetical Works of L. E. Landon.* Boston: Phillips, Sampson, 1856.

Langbauer, Laurie. *Women and Romance: The Consolations of Gender in the English Novel.* Ithaca and London: Cornell University Press, 1990.

Leder, Sharon, with Andrea Abbott. *The Language of Exclusion: The Poetry of Emily Dickinson and Christina Rossetti.* New York: Greenwood, 1987.

Le Gallienne, Richard. Review of *Poems,* by Christina Rossetti. *The Academy* 979 (February 7, 1891): 130-31.

Leighton, Angela. "'Because Men Made the Laws': The Fallen Woman and the Woman Poet." *Victorian Poetry* 27 (1989): 109-27. Reprinted in *New Feminist Discourses: Critical Essays in Theories and Texts,* ed. Isobel Armstrong, pp. 343-60. London and New York: Routledge, 1992.

———. Elizabeth Barrett Browning. Key Women Writers Series. Brighton: Harvester, 1986.

———. *Victorian Women Poets: Writing Against the Heart.* London and New York: Harvester; Charlottesville and London: University Press of Virginia, 1992.

———. "'When I Am Dead, My Dearest': The Secret of Christina Rossetti." *Modern Philology* 87 (1990): 373-88. Reprinted in *New Feminist Discourses: Critical Essays in Theories and Texts,* ed. Isobel Armstrong, pp. 343-60. London and New York: Routledge, 1992.

Leighton, Angela, ed. *Victorian Women Poets: A Critical Reader.* Oxford: Blackwell, 1996.

Leighton, Angela, and Margaret Reynolds, eds. *Victorian Women Poets: An Anthology.* Oxford: Blackwell, 1995.

Linley, Margaret. "Sappho's Conversions in Felicia Hemans, Letitia Landon, and Christina Rossetti." *Prism(s): Essays in Romanticism* 4 (1996): 1-35.

Lootens, Tricia. "Hemans and Home: Victorianism, Feminine 'Internal Enemies,' and the Domestication of National Identity." *PMLA* 109 (1994): 238-53.

———. *Lost Saints: Silence, Gender, and Victorian Literary Canonization.* Charlottesville: University Press of Virginia, 1996.

Loudon, Mrs. [J. W.], et al., eds. *Loudon's Encyclopædia of Plants.* New impression. London: Longmans, 1872.

"Lunar Warmth and Stellar Heat." *Fraser's Magazine* 81 (1870): 36-43.

Maas, Jeremy. *Victorian Painters.* London: Barrie and Rockliff, 1969.

MacDonald, George. *At the Back of the North Wind.* London: Strahan, 1871.

Marks, Elaine, and Isabelle de Courtivron, eds. *New French Feminisms.* Brighton: Harvester, 1981.

Marsh, Jan. *Christina Rossetti: A Literary Biography.* London: Jonathan Cape, 1994.

———. "Christina Rossetti's Vocation: The Importance of *Goblin Market.*" *VP* 32 (1994): 233-48.

———. "The Indian Mutiny and Christina Rossetti's First Appearance in *Once a Week.*" *Journal of Pre-Raphaelite Studies* n.s. 1 (1992): 16-19.

Marshall, Linda E. "'Abstruse the Problems!': Unity and Division in Christina Rossetti's *Later Life: A Double Sonnet of Sonnets.*" *VP* 32 (1994): 299-314.

———. "What the Dead Are Doing Underground: Hades and Heaven in the Writings of Christina Rossetti." *VN* 72 (1987): 55-60.

Marx, Karl. *A Contribution to the Critique of Political Economy.* 1859. Trans. S. W. Ryazanskaya. Ed. Maurice Dobb. New York: International Publishers, 1970.

———. *The Marx-Engels Reader.* Ed. Robert C. Tucker. New York: Norton, 1978.

———. *Marx and Engels on Malthus: Selections from the Writings of Marx and Engels Dealing with the Theories of Thomas Robert Malthus.* Trans. D. L. and R. L. Meek. Ed. R. L. Meek. London: Lawrence and Wishart, 1953.

Maxwell, Catherine. "The Poetic Context of Christina Rossetti's 'After Death.'" *English Studies* 76 (1995): 148-55.

Mayberry, Katherine J. *Christina Rossetti and the Poetry of Discovery.* Baton Rouge: Louisiana State University Press, 1989.

Mayhew, Henry. *London Labour and the London Poor.* 1851-61. 4 vols. New York: Dover, 1968.

McCulloch, J. R. *A Dictionary, Practical, Theoretical, and Historical, of Commerce and Commercial Navigation.* New ed. London: Longman, 1850.

McDowell, Paula. "Consuming Women: The Life of the 'Literary Lady' as Popular Culture in Eighteenth-Century England." *Genre* 26 (1993): 219-52.

McGann, Jerome J. "Christina Rossetti's Poems: A New Edition and a Revaluation." *VS* 23 (1980): 237-54.

———. "The Religious Poetry of Christina Rossetti." *Critical Inquiry* 10 (1983): 127-44.

———. "Rossetti's Significant Details." *VP* 7 (1969): 41-54. Reprinted in *Pre-Raphaelitism: A Collection,* ed. James Sambrook, pp. 230-42. Chicago and London: University of Chicago Press, 1974.

McGillis, Roderick. "Simple Surfaces: Christina Rossetti's Work for Children." In *The Achievement of Christina Rossetti,* ed. David A. Kent, pp. 208-30. Ithaca and London: Cornell University Press, 1987.

Merchant, Carolyn. *The Death of Nature.* London: Wildwood House, 1982.

Mermin, Dorothy. *Elizabeth Barrett Browning: The Origins of a New Poetry.* Chicago and London: University of Chicago Press, 1989.

———. "'The Fruitful Feud of Hers and His': Sameness, Difference, and Gender in Victorian Poetry." *VP* 33 (1995): 149-68.

———. *Godiva's Ride: Women of Letters in England, 1830-1880.* Bloomington: Indiana University Press, 1993.

———. "Heroic Sisterhood in *Goblin Market.*" *VP* 21 (1983): 107-18.

Meynell, Alice. *Alice Meynell: Prose and Poetry.* Intro. by V. Sackville-West. London: Jonathan Cape, 1947.

Michie, Helena. "'There Is No Friend Like a Sister': Sisterhood as Sexual Difference." *English Literary History* 56 (1989): 401-21.

Mill, John Stuart, with Harriet Taylor Mill. "On Liberty." 1859. *Essays on Politics and*

Society. Vol. 18 of *Collected Works of John Stuart Mill,* ed. John M. Robson, pp. 213–310. 33 vols. Toronto: University of Toronto Press; London: Routledge, 1963–91.

Milton, John. *Paradise Lost.* In *The Poetical Works of John Milton.* Ed. D. Masson. London: Macmillan, 1890.

———. *Paradise Lost.* Ed. Alastair Fowler. London: Longman, 1971.

Mintz, Sidney W. *Sweetness and Power: The Place of Sugar in Modern History.* New York: Sifton-Viking, 1985.

Mitchell, W. J. T. *Picture Theory: Essays on Verbal and Visual Representation.* Chicago and London: University of Chicago Press, 1994.

Moers, Ellen. *Literary Women.* New York: Oxford University Press, 1977; and London: Women's Press, 1978.

Moi, Toril, ed. *The Kristeva Reader.* Oxford: Blackwell, 1986.

Montefiore, Jan. *Feminism and Poetry: Language, Experience, Identity in Women's Writing.* 2d ed. London: Pandora, 1994.

Morris, William. Review of *Poems* by D. G. Rossetti. *The Academy* 1 (14 May 1870): 199–200.

A Naval Encyclopædia. Philadelphia: L. R. Hammersly, 1881.

Nead, Lynda. *Myths of Sexuality: Representations of Women in Victorian Britain.* Oxford: Basil Blackwell, 1988.

Noske, Barbara. *Humans and Other Animals.* London: Pluto, 1989.

"Notice of *Maude: Prose and Verse.*" *Bookman* 11 (December 1896): 57.

"Notices to Correspondents." *Gardeners' Chronicle and Agricultural Gazette* (31 December 1859): 1056.

Oliver, Kelly. *Reading Kristeva: Unraveling the Double-bind.* Bloomington and Indianapolis: Indiana University Press, 1993.

Orr, Mrs. [Alexandra] Sutherland. *A Handbook to the Works of Robert Browning.* London: G. Bell and Sons, 1927.

———. *Life and Letters of Robert Browning.* London: Macmillan, 1908.

Ottlinger, Claudia. *The Death-Motif in the Poetry of Emily Dickinson and Christina Rossetti.* Frankfurt: Peter Lang, 1996.

Packer, Lona Mosk. *Christina Rossetti.* Berkeley and Los Angeles: University of California Press, 1963.

———. "Christina Rossetti's Correspondence with Her Nephew: Some Unpublished Letters." *Notes and Queries* 204 (1959): 425–32.

Packer, Lona Mosk, ed. *The Rossetti-Macmillan Letters.* Berkeley and Los Angeles: University of California Press, 1963.

Padoan, Giorgio. "Colui Che Fece Per Viltà Il Gran Rifiuto." *Studi Danteschi* 38 (1961): 75–128.

Patmore, Coventry. *Principle in Art, Religio Poetae, and Other Essays.* London: Duckworth, 1913.

Paul, Sarah. "Strategic Self-Centering and the Female Narrator: Elizabeth Barrett Browning's *Sonnets from the Portuguese.*" *Browning Institute Studies* 17 (1989): 75-91.

Peterson, Linda H. "Restoring the Book: The Typological Hermeneutics of Christina Rossetti and the PRB." *VP* 32 (1994): 209-32.

Petrarch, Francesco. *Letters from Petrarch.* Trans. Morris Bishop. Bloomington: Indiana University Press, 1966.

Phillips, Henry. *Floral Emblems: A Guide to the Language of Flowers.* London: Saunders and Otley, 1831.

"Plum." *Encyclopædia Britannica.* 9th ed. New York: Scribners, 1878-89. 19:230.

Poe, Edgar Allan. "The Philosophy of Composition." In *Essays and Reviews.* New York: Literary Classics of the United States, 1984.

"Pomeloes or Forbidden Fruit." *Gardeners' Chronicle and Agricultural Gazette* (15 January 1859): 39.

Prins, Yopie. "Elizabeth Barrett, Robert Browning, and the *Différance* of Translation." *VP* 29 (1991): 435-51.

Proctor, Ellen. *A Brief Memoir of Christina Rossetti.* London: SPCK, 1895.

Proctor, Richard A. *The Moon: Her Motions, Aspect, Scenery, and Physical Condition.* London: Longmans, Green, 1873.

———. "Newton and Darwin." *Contemporary Review* 41 (1882): 994-1002. Reprinted in *Mysteries of Time and Space,* pp. 1-13. London: Chatto, 1883; new ed. 1892.

———. *Other Worlds Than Ours: The Plurality of Worlds Studied under the Light of Recent Scientific Researches.* 2d ed. London: Longmans, Green, 1870.

———. "The Rosse Telescope Set to New Work." *Fraser's Magazine* 80 (1869): 754-60.

———. "What, Then, *Is* the Corona?" *Fraser's Magazine* 83 (1871): 515-28.

Punch, or the London Charivari (16 April 1859): 161.

Rees, Joan. *The Poetry of Dante Gabriel Rossetti: Modes of Self-Expression.* Cambridge: Cambridge University Press, 1981.

Ricardo, David. *The Principles of Political Economy and Taxation.* 3d ed. 1821. Homewood, Ill.: Irwin, 1963.

Rich, Adrienne. *On Lies, Secrets, and Silence.* London: Virago, 1980.

Richards, Thomas. *The Commodity Culture of Victorian England: Advertising and Spectacle, 1851-1914.* Stanford, Calif.: Stanford University Press, 1990.

Riede, David G. "Elizabeth Barrett: The Poet as Angel." *VP* 32 (1994): 121-39.

———. "Erasing the Art-Catholic: Rossetti's *Poems, 1870.*" *Journal of Pre-Raphaelite Studies* 1 (1980-81): 50-70.

Robinson, Daniel. "Reviving the Sonnet: Women Romantic Poets and the Sonnet Claim." *European Romantic Review* 6 (1995): 98-127.

Robson, John M. Introduction to *Miscellaneous Writings.* Vol. 31 of *Collected Works of*

John Stuart Mill, ed. John M. Robson, pp. vi-l. 33 vols. Toronto: University of Toronto Press; London: Routledge, 1963-91.

Rockliff, Robert. *Literary Fables.* London, 1851.

Roe, Sue, ed. *Women Reading Women's Writing.* Brighton: Harvester, 1987.

Roll, Eric. *A History of Economic Thought.* 4th ed. London: Faber and Faber, 1973.

Rose, Jacqueline. *The Case of Peter Pan, or The Impossibility of Children's Fiction.* London: Macmillan, 1984.

Rosenblum, Dolores. *Christina Rossetti: The Poetry of Endurance.* Carbondale: Southern Illinois University Press, 1986.

Ross, Marlon B. *The Contours of Masculine Desire.* New York: Oxford University Press, 1989.

Rossetti, Christina. *Called to Be Saints: The Minor Festivals Devotionally Studied.* London: SPCK, 1881.

—————. *Christina Rossetti: Poems and Prose.* Ed. Jan Marsh. Everyman's Library. London: J. M. Dent, 1994.

—————. *Christina Rossetti: Selected Poems.* Ed. C. H. Sisson. Manchester: Carcanet Press, 1984.

—————. *Commonplace and Other Short Stories.* London: F. S. Ellis, 1870.

—————. *The Complete Poems of Christina Rossetti.* Variorum ed. Ed. R. W. Crump. 3 vols. Baton Rouge and London: Louisiana State University Press, 1979-90.

—————. "Dante, an English Classic." *The Churchman's Shilling Magazine and Family Treasury* 2 (1867): 200-205.

—————. "Dante. The Poet Illustrated out of the Poem." *The Century* 27 (1884): 566-73. n.s. vol. 5.

—————. *The Face of the Deep: A Devotional Commentary on the Apocalypse.* 2d ed. London and Brighton: SPCK; New York: Young, 1892.

—————. *The Family Letters of Christina Georgina Rossetti.* Ed. William Michael Rossetti. 1908. New York: Haskell, 1968.

—————. *Goblin Market and Other Poems.* Illustrated by D. G. Rossetti. London and Cambridge: Macmillan, 1862.

—————. *Goblin Market.* Illustrated by Laurence Housman. London: Macmillan, 1893.

—————. *Goblin Market.* Illustrated by Dion Clayton Calthrop. London and Edinburgh: T. C. and E. C. Jack, [1906].

—————. *Goblin Market.* Illustrated by Margaret W. Tarrant. London: Routledge, [1912].

—————. *Goblin Market.* Illustrated by Arthur Rackham. London: George G. Harrap, 1933.

—————. "Goblin Market: A Ribald Classic." Illustrated by Kinuko Craft. *Playboy* 20 (September 1973): 115-119.

—————. *Goblin Market.* Illustrated with Etchings by Martin Ware. London: Victor Gollancz, 1980.

————. *Goblin Market.* Illustrated by George Gershinowitz. Boston: David R. Godine, 1981.

————. *Goblin Market.* Illustrated by John Bolton. *Pacific Comics: Pathways to Fantasy* 1, no. 1 (1984): 9-18.

————. *Letter and Spirit: Notes on the Commandments.* London and Brighton: SPCK; New York: Young, 1883.

————. *The Letters of Christina Rossetti: Volume 1, 1834-1873.* Ed. Antony H. Harrison. Charlottesville and London: University Press of Virginia, 1997.

————. *Maude: Prose and Verse.* 1897. Ed. R. W. Crump. Hamden, Conn.: Archon Books, 1976.

————. *New Poems of Christina Rossetti Hitherto Unpublished or Uncollected.* Ed. William Michael Rossetti. London: Macmillan, 1900.

————. "Petrarca, Francesco." *The Imperial Dictionary of Universal Biography,* ed. John Francis Waller, 3:542-44. London: William MacKenzie, 1863.

————. *Poems by Christina Rossetti.* Illustrated by Florence Harrison. London, Glasgow, and Bombay: Blackie and Son, 1910.

————. *The Poetical Works of Christina Georgina Rossetti.* Ed. with a Memoir and Notes by William Michael Rossetti. London and New York: Macmillan, 1904.

————. *Seek and Find: A Double Series of Short Studies of the Benedicite.* London and Brighton: SPCK; New York: Young, 1879.

————. *Selected Prose of Christina Rossetti.* Ed. David A. Kent and P. G. Stanwood. New York: St. Martin's, 1998.

————. *Sing-Song: A Nursery Rhyme Book.* London: Routledge, 1872.

————. *Speaking Likenesses.* London: Macmillan, 1874.

————. *Time Flies: A Reading Diary.* London and Brighton: SPCK, 1885; Boston: Roberts Brothers, 1886.

Rossetti, Dante Gabriel. *The Collected Works of Dante Gabriel Rossetti.* London: Ellis and Elvey, 1888.

————. *Dante Gabriel Rossetti: His Family Letters.* With a Memoir by William Michael Rossetti. Ed. William Michael Rossetti. 2 vols. London: Ellis and Elvey, 1895.

————. *The House of Life.* In *The Pre-Raphaelites and Their Circle,* ed. Cecil B. Lang, pp. 79-129. 2d ed. Chicago and London: University of Chicago Press, 1975.

————. *Letters of Dante Gabriel Rossetti.* Ed. Oswald Doughty and John Robert Wahl. 4 vols. Oxford: Clarendon, 1965-67.

————. *The Works of Dante Gabriel Rossetti.* Ed. William Michael Rossetti. Rev. and enl. ed. London: Ellis and Elvey, 1911.

Rossetti, Frances. *Commonplace Book of Frances Rossetti.* 1816. University of British Columbia Angeli-Dennis Collection, Box 12, Folder 18.

Rossetti, Gabriele. *Disquisitions on the Antipapal Spirit which Produced the Reformation:*

Its Secret Influence on the Literature of Europe in General, and of Italy in Particular. Trans. Caroline Ward. 2 vols. London, 1834.

———. *Il Mistero dell' Amor Platonico.* 5 vols. London, 1840.

———. *La Beatrice di Dante.* London, 1842.

———. *La Divina Commedia di Dante Alighieri con Comento Analitico di G. Rossetti.* 2 vols. London, 1826-27.

Rossetti, Maria Francesca. *A Shadow of Dante: Being an Essay Towards Studying Himself, His World, and His Pilgrimage.* London, Oxford, and Cambridge: Rivington, 1871; Boston: Roberts Brothers, 1872.

Rossetti, William Michael. *The Comedy of Dante Allighieri: Part I—The Hell.* London: Macmillan, 1865.

———. *Dante and His Convito: A Study with Translations.* London: Elkin Mathews, 1910.

———. "Memoir." In *Dante Gabriel Rossetti: His Family Letters.* With a Memoir by William Michael Rossetti. Ed. William Michael Rossetti. Vol. 1. London: Ellis and Elvey, 1895.

———. "Memoir." In *The Poetical Works of Christina Georgina Rossetti,* ed. W. M. Rossetti, pp. xlv-lxxi. London: Macmillan, 1900, 1904, 1931; London: George Allen, 1899.

———. *Selected Letters of William Michael Rossetti.* Ed. Roger W. Peattie. University Park: Pennsylvania State University Press, 1990.

———. *Some Reminiscences of William Michael Rossetti.* 2 vols. London: Brown, Langham, 1906.

Rossetti, William Michael, ed. *Rossetti Papers: 1862-1870.* London: Sands, 1903.

———. *Ruskin: Rossetti: Preraphaelitism: Papers 1854 to 1862.* New York: Holt, Rinehart, and Winston; London: George Allen, 1899.

Rowton, Frederic. *The Female Poets of Great Britain, Chronologically Arranged with Copious Selections and Critical Remarks. A Facsimile of the 1853 Edition with a Critical Introduction and Bibliographical Appendices.* Ed. Marilyn L. Williamson. Detroit: Wayne State University Press, 1981.

Ruether, Rosemary Radford. *Sexism and God-Talk.* London: SCM Press, 1983.

Ruskin, John. *The Works of John Ruskin.* Ed. E. T. Cook and Alexander Wedderburn. 39 vols. London: George Allen, 1903-12.

Saul, M. "Fruit Prospects." *Gardeners' Chronicle and Agricultural Gazette* (14 May 1859): 424-25.

Schofield, Linda. "Displaced and Absent Texts as Contexts for Christina Rossetti's '*Monna Innominata.*'" *Journal of Pre-Raphaelite Studies* n.s. 6 (spring 1997): 38-52.

Scott, Joan Wallach. *Gender and the Politics of History.* New York: Columbia University Press, 1988.

Shakespeare, William. *A Midsummer Night's Dream* and *Othello.* In *The Riverside Shakespeare,* ed G. Blakemore Evans et al. Boston: Houghton Mifflin, 1974.

Sharp, William. "Some Reminiscences of Christina Rossetti." *The Atlantic Monthly* 75 (June 1895): 736-49.

Shaw, W. David. "Poet of Mystery: The Art of Christina Rossetti." In *The Achievement of Christina Rossetti,* ed. David A. Kent, pp. 23-56. Ithaca and London: Cornell University Press, 1987.

————. *Victorians and Mystery: Crises of Representation.* Ithaca and London: Cornell University Press, 1990.

Shelley, Percy Bysshe. *Shelley: Poetical Works.* Ed. Thomas Hutchinson. Revised by G. M. Matthews. Oxford and New York: Oxford University Press, 1970.

Sheppard, J. "Heating." *Gardeners' Chronicle and Agricultural Gazette* (1 December 1860): 1062.

Sherwood, Mrs. *The History of the Fairchild Family.* Wellington, Salop: F. Houlston, 1820.

Shires, Linda M. "The Author as Spectacle and Commodity." In *Victorian Literature and the Victorian Visual Imagination,* ed. Carol T. Christ and John O. Jordan, pp. 198-212. Berkeley, Los Angeles, and London: University of California Press, 1995.

Showalter, Elaine. *A Literature of Their Own: British Women Novelists from Brontë to Lessing.* London: Virago, 1978.

————, ed. *Maude; On Sisterhoods; A Woman's Thoughts about Women.* New York: New York University Press; London: William Pickering, 1993.

Sinclair, John D. *The Divine Comedy of Dante Alighieri with Translation and Comment: Inferno.* New York: Oxford University Press, 1939.

Singleton, Charles S. *The Divine Comedy, Translated with a Commentary. Inferno: Commentary.* Vol 1.2. Bollingen Series 80. Princeton, N.J.: Princeton University Press, 1970.

Sircar, Sanjay. "The Victorian Auntly Narrative Voice and Mrs. Molesworth's *Cuckoo Clock.*" *Children's Literature* 17, ed. Francelia Butler, pp. 1-24. New Haven and London: Yale University Press, 1989.

[Skelton, John]. "Our Camp in the Woodlands: A Day with the Gentle Poets." *Fraser's Magazine* 70 (1864): 204-13.

Smith, Adam. *The Wealth of Nations.* 1776. Reprint, New York: Everyman-Knopf, 1991.

[Smith, William Henry, and D. M. Moir]. "Mrs. Hemans." *Blackwood's Edinburgh Magazine* 64 (December 1848): 641-58.

Smulders, Sharon. *Christina Rossetti Revisited.* New York: Twayne, 1996.

————. "Woman's Enfranchisement in Christina Rossetti's Poetry." *Texas Studies in Literature and Language* 34 (1992): 568-88.

Somerville, Mary. *On the Connexion of the Physical Sciences.* 7th ed. London: John Murray, 1846.

Spencer, Herbert. "Recent Astronomy, and the Nebular Hypothesis." *Westminster Review* 70 (1858): 104-27 [American ed.]; 185-225 [British ed.]. Reprinted, with additional notes, as "The Nebular Hypothesis" in *Essays Scientific, Political, and Speculative,* 1:108-81. New York: Appleton, 1896.

Spivack, Charlotte. "'The Hidden World Below': Victorian Women Fantasy Poets." In *The Poetic Fantastic: Studies in an Evolving Genre,* ed. Patrick D. Murphy and Vernon Hyles, pp. 53-64. New York: Greenwood, 1989.

Stanwood, P. G. "Christina Rossetti's Devotional Prose." In *The Achievement of Christina Rossetti,* ed. David A. Kent, pp. 231-47. Ithaca and London: Cornell University Press, 1987.

Stephenson, Glennis. *Elizabeth Barrett Browning and the Poetry of Love.* Ann Arbor: UMI Press, 1989.

————. "Letitia Landon and The Victorian Improvisatrice: The Construction of L.E.L." *VP* 30 (1992): 1-17.

————. *Letitia Landon: The Woman Behind L.E.L.* Manchester and New York: Manchester University Press, 1995.

Stevenson, Lionel. *The Pre-Raphaelite Poets.* New York: Norton, 1972.

Stewart, Balfour, and P. G. Tait. *The Unseen Universe or Physical Speculations on a Future State.* 7th ed. London: Macmillan, 1886.

Stone, Marjorie. *Elizabeth Barrett Browning.* Macmillan Women Writers Series. London: Macmillan, 1995.

————. "Sisters in Art: Christina Rossetti and Elizabeth Barrett Browning." *VP* 32 (1994): 339-364.

"Supplement to the *Economist.*" *Economist* 25 (December 1858): 65-72; (18 February 1860): 89-96.

Surette, Leon. *The Birth of Modernism: Ezra Pound, T. S. Eliot, W. B. Yeats, and the Occult.* Montreal and Kingston: McGill-Queen's University Press, 1993.

Swinburne, Algernon Charles. *Swinburne's Collected Poetical Works.* 2 vols. London: Heinemann, 1927.

Tennyson, Alfred Lord. *The Poems of Tennyson.* Ed. Christopher Ricks. 3 vols. London: Longmans, Green, 1969; and Harlow: Longman, 1989.

Tennyson, G. B. "Afterword." In *The Achievement of Christina Rossetti,* ed. David A. Kent, pp. 346-55. Ithaca and London: Cornell University Press, 1987.

[Thackeray, William]. "A Word on the Annuals." *Fraser's Magazine* 16 (December 1837): 757-763.

Thomas, Frances. *Christina Rossetti.* London: Virago, 1994.

Thompson, Deborah Ann. "Anorexia as a Lived Trope: Christina Rossetti's 'Goblin Market.'" *Mosaic* 24, nos. 3-4 (1991): 89-106.

"Trade Report." *Times* [London] (11 December 1858): 5.

Troxell, Janet Camp, ed. *Three Rossettis: Unpublished Letters to and from Dante Gabriel, Christina, William.* Cambridge, Mass.: Harvard University Press, 1937.

Tucker, Herbert F. Review of *Victorian Poetry: Poetry, Poetics, and Politics,* by Isobel Armstrong. *VP* 33 (1995): 174-87.

Tucker, Herbert F., ed. *Critical Essays on Alfred Lord Tennyson.* New York: G. K. Hall, 1993.

Vaughan, Henry. *Henry Vaughan: The Complete Poems.* Ed. Alan Rudrum. Harmondsworth: Penguin, 1976; reprinted 1983.

Veblen, Thorstein. *The Theory of the Leisure Class: An Economic Study of Institutions.* 1899. New York: Random House, 1931.

Vincent, E. R. *Gabriele Rossetti in England.* Oxford: Clarendon, 1937.

Wallace, P. "On the Cultivation of Exotic Fruits." *Journal of the Royal Horticultural Society of London* o.s. 3 (1853): 47-52.

Waller, R. D. *The Rossetti Family, 1824-1854.* Manchester: Manchester University Press, 1932.

Watts-Dunton, Theodore. *Old Familiar Faces.* 1916. Reprint, Freeport, N.Y.: Books for Libraries Press, 1970.

Weathers, Winston. "Christina Rossetti: The Sisterhood of Self." *VP* 3 (1965): 81-89.

Weber, Max. *The Protestant Ethic and the Spirit of Capitalism.* Trans. Talcott Parsons. New York: Scribners, 1958.

Wenger, Helen H. "The Influence of the Bible in Christina Rossetti's 'Monna Innominata.'" *Christian Scholar's Review* 3 (1973): 15-24.

Whitla, William. "Questioning the Convention: Christina Rossetti's Sonnet Sequence 'Monna Innominata.'" In *The Achievement of Christina Rossetti,* ed. David A. Kent, pp. 82-131. Ithaca and London: Cornell University Press, 1987.

Wolfson, Susan. "Gendering the Soul." In *Romantic Woman Writers: Voices and Countervoices,* ed. Paula K. Feldman and Theresa M. Kelley, pp. 33-68. Hanover and London: University Press of New England, 1995.

Wollstonecraft, Mary. *Original Stories from Real Life.* London: J. Johnson, 1791.

Wood, Rev. J. G. *The Common Objects of the Sea Shore; Including Hints for an Aquarium.* London: Routledge, 1857.

Woolf, Virginia. *A Room of One's Own.* London: Hogarth, 1929.

Yaeger, Patricia. *Honey-Mad Women: Emancipatory Strategies in Women's Writing.* New York: Columbia University Press, 1988.

Yonge, Charlotte M. *History of Christian Names.* London: Macmillan, 1884.

Yourcenar, Marguerite. *Coup de Grâce.* Trans. Grace Frick. London: Secker and Warburg, 1957.

Zaturenska, Marya. *Christina Rossetti: A Portrait with Background.* New York: Macmillan, 1949.

Zipes, Jack, ed. *Victorian Fairy Tales: The Revolt of the Fairies and Elves.* New York: Methuen, 1987.

EDITORS AND CONTRIBUTORS

MARY ARSENEAU is Assistant Professor of English at the University of Ottawa, Canada. She has published articles on John Keats, Dante Gabriel Rossetti, and Christina Rossetti. She is currently working on a monograph on Christina Rossetti, commissioned for Macmillan's Women Writers Series.

JULIA BRIGGS is Professor of English at De Monfort University, Leicester. She has authored a history of the ghost story, *Night Visitors* (1977), a historical study of Renaissance literature, *This Stage-Play World* (1983, 1997), and a biography of the children's writer, *E Nesbit: A Woman of Passion* (1987). She is co-editor, with Gillian Avery, of *Children and Their Books: A Celebration of the Work of Iona and Peter Opie* (1989), and has also edited the work of Virginia Woolf for Penguin Books. She is currently editing, with Dennis Butts and Brian Alderson, a collection of essays on popular literature for children.

KATHRYN BURLINSON was Lecturer in English at the University of Southampton from 1990 to 1997. Her publications include *Christina Rossetti* (Writers and Their Work Series, 1998) and essays on Emily Brontë, Christina Rossetti, and nineteenth-century women's writing. She is now working in an international touring theater company, The Weird Sisters.

ALISON CHAPMAN is Lecturer in English at the University of Dundee, Scotland. She has published articles on Christina Rossetti and "feminine subjects" in Victorian poetry. Her book, *Christina Rossetti and the Aesthetics of the Feminine,* will be published in 1999 by Macmillan. She is currently working on a new study of Victorian poetry and technologies of the uncanny.

SUSAN CONLEY lectures in English at Melbourne University, Australia. She has published "'Poet's Right': Elegy and the Woman Poet" in *Victorian Women Poets: A Critical Reader* (1996), edited by Angela Leighton.

ANTONY H. HARRISON is Professor of English at North Carolina State University. He is currently editing the letters of Christina Rossetti and has edited several collections of critical essays. His authored books include *Christina Rossetti in Context* (1988), *Swinburne's Medievalism: A Study in Victorian Love Poetry* (1988), *Victorian Poets and Romantic Poems: Intertextuality and Ideology* (1990), and *Victorian Poets and the Politics of Culture* (1998).

LORRAINE JANZEN KOOISTRA is Associate Professor of English at Nipissing University, North Bay, Canada. A specialist in visual/verbal relations, she has published *The Artist as Critic: Bitextuality in Fin-de-Siècle Illustrated Books* (1995), a series of articles on illustrated editions of Christina Rossetti's work, and essays on Woolf, Joyce, Hopkins, and Beardsley. She is currently writing a book on Christina Rossetti and the visual imagination.

MARGARET LINLEY is Assistant Professor of English and a member of the Print Culture, 1700-1900 Graduate Program at Simon Fraser University, Vancouver, Canada. She has articles published or forthcoming on Tennyson, Felicia Hemans, Letitia Landon, Christina Rossetti, and the Literary Annuals.

LINDA E. MARSHALL has recently retired from her post as Associate Professor of English at the University of Guelph, Canada. She has published a series of essays on medieval and nineteenth-century texts, including a number of articles on Christina Rossetti.

CATHERINE MAXWELL is Lecturer in English in the school of English and Drama at Queen Mary and Westfield College, University of London, England. She is the editor of *Algernon Charles Swinburne* (Everyman's Poetry, 1997) and has published articles on Browning, George Eliot, Ruskin, the Rossettis, and Vernon Lee. She is currently writing a book on Victorian male poets.

RICHARD MENKE is a Ph.D candidate and Mabelle McLeod Lewis Fellow at Stanford University, where he is completing a dissertation on Victorian interiors. His articles on George Eliot and Martin Amis are forthcoming in *ELH* and *Modern Fiction Studies* respectively.

MARGARET REYNOLDS is Visiting Fellow at Clare Hall, Cambridge. She has coedited (with Angela Leighton) *Victorian Women Poets: An Anthology* (1995), prepared the variorum edition of Elizabeth Barrett Browning's *Aurora Leigh* (1992, 1996), and written many articles on nineteenth-century literature and women's writing.

MARJORIE STONE is Associate Professor of English and Women's Studies at Dalhousie University, Halifax, Canada. She is the author of *Elizabeth Barrett Browning* (1995), and of articles on Dickens, the Brownings, Gaskell, Christina Rossetti, Tennyson, the female body, and other subjects. She was the President of the Association of Canadian College and University Teachers of English in 1996-98. She is currently editing (with Judith Thompson) a book on literary couples and collaborators.

INDEX